Building the Population Bomb

Building the Population Bomb

Emily Klancher Merchant

OXFORD
UNIVERSITY PRESS

OXFORD
UNIVERSITY PRESS

Oxford University Press is a department of the University of Oxford. It furthers the University's objective of excellence in research, scholarship, and education by publishing worldwide. Oxford is a registered trade mark of Oxford University Press in the UK and certain other countries.

Published in the United States of America by Oxford University Press
198 Madison Avenue, New York, NY 10016, United States of America.

Library of Congress Control Number: 2021933733
ISBN 978–0–19–755894–2

DOI: 10.1093/oso/9780197558942.001.0001

For my family, planned and unplanned.

CONTENTS

FIGURES

ACKNOWLEDGMENTS

This book was a long time in the making, and I incurred many debts along the way. My earliest academic mentors, Gary Wilder, Pamela Smith, and Samuel Yamashita at Pomona College, sparked my fascination with historical research. At the University of Michigan, Sonya Rose, Kali Israel, Farina Mir, Nancy Hunt, and Gabrielle Hecht shepherded me through the early years of graduate school; Myron Gutmann and Barbara Anderson introduced me to demography and inspired me to pursue its history; John Carson, Howard Brick, and Paul Edwards saw me through the dissertation process and helped me land on the other end.

Thanks go to my family, who fed and housed me, held my hand, and even washed my hair when necessary: Karen Hilfman and Ken Levy; Jon Klancher and Joan Cucinotta; Nancy, Sophie, and Maya Klancher; Lesley, Richard, and Rebecca Hume; and Tania Verafield and Nadine Levyfield. Equally important are my Ann Arbor friends and colleagues, who celebrated my triumphs and helped me weather numerous defeats: Diana Mankowski, Laura Hilburn, LaKisha Simmons, Rebecca Grapevine, Crystal Chung, Lenny Ureña Valerio, Yan Long, Susan Hwang, Ken Garner, Dan Hirschman, Jamie Budnick, Liz Ela, Emily Marshall, Kristen Cibelli, Birgit and Florian Keusch, Clay Howard, Tandiwe and Nicole Aebi-Moyo, Liz Harmon, Robyn D'Avignon, Ashley Rockenbach, Paul Hébert, Ronit Stahl, Katie Rosenblatt, Laura Ferguson, David Merchant, Susan Leonard, Ken Sylvester, George Alter, Elizabeth Moss, Elizabeth Sikkenga, Mary Vardigan, and Sanda Ionescu.

At Dartmouth College, my mentors, colleagues, and friends helped me rethink the project at a critical moment: Leslie Butler, Bob Bonner, Richard Wright, Kes and Chris Domone, Kirstyn Leuner, Joe DiGrazia, Jennie Miller, Udi Greenberg, Michael Barany, Bethany Moreton, Pamela Voekel, Tish Lopez, and Nisha Kommattam. I couldn't be more grateful for my UC Davis colleagues, who have provided immeasurable encouragement and support: Colin Milburn, John Marx, Joe Dumit, Tim Choy, Gerardo Con Diaz, Lindsay Poirier, Marisol de la Cadena, Tim Lenoir, Meaghan O'Keefe, Jim Griesemer, Andrés Barragán, Duncan Temple Lang, Carl Stahmer, Pamela Reynolds, Dan Goldstein, Ian Campbell, and Daniel Stolzenberg.

Many people offered targeted help in the last year or so of the writing process. These include Audra Wolfe and Dan Bouk, who read the entire manuscript and gave invaluable feedback; Sohmer Kristensen, Dawn Warfield, Lily Hallmark, and Joshua Silver, who provided research assistance; my writing group—Jade Sasser, Ellen Foley, and Rajani Bhatia—who offered supportive and incisive critique; my writing coaches—Cathy Mazak, Rocío Caballero-Gill, and Gina Robinson—who made the process a lot more enjoyable; and my editors at Oxford University Press, Sarah Humphreville and Emma Hodgdon, who brought the book to fruition. Jenny Trinitapoli, Rina Bliss, and Susan Mizruchi provided much-needed encouragement in the final stages.

A very special thank-you goes to all of the demographers who patiently discussed this project with me over the past nine years, generously offering their insights and graciously letting me know when I was barking up the wrong trees: Jane Menken, Charlie Hirschman, Gretchen Condran, Pete Guest, Dennis Hodgson, John Weeks, Richard Easterlin, Ron Lee, Adrian Raftery, Sam Preston, Jeff Evans, Mike Spittel, Wendy Baldwin, Karen Hardee, James Trussell, Win Brown, Jason Boardman, John Haaga, Simon Szreter, Al Hermalin, Arland Thornton, John Knodel, Ren Farley, David Featherman, and Phyllis Piotrow.

This project received generous funding from many sources: the University of California, Davis; the American Philosophical Society and British Academy; the University of Michigan (Rackham Graduate School and Population Studies Center); Marshall Weinberg; the National Science Foundation; the Consortium for History of Science, Technology, and Medicine; the Rockefeller Archive Center; and the Society for Historians of American Foreign Relations.

My deepest thanks go to the Parkers. Patrick was by my side through much of the process, diverting me with comedy, card games, and ice cream when necessary. Hazel joined us while I was writing this book and gave me the motivation to finish; Nancy provided the child care that actually made it possible. I owe my infinite gratitude to everyone listed here, and to the many others I no doubt forgot to include.

ABBREVIATIONS USED IN NOTES

AESR	American Eugenics Society Records, American Philosophical Society Library, Philadelphia
AJCP	Ansley J. Coale Papers, Seeley G. Mudd Manuscript Library, Princeton University
AJLP	Alfred J. Lotka Papers, Seeley G. Mudd Manuscript Library, Princeton University
FHOP	Frederick Henry Osborn Papers, American Philosophical Society Library, Philadelphia
FWNP	Frank W. Notestein Papers, Seeley G. Mudd Manuscript Library, Princeton University
HMFC	Hugh Moore Fund Collection, Public Policy Papers, Department of Special Collections, Princeton University Library
JDR3	John D. Rockefeller III Papers, Rockefeller Archive Center, Sleepy Hollow, New York
MMFR	Milbank Memorial Fund Records, Yale University Library
NA	National Archives, Washington, D.C.
NAS	National Academy of Sciences Archives, Washington, D.C.
PCA	Population Council Archives, Rockefeller Archive Center, Sleepy Hollow, New York
PMHP	Philip M. Hauser Papers, Special Collections Research Center, University of Chicago Library
PREP	Paul R. Ehrlich Papers, Stanford University Library
RFA	Rockefeller Foundation Archives, Rockefeller Archive Center, Sleepy Hollow, New York
RPP	Raymond Pearl Papers, American Philosophical Society Library, Philadelphia

SPIA	School of Public and International Affairs, Seeley G. Mudd Manuscript Library, Princeton University
SSC	Sophia Smith Collection, Smith College
UNA	United Nations Archives, New York

Introduction

The camera started rolling. Wearing his signature bow tie and light blue lab coat, Bill Nye the "Science Guy" stood in front of a conveyor belt that moved colorful people-shaped sponges from the sponge-people machine into a small blue tub. The tub was full of water, which the sponge people rapidly absorbed. In his characteristic frenetic style, Nye scooped them up, squeezed them out, and put them back on the conveyor belt, only to have even more sponge people fall into the tub. "They're so absorbent!" he complained. Nye was filming the finale episode for the first season of his Netflix show, *Bill Nye Saves the World*. The episode was titled "Earth's People Problem," and the sponge people represented the growing human population soaking up Earth's limited resources.[1]

Nye's own concern about population growth had begun at the age of nine, when he visited the 1965 World's Fair in New York with his family. There he saw a scoreboard showing the world's population growing in real time. On the day he attended the fair, the scoreboard had just clicked over from 2,999,999,999 to three billion. When he filmed "Earth's People Problem" a half-century later, the world's population had more than doubled to 7.5 billion. Nye predicted that, by the time the episode aired, it would have increased by another million.

That the Earth's human population is growing is undeniable. At the time of this writing (2020), it has passed 7.7 billion.[2] Also undeniable is the fact that global population growth causes Americans considerable anxiety. As Nye explained, population growth "is bound up with lots of other difficult issues: the way we treat the environment, how our economies grow, migration of people, women's rights, access to healthcare, and contraception."

Building the Population Bomb. Emily Klancher Merchant, Oxford University Press (2021). © Oxford University Press.
DOI: 10.1093/oso/9780197558942.003.0001

Yet by the end of the episode twenty-six minutes later, Nye had done little to elucidate the connection between population growth and these other important issues. He even suggested that perhaps the population problem is not what we think it is. He explained, "close to a billion of us are undernourished" because "we can produce enough food for everybody, but we're not good at distributing it." He also noted that "Earth's people problem" isn't necessarily about too many babies. In some parts of the world there aren't enough young people to support rapidly growing elderly populations. Nye even admitted that the word "overpopulation" "has a lot of baggage" because, when people use it, they always attribute it to "those other people" rather than to themselves. Despite complicating population in these ways, Nye kept the episode firmly focused on the question of how to reduce the number of babies coming into the world.

More than anything, what this episode of *Bill Nye Saves the World* demonstrates is Americans' widespread confusion regarding human population. We know that the Earth's population is growing, and we have a sense that population growth is causing problems. We can't exactly explain why, though, and there is little scientific evidence to support that feeling. We are nevertheless certain that having fewer people on the planet would help, and we are frustrated because we don't exactly know how to make that happen. As a result, the challenges of controlling the world's population often stand in for evidence that the world's population needs to be controlled.

This book turns the clock back one hundred years to explain how Americans came to see population growth as the fundamental cause of—and population control the ultimate solution to—many of the world's most pressing problems, from poverty to climate change. It explores how human population became an object of intervention for governments, intergovernmental agencies, and nongovernmental organizations, and how some forms of intervention, such as increasing women's access to education and birth control, got classified as legitimate, while others, such as penalties for supposedly excess childbearing, were recognized as coercive. This distinction between legitimate and illegitimate modes of intervention played out in the central segment of the Bill Nye episode, in a debate among a panel of experts over how to solve "Earth's people problem." On one side, Nye and bioethicist Travis Rieder argued that, for the sake of the planet, we need strict limits on childbearing in the "developed world."[3] On the other side, reproductive biologist Rachel Snow and gynecologist Nerys Benfield recommended a focus on family planning and education for women.[4] They argued against "anything to incentivize fewer children or more children," pointing out that such policies inevitably penalize "poor women, minority women, disabled women." Nye, who seemed unaware of the history of eugenics in the United States, challenged this position, asking how these women were penalized, and suggested as an alternative better birth control for men.

The ongoing population debate, between moderates who advocate voluntary family planning and extremists who advocate compulsory childbearing limits, follows contours that were drawn globally between the 1920s and the mid-1970s. On the moderate side, demographers, the United Nations, and such nongovernmental organizations as the Population Council take the position that continued economic growth requires that population growth rates remain within a narrow (but generally unspecified) band. Populations must grow rapidly enough that there are ample workers to provide for children and retirees but not so rapidly as to divert money from capital accumulation for such everyday needs as food, clothing, and shelter. Proponents of this view maintain that the only legitimate way to keep population growth rates within the appropriate band is through education for women and the active promotion of family planning. The moderate side of the debate also includes those who argue that population in some parts of the world—notably East Asia and Europe—is growing too slowly, a perspective that Nye acknowledged and quickly skipped past. The extreme position is less prevalent today than it was fifty years ago, but support for it mounts as anxiety about climate change becomes more pervasive. This side is taken by population-oriented natural scientists, some ethicists, and such environmental organizations as Population Matters.[5] Its proponents contend that human population has already exceeded the planet's ability to provide for us and absorb our emissions, and that population growth must be reversed by limiting the number of children people are allowed to have.

Building the Population Bomb does not take one side or the other. Rather, it argues that today's population debate presents a false set of choices, focusing attention on how to control the world's population and foreclosing the question of whether doing so would actually solve any of the world's problems. This book transcends the debate by demonstrating that the moderate and extreme positions emerged in tandem and have supported and sustained one another, each attributing some of the world's most pressing problems to population, thereby eliding the true causes of those problems and substituting population control—whether of the moderate or the extreme variety—for more appropriate solutions. Most histories of population thought and policy, even those that are critical of population control, are told from within the terms of this debate. They generally begin from the assumption that human population growth is a problem and that we need noncoercive means of slowing it down.[6] Some explain how experts came to recognize that population is a problem,[7] while others tell the story of how the enormity of this problem led to enthusiasm for coercive solutions that did not respect women's rights.[8] Yet others warn that our enthusiasm for women's rights has led us to overlook the enormity of the population problem.[9]

Instead of beginning with those assumptions, this book asks where they came from.[10] It finds that demography, the social science of human population dynamics, is the key to answering that question. Demography has been mostly absent from existing histories, and its absence has gone almost entirely unremarked. Demographers make cameo appearances, but they are generally assumed to speak in unison and in unqualified support of population control. I was able to piece together a more complete story only through a lengthy research process that involved traveling to archives around the country, training in demography and working in a historical demography lab, interviewing demographers and attending their meetings, reading as much of the demography literature as I could, and programming computers to read what I couldn't.[11] What I found is that historicizing demography unravels the presumed scientific foundation of the entire population debate; it was the debate itself that provided the impetus for the establishment of demography between the world wars and its meteoric growth in the decades following World War II. Only by taking a step back from the debate over how to solve the population problem does it become possible to ask how population growth came to constitute a problem, to identify demography's contributions and challenges to that process, and to recognize that the moderate and extreme positions evident on *Bill Nye Saves the World*, though generally framed as oppositional, are mutually constitutive.

Building the Population Bomb documents the history of "Earth's people problem" by tracing the material circulation of ideas about human population among and between scientists (of various kinds), philanthropists, businessmen, diplomats, the media, and policymakers in the United States and throughout the world. It demonstrates that each side of the debate aired on *Bill Nye Saves the World* represents an *assemblage*: a specific configuration of people, theories, data, analytics, institutions, organizations, publications, slogans, and devices.[12] While the two sides of the debate are distinguishable from one another, their assemblages are entangled. Each has contributed to the promotion and perpetuation of the other. Even the conflict between them has helped to advance their primary point of agreement, which is that population growth is a problem that needs to be solved. The emergence of these population assemblages in the interwar United States was neither natural nor inevitable but rather the result of specific people working toward specific ends with the tools at their disposal. Their continued existence has never been an accomplished fact. Rather, the maintenance and transformation of these populationist assemblages over the past hundred years has always been the product of active work by their witting or unwitting supporters.

This book shows who put each piece of each assemblage into place and what implements they used to secure it. Identifying this historical process required following specific concepts—and even turns of phrase—as they moved between contexts and across time, tracing their travels between people, institutions, and publications. It involved constructing family trees and intellectual and professional networks that made it possible to document the circulation of ideas among people, people among institutions, and money between people and institutions. The book relies on archives of demographers, their employers, and their interlocutors, and on oral history interviews with demographers and other key players in the story.[13] This research demonstrates that, while science often legitimated population control projects, money was the most powerful tool for constructing the assemblages and holding them in place. Those who had the money wielded considerable influence over what science got done and how and to whom its results were communicated.

Although this book deals with global population, it is centered on the United States. Since World War II, U.S.-based actors have exercised an outsized influence on population thought and policy worldwide. Digging below the surface of such multilateral organizations as the United Nations Population Fund usually reveals that the bulk of the leadership and money comes from the United States.[14] This book therefore tells the story of how Americans understood and shaped the world's population in the twentieth century, though it also demonstrates that they did not do so alone and that they often faced resistance.

Building the Population Bomb furthers our understanding of the history of the social sciences[15] and of the role of the United States in promoting global development in the second half of the twentieth century.[16] Critically, it brings together these largely separate areas of historical inquiry, showing how social scientific research not only informed American efforts to promote economic development abroad during the Cold War but also legitimated those efforts and traveled along with them, often smoothing the way. In a postwar and postcolonial world organized around national sovereignty, carrying the authority of science allowed the U.S. government and U.S.-based nongovernmental organizations to step across international borders and intervene in the most intimate aspects of life in other countries.

This book also furthers the contemporary project of reproductive justice, which advocates "the human right to maintain personal bodily autonomy, have children, not have children, and parent the children we have in safe and sustainable communities."[17] In the United States, white middle-class and wealthy women generally take these rights for granted. The reproductive justice movement was born out of the struggles of women of color and poor women to achieve the same basic rights regarding their reproductive capacity. The United States has a long history of sometimes suppressing and sometimes promoting the reproduction of poor women and women of color for the benefit of the country's white middle-class and wealthy. In the twentieth century, population size and the rate of population growth emerged as scientific justifications for denying women of color and poor women the right to have children, not just in the United States but throughout the world. This book explains how. It further explains how supposedly legitimate approaches to population control, namely family planning programs, were neither safe nor dignified approaches to fertility management. Such programs aimed to convince women that their poverty was caused by the number of children they had rather than by the structure of the global economy, and clinics often disappeared after they had put IUDs in what governments and scientists deemed enough women, leaving the women without medical care to deal with complications or to remove the devices when they wanted to have children.

This book shows how population professionals, most of them elite men, transformed the reproduction of poor and nonwhite women into a problem that required their intervention. At the same time, those professionals denied poor and nonwhite women the right to parent the children they had in safe and sustainable communities. By attributing individual poverty to family size and nation-level poverty to high birth rates, population professionals foreclosed opportunities for redistribution between and within societies. By attributing ecosystem degradation to human numbers, they naturalized the industrial, military, and governmental activities and decisions that pollute our air, water, and soil and that warm our climate. Further, they elided the fact that pollution-generating installations are intentionally sited in poor communities and communities of color, the issue at the heart of today's environmental justice movement. Achieving economic, environmental, and reproductive justice requires challenging the attribution of the world's problems to reproduction, whether the supposedly excessive reproduction of poor people in high-fertility countries or the supposedly inadequate reproduction of middle-class people in low-fertility countries.

Building the Population Bomb reveals, layer by historical layer, the scientific and political foundation on which the "Earth's People Problem" episode stands. Seeing the accretion of those layers, understanding where they came from, and recognizing whose ends they have served is key to realizing that the emperor of population is wearing no clothes. To be sure, there is a theoretical limit to the number of people the Earth can sustain. That limit, however, depends on how humans interact with the Earth; at current rates of population growth, we are unlikely to reach it.[18] The story told here challenges the implication of reproduction (whether thought to be excessive or inadequate) in the creation and perpetuation of such global problems as poverty and environmental degradation by demonstrating how population came to take the blame in the first place. It does not, however, advocate for dispensing with the concept of population altogether, as some science and technology scholars have recommended.[19] As will become clear, demography and the demographic concept of population provide powerful tools for thinking in terms of social (not natural) aggregates, for planning the provision of human services, and for interrogating and addressing the causes of inequality.[20]

The story begins in the 1920s, with the emergence of two scientific approaches to human population. Natural scientists, focusing on population growth in the aggregate, warned that the United States and the world as a whole were headed for overpopulation. Statisticians, meanwhile, developed new vital rate indices that suggested that population growth in North America and Western Europe was slowing and would soon reverse course. Instead of overpopulation, they claimed, countries in those regions faced the danger of depopulation. Chapter 1 demonstrates that these divergent scientific positions emerged from different ontologies of population and supported opposing political projects. They could not be reconciled scientifically, as they relied on incompatible analyses of the same data. Despite these differences, natural scientists and statisticians from the Americas, Europe, and Asia came together in 1928 to form an international professional organization to promote the emergent science of population. Their project crumbled in the 1930s, however, under the weight of the political tensions that had begun to tear Europe apart. As various European countries weaponized their population policies, they looked to the new organization for scientific legitimacy, and scientists found themselves unable to distinguish scientific questions about population from political ones. In their attempts to draw those boundaries, American participants laid the foundation for demography, a social science of human population based on the vital rate indices developed by statisticians in the 1920s.

Chapter 2 demonstrates that the American social scientists who began to identify as demographers between the wars formed an alliance with a new brand of eugenics that emerged in the United States in the 1930s. This updated version of eugenics eschewed the intra-European racism that had become associated with European fascism. Its proponents aimed to replace government control over who reproduced and who did not with social and market control. While the older eugenicists who continued to espouse nativism and intra-European racism looked to the natural science of population and its predictions of overpopulation for scientific legitimacy, younger eugenicists instead embraced demography and its vital rate indices, which continued to suggest that depopulation was just around the corner. As the Great Depression opened seats at the policy table for demographers, demographers turned their research focus to the development of eugenic pronatalist policies. At the heart of this agenda was a new combination of birth control legalization and social engineering that would encourage the wealthy to have large families and the poor to have small families, without overt state control. Supporters of this project termed it "family planning."

Chapter 3 explains how, following World War II, the new United Nations conceptually reorganized the world from a small collection of empires into a large community of nation-states, each responsible for statistically constituting and technocratically governing its own population and economy. The experts who advised the UN expected that, once populations and economies had been measured, they could be compared and adjusted relative to one another if necessary. UN demographers initially attempted to bring this world of nation-states into being through the establishment of democratic governments and national statistical infrastructures. This effort failed, however, as disputes over sovereignty at local, national, and international levels rendered population data either uncollectable or untrustworthy. The UN ultimately turned to demographic theory and models to fill in the persistent gaps in its data tables, producing a statistical image of the world as a series of populations and rendering those populations tractable to control.

Chapter 4 documents the development in the 1950s and 1960s of a global consensus regarding population that briefly united the two scientific positions that had emerged in opposition to one another between the wars. Whereas interwar natural scientists had contended that the world's population was nearing its natural limit, postwar natural scientists argued that the limit had already been exceeded, pointing to soil erosion and resource depletion as evidence. Demographic theory, meanwhile, suggested that modernization would both expand the Earth's human capacity and keep human population well below it. But demographers worried that rapid population growth in certain countries of Asia and Latin America could prevent modernization, and they began to promote family planning as the solution. Working together, demographers and natural scientists generated and popularized the belief that population growth in developing countries was one of humanity's most pressing challenges and that it could be averted through family planning. This consensus allowed the U.S. government to embrace family planning as a tool of domestic and foreign policy by moving it from the realm of religious and political debate to the realm of scientific and technological certainty.

Chapter 5 explains how, during the 1960s, the (over)population consensus supported the growth of demography, which in turn promoted the international spread of the consensus. U.S.-based organizations devoted to overseas population control recruited demography graduate students from developing countries and funded their education in the United States, with the understanding that they would return home to advocate for population control as a means of promoting economic development. These organizations also funded field studies by American demographers in Africa, Asia, and Latin America that promoted small-family norms and the distribution of new systemic contraceptive technologies. This research documented the existence of what demographers termed "unmet need" for family planning services, legitimating the establishment or expansion of family planning programs by governments, international agencies, and nongovernmental organizations.

Chapter 6 documents the fragmentation of the postwar population consensus. It explains how, as American power in the world became more tenuous at the end of the 1960s and the beginning of the 1970s, the consensus broke down under attack from two directions. On the right, natural scientists abandoned their support for family planning and instead advocated more direct population control measures. Pointing to the growing environmental crisis, these erstwhile participants in the population consensus contended that family planning would not reduce population growth quickly enough to prevent massive famine, ecosystem collapse, and global political catastrophe. On the left, Latin American social scientists, amplified by a new generation of demography graduate students in the United States, contended that no approach to population control would ever solve the world's problems because those problems had their roots in the structure of the global capitalist economy, not human numbers. American demographers, who continued to espouse family planning as a stabilizing force in an increasingly chaotic world, found themselves embattled at the 1974 UN World Population Conference, which marked the demise of the postwar population consensus.

The epilogue brings the story to the present. It follows the demographic and natural scientific versions of the population problem into the twenty-first century and demonstrates how debates between these two positions on population have largely silenced and co-opted voices that refuse to attribute the world's woes to expanding human numbers. I contend that the real problem with population is that it remains a prominent scapegoat for nearly all of the world's ills. Efforts to control population distract publics and policymakers from the actual causes of human suffering and environmental degradation. The framing of the world's pressing issues as "the population problem" diverts resources from just and equitable solutions at the expense of the world's most vulnerable people and of the planet itself.

Feminist science and technology scholars Adele Clarke and Donna Haraway have recently made a new appeal for limiting the number of humans on Earth, equating sanguinity about population growth with climate denialism.[21] This book challenges that position, contending that blaming population growth for climate change is much more akin to climate denialism, as it obscures the role of fossil-fuel-driven global capitalism and deters regulatory solutions. I certainly do not dispute that population has grown enormously in the past hundred years or that anthropogenic climate change is threatening our very existence on Earth, but research has shown that the former is not the cause of the latter.[22] As feminist environmental geographer Joni Seager explains, "there is only the loosest correlation between numbers of people and environmental stress," so "an environmental analysis that focuses on population numbers is largely diversionary."[23] This book explains who has diverted our attention and from what.

Advocates of population limitation often complain that ideological opposition to birth control and abortion keep birth rates dangerously high or that the dark history of eugenics and population control have rendered suspect any efforts to make birth control and abortion more readily accessible. Ideological opposition to birth control and abortion, and the long history of eugenics and population control, are real issues that need to be addressed. But these are reproductive justice problems, not population problems. To adequately solve them, we must challenge the assumption that population is the source of such complex issues as global poverty and climate change. This book tells the story of how these separate concerns—human population growth, the natural environment, social inequality, eugenics, racism, and the legality and availability of birth control and abortion—got entwined. In particular it documents the role of demography in both bringing them together and teasing them apart.[24]

Prior to the COVID-19 pandemic, the UN predicted that the world's human population would peak at 11 billion around the year 2100.[25] This book explains where such numbers come from and how Americans have been taught to view them with alarm—really to view *any* prediction of future population growth with alarm. It is only by recognizing that the anxiety we feel about future population growth is learned and not obvious that we can see that population growth itself is not a barrier to economic, environmental, and reproductive justice. Rather, it is our anxiety about population growth that distracts us from the pursuit of those urgent goals.

CHAPTER 1

Quantity and Quality

On August 29, 1927, the former registrar-general of England and Wales Sir Bernard Mallet welcomed invited guests to the Salle Centrale in Geneva for the World Population Conference, an international meeting of scientists to discuss "the problems of population."[1] Ninety years later, when Bill Nye filmed "Earth's People Problem," the title itself asserted the cause of the world's problems and suggested a potential solution. In 1927 phrases like "the problems of population" and "population problems" served a similar function, attributing all of the challenges of urban industrial society in the Gilded Age and Progressive Era—inequality, corruption, poverty, crime, and social strife—to population size and composition, or "quantity" and "quality" in the lexicon of the day. These phrases blamed a variety of social issues on there being too many people, or not enough, or too many of the wrong kind of people and not enough of the right kind. They also pointed to a scientific remedy: changing either the number or the type of people who composed the nation. Advocates for and opponents of population-oriented political programs—eugenic sterilization, selective pronatalism, immigration restriction, and birth control legalization—presented them as cures for ills caused by population and called on science to support their agendas. Scientists themselves took part in political advocacy and focused their research on the dynamics of human population in order to find solutions to the most pressing problems of their time.

The 1927 conference was put on by the American birth control activist Margaret Sanger and a Johns Hopkins University biologist named Raymond Pearl in an uneasy partnership that would not survive the meeting. Each saw the establishment of an international organization of

Building the Population Bomb. Emily Klancher Merchant, Oxford University Press (2021). © Oxford University Press.
DOI: 10.1093/oso/9780197558942.003.0002

scientists working on questions of human population as a critical step toward meeting their own ultimate goals. For Sanger, that goal was the worldwide legalization of birth control; for Pearl, it was the integration of human population dynamics into biology. The organization that emerged from the meeting, the International Union for the Scientific Investigation of Population Problems (IUSIPP),[2] proved just as fragile as Sanger and Pearl's partnership. Composed of committees from each of its constituent countries, the IUSIPP served as a forum for debate over the scientific basis of nationalist population policies that were rapidly becoming oppressive and even genocidal. Practitioners of the emergent science of demography found themselves unable to demarcate a boundary between population science and population politics, and the IUSIPP fell victim to the same political tensions that were tearing Europe apart. Yet even as this attempt at demographic internationalism failed, it fostered the development of the mathematical foundation for demography, which provided scientific cover for fascist population policies in the 1930s and for efforts to shape the world's population over the next fifty years.

THE POPULATION PROBLEM

Sanger's alliance with Pearl and other scientists was part of a new strategy for birth control legalization that Sanger adopted after her second arrest. She had been arrested the first time in 1914 for mailing her newsletter, *The Woman Rebel*, which advocated contraception as part of a feminist and pro-labor agenda. Sanger saw in birth control—a term she coined to denote women's control of their reproductive capacity—the potential to increase female sexual autonomy and empower workers to abstain from reproducing capital's surplus army of labor.[3] She was arrested again in 1916 for providing information about birth control through a clinic in Brooklyn. After the trial, Sanger decided that, rather than fighting an uphill battle to distribute birth control information illegally, she would work to change the law by recruiting to her cause those whose opinions would have the most influence in the legislative realm: professional men. The only problem was that few of the doctors, judges, clergy, scientists, and writers Sanger hoped to enlist cared about female reproductive autonomy or workers' rights. To attract their support, therefore, Sanger began to promote birth control as a solution to "the population problem."

The phrase "the population problem," though certainly not new, was heard with increasing frequency in the decades between the world wars.[4]

It referred not to a specific *problem* but rather to a *framework* for understanding and ameliorating the most urgent social and political issues of the day, those stemming from the extreme inequality that characterized urban industrial modernity in the United States and Western Europe, and the even starker inequality between these metropoles and their colonial peripheries. In rapidly expanding metropolitan cities, dazzling wealth abutted abject poverty, which was accompanied by crime, disease, and strife. Globally, extreme climatic events collaborated with imperial economies to produce devastating famines.[5] In the first decades of the twentieth century, reformers proposed social and political solutions to these problems.[6] Following World War I, progressive reform took a decidedly biological turn as experts in a variety of domains adopted the view that social problems originated in the biology and genealogy of society's most vulnerable members.[7] If people were starving, there must be too many of them. If pauperism, illness, and criminality were hereditary conditions with biological origins, then poverty, disease, and crime could be alleviated through selective breeding, also known as eugenics.[8]

Between the wars, "eugenics" referred both to the science of human breeding and to political programs and social movements aimed at either limiting the reproduction of those thought to be hereditarily predisposed to poverty or antisocial behavior (negative eugenics) or promoting the reproduction of those thought to be hereditarily predisposed to socioeconomic and professional success (positive eugenics). Eugenics was both a national and an international phenomenon: every inhabited continent boasted at least one organization aimed at improving the population of a given country through selective breeding; these nation-level organizations communicated and coordinated with one another through international eugenics conferences and publications.[9] In the United States, the Eugenics Record Office at Cold Spring Harbor, New York, integrated science and politics, pursuing research on human heredity and using the results to promote state-level legislation for compulsory sterilization. Between 1907 and 1940 more than thirty states enacted such laws.[10] Most interwar professionals, including those Sanger hoped to recruit to her cause, considered the biological heredity of socioeconomic characteristics a scientific fact and supported eugenic legislation as "a major breakthrough in the application of rational, scientific methods to the problems of a complex urban and industrial society."[11] In their minds, such problems inhered in what they termed the "quality" of the population, not the structure of society.

Population was itself a relatively new concept, a product of novel forms of democratic governmental rationality that had emerged in the nineteenth century and that focused on the counting and classification of those who were subject to and subjects of state power. Populations are statistical artifacts produced in the process of census-making.[12] Though censuses have much older antecedents,[13] the present-day practice of census-making originated in the United States, mandated by the Constitution as the quantitative basis for representative democracy.[14] Censuses enumerate the individuals who are to be represented by government. In so doing, they simultaneously constitute both the government itself and its citizens and subjects, who collectively constitute the nation governed by the state: the state's national population.

Making a census reflects and facilitates the power of the organization carrying out the project, which is almost always a state. One of the defining features of a census is its universality. It counts and describes every person meeting a given set of criteria. Achieving universality requires sufficient resources to locate all qualifying individuals and sufficient power to compel them to submit to enumeration. Typically only states have the resources and power to do this, and censuses typically include only those living within the boundaries of a state *and* subject to its jurisdiction.[15] The primary activity of census-making is enumeration, which involves locating each person and household in administrative and geographic space and classifying each person along a set of social and biosocial axes that mark some as subjects of state power and others as subject to it.[16] Censuses measure both the total size of national populations, which interwar observers termed "population quantity," and the distribution within that total number of such characteristics as age, sex, race, nativity, occupation, and education. Interwar observers termed the distribution of these traits "population quality."[17]

Population quality was both a descriptive and a normative term. It was descriptive in that it referred to the *qualitative* (nonquantitative) or categorical characteristics of individuals, such as race, national origin, and occupation. It was normative in the sense that it equated high population quality with high proportions of people in socially favored categories (white, native born, professional). The concept of population quality conflated social characteristics that could be measured in censuses with traits that could not be measured in censuses (or in any other way at the time), namely genetic makeup. For proponents of eugenics, the statistical portraits painted by censuses reflected the biological quality of a nation's population. Eugenicists equated social inequality with genetic diversity, attributing poverty not to the exploitation of labor by capital but rather to what they termed "differential fertility," or the higher birth rates of the poor relative to the middle class and wealthy.

In the United States, eugenics was a project of white racial hygiene given urgency by the fact of an increasingly multiracial nation. Its proponents believed that the global political and economic power of the United States depended on white political, economic, and social hegemony at home. They therefore aimed to police the internal and external boundaries of American whiteness by restricting reproduction and immigration. To be sure, nonwhite reproduction and immigration were always more stringently proscribed than were white reproduction and immigration. Segregation, Asian exclusion, Mexican repatriation, and a host of other *racial* projects targeted the reproduction and migration of nonwhites.[18] The *eugenic* project, however, targeted the reproduction of poor whites and the immigration of Southern and Eastern Europeans in the service of the racial projects to which it was articulated.[19]

American eugenics therefore had a strong nativist bent, at least in the first two decades of the twentieth century. The growth of industry at the end of the nineteenth century had drawn immigrants from Southern and Eastern Europe, as well as from Asia and Latin America, to work in new low-paying jobs. The eugenic worldview assumed that markers of socioeconomic status reflected genetic quality. Correlations between socioeconomic status and race or national origin were therefore thought to reflect biological differences at the group level. As industrial poverty became more prevalent, visible, and concentrated among recent immigrants, many observers attributed it to the genetic deficiencies of immigrants rather than the structure of the labor market. Prior to the 1930s, most American eugenicists subscribed to Madison Grant's typology of intra-European racial distinctions. In his 1916 bestseller, *The Passing of the Great Race*, Grant attributed urban poverty to the fact that "old stock" Americans, descended from the "Nordic" race of Northwest Europe, were in danger of being outnumbered by new migrants who represented the inferior "Alpine" and "Mediterranean" races of Southern and Eastern Europe.[20] American eugenicists typically supported restrictions on immigration from Southern and Eastern Europe and included in their conception of differential fertility the higher birth rates of foreign-born whites relative to native-born whites.

Sanger began to align birth control with eugenics while in exile in London after her first arrest.[21] After her second arrest, she wholeheartedly embraced eugenics as a vehicle for the legalization of contraception, refashioning birth control from a tool for the sexual autonomy of women or economic liberation of workers into a solution to "the population problem" and a tool for "the improvement of the race."[22] Her new strategy took institutional form with the 1917 launch of the *Birth Control Review* and the 1921 establishment of the American Birth Control League (ABCL), which aimed to attach scientific authority to birth control advocacy. Sanger recruited to the ABCL's National Council eugenically minded natural and social scientists. The social scientists included anti-immigrant sociologists Edward A. Ross, Henry Pratt Fairchild, and Franklin Giddings. The natural scientists included biologists Clarence Cook ("C. C.") Little, Edward East, and Raymond Pearl, who have been described by historian Daniel Kevles as members of the "eugenic priesthood" in the interwar United States.[23] In the *Birth Control Review* and at a series of regional, national, and international conferences, these men and other members of the ABCL's National Council made the scientific case for birth control legalization. For them, the value of birth control inhered not in its potential to increase individual reproductive autonomy or even individual health, but rather in its potential to increase the control of governmental and scientific authorities over the reproduction of desired and undesired segments of national populations.

If the population problem was entirely one of quality, however, birth control was not necessarily an obvious solution. In fact, many American eugenicists in the first decades of the twentieth century opposed its legalization. Since birth control was in more common use among the native-born professional middle class than among the poor or foreign born, eugenicists often decried it as a cause of differential fertility.[24] Eugenic theory (if not eugenic practice) generally combined antinatalism for those considered genetically inferior with pronatalism for those considered genetically superior. Sterilization was the preferred vehicle for the antinatalist project and birth control often seemed a hindrance to the pronatalist project. The scientists who allied themselves with Sanger, however, invoked rising population *quantity* as a primary cause of declining population *quality*. They did so by citing resource limitation as the link between population quantity and population quality.

Sanger's social scientific supporters focused primarily on immigration and high birth rates among immigrants as the major sources of population growth. In 1896 Francis Amasa Walker, superintendent of the 1870 and 1880 U.S. censuses and then president of MIT, contended that immigration drives down the native white birth rate by generating competition over scarce resources, an outcome he termed "displacement."[25] Sociologist Edward Ross described this effect in 1901 as "race suicide" (a term later popularized by President Theodore Roosevelt),[26] warning that, if immigration continued, native-born whites would be replaced by "masses of fecund but beaten humanity from the hovels of far Lombardy and Galicia."[27] He published the anti-immigrant *Standing Room Only?* in 1927. Fellow sociologist and Sanger supporter Henry Pratt Fairchild published *Immigration* in 1913, *The Melting Pot Mistake* in 1926, and *The Alien in Our Midst* in 1930.

Although immigration restriction was the primary political goal of these men, they supported the legalization of contraception as a means of reducing the birth rates of immigrants already in the United States.

The natural scientists who supported Sanger belonged to an intellectual tradition that blended eugenics with conservation.[28] Drawing from principles of wildlife management later popularized by Aldo Leopold, these scientists cautioned that the health of a species depended on the health of its environment, which was threatened by overstocking.[29] For these eugenicists, the carrying capacity of the natural environment legitimated restrictions on immigration and reproduction. Edward East's 1923 *Mankind at the Crossroads*, which Sanger praised as "one of the finest contributions given to the literature on the age," exemplified the natural science argument for immigration restriction and a eugenic birth control program, the necessity of which he justified with reference to the soil erosion that was beginning to threaten U.S. agriculture.[30] East and Little, then president of the University of Michigan, leveraged their scientific credentials to advocate for eugenic sterilization, immigration restriction, and birth control legalization as means of limiting population quantity and thereby improving population quality.[31] Their colleague Raymond Pearl went a step further, launching a new research program into human population dynamics.

A BIOLOGICAL SCIENCE OF POPULATION

Raymond Pearl was a large and outspoken man, described by his contemporaries as "flamboyant."[32] Born in 1879, Pearl attended Dartmouth College, where he initially intended to study classics. He soon became obsessed with genetics, however, under the influence of biologist Herbert Spencer Jennings, a former student of Charles Davenport, the founder of the Eugenics Record Office.[33] When Pearl graduated from Dartmouth in 1899, he followed Jennings to the University of Michigan, where he completed a Ph.D. in zoology in 1902 with a dissertation on the behavior of flatworms.[34] Between 1905 and 1906 Pearl studied biometrics—the statistical analysis of biological material—with Karl Pearson, who was then director of the Galton National Eugenics Laboratory in London.[35] Pearl and Pearson became quite close, but had a falling-out after Pearl returned to the United States, when his research on hen breeding produced support for the Mendelian model of heredity and against the "ancestral inheritance" (blending) mechanism of heredity at the heart of Pearson's biometric tradition.[36]

During World War I, Pearl served under Herbert Hoover as chief of the Statistics Division of the U.S. Food Administration.[37] Reading Thomas Robert Malthus's 1798 *Essay on the Principle of Population* sparked Pearl's interest in human population growth and the relationship between population and food supply.[38] Food had recently become a concern of scientists worldwide with the discovery of the nitrogen cycle and the realization that the already limited supply of the usable form of this element—essential for all food production—was rapidly dwindling.[39] Pearl began researching human population growth in earnest in 1919, prompted by a fire that devastated his work in progress shortly after he was hired as the first professor of biometry and vital statistics at the new School of Hygiene and Public Health at Johns Hopkins University, where he had again followed Jennings. Over the next year Pearl developed the natural law of population growth that he would spend much of his life promoting and defending.

Pearl's natural law of population was grounded in the same Malthusian perspective that undergirded East's *Mankind at the Crossroads*. It would later become a foundational principle of the new field of (nonhuman) population ecology.[40] The law rested on two premises, which Pearl attributed to Malthus. The first was that all human and nonhuman populations will grow until they reach the limits of subsistence resources in the territories they occupy. According to this premise, the maximum size of a population is determined by the potential food supply in the territory available to it, and it cannot grow beyond that biologically determined size. The second premise was that the finitude of subsistence resources was the only thing that could affect the rate of population growth. According to this premise, any slowing or cessation of growth indicates that the population in question has begun to feel or anticipate the encroaching limit of the food supply. Pearl's innovation was to suggest that the growth of a population would slow as it neared its maximum size, resulting in an S-shaped growth curve that could be described mathematically by the logistic equation shown in Figure 1.1.[41]

In this image, the x-axis represents calendar time in years and the y-axis represents population size at any given time. The letter e is Euler's number, and a, b, and c are population-specific constants. These three unknowns were to be discovered empirically for each population by fitting the curve to historical census data. Once the constants were known, it became possible to calculate the maximum size the population would reach, given by b/c. Pearl described this value as the population's "saturation point." The date at which a population would reach saturation could be identified by setting y equal to b/c and solving for x. The size of the population at any given date, past or future, could be calculated by setting x equal to that date and solving for y. Pearl contended that the curve did

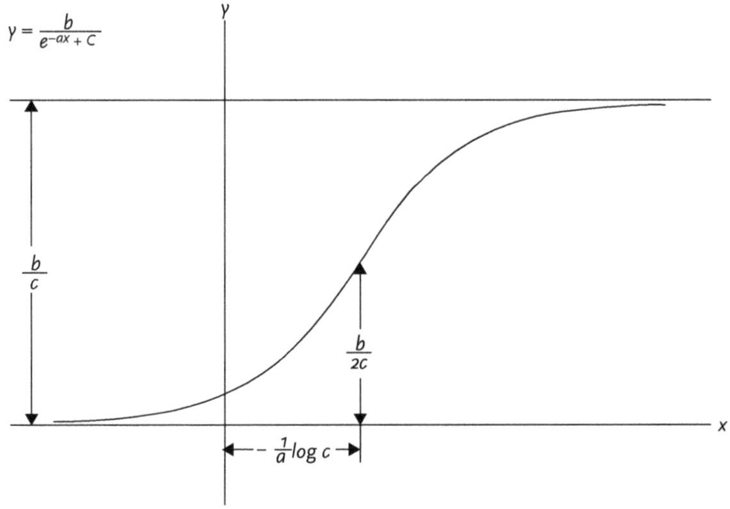

Figure 1.1 Raymond Pearl's logistic curve.
Source: Raymond Pearl, *The Biology of Death* (Philadelphia: J.B. Lippincott, 1922), 249.

not simply *describe* a general pattern of population growth; rather, the logistic equation was itself a *natural law* of population growth. Populations, human and nonhuman alike, he claimed, were biologically constrained to follow a logistic growth trajectory. He compared his law of population growth to the equations that describe planetary motion, claiming that, just as those equations could predict the location of a planet at any point in time, so too could the logistic equation "construct the entire orbit of population" and thereby indicate its size at any date in the past or the future.[42]

Pearl's approach to all areas of biology was holistic, focusing on entire organisms rather than their component parts or processes.[43] In this case, the population as a whole and its growth trajectory were his objects of analysis. He described populations as "super-organisms" that expanded over the course of national life cycles. He chose the logistic equation to describe population growth because the logistic had been identified a decade earlier as the growth trajectory of individual organisms.[44] Pearl had little to say about the people composing populations or about the processes of birth, death, and migration that made populations grow or shrink. In his view, individuals and their vital processes were no more independent than were the cells of an organism. Cells could die or be generated, but those activities were governed by the dynamics of the organism to which they belonged. For human populations, that organism was the state that constituted its population through census-making and controlled the territory that provided for its population's subsistence.

Pearl's logistic law therefore assumed the kind of organic relationship between state, territory, and people claimed by nationalist movements of the nineteenth century.[45] He conceived of the logistic growth trajectory as a process of national maturation, through which states and their populations advanced from youth to senescence.[46] When he found that historical censuses for the United States, France, and Serbia corresponded to different portions of the logistic curves he fit to those populations (Figure 1.2), he explained that the observed data for the United States traced the bottom (left) of the curve because it was a "comparatively new country," while the observed data for France traced the top (right) of the curve because it was "an old country" that had only recently introduced censuses. Observed data for Serbia, which Pearl considered a middle-aged country, traced the middle.[47] Pearl was not troubled by his inability to find a country whose observed historical growth trajectory traced an entire logistic curve.[48] He explained that, given the recency of census-making and the slow growth of human populations, the period covered by censuses represented only a fraction of human history.

Pearl took to his laboratory to validate the claim that population growth was as predictable as celestial motion. If the logistic curve represented a natural law of population growth, then all populations, both human and nonhuman, should follow a logistic growth trajectory. Faster-growing nonhuman populations could therefore stand in for slower-growing human populations for the purpose of scientific analysis. As Pearl put it, "a real understanding of the problem to which Malthus addressed himself is going to come more from the intensive study of lower forms of life in the laboratory, under physically and chemically controlled conditions, than from the manipulation of never quite satisfactory demographic statistics."[49] He demonstrated that a pair of *Drosophila* (geneticists' favorite fruit fly) in a bottle would reproduce, and that the growth of the population of offspring would follow a logistic trajectory. Neglecting the many differences between a bottle of flies and the human population of a country, Pearl presented this finding as evidence that the logistic was also the pattern of growth a human population would exhibit if it could be watched long enough.[50]

Pearl published his logistic law in a range of scientific and popular periodicals. In each of these venues, he raised alarm bells about the imminent overpopulation his logistic law appeared to predict. A 1922 article in the *New York Times* began with the provocative statement "they breed like flies!" Pearl continued, "most cynical persons who make this remark about the inhabitants of the congested quarters of our great cities do not realize

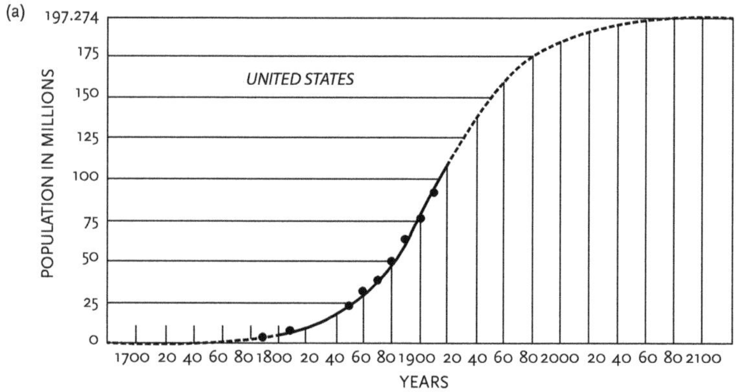

Fig. 61.—Showing the curve of growth of the population of United States. For further explanation of this and the two following diagrams, see text.

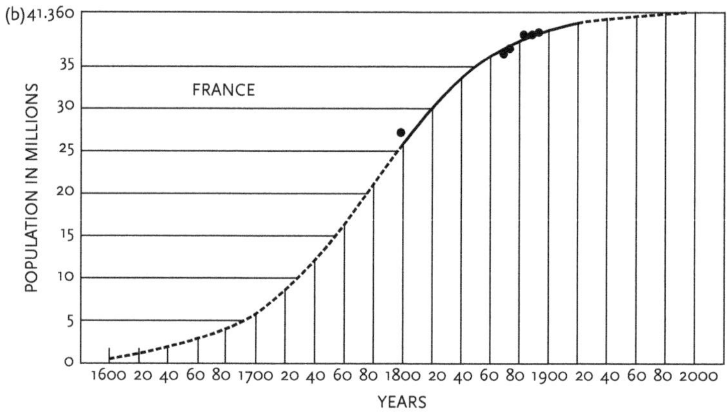

Fig. 62.—Showing the curve of growth of the population of France.

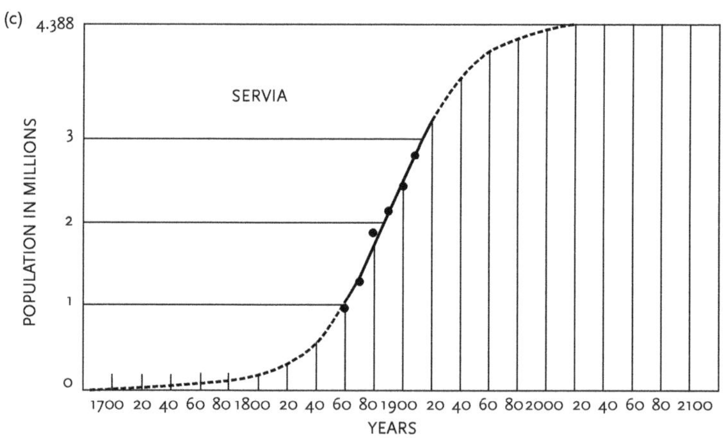

Fig. 63.—Showing the curve of growth of the population of Serbia.

Figure 1.2 Raymond Pearl's logistic growth curves for the United States, France, and Serbia.
Source: Raymond Pearl, *The Biology of Death* (Philadelphia: J.B. Lippincott, 1922), 250–253.

that this is an accurate statement of scientific fact." He then described his *Drosophila* experiments and presented his logistic calculation for the United States, according to which the country would reach its saturation population of 197 million around the year 2100.[51] Pearl did not explain that, according to his theory, the wealthy too bred like flies. Instead his article suggested that, due to the hypersexuality of the poor, the United States was headed inexorably toward overpopulation.

The impending overpopulation Pearl claimed to have discovered, however, was the starting point of his analysis, not its outcome. He began with the Malthusian assumption that each national population was growing toward the carrying capacity of the territory its state controlled, and that population growth was wholly determined by the difference between the current population size and the saturation point. He then fit logistic curves to historical population data and claimed that the curves he fit proved that the populations in question were in fact growing along logistic trajectories toward their maxima. Pearl never subjected any of these assumptions to empirical examination, nor did he compare the saturation point he calculated for any population to independent estimates of carrying capacity.[52]

Unlike his colleagues, who raised the threat of overpopulation in order to advocate for immigration restriction and birth control legalization as means of averting disaster, Pearl contended that the overpopulation he predicted was inevitable. The logistic was a *law* of population growth, not a suggestion. Admitting the possibility of preventing the overpopulation it forecast undermined its credibility as a law of nature and its value as a predictive tool. According to Pearl's theory, population growth was predetermined. It could be predicted but not controlled, and it could be predicted only *because* it could not be controlled. But if population *quantity* was predetermined, Pearl contended that population *quality* was not. He offered tempered support for birth control legalization in his 1922 *New York Times* article with the statement that "man, in theory at least, now has it completely in his power to determine what kind of people will make up the earth's population when saturation is a fact" through "birth control, directed along eugenic lines."[53] In accord with other eugenicists of his time, Pearl pointed to the threat of rising population quantity to justify policies aimed at manipulating population quality.

Pearl's logistic law of population growth generated both admiration and criticism. Critics decried its biological determinism and challenged its logical inconsistencies. Some pointed out that it produced improbable figures for population size in the distant past or future. Even those who accepted the curve as an accurate empirical description of past population size rejected Pearl's claims that it represented a law of population growth or that it could accurately forecast future growth.[54] Pearl's harshest critic, Harvard University mathematician Edwin B. Wilson, began as an enthusiast but found that the logistic law did not hold up to his scrutiny. When Wilson tried to fit logistic curves to some of the same populations Pearl had discussed in his publications, he found that he was unable to achieve the same results and that different methods of curve fitting produced different saturation limits for the same population.[55] Wilson also discovered that logistic curves are not additive; that is, if curves for, say, the United States, Canada, and Mexico were summed to produce a population forecast for the whole of North America, that aggregate population trajectory would not itself necessarily trace a logistic curve. Perhaps most disturbing, Wilson discovered that the saturation population he calculated for the three states of New York, New Jersey, and Connecticut was *less* than the saturation population Pearl had calculated for just the New York City metropolitan area, which is fully contained within those three states.[56]

Although they had been friends, Pearl refused to discuss Wilson's challenge to his theory, accusing Wilson of attacking him personally. In response, Wilson did begin to make the critique personal, accusing Pearl of failing to adhere to the norms of the scientific community, according to which methods are presented in such a way as to make results replicable. Feigning modesty, Wilson explained what his inability to reproduce Pearl's results must mean: "either I am a very bad curve fitter, which I admit, or . . . you don't actually fit your curves in the precise way that you say you fit them, or . . . you state so indefinitely the method of fitting them that one cannot reconstruct it from this statement."[57] While Pearl seems to have expected that the logistic law of population would be accepted as fact if he simply asserted it frequently enough, Wilson countered that "no method of scientific investigation is really accepted in the scientific world until it has spread out from its original author and been adopted in a larger or smaller part by other investigators."[58] Pearl never engaged with Wilson's critique, which had escalated from questioning Pearl's theory of population growth to denigrating his behavior as a scientist. Instead Pearl denied, in a private letter to Wilson, that he had ever claimed the logistic curve represented a natural law of population growth, even as he continued to promote it as such in public.[59] This exchange would come back to haunt Pearl later in the decade, when Wilson sabotaged Pearl's chance for a job at Harvard.[60] By the time of his death in 1940, Pearl himself had fully repudiated the logistic law of population growth.

Wilson's opinion notwithstanding, Pearl was generally well respected as a scholar. He was elected to the National Academy of Sciences in 1916, when he was only thirty-seven years old, and was also a member of the American Philosophical Society, the American Academy of Arts and Sciences, and the National Research Council. He served as president of the American Society of Zoologists (1913), the American Society of Naturalists (1916–1917), the American Statistical Association (1939), and the American Association of Physical Anthropologists (1935–1936).[61] In all, he published seventeen books and nearly seven hundred articles covering a wide swath of biological topics, including animal behavior, disease, genetics, alcohol and tobacco, population growth, and birth control.

Pearl understood all of these inquiries to be part of a new field he was pioneering, human biology, which explored the human animal through statistical methods and experimentation on nonhuman animals. With a five-year grant of $175,000 from the Rockefeller Foundation, he established a new Institute of Biological Research within the Medical School at Johns Hopkins in 1925 as the epicenter for this work. The grant allowed him an annual salary of $15,000, making him Hopkins's highest-paid professor.[62] When existing scholarly journals didn't provide adequate outlets for his work, Pearl founded new ones: the *Quarterly Review of Biology* in 1926 and *Human Biology* in 1929. He popularized his own work, publishing in such venues as *Ladies' Home Journal* and *Readers' Digest*. He was a close friend of H. L. Mencken and a member of Mencken's Saturday Night Club, which met weekly during Prohibition to drink and jam in impromptu instrumental ensembles. (Pearl played the French horn.)[63] He also wrote a number of articles for Mencken's *American Mercury*. He was well enough known by 1925 that Sinclair Lewis included him as a character in his novel *Arrowsmith*.

It was Pearl's influence that turned the focus of the 1927 meeting in Geneva from birth control to population. Sanger had initially planned the meeting as a follow up to the sixth Neo-Malthusian and Birth Control Conference, which she had hosted in New York in 1925. But when she sought Pearl's assistance, he suggested that the meeting should instead launch a new international union for population science, modeled after existing international scientific unions. There was, at that time, no such thing as population science. Pearl and other scientists were only just beginning to investigate the dynamics of human population, which were still largely the province of government statisticians and insurance actuaries. He nonetheless envisioned population becoming a subfield of human biology and recognized that, in order to raise funds to support his vision, the emergent science needed to take institutional form. Sanger agreed to Pearl's suggestion, imagining the new field as a valuable source of intellectual capital for the legalization of birth control.

In preparation for the conference, Pearl began to draw boundaries around the nascent science of population, distilling it from the contraceptive and eugenic activism out of which it had precipitated. He insisted that the scientific credibility of the conference depended on birth control being excised, as it still carried the taints of politics, sex, and feminism.[64] Bernard Mallet, who agreed to preside over the conference at Sanger's invitation, similarly felt that it would be unseemly for government statisticians to participate in a conference in which birth control was discussed openly.[65] Although there was nothing inherently unscientific about contraception, it had to that point been the subject of very little scientific investigation.[66] Pearl had initially viewed research on birth control as a legitimate task of population science, and in 1926 he asked Sanger for clinical data from the ABCL that he could use for statistical analysis. Sanger was enthusiastic about Pearl's research but unwilling to grant him *exclusive* access to the data, without which he refused to undertake the study.[67] By prohibiting discussion of birth control at the Geneva conference, Pearl brought population science into existence by demarcating it from the feminine world of the birth control clinic and the political world of birth control activism. Sanger acquiesced, reasoning that the success of population science would further her cause even if no explicit mention of birth control was made at the meeting.[68] She sat silently throughout the conference but managed to make her presence known to the historical record by editing its proceedings.[69]

Pearl also sought to exclude from the conference the elements of the eugenics movement that he understood to be scientifically unsound.[70] Like other scientists of his time, he believed that most social problems resulted from the excessive reproduction of those who were hereditarily predisposed to low intelligence and antisocial behavior, and he thought it was at least theoretically possible to improve society through selective breeding. His own research, however, had demonstrated that such improvement would be more difficult than most proponents of eugenics recognized. Genotype was not transparently reflected in phenotype. Laws limiting reproduction could therefore noticeably raise the quality of the population only if they covered not just "actual defectives," as Pearl put it, but also their "somatically normal" parents.[71] Pearl thought it unlikely that a democratic society would acquiesce to such a program.

In a 1927 article in Mencken's *American Mercury*, Pearl complained of advocates for eugenics that, "in preaching as they do, that like produces like, and that therefore superior people will have superior children, and inferior people inferior children, the orthodox eugenicists are going contrary to the best established facts of genetical science and are, in the long run, doing their cause harm."[72] Recent readers have interpreted this article as Pearl's repudiation of his 1908 statement that "for the welfare of the state or nation those stocks which are on the whole endowed with the best traits should contribute more, many more, individuals to the next generation than should those stocks whose characteristics are on the whole bad."[73] Some have even interpreted it as Pearl's wholesale rejection of the eugenic project.[74] Pearl himself, however, claimed otherwise. He continued to believe that those representing the best "stock" should reproduce more than others but had come to realize that quality of "stock" was not readily apparent. Although his article included a lengthy quote from geneticist Thomas Hunt Morgan explaining why genetic inferiority or superiority should not be ascribed "to whole races, by which is meant not races in a biological sense but social or political groups bound together by physical conditions, by religious sentiments, or by political organizations,"[75] Pearl remained staunchly racist and anti-Semitic.[76] Before their falling-out, he complained to Wilson that the National Academy of Sciences was "on the high road to becoming a home for incurable Hebrews," and he praised the measures taken by Johns Hopkins University to limit enrollment of Jewish students.[77] As Pearl explained to Wilson, he was not withdrawing his support from eugenics but simply trying "to make a more or less subtle distinction between eugenics with a good genetics foundation and eugenics with a bad genetics foundation."[78] In contrast to birth control, which received virtually no mention at the 1927 conference, eugenics saturated the program in the form of research on heredity and differential fertility.

By excluding birth control and the elements of eugenics he termed "propagandist," Pearl aimed to attract the support of American foundations to the organization that emerged from the conference, the IUSIPP. He initially courted the Laura Spelman Rockefeller Memorial (LSRM). As an organization devoted to supporting the social sciences, however, the LSRM was reluctant to fund a population organization led by a biologist.[79] The Milbank Memorial Fund, on the other hand, was eager to offer its patronage.[80]

A public-health-oriented philanthropy based in New York, the Milbank Memorial Fund had begun to involve itself in population-related issues at the insistence of board member Thomas Cochran, a partner in J. P. Morgan and Company. Cochran demanded that the Fund include birth control in its services to the poor and even threatened to withhold support from other Milbank projects if this demand was not met.[81] He saw birth control as a technological solution to poverty and a cost-saving measure for philanthropists that would allow them to devote more of their largesse to causes benefiting the wealthy than to causes benefiting the poor.[82] Cochran's own pet cause was his alma mater, Phillips Academy Andover, of which he was a trustee.[83] The Fund's executive director, a friend and neighbor of Sanger, supported Cochran's proposal, but there was little scientific evidence that birth control even prevented conception, much less reduced the prevalence of poverty. The Fund therefore began by hiring Edgar Sydenstricker, a former statistician of the U.S. Public Health Service, to direct a research program into the relationship between birth control and differential fertility.[84] Sydenstricker hoped that supporting the IUSIPP would advance research in this area, and it probably helped the IUSIPP's case that Pearl's Hopkins colleague William Welch was then chair of the Milbank Memorial Fund's Advisory Council.[85] The Fund committed $10,000 per year for the IUSIPP's first three years. Over the next forty years it would spend more than $2.75 million on population-related activities, mostly research, training, conferences, and publications.[86]

The grant from the Milbank Memorial Fund covered about a third of the IUSIPP's operating expenses. Pearl continued to try to raise the remaining funds, first from the LSRM and then from the Rockefeller Foundation, which absorbed the LSRM in 1929. Though he never did manage to secure Rockefeller patronage, Pearl attempted to win the Foundation's favor by recruiting American statisticians to the IUSIPP. As these men became invested in the interdisciplinary project of population science, the emergent field began to transform under their influence.

A MATHEMATICAL SCIENCE OF POPULATION

The statisticians Pearl recruited came from the Metropolitan Life Insurance Company (MetLife), which was the origin of new mathematical approaches to human population. Developed by Alfred James ("Jim") Lotka and popularized by his colleague Louis Israel Dublin, these analytic methods are still fundamental components of demography's toolkit. They arose from an ontology of population that differed dramatically from Pearl's, one that conceived of populations as aggregates of individuals rather than organic wholes. Lotka and Dublin understood population growth not as a biological response to food availability but as the sum of separate vital processes (fertility, mortality, and migration), which were themselves subject to social, political, and economic influences. Whereas Pearl's logistic law pointed to impending overpopulation, Lotka and Dublin's pointed to looming depopulation.

Unlike Pearl and East, who called on population analysis to support birth control legalization and immigration restriction, Dublin and Lotka used their population analysis to advocate against birth control legalization and in favor of immigration. Both men had been born in Europe, though Lotka's parents were U.S. citizens and Dublin had moved to New York at the age of four. Dublin completed an undergraduate degree at the City College of New York in 1901 and a Ph.D. in 1904 at Columbia University, where he was inspired by the anthropologist Franz Boas, a vocal critic of Madison Grant's racial eugenics.[87] Dublin took a position at MetLife in 1909, and in the 1920s became a member of the Milbank Memorial Fund's Advisory Council.[88] Lotka joined Dublin at MetLife in 1924, after completing the majority of his education in Europe and working in Pearl's lab at Johns Hopkins for about four years.[89] In 1925 Lotka and Dublin published the article that would provide the basis for mathematical (formal) demography.

Prior to this publication, most observers had conceptualized population growth in terms of overall change, crude birth and death rates (births or deaths per thousand population), and crude rates of natural increase (births minus deaths per thousand population).[90] These crude rates were accurate measures of how quickly a population was growing at any given moment, but they offered no indication of how a population would grow over the long term. Working in the insurance industry, Dublin and Lotka were well-versed in life tables, which quantify the risk of death for men and women at each age of life. Their key insight was recognizing that the risk of giving birth also varies by age and sex.

Lotka and Dublin determined that crude birth and death rates (and therefore crude rates of natural increase) are a function of age-specific fertility and mortality rates (births or deaths within an age group divided by the number of people in that age group) and the age-sex structure of the population (the proportion of the population in each age-sex category). They found that, since mortality rates are higher among the elderly than among young adults, a population with a higher proportion of elderly people will have a higher crude death rate than one with a lower proportion of elderly people, even if both populations have the same age-specific mortality rates. Similarly, since fertility rates are higher among young adults than among the elderly, a population with a higher proportion of young adults will have a higher crude birth rate, even if both populations have the same age-specific fertility rates. Lotka and Dublin realized that, due to a precipitously falling birth rate and the sharp curtailment of immigration to the United States, the country would soon have a higher proportion of elderly people and a lower proportion of young adults, which meant that the crude rate of natural increase would likely be much lower in the near future. The measure they developed, which they called the "true" rate of natural increase and which demographers today call the intrinsic growth rate, accounted for these impending changes, representing *the rate of natural increase that would obtain with current age-specific mortality and fertility rates if those rates were to continue indefinitely.*[91]

At the time of their writing, the crude rate of natural increase in the United States was 11.0 per thousand annually, but Lotka and Dublin calculated a true rate of only 5.5 per thousand.[92] This meant that, although the U.S. population was, at that time, increasing at an annual rate of 11.0 per thousand (1.1%) through the difference between births and deaths (ignoring immigration), if then-current age-specific rates of fertility and mortality were to continue into the future, those same age-specific fertility and mortality rates would produce a future crude rate of natural increase (growth excluding immigration) of only 5.5 per thousand, or 0.55%. Dublin alluded to this discrepancy in a scathing review of East's *Mankind at the Crossroads*, which had predicted imminent overpopulation in the United States by assuming that then-current crude rates of natural increase would continue unabated in the absence of birth control legalization and immigration restriction.[93] The true rate of natural increase demonstrated that, given the age structure of the U.S. population, *if the family-formation processes of Americans remained the same into the future*, the crude rate of natural increase would eventually be reduced by half. The aggregate ontology of population underpinning the true rate provided the conceptual foundation for nearly all of demography. After his death in 1951, Lotka would be credited with formulating demography's "entire central core of analytical development"[94] and dubbed "the father of demographic analysis."[95]

Pearl was an important influence on Lotka, having made him question his prior belief that populations always grow exponentially.[96] In their work on the U.S. population, Dublin and Lotka predicted more or less the same pattern of future population growth that Pearl had predicted: a slowing rate of increase followed by stationarity (constant size).[97] But whereas Pearl saw the *S*-shaped growth trajectory in the United States (and everywhere) as the *inevitable* result of population expanding to fill the space available to it, with growth slowing as the given territory became more densely populated, Dublin and Lotka saw it as the *contingent* result of millions of individual births, deaths, and migrations and of trends in aggregate fertility, mortality, and migration rates. They did not entertain the idea that the biological limits of subsistence played any role in directing population growth. The biology in their analysis was that of the individual life cycle, expressed in age-specific probabilities of dying or giving birth. Within the limits of that life cycle, births, deaths, and migrations were wholly determined by social, economic, and political factors.

Although Pearl, Lotka, and Dublin all foresaw an imminent end to population growth in the United States, they interpreted looming population stationarity very differently. Pearl took a Malthusian view, in which stationarity was synonymous with overpopulation. It would occur only when a population had reached the limits of subsistence and would be characterized by competition over scarce resources. Lotka and Dublin, however, interpreted stationarity through the older theoretical lens of mercantilism, according to which population growth both reflected and generated economic dynamism and geopolitical strength.[98] According to their mercantilist perspective, population stationarity signaled economic stagnation and geopolitical weakness. Whereas Pearl believed a population could only grow or remain the same size, Dublin warned that "if a population can increase in a geometric ratio, it can also decrease in the same ratio," an outcome even worse than stationarity from a mercantilist perspective.[99] Demographer Frank Notestein would later credit Lotka with reorienting population concerns in the United States and Western Europe. As he put it, "the fear that population growth would outstrip the means of subsistence gave way to the contrary fear that the population of the countries of the West were [*sic*] heading for ultimate decline."[100]

Dublin pointed to the true rate and the possibility of depopulation to counter calls for birth control legalization and immigration restriction. Although his policy preferences were diametrically opposed to those of Pearl and East, he too legitimated his efforts to control population *quality* with reference to population *quantity*. As president of the American Statistical Association in 1924, Dublin organized a conference titled "The Statistician and the Population Problem." He defined "the population problem" as *unfounded anxiety about the threat of overpopulation*, which fostered nativism and its expression in immigration restriction and calls for birth control legalization. Dublin contended that immigration restriction had no scientific basis; rather "the stream of papers and books in recent years which has crystallized into an organized propaganda for the Nordic races in America is simply an effort to give the appearance of respectability and of science to what is fundamentally an expression of unreasoned prejudice."[101] He thereby discredited claims of impending overpopulation as having been invented in the service of Madison Grant's intra-European racism.

But while Dublin challenged claims of Nordic superiority, he did not eschew eugenics altogether. He cautioned that "we must exercise particular care, as we approach the point of a stationary population, not to weaken its internal composition by increasing the proportion of defective stock,"[102] even as he disputed the idea that Southern and Eastern European "stocks" were necessarily "defective." Birth control legalization, Dublin feared, would have "its greatest effect on those groups of the population whom it is for obvious reasons a great misfortune to have less well represented in the populations of the future" and its "least effect . . . among the illiterate, the poor, and the wretched, among whom a curtailment of reproduction would be a social blessing."[103] Although Dublin did not share his contemporaries' enthusiasm for birth control or their antipathy toward immigrants, he did share the belief that American society could be improved by selective breeding. Even as he rejected claims of intra-European racial difference, he validated claims that socioeconomic status was genetically inherited. Whereas East and Pearl had pointed to impending overpopulation to lend urgency to the argument for selective breeding, Dublin pointed to impending depopulation.

Despite his long-standing relationship with Lotka, Pearl invited neither Lotka nor Dublin to the 1927 World Population Conference. Their exclusion likely resulted from personal animosity between Pearl and Dublin, political differences between Pearl and East on the one side and Lotka and Dublin on the other, and the incompatibility between Dublin and Lotka's aggregate ontology of population and Pearl's organic ontology.[104] But when potential funders of the IUSIPP demanded more American representation in the organization, Pearl asked Dublin and Lotka to join and the statisticians agreed. At the insistence of the IUSIPP's patrons, Dublin became chair of the American Committee. Pearl also recruited to the American Committee a Brookings Institution statistician, Robert René Kuczynski, who was then in the process of popularizing a vital rate index known as the net reproduction rate (NRR), a close analogue of Lotka and Dublin's true rate of natural increase.

Developed at the Berlin Statistical Office in the late nineteenth century, the NRR summarizes a population's age-specific rates of fertility and mortality into an index that indicates whether fertility is sufficient for the population to replace itself over the long term, assuming that age-specific birth and death rates remain constant into the indefinite future.[105] Technically the NRR summarizes age-specific *female* birth and death rates (births of girls and deaths of girls and women) to calculate the number of daughters who will replace their mothers by living long enough to bear their own children.[106] A population with an NRR of one (unity) is at replacement fertility and has a true rate of natural increase of zero. An NRR below one (analogous to a negative true rate of natural increase) indicates long-term population decline (negative growth); an NRR above one (analogous to a positive true rate of natural increase) indicates long-term population growth.[107]

Like the true rate of natural increase, the NRR is a measure of *current* age-specific fertility and mortality rates expressed in terms of their *potential* long-run effects on the population's size and age-sex structure. Also like the true rate, it says nothing about current rates of overall population growth. An NRR of one, or a true rate of zero, does not necessarily mean that a population is currently stationary, only that it *would become stationary if current age-specific rates of fertility and mortality were to continue indefinitely*. It includes no indication of whether or not those rates *will* continue, or how much a population with an NRR of one would increase before reaching stationarity. Also, like the true rate of natural increase, the NRR ignores immigration entirely.

The NRR and the true rate are both one-sex models, calculating population growth on the basis of fertility rates experienced by women.[108] Counting births to men and to women would double-count fertility, but there is no inherent reason why the number of women of childbearing age should be used as the denominator of the fertility rate rather than the number of men of childbearing age, since men are also involved in conception. There are, however, practical reasons to attribute births to mothers rather than to fathers that arise from the physiological process of childbearing. Mothers are simply easier to account for, as they are always present at a birth. Their childbearing is also easier to model than is the childbearing of men because women can bear children only during a particular age span (usually considered by demographers to be fifteen to forty-nine), and rarely give birth to more than one child per year. Conception, however, involves two parties, so the rate at which women give birth will necessarily depend on the ratio of and relationship between men and women in a society.

Kuczynski popularized the NRR in a two-volume work, *The Balance of Births and Deaths*, published in 1928 and 1931. He demonstrated that the NRR had dropped below one in much of Western Europe, forecasting absolute population decline in the near future. The NRR remained above one in many countries of Southern and Eastern Europe, suggesting that population growth would continue, though—with the exception of the Soviet Union—most of these countries were also experiencing rapid declines in their birth rates. Taking a mercantilist view of population growth, Kuczynski warned that these numbers could indicate an impending eastward shift in Europe's balance of power. Kuczynski's books sparked widespread concern about depopulation in Great Britain, where the NRR was popularly known as the "Kuczynski rate," and in Italy, where the NRR provided scientific support for Mussolini's pronatalist policies.[109] Family planning programs sprang up in several British colonies, aiming to reduce colonial population growth so as to preserve metropolitan power.[110] The female-centric nature of NRRs calculated by Kuczynski and others for European countries between the world wars made the trend seem particularly dire. The enormous cost of World War I in terms of male lives had produced extreme sex imbalances among young adults in most countries of Europe. Under such conditions, a female NRR can be well below a male NRR, or can even indicate below-replacement fertility while the male NRR indicates above-replacement fertility, as was the case in interwar France.[111]

In addition to setting off a panic in several countries about what appeared to be a crisis of depopulation, Kuczynski's books sparked a feud within the emergent field of demography over the origins and proper attribution of the new vital rate indices. Ultimately the feud solidified the formation of a new form of demographic expertise around the calculation and use of these measures. Brookings Institution director Edwin Griswold Nourse conceded that the dispute could "be adequately dealt with only by one who is not merely an able mathematician but also one who has a very considerable familiarity with vital statistics and demographic concepts," acknowledging that the vital mathematics of the true rate and the NRR were part of a new field of scientific inquiry that was not reducible to any existing discipline and could not be adequately judged by those external to it.[112] Sociologist Frank Hankins made the same observation in a 1933 review of Kuczynski's *Fertility and Reproduction*, a methodological sequel to *The Balance of Births and Deaths*, declaring that "if science deals with abstraction, this 'stable' population method is science at its best. The mathematics involved are beyond the reviewer's critical capacity. If sound, they mark the beginning of a new epoch in demographic analysis."[113]

With the true rate of natural increase and the NRR, Lotka, Dublin, and Kuczynski claimed a new kind of expertise over population based on the calculation of vital rate indices. A population's overall size and current aggregate growth rate, they argued, though readily comprehensible, were misleading indicators of population dynamism. Rather, the true measure of a population was its potential for long-term growth, or what Dublin and Lotka called its "reproductive vitality," which could be assessed only through the application of sophisticated mathematical techniques to age-specific vital rates.[114] These methods were incredibly data-intensive, requiring mortality and fertility rates by sex and five-year age groups. The requisite data had only recently become available for the United States and could be found in several countries of Western Europe, but were not more widely available. Readers even questioned whether the NRR values Kuczynski had published for some of the countries of Eastern Europe were based on actual data. If sociologists and economists found these emerging metrics inscrutable, they were even more opaque to natural scientists and the general public.

The true rate and the NRR pointed to a "population problem" that was very different from that supposedly identified by Pearl's logistic law. Whereas the logistic law assumed that all populations would soon experience a slowing and cessation of growth because overpopulation was imminent within each country and at the global level, the true rate and the NRR suggested that some countries had more "reproductive vitality" than other countries and that this inequality would increase the relative political, military, and economic power of the faster-growing countries relative to the slower-growing countries. Indeed Germany, Italy, and Japan had begun to cite their rapid population growth rates to justify claims on the territory of neighboring countries and enacted pronatalist policies to aid them in their anticipated military endeavors.[115] These competing versions of "the population problem" pointed to divergent remedies: immigration restriction and birth control legalization to solve the Malthusian problem of impending overpopulation; pronatalism and immigration to solve the mercantilist problem of impending depopulation in the countries of North America and Western Europe combined with rapid population growth elsewhere. Both versions supported eugenic policies to improve the quality of either too-large or too-small populations.

The question of whether the countries of North America and Western Europe were staring down the barrel of imminent overpopulation or depopulation could not be answered with even the most accurate or detailed population data. The biological and mathematical models that underpinned the two sides of the debate relied on incompatible analyses of the same numbers and opposing interpretations of the expected leveling-off of population growth. The Malthusian overpopulation view was more readily embraced in the United States, where observers routinely attributed urban poverty to rapid population growth and high immigration rates. The mercantilist depopulation view was more readily embraced in Europe, where World War I and the influenza pandemic had produced higher casualty rates and where international tensions were increasingly understood in terms of population. Within the United States, the Malthusian biological model held more sway among natural scientists, who conceptualized population in the context of natural resources. Older social scientists, particularly those with less quantitative facility and those who were ideologically committed to immigration restriction and the intra-European racism that supported it, also embraced this model, while younger social scientists who were more adept with numbers and less committed to Nordic superiority preferred the mercantilist mathematical model.

As American statisticians and younger social scientists became more involved with the IUSIPP, their approach to population growth predominated within the emerging science of population. The American philanthropists who were beginning to fund demographic research may have preferred the mathematical model as well because, contrary to Pearl's claims, it suggested that future population growth was malleable, open to intervention. For this reason it was also attractive to European governments, which were beginning to adopt a variety of measures to increase the quantity and quality of their populations.

THE RISE OF FASCISM AND THE FALL OF DEMOGRAPHIC INTERNATIONALISM

As European governments began to institute policies aimed at increasing the size and altering the composition of their populations, they sought legitimacy in science, and particularly in the emerging science of demography. Government statisticians in Italy, Germany, and France leveraged their connections with the IUSIPP to produce scientific support for their countries' pronatalist, expansionist, anti-immigrant, and genocidal policies. Population scientists from the United States and the United Kingdom, however, increasingly rejected the intra-European racial taxonomies that underpinned the work of their Continental colleagues, describing them as "political" or "emotional" rather than "scientific." The debate between these scientists over the boundary between population science and population politics ultimately destroyed the organization.

This boundary dispute began almost as soon as the IUSIPP formed. Modeled on existing scientific unions in other fields, the IUSIPP was a union of national committees rather than an association of individual scientists. Pearl was its first president; chairs of the British, French, German, and Italian committees served as vice presidents. At the IUSIPP's founding, it was decided that the next International Congress (scientific conference) and General Assembly (business meeting) would be sponsored by the Italian Committee and held in Rome in 1931. Informally, Pearl planned to step down as president at that point, with the expectation that Vice President Corrado Gini, head of Italy's National Institute of Statistics, would replace him. However, by 1930 the American statisticians Pearl was trying to recruit to the IUSIPP and the organization's American patrons had become deeply suspicious of Gini.

In 1929 Gini delivered three public lectures at the University of Chicago in which he attributed population growth and decline to racial dynamism. He argued that birth rates were falling in Northern, Western, and Central Europe because the national races of those regions were decaying. In contrast, he attributed Italy's higher birth rates not to Mussolini's pronatalist policies but to the fact that Italy's recent national unification had created a new race that was entering a period of expansion.[116] Already by then, most of the younger social scientists of the United States had rejected the idea of racial distinctions among those of European descent, as evident in a review of Gini's lectures that described his position as "so untenable and vulnerable at so many points that, under other authorship and other auspices, one would dismiss it as a vagary of the human mind operating unscientifically and without a command of the facts."[117] Pearl described Gini's work as "a good deal influenced by the dictatorial philosophy of Mussolini."[118] The leaders of both the Milbank Memorial Fund and the Rockefeller Foundation made it clear to Pearl that they would have nothing to do with an organization led by Gini.[119]

Pearl saw an opportunity to break with Gini when Gini refused to allow the IUSIPP to exercise oversight in the planning of the 1931 Congress. Pearl and Vice President Bernard Mallet moved the General Assembly to London, where the English cartographer Charles Close, retiring president of the Royal Geographical Society, was elected president.[120] The Italian Committee did not show up.[121] The Congress proceeded in Rome as scheduled, but occurred wholly under the auspices of the Italian Committee, funded by the Italian government and presided over by Mussolini.

The schism between the Italian Committee and the IUSIPP was only the beginning of the organization's political woes. At the 1931 General Assembly in London, the IUSIPP's leadership decided that the next General Assembly and International Congress would be held in 1934 in Berlin. Close recommended that the physical anthropologist Eugen Fischer, chair of the IUSIPP's German Committee, be elected as his successor at that meeting. As early as 1928 Pearl had expressed concern that Fischer, a disciple of Madison Grant, was "a great Nordic propagandist, and under cover I am told, an anti-Semite."[122] As the Nazi government tightened its control over intellectual production in Germany in the mid-1930s, Fischer toed the party line and ensured that other members of the IUSIPP's German Committee did so as well. In 1933 Dublin, who was then chair of the American Committee, recommended that the Berlin Congress be postponed, as it was becoming clear that it would be difficult to ensure the intellectual freedom of a conference held in Germany.[123]

After Fischer announced that he would not stand for election to the presidency of the IUSIPP, citing other commitments, the Congress went ahead in Berlin in 1935, a year later than originally planned. It was financed entirely by the German government. The meeting featured science in the service of Nazi population policy, with several Party officials listed on the program as participants. The IUSIPP's leadership felt it could do nothing about the situation. As Close put it, "he who pays the piper has [the] right to call the tune."[124] The U.K. and U.S. committees of the IUSIPP officially boycotted the conference, though some Americans and Britons attended in other capacities, including sociologist Frank Hankins, who went on to publish a favorable summary of German population policy in the *American Journal of Sociology*;[125] Clarence Gordon Campbell of the Eugenics Research Association, who appeared "as a champion of Nazi racial principles";[126] Harry Laughlin of the Eugenics Record Office, who proposed a toast to Hitler at one of the social events connected to the meeting;[127] and Wickliffe Draper, who went on to found the overtly racist Pioneer Fund in 1937.

Although blatant anti-Semitism was omitted from the program, press reports made it clear to Pearl, who was not in attendance, that "the Berlin Congress could not by any stretch of the imagination be regarded as a disinterested scientific discussion of the problems of population; but was, on the other hand, essentially propaganda under the aegis of the International Union for the nationalistic political philosophy of the government of Germany."[128] British demographer David Glass, who attended as a delegate of the Eugenics Society of Great Britain, reported in the *Eugenics Review* that the overriding theme of the meeting was "race prejudice" and that the content of the presentations did not conform to the scientific standards set by the IUSIPP.[129] It was only through these disputes, however, that American and British demographers began to promulgate standards for the new science of population. They bounded their field at the emerging distinction between eugenics and the Madison Grant–style intra-European racism that had been rejected by the statisticians whose models were coming to characterize demography.[130] More subtly, they also began to describe as unscientific government policies that determined who could reproduce and in what quantity.

Following the Berlin Congress, the American Committee of the IUSIPP resolved that it would not endorse any future Congress over which the IUSIPP "does not exercise effective control."[131] Pearl felt that "about one more nationalistic international population Congress would completely ruin any hope for real cooperation in the study of population problems scientifically."[132] The IUSIPP's leadership nonetheless accepted the offer of Adolphe Landry, chair of the French Committee, to host the next Congress and Assembly in Paris in 1937.[133] Landry was a prominent demographer, best known for his 1934 book *La révolution démographique* (*The Demographic Revolution*), which utilized the NRR to argue that, as a result of the widespread adoption of birth control, France was on the verge of depopulation. Landry was also a politician, representing Corsica in the French Parliament, where he advocated pronatalist policies modeled on those of Germany and Italy.[134] Perhaps unsurprisingly, the 1937 Paris meeting has been described as "the scene of an intense ideological struggle."[135] Urged by Fischer, the

German government sent fifty-six scientists to advocate for Nazi population policy. The organizers did not bar openly racist papers, but grouped them together in a single session, with Franz Boas vigorously critiquing them in the role of discussant. Each side presented itself as scientific and the others as political. The 1937 meeting was the last to be held by the IUSIPP, which effectively ceased to function when World War II broke out in 1939.

The men who established the IUSIPP had successfully leveraged the interwar politics of population to garner support for their scientific activities, which developed in tandem with their political sympathies. Their project of demographic internationalism failed, however, when scientists proved unable to extricate demography from the nationalist politics that were consuming Europe. Nonetheless, by the time Europe erupted in war, demography had solidified into a small but recognizable field of research in the United States. There its development was closely tied to the emerging New Deal welfare state and to a new brand of eugenics that supporters claimed was free of racial baggage and compatible with American democracy.

CHAPTER 2

Family Planning

As the members of the IUSIPP's American Committee worked to distance their nascent science of demography from the fascist population politics of interwar Europe, they simultaneously angled for a seat at the policymaking table in the United States. Efforts to utilize demography to inform U.S. population policy began in 1930, when Margaret Sanger and NYU sociologist Henry Pratt Fairchild, both of whom had been involved in the founding of the IUSIPP but were subsequently marginalized, tried again to marshal science in support of their contraceptive and eugenic projects, this time through a U.S.-based organization devoted to the investigation and solution of domestic "population problems."[1] The organization they founded, the Population Association of America (PAA), quickly became the professional society for U.S.-based demographers. It also became a source of scientific legitimacy for a new political program that fused birth control and eugenics, known as family planning.

Family planning was the brainchild of eugenicist Frederick Henry ("Fred") Osborn, who saw in demography a scientific ally for his life's project: a eugenics program that would improve the quality of the American population without violating the country's democratic ideals. Wealthy and well-connected, Osborn secured patronage for demographers and their new institutions, spearheading the establishment of the PAA and of demography's first graduate training program in the United States. His social ties to Franklin and Eleanor Roosevelt helped Osborn find an audience for demographic research in the emerging New Deal welfare state. Because he was demography's primary champion and the critical link between the new science and its patrons and audiences, Osborn exerted considerable

Building the Population Bomb. Emily Klancher Merchant, Oxford University Press (2021). © Oxford University Press.
DOI: 10.1093/oso/9780197558942.003.0003

influence over the field's institutional structure and the content of its research. As demographers made a place for themselves in the interwar intellectual landscape and developed a distinct interdisciplinary identity, they did so in the service of Osborn's new family planning program, which advocated the legalization of birth control in the service of eugenics.

MAKING EUGENICS SAFE FOR DEMOCRACY

Osborn came to the attention of the American demographic community at the official launch of the PAA in 1931.[2] In attendance were eugenicists, birth control advocates, and most of the newly formed American Committee of the IUSIPP, including Jim Lotka, Louis Dublin, and Robert Kuczynski.[3] Fairchild and Sanger had been nominated for election to the offices of president and vice president, respectively. Before the vote could occur, however, Osborn contested Sanger's nomination, asserting that an official connection to the birth control movement would undermine the new organization's scientific authority.[4] Sanger agreed to stand down, reasoning, as she had done in the formation of the IUSIPP, that the PAA could have a stronger political influence if it did not have explicitly political aims. Fairchild was still elected president, but University of Chicago sociologist William Fielding Ogburn was elected first vice president and Kuczynski second vice president.[5] To preserve the scientific reputation of the organization, its members decided that the American Committee of the IUSIPP should form a College of Fellows within the PAA as a scientific elite that would appoint the organization's officers.[6] Led by this "gentleman's club," as an early female demographer would describe it, the PAA sidelined the feminist birth control movement while embracing Osborn's version of eugenics.

Fred Osborn was born in 1889 to a rich family with close ties to powerful people. During the 1930s he leveraged his familial network, shown in Figure 2.1, to build a professional network of social scientists recognized as population experts, the foundation for today's interdisciplinary field of demography. Their research would, in turn, inform and legitimate Osborn's vision for a postracial democratic eugenics.

Osborn's grandfather, William Henry Osborn, had grown wealthy doing business in the Philippines during the first half of the nineteenth century. William Henry settled in New York in 1850 and married Virginia Sturges, taking over her father's presidency of the Illinois Central Railroad and joining the family's culturally rich social life. William Henry became

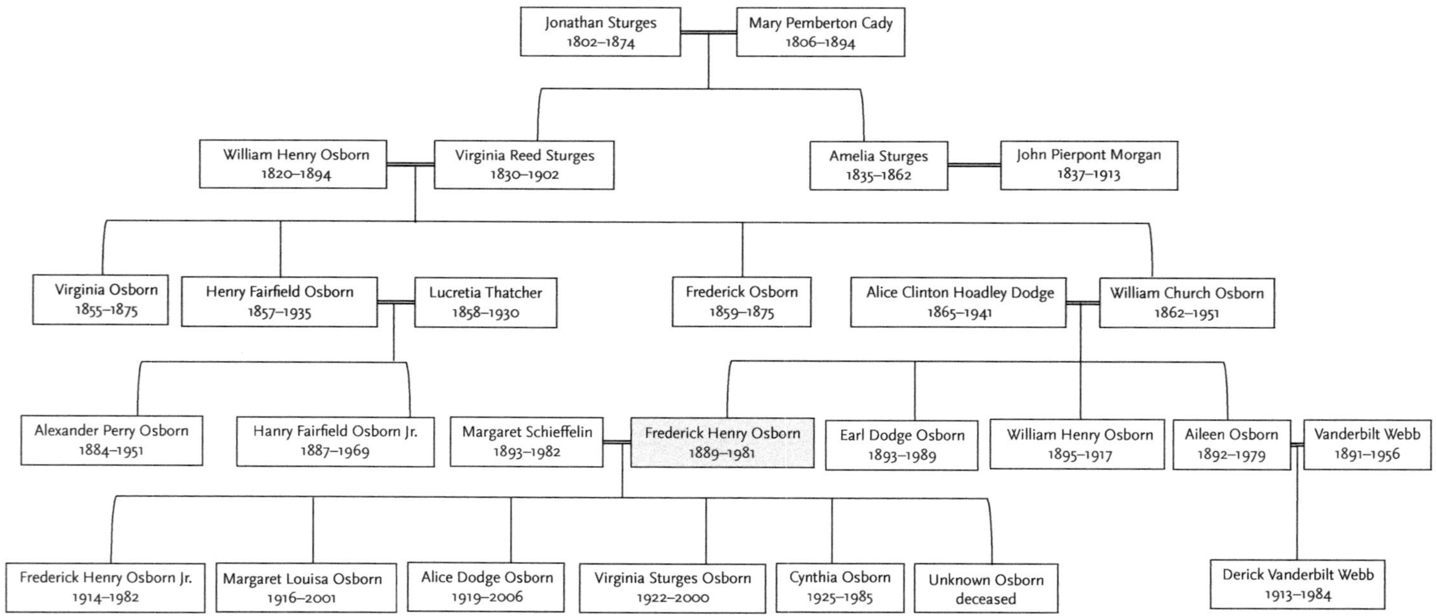

Figure 2.1 Osborn family tree.
Produced by the author.

close with Virginia's brother-in-law, banker John Pierpont Morgan, and even closer with artist Frederic Church, to whom he served as both patron and agent.[7] William Henry named two of his children for the painter: his second-born son, Frederick, and his youngest son, William Church. Fred Osborn of the PAA was the oldest child of William Church and Alice Dodge. He was named for William Church's older brother Frederick, who had drowned in the Hudson River at the age of sixteen. The original Frederick had been a close boyhood friend of Theodore Roosevelt,[8] and the Osborn and Roosevelt families remained close. Fred's younger sister Aileen later befriended Eleanor Roosevelt, hosting her frequently at the Osborn family estate in Garrison, New York, which was only twenty-five miles from the Roosevelt residence at Hyde Park.[9]

Fred adhered to his family's educational tradition, completing an undergraduate degree in English at Princeton University in 1910. After a postgraduate year at Trinity College, Cambridge, he joined the Detroit, Toledo, and Ironton Railroad as treasurer, and within five years had become its president. He married Margaret Schiefflin, a descendant of John Jay, in 1916. Fred served in the Red Cross in France during the last year of World War I. On his return to the United States, he went into industrial management and stock brokerage and joined the boards of several large corporations. Together with his uncle Henry Fairfield Osborn, president of the American Museum of Natural History, Fred was a founding member of the American Eugenics Society (AES) in 1926, though he was not admitted to the more exclusive Galton Society until 1928.[10] By then Fred Osborn, age forty, had earned enough money to retire from business. He installed himself as a research associate at his uncle's museum and pursued a course of reading recommended to him by the eugenicist anthropologist Clark Wissler, becoming an armchair expert in the scientific fields from which eugenics drew its theories.[11]

Osborn quickly realized that his uncle's brand of eugenics was falling out of favor among scientists. Yet he felt that the need for eugenics was more urgent than ever. He attributed the poverty and social strife he witnessed in New York to the municipal sanitation, clean water, food safety, and other hygienic practices inspired by recent discoveries in microbiology, all of which had reduced mortality rates and—in Osborn's mind—disrupted the process of natural selection. Osborn decried the fact that, whereas previously many of the supposedly inferior members of the U.S. population had died before reaching childbearing age, now most children who were born lived long enough to reproduce. The differential use of contraception by the professional classes only compounded the situation, as it reduced the size of the families Osborn thought should be contributing the most members of the next generation. He viewed eugenics as a necessary replacement for natural selection, a new type of conscious selection that would operate through birth rather than death. His desire to limit births among "the marginal economic groups" and encourage large families among those of "fine blood strains," indicates his conflation of socioeconomic success with genetic capacity and belief that the former reflected the latter.[12]

As Americans began to express disapproval of the fascist eugenic policies that were devouring Europe, Osborn aimed to salvage eugenics for the United States by adapting it to comport with American democratic ideals. He did this in three ways. First, he jettisoned the intra-European racism that had underpinned the 1924 Johnson-Reed Immigration Act, which set low quotas for immigration from Southern and Eastern Europe and much higher quotas for immigration from Northern and Western Europe. (Immigration from Asia was barred altogether.)[13] Second, he proposed that selection for reproduction be made on the basis of individual genetic quality rather than on the basis of such social characteristics as race, class, or national origin. Third, he suggested that eugenic selection should operate through the private sector rather than the state, and in a way that appeared voluntary.

When Osborn became secretary of the AES in the 1930s, he transformed it into an institutional home for his new eugenics program. At its peak in 1930, the AES boasted around 1,260 members, representing every state. Osborn later described its membership at that point as "a veritable blue book of prominent and wealthy men and women," including scientists who were "heavily involved with large general ideas based on subjective evaluations, and with a strong propagandist bent," by which he meant that their work was suffused with intra-European racism.[14] As the decade wore on, American scientists began to turn against racism, and Osborn brought the AES along with this trend, salvaging the organization's scientific reputation, though at the expense of alienating many of its wealthy nonscientific members.[15] Yet intra-European racism remained alive at the Eugenics Record Office (ERO), which continued to attribute favorable traits, such as inventiveness, to the "Nordic race" and unfavorable traits, such as criminality, to other racial groups.[16] Osborn worked to undermine the ERO's credibility by convincing its funders that its work was "emotional rather than scientific,"[17] drawing the boundary between "science" and "emotion" at the same line between eugenics and racism that Raymond Pearl and David Glass had demarcated in their evaluation of the 1935 IUSIPP meeting in Berlin. As a result of Osborn's efforts, the ERO closed in 1939, leaving the AES as the leading eugenics organization in the United States. The agenda it promoted drew racial boundaries around, rather than within,

Europe. Unlike the leaders of the ERO, Osborn would not use national origin as a proxy for genetic quality among whites, though he continued to advocate against marriages between whites and nonwhites.[18]

Osborn envisioned a eugenic program in which "selection"—the determination of how many children a person or couple could have—would not be based on national origin, race, or any other social characteristic, but instead would be made on the basis of individual genetic quality. That is, he advocated for selection *within* rather than *between* social categories. He acknowledged that scientists were "not at all sure that any races or social classes in this country are above or below others in biological capacity for developing socially valuable qualities."[19] He therefore advocated that "if we are to breed a constantly improving stock, it must be done by raising in every group available for reproduction a greater proportion of children among those couples who are above the national average of hereditary capacity, and in every group a lesser proportion of children among those members of the group who are below the national average in hereditary capacity."[20] There was, however, no way to measure "hereditary capacity."

Osborn recommended that within-group eugenic selection be made on the basis of the quality of the home environment parents provided to their children.[21] He insisted that this was an individual and egalitarian criterion as "no race and no social class has a monopoly on the quality of the home environment."[22] As a result, Osborn's contemporaries and even more recent scholars have overwhelmingly described his program as less "hereditarian" (attributing social qualities to nature) and more environmental (attributing social qualities to nurture) than orthodox eugenics.[23] This characterization, however, misconstrues Osborn's own eugenic recommendations. Just like Pearl, Osborn was a hard hereditarian, assuming that social qualities were biologically inherited and that society could be improved through selective breeding. Although Osborn recognized that a harsh home environment could hinder the achievements of genetically endowed children, he did not expect that a nurturing environment would help those who were not genetically predisposed to success. He recommended that parents providing a good home environment should have more children, not because the home environment made much of a difference in and of itself but because it was "an indication of [parents'] genetic qualities."[24] Osborn maintained that "children born to parents who are above the average of the group in social valuable qualities *as expressed in home conditions or productive achievement*, will in the great majority have a *better than average genetic constitution*."[25] Even the equalizing measures he recommended, such as free school lunches and public housing, were intended not to produce equality of outcomes but rather to remove obfuscating factors in the identification of genetic quality.

Osborn acknowledged that there was no biological marker for the type of genetic quality he sought. He therefore anticipated that the quality of the home would be the best proxy for a long time to come, as "the science of genetics will have to make many forward steps before a better measure of genetic quality can be made available."[26]

Perhaps the most innovative aspect of Osborn's eugenic program was that it endowed no hereditary court or other scientific, medical, or governmental body with the authority to decide who would reproduce and who would not. He downplayed involuntary sterilization, not because he opposed it in principle (he did not) but because he thought it unlikely that Americans would support a sterilization program on such a scale as would be necessary to markedly change the quality of the U.S. population. He hoped scientists would eventually be able to identify the genes responsible for poverty and antisocial behavior, but he recognized that success in that realm was possibly decades in the future and that sterilizing people merely suspected of harboring deleterious recessive alleles was incompatible with democracy. He recognized too that, without scientific evidence linking social and character traits to specific genetic markers, and with government control over reproduction increasingly associated with fascism, the American public was unlikely to cede control over childbearing. Speaking at a maternity center luncheon at the Waldorf Astoria in 1936, Osborn assured his audience that "there is no need for controversy about the basis of eugenic selection, nor, indeed, as to who should do the selecting. No group is proposing to arrogate to itself such a function. The decision as to number of children in a family must remain, as always in the hands of the parents."[27]

But how could parents be entrusted to have the appropriate number of children? Osborn conveniently believed that inferior parents actually wanted smaller families but couldn't be bothered to get information about birth control, while superior parents actually wanted larger families but used birth control out of a sense of responsibility that prevented them from having more children than they could support.[28] He therefore made two recommendations: first, that contraceptives be made freely and universally available so that the irresponsible could easily choose to have smaller families; second, that the government offer financial support to more responsible parents, who would likely choose to have more children if they could afford to raise them. He explained:

> Under a system of freedom of parenthood, we believe that on the whole the finest parents in every group of people would have the most children. That is, those parents most distinguished by their willingness to carry responsibility,

> those with the greatest capacity for affection and cooperation, those with the best health and other good qualities; and that people who are most selfish, least strong, and least responsible, would have the fewest children.[29]

Osborn reasoned that measures such as free school lunches, public housing, and college scholarships, rather than family or child allowances, would encourage genetically endowed parents to have the large number of children that their genetic superiority made them desire without incentivizing genetically inferior parents to have more children than they naturally wanted. Yet in recommending that the child tax credit be proportional to parents' income and that only college graduates be promised scholarships for their children, he conflated socioeconomic success with genetic quality and reserved childbearing incentives for the already well-off.

Osborn called for assistance on "those who are in any way helping to form and direct public opinion, or to advise and assist in the lives of others." In particular, he sought the help of teachers, medical professionals, and clergy to encourage promising young couples to have large families and other couples to have small families. He encouraged "all leaders of thought" to

> have constantly in mind that parenthood is desirable and valuable to society and to the parents themselves, in proportion as the parents stand out above the average of the group of which they are a part, and that in proportion as the quality of the parents lies below the average of the group to which they belong, large families are injurious to society and to the children, and a burden to the parents' own relative inadequacy.[30]

Osborn thereby encouraged the development of "a public opinion which will not tolerate families of more than one or two children among the socially inadequate, the dependent, the marginal economic, and others who do not provide home surroundings proper for child nurture, or among those likely, though not certain, to pass on hereditary defect."[31] He called for the sterilization of those known to carry a "hereditary defect" but allowed other "socially inadequate" parents one or two children, as long as the families of "socially adequate" parents were larger. For those parents, Osborn recommended five or more children. He and Margaret had six.

Osborn described his program as "a system of freedom of parenthood," but it embodied a tension that would also characterize postwar population control programs. On the one hand, the legalization of birth control would empower couples to choose the size of their own families. On the other hand, those choices would always be made within the context of public policies, economic constraints, and social norms that would direct some couples to have more children and other couples to have fewer. Couples could make their own choices, as long as their childbearing calculus optimized the quantity and quality of the population to which they belonged. Osborn's eugenic program therefore relied on reproductive autonomy in the context of social control.

What may be hard to realize from the vantage point of the twenty-first century is the fact that the reproductive autonomy side of Osborn's program was more controversial at the time than was the social control side. Between the world wars, choosing the number of children one had was not considered a right the way it (generally) is today. Birth control and abortion were illegal in most states of the United States and most countries of Europe. In other parts of the world, social and religious institutions governed childbearing. Osborn advocated for the legalization of birth control, not because he favored individual reproductive autonomy but because he planned to develop new social, legal, and technological mechanisms that would direct individual childbearing decisions.

Inspired by the behaviorism that was gaining traction among the social scientists of his day,[32] Osborn hoped to simultaneously make birth control widely available and turn American society into a Skinner box that would guide the wealthy and well-educated toward large families and the poor and uneducated toward small families. In advocating for reproductive autonomy in the context of social control, he drew a boundary between coercive and legitimate approaches to eugenics, just as he drew a boundary between "scientific" and "emotional" eugenics. Legislating the number of children people could have was beyond the pale, as was sterilization of anyone not definitely known to harbor a "hereditary defect." Manipulating the social and economic contexts in which childbearing decisions were made in order to encourage some people to have more children and other people to have fewer children was perfectly fine. The only problem was that nobody knew exactly how to do it. To solve that problem, Osborn turned to demography.

DISCIPLINING DEMOGRAPHY

Though he lacked any kind of scientific credential, Osborn was elected to the PAA's College of Fellows and became a member of the IUSIPP's American Committee. His research assistant, Frank Lorimer, became the PAA's first secretary-treasurer, a professional position with a salary provided by the Milbank Memorial Fund. Lorimer and Osborn earned their place in the world of population science with their coauthored *Dynamics of Population: Social and Biological Significance of Changing Birth Rates in the United States*. Published in 1934, the book utilized metrics developed by Lotka, Dublin, and Kuczynski to argue that differential fertility was undermining the quality of the U.S. population.[33] Lorimer, then forty, has been described by contemporaries as "remarkably young for his age . . . in terms of interest in people, in events, in size-up of things."[34] He was an idealist and a liberal and was always willing to give people the benefit of the doubt. He has been credited with turning Osborn away from his uncle's eugenics and toward a version that, at least on its surface, seemed less racist and more democratic.[35] Lorimer remained secretary-treasurer of the PAA until 1940. Relative to their late arrival in demography, Osborn and Lorimer played outsized roles in the field's development. Lorimer oversaw some of the early projects through which the PAA defined demography, including a census of scholars involved in population research,[36] the production of a standard demographic lexicon,[37] and the compilation of a quarterly bibliography of population-related publications.[38] Recognizing that a full-fledged science of human population would require a reliable way of reproducing itself, Osborn singlehandedly created the first graduate training program in demography in the United States.

After the publication of *Dynamics of Population*, Osborn became a trustee of the Milbank Memorial Fund, which had continued to support the activities of the IUSIPP and its American Committee. From that position, he secured a grant from the Fund to establish a research center and graduate training program in demography at a prestigious U.S. university. The next step was finding a university that would accept it. After Harvard turned him down, Osborn moved on to his alma mater, Princeton, where his father and Albert Milbank, head of the Milbank Memorial Fund, were both trustees.[39] Princeton's president Harold Dodds agreed to house the new center, the Office of Population Research (OPR), in the School of Public and International Affairs (SPIA). Osborn's father and Albert Milbank had both played important roles in SPIA's 1930 establishment as an interdisciplinary training program for "men who expect to enter public life or public administration, whether national, state, or municipal, or to engage in international business and affairs, as well as those who contemplate careers in journalism and law."[40] The establishment of SPIA reflected the growing sense in the 1930s that real-world problems needed to be addressed by interdisciplinary inquiry.[41] By housing OPR at SPIA, Osborn and Dodds positioned demography as a practical interdisciplinary science that would inform policy.

Osborn selected Frank Notestein of the Milbank Memorial Fund's research department to direct OPR. Notestein, then thirty-four, had completed a Ph.D. in economics at Cornell University in 1927 under the direction of Walter Willcox, chief statistician for the 1900 census and one of the most well-known vital statisticians of his time. Willcox was a member of the Milbank Memorial Fund's Advisory Council and had linked Notestein to the Fund's health demonstration project in Cattaraugus County, New York, to supply data for his dissertation. After Notestein completed that project, the Fund hired him full time to pursue research on the relationship between birth control and differential fertility. Despite his youth and inexperience, the PAA's College of Fellows and the IUSIPP's American Committee warmly welcomed Notestein as a representative of demography's primary patron.[42] When Osborn chose Notestein to direct OPR, he explained to SPIA director Dewitt Clinton Poole that Notestein's "people come from Alma, Michigan, having moved there very early from the East where they had settled before the Revolution. . . . It is quite a German community and the Notesteins are mostly farmers and teachers."[43] Given Notestein's name, this was likely Osborn's way of reassuring the Princeton administration that Notestein was neither Jewish nor part of the recent wave of immigration from Eastern and Southern Europe.[44]

The Milbank Memorial Fund pledged $10,000 annually to OPR. This grant paid Notestein's salary and OPR's operating expenses. Milbank additionally funded a fellowship for one graduate student each year. Notestein saw this fellowship as critical to bringing in students because "no economist wants to be a demographer."[45] The first Milbank Fellow was John Durand, a former Census Bureau employee, who completed a Ph.D. in economics in 1939 under Notestein's supervision. Durand described his training as "haphazard." He learned mainly from proximity to Notestein, who "would discuss at the drop of a hat most anything having to do with population questions" and would occasionally send Durand off to do further research on topics that came up in their conversations.[46] The next Milbank Fellow, Ansley Coale, would become one of the most eminent demographers of the second half of the twentieth century. Coale had had no particular interest in demography until he was offered the Milbank Fellowship. He explained in 1979, "I had no money so the only way I could go to graduate school was with a full ride. I was willing to have an interest in population in order to have a fellowship that would pay my way."[47] The Milbank Memorial Fund continued to provide this fellowship until 1968, and many prominent demographers entered the field as Milbank Fellows.[48]

Osborn's influence on the establishment and development of demography, and on the careers of demographers in Notestein's generation, has not previously been recognized[49] but cannot be overstated. Notestein, who went on after World War II to direct the UN Population Division and preside over the nongovernmental Population Council, would acknowledge in 1968 that Osborn had "created all of the opportunities that came to us. . . . Without [Osborn's] sponsorship there would have been no Office of Population Research in Princeton, and I probably would've had no role either in the United Nations or in the Population Council."[50] Without Osborn, there may not have even been a Population Council.

A SEAT AT THE POLICY TABLE

Osborn's project to develop demography as a scientific tool for the crafting of population policy received a boost from the nascent American welfare state, which created seats at the policy table for the social scientists who were beginning to identify as demographers. By the time the Great Depression hit, the U.S. government had begun to take an interest in social science as a tool for crafting policy. In December 1929, President Herbert Hoover, an engineer who saw in social science the potential to solve the growing social problems associated with the speculative capitalism of the 1920s and the resulting stock market crash, launched the Recent Social Trends project. Under the leadership of economist Wesley C. Mitchell, the project aimed to paint a statistical portrait of American society, producing a compendium of social indicators that would document problems and point to policy solutions.[51] University of Chicago sociologist William Fielding Ogburn served as research director with the assistance of University of North Carolina sociologist Howard Odum.

Ogburn and Odum had each completed a Ph.D. at Columbia University under the direction of Franklin Henry Giddings, an ally of Margaret Sanger. Often described as one of the "four founders" of sociology,[52] Giddings might also be considered a grand-founder of demography, though he has not been widely recognized as such. Giddings became the first professor of sociology at Columbia University in 1894. At the time, Columbia was transforming from a small college into a major research university and developing its strength in statistical approaches to social science. Franz Boas, already an eminent anthropologist by that point, arrived in 1896. Giddings was much less distinguished, having come to sociology with no graduate training, by way of a career in journalism. Giddings and Boas both utilized statistical methods to assert the scientific value of their newly forming disciplines.[53] However, while Boas emphasized anthropometric variation in order to undermine theories about intra-European racial difference, Giddings measured the central tendencies of social aggregates in order to rank the prestige of various racial, ethnic, and religious groups.[54] Between 1908 and

1919 nearly half of the sociology Ph.D.s granted in the United States came from Columbia University, and virtually all of those who earned a doctorate in sociology at Columbia worked with Giddings. Giddings's students self-consciously styled themselves as his disciples, "Giddings men." Those most favored formed the "F.H.G. Club," which met regularly at Giddings's home.[55] Giddings is widely recognized as the pioneer of quantitative methods in sociology, but his enthusiasm for statistics exceeded his facility with them. He left it largely to the "Giddings men" to develop quantitative approaches to social questions. Ogburn and Odum were perhaps the students who did the most to bring these methods to the next generation of sociology. When policymakers sought objective scientific knowledge, the quantitative work of Ogburn, Odum, and other intellectual descendants of Giddings seemed to best fit the bill. In turn, government recognition of their expertise raised the status of these men and their quantitative methods within sociology.

Ogburn and Odum recruited Warren Simpson Thompson and Pascal Kidder ("Pat" to his friends and "P. K." in print) Whelpton to write a monograph on population as part of the Recent Social Trends series. Thompson and Whelpton were the research staff of the Scripps Foundation for Research in Population Problems at Miami University in Ohio. Newspaper magnate Edward Scripps had established the Foundation in 1922 after reading Thompson's 1915 dissertation, written at Columbia University under Giddings's direction. Giddings had suggested population as the topic because population data were becoming more readily available but had been little analyzed outside of government statistical offices and insurance companies.[56] Scripps found Thompson's dissertation in 1918 and took it with him on a yacht trip around the world. Although the dissertation did not address Asia, it helped Scripps make sense of the poverty he witnessed there, as it suggested that some populations had simply grown too large. Thompson's dissertation, linking quantity and quality, suggested that, if population growth in the United States continued apace, the result would be ever-worsening poverty there as well. Reflecting his mentor's anti-immigrant Malthusian perspective, Thompson suggested that eugenics and immigration restriction could preserve population quality in the face of rising quantity.

When Scripps created his eponymous Foundation, he did not perceive population growth in the United States as a pressing concern.[57] He expected that it would become more urgent over the next few decades, however, and aimed to recruit a research staff that could come to an understanding of "the population problem" and develop solutions well in advance. Scripps therefore sought young scientists who would be able to work on the project for a long time. Since he intended his staff to solve problems that were not currently receiving sufficient attention, he may have thought young scientists more likely to develop creative new approaches.[58] Scripps also could not afford to pay a salary of more than $4,000 per year, which at the time was not enough to lure "a man who is well established in his work in some good university."[59] Thompson, age thirty-five, was Scripps's first hire. The second was Pat Whelpton, who seems to have been selected for his youth rather than his expertise.[60] Whelpton had earned an undergraduate degree in agricultural economics at Cornell in 1915 and had no prior experience in population research. As a close colleague later put it, "it seems doubtful that he had previously known or cared much about demographic questions at all."[61] To be fair, very few people at the time had.

Thompson and Whelpton's research explored the social determinants of population growth in the United States. They found that farm-dwellers had more children on average than did their urban counterparts, that foreign-born couples had more children than native-born couples, and that African Americans comprised a smaller fraction of the U.S. population than they had in the past.[62] Their work suggested that population growth was not determined by the biology of subsistence, as Raymond Pearl had argued, but rather by such complex social and political factors as immigration, industrialization, urbanization, and racial discrimination. Thompson and Whelpton's approach integrated analysis of population quantity with that of population quality by demonstrating that population quality—the proportion of the population that was urban as opposed to rural, white as opposed to nonwhite, and native-born as opposed to foreign-born—was both cause and effect of changes in population quantity.

The Scripps Foundation's major contribution to demography was a new method for predicting population growth, published by Whelpton in 1928.[63] Scripps had asked Thompson and Whelpton to anticipate population problems that would arise for the United States over the next several decades, so predicting growth during those decades seemed the best place to start. Rather than using Pearl's logistic curve, however, they developed their own approach.[64] Now known as the cohort component method of population projection, it remains the standard model used by demographers worldwide.[65]

The cohort component method rests on the same aggregate ontology of population as Lotka and Dublin's true rate of natural increase and Kuczynski's net reproduction rate. In contrast to Pearl's logistic law, which assumed downward causation from a territory's subsistence resources to total population size to individual vital processes, the cohort component method assumes upward causation from individual vital events, summarized as averages across the population, to total population size and structure. The cohort component method derives future population size and structure by applying expected future age-specific vital rates (fertility, mortality, and migration) to the current population age-sex structure (number of males and females at each age). In his 1928 publication, Whelpton predicted the size of the U.S. population at five-year intervals from 1925 to 1975. He also subdivided the U.S. population by what seemed to be the most relevant qualitative characteristics—race, nativity, and urban/rural status—producing predictions of future population quality in addition to predictions of future population quantity.[66]

By including population in the Recent Social Trends project, Ogburn and Odum claimed human population dynamics as an object of social scientific analysis. By selecting Thompson and Whelpton—rather than Pearl or any other biologist—as the relevant experts, Ogburn and Odum endowed the cohort component projection method with the government's imprimatur, validating the aggregate population ontology it embodied and the mercantilist perspective that traveled along with the aggregate ontology. Even Thompson—whose earlier work had espoused Giddings's anti-immigrant Malthusianism—withdrew his earlier support for immigration restriction and began to argue the mercantilist position that the United States was headed for depopulation rather than overpopulation when he shifted his analytic focus from overall growth (organic ontology) to age-specific vital rates (aggregate ontology).[67]

By the time they were selected to write about population for Recent Social Trends, Thompson and Whelpton had become key figures in the new science of demography. Pearl invited them to join the IUSIPP's American Committee, and they were founding members of the PAA. It was younger social scientists like Thompson and Whelpton, as well as students of Ogburn and Odum, those who utilized quantitative methods and embraced Lotka and Dublin's aggregate population ontology, not the natural scientists like Pearl or the older anti-immigrant sociologists like Giddings and Fairchild, whose work was coming to characterize demography.

When the U.S. government became an audience for population forecasts, Thompson and Whelpton adapted the cohort component method to emphasize the effects of policy on population. In so doing, they made the shift from population *forecasting* or *prediction* to population *projection* or *simulation*. In contrast to Whelpton's 1928 article, which included only one vision of the future, the monograph Thompson and Whelpton wrote for the Recent Social Trends project included ten possible futures, a set of *projections* rather than a single *prediction*. These projections combined five possible future fertility trajectories, three possible mortality trajectories, and six possible immigration rates, emphasizing the dependence of overall population size and structure on vital rates. The accompanying text emphasized the dependence of vital rates on government policy.

In contrast to Pearl, who had contended that future population size *could be known with certainty because it could not be controlled*, Thompson and Whelpton described future population size as something that *could not be known with certainty because it could be controlled*. Whereas Pearl had claimed that the logistic equation could accurately *forecast* future population size, the cohort component method allowed analysts to *simulate* the effects of various fertility, mortality, and migration rates—all ostensibly under human control—on future population size and structure. In the 1930s there was no empirical basis for favoring one method over the other; not enough time had elapsed to judge the accuracy of the predictions. The growing political desire to control the future of human population quantity and quality, however, generated support for the cohort component method, which made population control theoretically possible and provided tools to calculate the effects of potential changes in vital rates on aggregate quantity and quality.[68] Throughout the 1930s the U.S. government continued to commission population projections from the Scripps Foundation.[69]

In their projections for Recent Social Trends, Thompson and Whelpton presented population as something that could be *planned* as well as something that could be *planned for*. They contended that, in the absence of active intervention, the population of the United States would soon reach stationarity, meaning that growth would cease. Their vision of stationarity was not Pearl's Malthusian vision of overpopulation and resource scarcity but Lotka, Dublin, and Kuczynski's mercantilist vision of depopulation, economic stagnation, and geopolitical weakness. Thompson and Whelpton described strategies the government could utilize to promote economic growth under a stationary population, an example of planning *for* population.[70] But they also suggested that the government could head off impending population stationarity with policies aimed at increasing either fertility or immigration, an example of planning population itself.

Thompson and Whelpton legitimated explicit government planning of population by arguing that public policy had always influenced population growth. They pointed out that, "though perhaps it is not generally realized, it is nevertheless a fact that the United States has had a definite and effective policy regarding the increase of population practically from the commencement of white settlement."[71] The goal of that policy, they contended, was to increase and whiten the population of the United States by encouraging immigration from Northern and Western Europe, limiting immigration from other regions, and preventing the spread of contraceptive knowledge. They recommended that, "if it is believed that the present population is not too large, or that still further increase is needed, then the financial burden of raising the next generation, which is very unevenly distributed at the present time, should be redistributed so that those who raise the children will not be compelled to forego their reasonable share of the material enjoyments of life."[72] In other words, they suggested that the U.S. government could—and probably should—raise the birth rate by subsidizing childbearing. When the government took a step in this direction by including Aid to Dependent Children in the 1935 Social Security Act, it implicitly favored white childbearing by excluding the children of agricultural and domestic workers.[73]

Published in 1933, Thompson and Whelpton's Recent Social Trends monograph advocated the kind of active role the federal government would begin to take in the U.S. economy with President Franklin Roosevelt's New Deal. The Great Depression demonstrated to economists and policymakers that unregulated markets could not effectively allocate resources or ensure long-term prosperity in industrial societies. The Roosevelt administration instituted new forms of social and economic planning, some intended to overcome the current crisis and others intended to provide Americans with a permanent social safety apparatus. The growth of the welfare state increased the government's demand for demographic expertise.[74] Beginning in 1934 the Federal Emergency Relief Administration hired several PAA members, mainly sociologists whose intellectual lineages went back to Giddings.

Henry Pratt Fairchild, who was still president of the PAA at that point, suggested that the organization hold its 1935 meeting in Washington, DC, and invite representatives of government agencies so as to "impress the public with the importance of scientific research in population for national planning."[75] This meeting cemented the relationship between the PAA, demography, and the federal government that had begun with Recent Social Trends. Its program included a conversation between demographers and Census Bureau officials, as well as sessions on public health and vital statistics, population studies in relation to social planning, population distribution and internal migration, and the place of population studies in university curricula. Fred Osborn took part, presenting a paper in a session on differential fertility that was cosponsored by the AES. Eleanor Roosevelt attended this session, reportedly with knitting in hand, escorted by Osborn.[76] Afterward the Roosevelts invited the PAA's leaders to tea at the White House.[77] The image of Osborn escorting Roosevelt to the PAA meeting symbolizes his role in the new field of demography. He mediated demographers' relationships to their patrons and their audiences, in effect controlling what research would be done and by whom it would be received.

Over the remainder of the decade, Osborn oriented demography toward the scientific questions raised by his eugenics program.

DEMOGRAPHY FOR EUGENICS

The birth rate in the United States fell dramatically throughout the 1930s, and Thompson and Whelpton continually revised downward their projections of future population growth, shown in Figure 2.2. All of these projections were lower than the one Pearl had produced in 1920 on the basis of his logistic law. In 1940 Lotka calculated that 100 girls born in the United States in 1936 could be expected to have only 95 daughters and 90 granddaughters, a net reproduction rate of 0.95.[78] The United States was not headed for population stationarity, he warned, but for depopulation. Only a decade earlier, Pearl and East had predicted that agriculture in the United States would not be able to keep up with population growth. Now Whelpton called on farmers to reduce their output to avoid overproduction.[79] USDA economist Oliver E. Baker observed as early as 1929 that, due to falling birth rates, "food is now pressing on population rather than

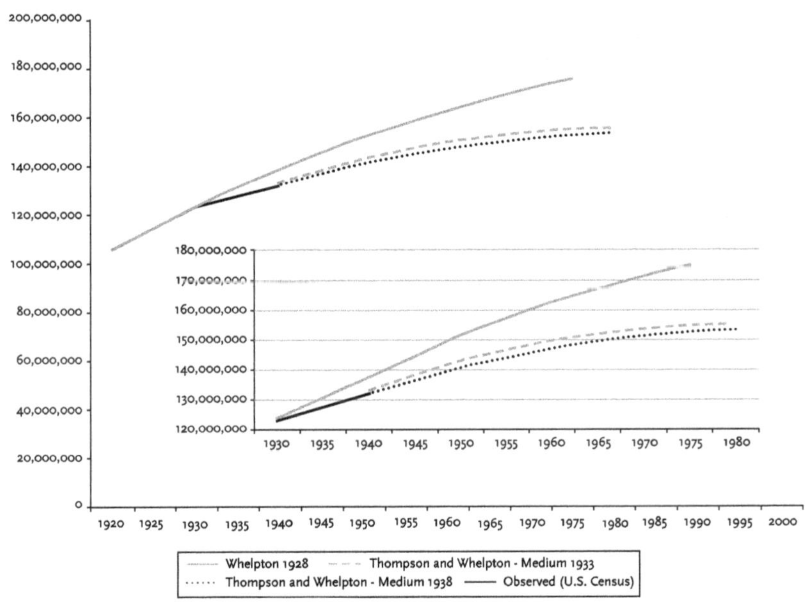

Figure 2.2 Observed U.S. population, 1920–1940, and U.S. population to 1980 as projected by Pascal Kidder Whelpton in 1928 and by Warren Simpson Thompson and Pascal Kidder Whelpton in 1933 and 1938.
Produced by the author.

population on food."[80] Indeed during the following decade, the New Deal state would begin to pay farmers to take land out of production. An exhibit in the Hall of Man at the 1939–1940 World's Fair in New York brought this depopulation anxiety to the general public by demonstrating that families were shrinking in size, as was the proportion of women in the reproductive ages, setting the country up for absolute population decline in the near future.[81]

By the end of the decade, Congress had begun to discuss potential pronatalist legislation. Osborn worried that hastily passed measures would focus on restricting access to contraception and that such an approach would exacerbate existing patterns of differential fertility, promoting larger families among the poor rather than the middle class and wealthy, thereby further reducing population quality and leaving the United States vulnerable to internal strife and external attack.[82] To avert this potential disaster, Osborn leveraged his connections to demography's patrons, coordinating the research programs of OPR, the Milbank Memorial Fund, and the Scripps Foundation to figure out how to address the falling birth rate by increasing births only among those he considered worthy of producing future generations of Americans: native white Protestant members of the professional middle class. To this end, interwar demography research focused on three questions:[83] Were the poor having more children than the middle-class and wealthy? Was the spread of birth control responsible for the overall decline in the birth rate and for differential fertility? What determined which couples used birth control and which did not? Osborn hoped that the answers to these questions could point the way toward policies that would increase the overall birth rate while redistributing births from poorer families to wealthier ones.

Notestein answered the first question while he was still working at Milbank.[84] Using previously untabulated data from the 1910 census, he examined the dimensions of fertility differentials (income, education, occupation, etc.) and their stability over time. As expected, he found that family size was inversely proportional to socioeconomic status, meaning that wealthier couples had fewer children.[85] Contrary to popular belief, however, the receipt of public benefits did not incentivize the poor to have more children. Although families receiving welfare were, on average, larger than other families, they had been large prior to obtaining relief and had not grown as a result.[86] But was birth control the reason some families were smaller than others?

While it now seems obvious that contraception was behind the falling overall birth rate and that the uneven use of birth control was behind differential fertility, there was no scientific consensus on this matter until the mid-1930s. In a 1931 press release, the Milbank Memorial Fund announced that, "in the country as in the city, the higher the economic and social status of the parents, the fewer are the children born. . . . Whether this limitation of babies is accomplished entirely by birth control or is partly the result of diminished fecundity, it is impossible to say."[87] Many scientists, particularly natural scientists and most vocally Raymond Pearl, attributed differential fertility (actual birth rates) to differential fecundity (biological capacity for reproduction). Any biological explanation for changes in the birth rate over time, or for inter- or intranational fertility differentials, would need to account for the fact that birth rates were falling mainly in the countries of North America and Western Europe, and within those countries they were falling most rapidly among the middle and upper classes. Interwar scientists advanced a variety of hypotheses, including a biological response to urban crowding, "some loss of natural capacity to bear children" associated with "civilization," a "cyclical rise and fall of racial reproductive vigor," a metabolic trade-off between economic success and reproduction, and a higher frequency of sexual activity among the poor because they had fewer nonsexual activities with which to dissipate "nervous energy."[88] The fact that contraceptive technologies were rudimentary and—in many places—illegal made these theories seem more plausible.

Very little contraceptive research had been done to that point.[89] What studies did exist examined the efficacy with which various birth control methods prevented pregnancy in individual women, not the prevalence of birth control use in the country as a whole or its effect on aggregate birth rates. The research sponsored by the Milbank Memorial Fund explored these population-level questions, asking whether the spread of birth control was responsible for overall reductions in fertility and for the observed correlation of family size with poverty.[90] This question was critical to the Fund's work, which rested on the assumption that "the limitation of certain families would have a direct influence on the social and economic development of society."[91] Research into this matter was carried out mainly by Notestein and Pearl and published primarily in the *Milbank Memorial Fund Quarterly*, which was becoming a major outlet for demographic research.[92]

By 1934 the results of these studies had obliterated any vestige of doubt that the differential spread of birth control was responsible for recent fertility patterns.[93] Notestein and Pearl discovered widespread knowledge of basic contraceptive principles. Most people knew that they could avoid getting pregnant through abstinence and at least reduce their chances through withdrawal. Condoms, diaphragms, and spermicides were readily available to those who knew where to look for them, though they could not be advertised as contraceptives. Notestein found that these methods "could fully account for the downward course of fertility"[94] in the aggregate, even if individual couples had less than perfect success rates.[95] Pearl announced that "this evidence destroys most of the basis of my life's work," repudiating his logistic law of population growth, which had depended on fecundity decreasing as a biological response to increasing population density.[96] Despite having resigned from the National Council of Sanger's American Birth Control League in 1928—at the time forswearing any involvement in "propagandist" activities—Pearl called publicly for the legalization of birth control as a means of poverty relief, arguing that "poverty and unemployment are being encouraged by the national policy of prohibiting the free dissemination of scientific birth control information."[97]

Yet it was not at all clear that simply legalizing birth control, or even distributing it for free, would equalize birth rates across racial or socioeconomic strata. Notestein found that, although knowledge of contraception was relatively widespread, the couples who were most interested in limiting their family size were members of the new professional middle class that had emerged with the growth of large industrial corporations at the turn of the twentieth century.[98] Poor and nonwhite couples had larger families not only because they lacked *access* to contraception, he contended, but also because they lacked the *motivation* to seek it out and use it. Pearl argued that the poor and nonwhite also lacked the skill and intelligence necessary to use available methods successfully.[99] For these reasons, Notestein and Pearl suggested that "birth control as an isolated movement—an inexpensive panacea—has small chance for success" as a means of reducing birth rates among the American poor.[100] What was needed instead was an expansion of middle-class living standards, which would also expand bourgeois "values and interests," as well as the development of simpler contraceptive methods that would make it easier for couples to act on their new interests.[101]

Notestein's focus on the effects of birth control on the aggregate birth rate rather than the efficacy of birth control as used by individual couples reflects demography's unit of analysis. Demographers, beginning with Lotka and continuing to the present day, analyze *aggregate rates*, not *individual experiences*. Osborn saw demography as the ideal scientific ally for eugenics because eugenics also had an aggregate aim: seeking improvement in *population quality*, not individual quality of life.

In the late 1930s Osborn's advocacy for eugenics and Sanger's advocacy for birth control legalization converged on family planning. For Sanger, the term was a euphemism for birth control that de-emphasized individual reproductive autonomy; for Osborn, it was a euphemism for eugenics that de-emphasized social control over family size. Family planning therefore signified birth control for eugenic ends: individual control over conception in the service of social control over reproduction.

When Sanger combined the Birth Control Clinical Research Bureau with the National Committee on Federal Legislation for Birth Control to form the Birth Control Federation of America at the end of the decade, she invited Osborn, Notestein, Lorimer, Whelpton, and Thompson to serve as an advisory committee on population.[102] In 1941 Osborn and Notestein pressured Sanger to change the name of the Birth Control Federation of America to the Planned Parenthood Federation of America, threatening to withdraw from the Federation's population committee if she didn't acquiesce.[103] The change of name indicated an official shift in the organization's aims from birth control to family planning, and from female sexual and reproductive autonomy to social control over childbearing. The renamed organization drew massive support from the business and medical communities. Prescott S. Bush, father of George H. W. Bush and grandfather of George W. Bush, served as treasurer of Planned Parenthood's first national fundraising campaign in 1947. Prescott Bush's support for Planned Parenthood, and that of his son—which earned him the nickname "Rubbers" during his stint in the U.S. House of Representatives twenty years later—makes sense only in light of the fact that family planning was not a synonym for birth control. Instead it connoted eugenics through birth control.[104]

SURVEYING FERTILITY

Osborn hoped that demography could point the way toward making family planning work by converting social control over reproduction from fantasy to reality. To that end, he proposed that the Milbank Memorial Fund and the Carnegie Corporation—of which he was also a trustee—fund a study on the social and psychological determinants of childbearing among couples whose reproduction he considered most desirable. Osborn had already directed a similar study under the auspices of the Pioneer Fund. The Study of the Family Life of Army Aviators had aimed to discover the reasons behind childbearing decisions and thereby determine how to encourage larger families among aviation officers, whom Osborn believed to be "descended predominantly from white persons who settled in the original thirteen states prior to the adoption of the Constitution of the United States."[105] The new project, titled Social and Psychological Factors Affecting Fertility, would be carried out jointly by the Scripps Foundation, the Milbank Memorial Fund, and OPR. Indianapolis was selected as the research site, and the project was informally known as the Indianapolis Study.

Osborn expected that the new field of survey research would help demographers figure out how couples determined the size of their families and how to influence the way those decisions were made. Today the term "survey" immediately brings to mind a questionnaire aimed at eliciting information about individuals that may include facts, opinions, or both. This meaning originated in the 1930s, when opinion pollsters such as George Gallup and Elmo Roper began to use the word to describe their methods. For social scientists, "survey" had previously signified something more akin to the work of a land surveyor, a systematic investigation of the entire social structure and life of a given place or people.[106] In the 1930s quantitatively oriented social scientists began to adopt and adapt the methods of opinion polling to social research, redefining the survey as a questionnaire- or interview-based approach to capturing and analyzing individual perspectives and experiences.[107] They touted the survey as a way to elicit the same information that could be discovered through case histories or community studies, but on a larger scale and more cost-effectively. With a standardized questionnaire and multiple-choice answers, it became possible to scale up a small study, even to the national level. Some of the earliest work on survey research in the social sciences occurred at Princeton University's Office of Public Opinion Research, established in 1939 alongside OPR in SPIA, which by then had been renamed the Wilson School after the former U.S. president and former Princeton University president Woodrow Wilson.[108]

Demographic analysis had previously relied on census and vital registration data, which recorded outcomes. Survey research promised to uncover the behavior that produced those outcomes and the attitudes that influenced behavior. Osborn hoped that policymakers would use such information to design eugenically sound pronatalist policies, just as politicians used the results of opinion polls to attract voters and businesses used market research to influence purchasing decisions. The Indianapolis Study set the model for postwar fertility surveys worldwide and was therefore the first of what would become a series of national and international surveys of fertility and family planning. Several prominent postwar demographers cut their analytic teeth on data from the Indianapolis Study as graduate students and junior faculty.[109]

Since demographers and their sponsors were concerned about the differential use of birth control among those whose fertility they hoped to increase, the Indianapolis Study focused on those whose fertility they considered most socially valuable and those they perceived as being in the vanguard of contraceptive trends: white, Protestant, native-born, middle-class couples. Although Jews had higher rates of contraceptive use than did

Protestants, the study focused on Protestants because it was their childbearing that Osborn hoped to encourage.[110] Those selected for the study were visited by "women with graduate training in psychology, sociology, or social case work," who asked "a large number of highly personal questions" that tried to link a couple's social and psychological characteristics to their childbearing history on the basis of Osborn's eugenic theories.[111] In addition to recording respondents' answers to these questions, each interviewer also recorded "her personal evaluation of the husband and wife on a series of attributes," including her perception of their economic security, on an "Interviewer's Rating Scale."[112]

The Indianapolis Study identified socioeconomic status as the strongest predictor of family size but found that its effects were not consistent. In the sample as a whole, socioeconomic status was *inversely* correlated with family size, meaning that wealthier families had fewer children. But among the subset of couples whose families were completely planned—that is, each birth intended at the time it occurred and unintended births averted through contraceptive use—the pattern was reversed. In planned families, the number of children was *directly* correlated with socioeconomic status, meaning that wealthier families were larger.[113] This finding provided support for Osborn's contention that the diffusion of birth control throughout society could reverse the prevailing socioeconomic fertility differential. It also laid the foundation for postwar economic theories of childbearing that compared fertility decisions to consumer choices.[114]

The Indianapolis Study found that couples whose relationships seemed stronger had been better able to achieve their desired family size, whether small or large. Given that the methods of birth control available at the time—abstinence, rhythm, withdrawal, condoms, diaphragms, and spermicides—required the cooperation or at least the consent of both sexual partners, it is perhaps not surprising that family planning "was most successful among couples in which both the wife and husband state that responsibility for contraception was a fifty-fifty proposition, and was least successful among couples in which each spouse said that the other should take the responsibility. . . . When each wished the burden on the other, apparently neither spouse took much responsibility."[115] After World War II, feminist efforts to give women more control over childbearing, together with the search for simpler contraceptives for use in the Global South, would lead to the development of systemic contraceptive technologies that worked directly on women's bodies, eliminating the need for male cooperation and turning birth control into a female concern rather than one of couples.

The Indianapolis Study taught demographers important lessons about survey research. They learned that it is very hard to determine causality with a cross-sectional study, in which independent and dependent (input and outcome) variables are measured at the same point in time. Did a couple's family size reflect long-standing attitudes toward children, or did attitudes toward children reflect current child care responsibilities? Answers were also subject to recall bias and post-hoc rationalization. Would a couple admit if one of their pregnancies had not been desired at the time it occurred?[116] As he analyzed data from Indianapolis, demographer Clyde Kiser of the Milbank Memorial Fund began to wonder whether standardized survey questions and statistical measures could effectively identify childbearing decisions "made by individuals with multiple and complex motivations."[117] Despite this doubt, demographers would come to rely more heavily on survey questionnaires and statistical analysis over the next few decades, though by the end of the century some would also begin to incorporate ethnographic methods into fertility research.[118]

The interview phase of the Indianapolis Study was completed in the summer of 1941, but the bombing of Pearl Harbor and subsequent entry of the United States into World War II required that analysis be put on hold while demographers turned their attention to the war effort. Osborn was already in Washington, DC, by then, having arrived in 1940 at the invitation of President Roosevelt. Despite Osborn's opposition to the New Deal, Roosevelt remained a friend, and he chose Osborn to chair the Committee on Selective Service, which would lay the legal and constitutional foundation for the wartime draft.[119] Osborn used that position to continue lobbying for eugenic policies in the United States. He claimed that, among men who were deemed unfit to serve, "a majority of their defects have a constitution, that is a hereditary basis." He recommended that the U.S. government "reduce the incidence of persons born with a tendency to defect," through "registration, segregation and refusal of marriage license to the feebleminded; use of contraceptives under medical advice by mentally normal carriers of defect; extensive search for bad family strains."[120] Osborn contended that America's success in the war, and therefore its democratic future, depended on such measures. Although he did not advocate sterilization directly, in a publication on the Selective Service, he approvingly cited the pro-sterilization opinion of Justice Oliver Wendell Holmes in the 1927 Supreme Court case *Buck v. Bell*. These negative measures, however, were only half of Osborn's eugenic prescription for safeguarding democracy. In his official capacity, Osborn contended that it was also critical that "the abler stocks from every class and section of the country have good-sized families," though he maintained that they must do so as part of "a natural, largely unconscious process," not the dictatorial control of births by the government.[121] In other words, through family planning.

By framing family planning as the solution to the interwar problem of imminent population decline and the wartime problem of military manpower, Osborn advanced the legalization of birth control while subordinating female autonomy over childbearing to social control over reproduction. He also advanced the professional fortunes of demographers, linking these population scientists to patrons and audiences, earning for himself the informal title of "demography's statesman."[122] In the 1930s American demographers focused almost exclusively on the U.S. population and its imminent decline. They were aware that population was growing rapidly in some other places, particularly Southern and Eastern Europe and South and East Asia, but it was not their primary concern.[123] Indeed very little information was available about population in much of the world. The entry of the United States into World War II, however, refocused their gaze on the international horizon. After the war ended, Osborn and other eugenicists would likewise widen the scope of their population projects to the world as a whole.

CHAPTER 3

Global Population

By the end of World War II, the Allied powers had begun to reimagine the world as a large collection of sovereign and coequal nation-states rather than a small club of Europe-based empires. In this aspirational new postwar order, each nation-state would be responsible for governing its population (the people counted by its censuses) and managing its economy (the transactions occurring within its borders). This emergent international community of nation-states was at the heart of the Bretton Woods vision of an interconnected global economy meant to ensure worldwide peace and prosperity.[1] Instantiating that vision would be the job of the new United Nations.

Transforming the world into a series of populations and economies required that each country bring its population into being through a census and bring its economy into being through national income accounting. The idea that each country had a population was not new, though methods of counting and constituting populations varied widely. The idea that each country had an economy *was* new, having emerged between the wars with the invention of macroeconomic statistics.[2] In the decades following World War II, scientists would recommend family planning as a means of keeping national populations in balance with national economies and global population in balance with the Earth's resources. That story will be the subject of the next three chapters. This chapter tells the story that is missing from existing accounts of postwar population control and economic planning, examining how scientists and policymakers transformed the world into a collection of national populations that could be harnessed to economies in new per capita measures and aggregated to produce population estimates

Building the Population Bomb. Emily Klancher Merchant, Oxford University Press (2021). © Oxford University Press.
DOI: 10.1093/oso/9780197558942.003.0004

for the world as a whole. It was not until national populations could be measured and global population calculated that scientists could project their futures and declare them a problem to be solved. That is, populations had to be constructed quantitatively before they could be construed as problematic.

Demography played a starring role in the generation of population numbers. In the decades following World War II, the UN established a Population Division, charged with collecting and publishing population data for every country of the world, and a Population Commission, which oversaw that work. Its demographers encouraged each country to establish standard mechanisms for census-making that would produce internationally comparable data. This project faltered, however, as the politics of demographic data collection proved inseparable from struggles over sovereignty at national and international levels. Populations are constituted through technologies of governance. Censuses therefore do more than simply count noses: they also assert and reflect the power of states over bodies. Where that power is contested, so too are the numbers produced by censuses. The process of converting the world into a community of populations was therefore inextricably bound up with imperial, anticolonial, and nationalist projects at a variety of scales.

When counting the world's populations proved to be anything but straightforward, the Population Division turned to demographic theory and models to fill in the persistent gaps in its statistical tables. With these techniques, demography was finally able to statistically represent the world as an international community of populations that could be planned and planned for. Yet the scientific rather than governmental constitution of the international community replaced the actual histories of the world's countries with the timeless past assumed by modernization theory and transformed the world's populations from political entities that would govern themselves democratically into natural objects that would be managed scientifically from outside.

A DEARTH OF DEMOGRAPHIC DATA

Prior to World War II, American demographers had focused primarily on the population of the United States and had worked almost exclusively with U.S. data.[3] During the war, however, OPR became the epicenter of global population analysis. Princeton's Institute for Advanced Study provided a haven for émigré intellectuals fleeing Europe, including economists and statisticians from the League of Nations secretariat.[4] As the League turned its attention to the inevitable challenge of postwar reconstruction, it asked Frank Notestein and his team to project population growth in Europe for the remainder of the century. Fred Osborn secured funding for this project from the Carnegie Corporation. After the United States entered the war, the Department of State also turned to OPR for population estimates and projections in the rest of the world. The Carnegie Corporation paid for these as well.[5]

Notestein and his team were able to obtain most of the data they needed to project the future population of Europe. When they looked to other continents, however, they found that, in many places, the requisite demographic data simply did not exist. Midcentury demographers had previously given little thought to why states collect demographic data. They were therefore surprised, when they tried to estimate and project population in the rest of the world, to find that the data they could easily acquire for the United States were not available everywhere. They do not seem to have realized that the institutions that produced the data they took for granted were products of liberal democracy, so it did not occur to them that societies with other forms of government would collect different kinds of population data, or perhaps would not collect population data at all.

The metrics American demographers had developed to estimate population size and project population growth relied on the data that were close to hand for them: information about population stock (the number of people in a specific place at a specific moment) from censuses and information about population flow (the number of births, deaths, immigrations, and emigrations) from vital registration. These data were produced not primarily for demographic analysis but for the purposes of democratic self-government and public health. In the United States, the first country to institute a regular census, population enumeration determined how seats in the House of Representatives would be allocated among the states. Enumeration and vital registration (which began later for public health purposes) enrolled the citizens of democratic countries in the project of self-government. As other countries in Western Europe and the Americas established liberal democratic governments, they also built the institutions responsible for population enumeration and vital registration. These institutions were expensive to maintain, however, and they relied on powerful states with territories well-connected by communication and transportation infrastructures. States that lacked resources, infrastructure, or authority were unable to carry out regular censuses. Therefore, when OPR demographers began to look for data in Latin America, they found that

Bolivia had not had a census since 1900, Uruguay had not had one since 1908, and Argentina had not had one since 1914.[6]

Many countries that did not have liberal democratic traditions—including Afghanistan, Bhutan, Ethiopia, Iraq, Kuwait, Nepal, Saudi Arabia, and Yemen—had no need for censuses and did not carry them out.[7] In 1940 the vital statistician Walter Willcox estimated that approximately one-third of all people in the world had not been counted by a census, though he did not elaborate on his method of quantifying the uncounted portion of the world's population.[8] China was, by far, the largest country that lacked a census. Several estimates of China's population size were floating around at the end of World War II; Notestein admitted in 1944, "opinions concerning the size of the present population [of China] differ by more than the total population of the United States."[9]

The governments of many French, British, and Dutch colonies in Asia, Africa, and the Caribbean did carry out censuses, but they were very different from the detailed individual enumerations that had become routine in France, Great Britain, and the Netherlands. Midcentury demographers simply deemed them bad censuses, but they should instead be recognized as censuses designed for the purpose of colonial administration rather than democratic self-government. European censuses established and reflected dynamic political relationships between states and citizens. Colonial censuses were more like inventories of the overseas human resources available to European empires. They counted population unevenly, covering urban areas in more detail than rural areas and enumerating expatriates more precisely than indigenes. It has been estimated that the 1931 censuses in Anglophone West Africa counted nearly all Europeans and Asians but only about 4% of Africans.[10] The sizes of indigenous populations were often simply estimated on the basis of tax or employment records.[11]

Who counted as African, Asian, or European differed from place to place and was highly contested within any given place, reflecting local social, economic, and political conditions. Analysis of the 1931 census of British Malaya found that

> of the 2,376 non-British Europeans, 825 were returned as "Dutch," but it is probable that many of these should have been included under Eurasians, the same being true in the case of the 117 "Portuguese." As to the Dutch, it must be borne in mind that, in the Netherlands Indies, whence comes the great majority of these people, the distinction between European and Eurasian is not maintained as we maintain it, and for census and other administrative purposes, the two classes are grouped together as "Europeans and those assimilated with them" or "Europeans" simply.[12]

Colonial censuses were themselves one of the mechanisms though which racial distinctions were established, maintained, and negotiated.[13]

Colonial censuses produced vague figures for total population. Nigeria's 1931 census, for example, concluded that "the population was probably not under 18,500,000 and not over 22,000,000."[14] Colonial censuses also lacked the detail necessary to determine the population's age-sex structure, a key input to the cohort component projection method. In contrast to censuses in North America and Western Europe, which enumerated each person individually, colonial censuses often simply returned the estimated number of adult men, adult women, and children. This tripartite division facilitated colonial rule and the extraction of labor and taxes, but not population projection.

Where colonial censuses happened at all, they did not necessarily occur on a regular basis. In many parts of the British Empire, the 1931 census had been postponed indefinitely as a result of the global economic depression. The 1941 round was scrapped entirely when World War II broke out. Vital statistics (birth and death rates) in colonial territories were even less complete than were censuses. Despite the fact that registration of births and deaths was, by 1926, compulsory throughout the British Colonial Empire (the British Empire, minus India and the self-governing Dominions), it actually covered only a small fraction of the population. Vital registration systems in West Africa included about 6% of the African population in Sierra Leone, 7% in Gambia, 1% in Nigeria and the Cameroons, and 9% in Gold Coast and Togoland (now Ghana and Togo).[15]

Colonial governments may simply have been too weak and underfunded to produce more detailed population data. They may have been unable to locate all of the people in the territory they controlled on paper, and they may have encountered resistance to enumeration that was done for the purposes of taxation or extraction but not representation. It is also possible that colonial governments simply had no need for the kind of detailed population data produced by metropolitan-style censuses and vital registers and therefore devoted to the task only the financial and human resources necessary to produce data relevant to colonial administration. Metropolitan censuses forged a direct relationship between individuals and governments, simultaneously constituting the state as a legitimate representation of the nation and its subjects as citizens of a democratic state. In contrast, colonial censuses facilitated the management of populations en masse.[16] Frederick Cooper has argued that colonial power was "more arterial than capillary," contrasting the macro scale of colonial rule to the micro-level diffusion of power throughout European and North American societies that Michel Foucault attributed to such forms of discipline as prisons, clinics, educational institutions, and statistics.[17] Colonial censuses, in fact, resembled methods of political arithmetic that early modern European governments had used to estimate the population that was available to a sovereign for labor or military conscription more than they resembled the censuses that produced modern self-governing metropolitan citizens.[18] The data they generated may have worked for colonial purposes but were not adequate to the task of estimating or projecting global population.

A WORLD OF POPULATIONS

When Notestein arrived the UN Population Division in 1947 as its first (interim) director, he brought this problem with him. The technical work of the Population Division was overseen by the Population Commission, which comprised delegates from twelve UN member countries. It was expected that membership would rotate, but the United States ended up maintaining a permanent presence, and thereby exercising considerable influence, initially focusing the work of the Population Commission and Population Division on demographic data collection.

The first U.S. representative to the Population Commission was a demographer, Philip Hauser.[19] At the time he took on this role, Hauser had just accepted a faculty position in the Sociology Department at the University of Chicago, where he had completed his Ph.D. in 1938. In between, Hauser served the New Deal state, first in the Federal Emergency Relief Administration and then in the Census Bureau. He worked in the Research Branch of the Information-Education Division of the army during World War II,[20] after which he returned to the Census Bureau as deputy director. There he established rapport with Secretary of Commerce and former vice president Henry A. Wallace, becoming Wallace's personal assistant.[21] Although he had job offers in academia, Hauser remained at the Census Bureau until Wallace was pushed out of Commerce, after which Hauser took the job at the University of Chicago.[22] He returned to the Census Bureau to direct the 1950 Census in an interim capacity, commuting back to Chicago every weekend to teach.[23]

As a result of his association with Wallace, Hauser came under the suspicion of the Loyalty Board of the Department of Commerce in the lead-up to the 1950 Census and was informed that "reasonable grounds may exist to believe that you are disloyal to the Government of the United States and therefore unsuited for Federal employment."[24] At Hauser's request, Notestein filed a sworn affidavit recounting Hauser's demonstrations of loyalty, particularly in his activities as U.S. representative to the UN Population Commission, where Hauser dutifully carried out directions supplied by the State Department.[25] Hauser was permitted to continue his work with the Census Bureau and remain on the UN Population Commission, but other demographers who came under suspicion were not so lucky. Hope Eldridge, who had volunteered in Wallace's 1948 presidential campaign, was dismissed from her position in the UN Food and Agriculture Organization for invoking the Fifth Amendment when questioned by the Internal Security Subcommittee of the U.S. Senate.[26]

Hauser and his advisors in the U.S. government saw in the UN a vehicle for the global extension of the New Deal and viewed the collection of population data as key to the social and economic planning that would be required to effect economic development worldwide.[27] They therefore envisioned the UN Population Division as a hub for the collection and dissemination of global population data, what Bruno Latour has termed a "center of calculation."[28] Hauser described the other delegates to the Population Commission as "mature demographers, sociologists, economists or statisticians, well aware of the world population situation at the time and of the gaps in demographic statistics and knowledge," suggesting that they had a similar focus on data collection and were more interested in planning for population than in planning population itself.[29] Malthusianism was not absent from the UN, however. Its main champion there was biologist Julian Huxley, first director of the UN Educational, Scientific, and Cultural Organization.[30] But the Population Commission paid him little attention. When Huxley proposed a world population conference in 1949, demographers Dudley Kirk of the U.S. State Department and Abram Jaffe of the U.S. Census Bureau advised Hauser that "it is not desired to have a conference simply for the sake of having one, or for the purpose of broadcasting Malthusian prophecies or birth control propaganda."[31] The primary concern of the U.S. Department of State and the UN Population Commission was with collecting population data from the countries of the world on a regular basis and compiling them into tables that would be published annually in the *UN Demographic Yearbook*. Doing so would accomplish three objectives.

First, it would encourage the governments of the world, especially those of new postcolonial states, to make censuses and thereby constitute the populations for which they were responsible. Once the UN began to request population data from member states, census-making became a norm of the international community, and governments that wanted to be recognized as part of that community obliged. Following Nigerian independence in 1960, the federal minister of economic development acknowledged Nigeria's obligation to provide population data to international agencies in a 1962 statement:

> It is our duty as a nation to see to it that we produce population census results which have been thoroughly conducted, verified and appraised, and [are] therefore acceptable, without any shadow of doubt, to all governments of the world and to all international bodies such as the United Nations and its agencies, the World Bank, etc. . . . The impressions of the manner in which a country conducts its affairs are one of the factors which earn for it the respect or disrespect of the rest of the world.[32]

For newly established countries, census-making facilitated internal authority by locating, counting, and classifying subjects and citizens; reporting the results secured external legitimacy with respect to international institutions.

Second, the publication of population data from each country of the world would make those countries legible to one another, to the multinational businesses that sought to coordinate labor and markets, and to the international agencies and nongovernmental organizations that hoped to promote reconstruction in Europe and economic development in Africa, Asia, and Latin America. The concept of economic development had two meanings that began to converge after World War II. The older meaning, typically applied to colonial territories, was the extraction and marketing of raw materials.[33] The newer meaning was modernization and the improvements to the human condition that were expected to accompany modernization. The two definitions of development intersected in response to calls for decolonization after World War II, when colonial and postcolonial governments began to promote economic development in the older sense (extraction of natural resources) as a route to economic development in the newer sense (modernization). The two meanings of development were connected by novel methods of national income accounting that constituted national economies as objects of sociotechnical expertise or, as Timothy Mitchell puts it, "effects" of "a series of iterated calculations."[34] With these new calculations, national economies could be measured, either in absolute terms (gross national product; GNP, a forerunner to today's gross domestic product) or relative to population (GNP per capita). Development in the older sense increased GNP, which was understood to index development in the newer sense. The possibility of economic growth offered the promise of prosperity without redistribution, either within or between countries.[35] Measuring GNP per capita required both national income accounting and population enumeration. Stimulating its increase required projection and planning, either for or of population.

Third, the aggregation of data from each country of the world would constitute the global population. Unlike national populations, global population couldn't be counted. Even the UN lacked the resources and authority to carry out a global census. Because the UN's framers had envisioned the world as a community of sovereign nation-states, each responsible for constituting its own population through enumeration, no entity had the authority to count the population of the world as a whole. Global population could therefore only be constituted through calculation.

Calculating and projecting global population required standard and commensurable data for all countries of the world. Notestein first attempted to acquire these by circulating paper forms that solicited vital rates and total population figures classified by age and sex from each government. He expected that statistical agencies in each country would simply fill in the forms with what Latour calls "immutable and combinable mobiles," or stable, portable, and commensurable numeric data.[36] The UN Population Division would then compile the data into what Ted Porter calls a "thin description" of global population: a set of numbers that is supposedly self-explanatory and value-free.[37] UN demographers quickly realized, however, that population data from various parts of the world bore the indelible imprint of the political purposes for which they were collected, making them irreducibly "thick" in the sense that comparing or aggregating them, if possible at all, required detailed explanation of how the data for each country had been collected and reported. In other words, the data compiled by the Population Division resisted comparison and aggregation because they were not commensurate.

Demographers often describe census-making as "counting noses," an exercise that enumerates population in a standard unit: people (since most people have exactly one nose). Comparing and aggregating the resulting data should therefore not require an act of commensuration, which sociologists Wendy Espelend and Mitchell Stevens define as "the expression or measurement of characteristics normally represented by different units according to a common metric."[38] Commensuration is necessary only for the *quantitative* aggregation or comparison of things that are *qualitatively* different, as "commensuration transforms qualities into quantities, difference into magnitude."[39] For example, in animal husbandry, the number of animals that can be stocked on a given plot of land is calculated in terms of animal units, which quantitatively convert the grazing land required by any given animal to that required by a cow with a calf, which is the point of reference. That is, if a plot of land can support five animal units, that means it can support either five cows with calves or any numerical equivalent, where a horse is 1.25 animal units, a lamb is 0.15 animal units, and a mature elk is 0.6 animal units. Animal units facilitate commensuration because they allow the quantitative aggregation and comparison of animals that are qualitatively different.

If all humans are assumed to be equivalent for the purpose of population enumeration, then aggregating and comparing human populations does not require commensuration. Commensuration can, however, be used to assert human nonequivalence and to naturalize social inequality. For example, Article 1, Section 2 of the U.S. Constitution, which mandates a decennial census, establishes the numerical nonequivalence of "free Persons" and "all other Persons" by specifying a formula for their commensuration. For purposes of representational apportionment, enslaved persons were to count as three-fifths of free persons. In this case, specifying a quantitative formula for commensuration asserted the human nonequivalence of free and enslaved persons and naturalized the legal inequality that underpinned the system of racial slavery. Less explicitly, governments establish systems of human commensuration by determining who will be counted in a census and how they will be classified.[40]

Censuses are tools of governance that count people in ways that facilitate specific policies. Different policies translate into a variety of census methods; the data these methods produce often cannot be directly compared or aggregated between countries. For example, some countries have *de jure* censuses, which count the legally resident population, while others have *de facto* censuses, counting the population physically present on census day.[41] In regions with high rates of temporary international labor migration, these methods could produce very different results that are legitimate on their own but become misleading when compared or aggregated.[42] Censuses in different countries also resisted aggregation and comparison because they had been taken at different dates, had varying levels of detail, and employed disparate methods of estimating population where complete enumerations were not carried out. Vital statistics, produced by the governmental registration of births and deaths, were even sketchier, their variation often reflecting differences in the completeness of registration systems rather than differences in actual rates and trends therein.

As a result of this data friction, the UN Population Division was simply not able to produce the thin statistical tables its leadership envisioned.[43] The first issue of the *Demographic Yearbook* was delayed more than a year and included a considerable amount of text explaining the data it presented.[44] Nonetheless it was still deemed to include "patently defective data about which the consumer is not adequately warned." The Population Commission lamented that "the reproduction of these figures by the United Nations Statistical Office gives an aura of spurious authenticity, which has given rise to misinterpretation and misuse of these data by unwary readers."[45]

COUNTING THE WORLD'S POPULATIONS

The Population Commission's first attempt to elicit thinner and more comparable data from constituent countries was the 1950 World Census Program. This program piggybacked on the Census of the Americas, a project led by the Inter American Statistical Institute that was heavily subsidized by the U.S. government.[46] The Census of the Americas aimed to produce a coordinated 1950 census among all Western Hemisphere countries that would generate standardized data. Backers in the United States expected that it would produce valuable information for the Department of State and for American businesses. State Department staff imagined World War III looming just over the horizon. They expected it would be another total war, with enemies targeting the civilian populations of the United States and its satellites.[47] Keeping track of those populations was therefore critical to hemispheric defense. American businesses were heavily invested in Latin America as a source of materials and labor and as a market for manufactures, and hoped that censuses in Latin American countries could guide business strategy. The Census of the Americas program itself was a boon to U.S. companies that produced business equipment, as it increased international demand for tabulating machines, filing cabinets, and other requisite gear for the collection, analysis, and storage of large quantities of data.[48] The U.S. Census Bureau provided training in data collection and analysis to statistical personnel from the other countries of the Western Hemisphere, and an international committee planned census questionnaires that it hoped would produce synoptic and commensurate data. The experts involved were not optimistic, however. Some of the concepts used in the U.S. Census had no Spanish-language equivalent.[49]

Despite this wariness, the UN Population Commission extended the Census of the Americas program worldwide, recommending "that all such member states as are proposing to take censuses in or around 1950 use comparable schedules."[50] The language "in or around 1950" acknowledged that, while some countries, notably the United States and France and its colonies, typically conducted censuses in years ending with zero (1940, 1950, etc.), the U.K. and its colonies typically took theirs in years ending with one (1941, 1951, etc.). The UN lacked the power to compel any country to change its census date. The date also had to be approximate because, in countries that did not have a tradition of census-making and therefore did not already have the necessary infrastructure in place, a census planned for 1950 might not actually happen until a later year or might take longer than a year to complete.

The Population Commission emphasized to member states the importance of producing internationally comparable data. All countries were instructed to collect information about each person's sex, age, marital status, place of birth, citizenship, native language, educational attainment, fertility, economic characteristics, and relationship to household head, and to count the total population and the number living in rural and urban areas.[51] But, as the leaders of the Census of the Americas anticipated, the Population Commission found it difficult to create a schedule that would work for all countries.[52] Commission members also recognized that, within the list of information it requested, definitions and categories were not obvious. It is perhaps unsurprising that marital status might be divided into different categories under different legal and religious systems, or that the distinction between employment and unemployment might have little relevance in subsistence economies.[53] But even "total population," seemingly the most straightforward measure, was not unambiguous. The UN lacked the authority to impose a definition on member states, but it did recommend one: everyone resident in a country on census day, excluding foreign military and diplomatic personnel and including the country's own military and diplomatic personnel living abroad.[54] Censuses were to include everyone subject to the authority of the state carrying it out—that is, everyone who could be compelled to submit to enumeration—thereby constituting the population to be governed.

The Population Commission acknowledged that member states might want information about their residents that was not included in the standard schedules, but implored them not to sacrifice international comparability in these areas for the sake of country-specific information.[55] The World Census Program therefore asked countries to privilege international legibility over national governance. Accordingly, member states were asked to collect information desired by UN demographers that may not have been relevant to their own governmental purposes. One such example is age, another seemingly straightforward category that proved more difficult to standardize than the Population Commission expected.

The quantification of age is a cultural practice. The same person can be a year older or younger depending on which country they are in. Moreover people tend to know their exact age only when age is relevant for social, cultural, economic, or political reasons.[56] In some places where people typically didn't know their age, census enumerators used the appearance of respondents or their marital status and childbearing histories to guess, though such methods often imposed the enumerators' ideas and values—regarding, for example, how old a married woman "must" be—onto the people they recorded. Nigeria took another approach. In preparation for its 1962 census, the Census Office asked each local and district council to set up a Historical Events Committee, which would submit to the Census Office lists of local historical events that could be used to estimate individual ages. Such events included the deaths of prominent citizens; the building of roads, hospitals, schools, and other public institutions; disasters, riots, and murders; spectacular social events, such as weddings and funerals; and memorable political events such as independence.[57] The Census Office compiled and standardized the list for each locality and for the country as a whole. Census enumerators then used the list to calculate respondents' ages based on their memories of these events.

Following the 1950(ish) round of censuses, the UN developed special training programs to guide government statisticians in the analysis of their new data.[58] Censuses are, by nature, big data affairs.[59] They have four defining characteristics, which distinguish censuses from other surveys and enumerations. Censuses are universal, individual, instantaneous, and periodic. That is, a census records information about each person resident in a country on a specified "census day" at regular intervals, usually every ten years. The 1950 U.S. Census asked approximately twenty questions of each of the 150,697,361 individuals resident in the United States on April 1,[60] generating billions of data points. Today, seventy years later, a data set this large still cannot be readily analyzed using a single computer. But even this massive trove of data constituted a highly stylized image of the U.S. population, one that reduced an infinite diversity of human ways of life to a set of categories that could fit on a punch card.

Census returns had been tabulated mechanically using Hollerith machines and similar devices since the late nineteenth century. To tabulate the 1950 data, the U.S. Census Bureau leased thirty-two of IBM's newest device, the Model 101.[61] In most other countries, this kind of tabulating machinery was well out of reach. The UN planned to help government statistical agencies by establishing permanent centers for training in demographic data collection and analysis in Chembur, India, Santiago, Chile, and Cairo, Egypt, though putting these in place would require external funding that the UN did not acquire until later in the decade. In the interim, the Population Commission and Population Division loaned personnel to member states to train the staffs of their statistical agencies. In this capacity, Philip Hauser spent fifteen months in Burma immediately after completing the 1950 U.S. Census.[62]

Nearly all Western Hemisphere countries took censuses in 1950 (1951 in Canada), and some countries in other parts of the world carried out their first censuses as part of the 1950 UN World Census Program. By 1954 the Population Division had released estimates of the population of each continent for each decade from 1920 to 1950 and had projected the population of each continent to 1980. The numbers the Population Division published, however, including those for *past* dates, came with strong qualifications. Text accompanying the data tables warned that "many of these estimates [of population in the past] are subject to various errors and . . . even the resulting continental totals are not entirely trustworthy."[63] Challenges to generating "trustworthy" estimates stemmed both from the complications of producing comparable censuses between countries and from the difficulty in carrying out national censuses in countries that lacked transportation and communication infrastructure. Censuses are also expensive propositions; the 1950 U.S. Census was estimated to cost $85 million.[64] The UN recognized that the price tags on the censuses it requested were large compared to the financial resources of many member states, particularly those that had just wrested their independence from imperial powers.

The uses to which censuses were put domestically at times inhibited their utility as an international source of data. People often evaded enumeration by colonial censuses, fearing that results would be used for taxation or for labor or military conscription. In some newly independent countries, citizens sought to inflate census counts when the results were to be used for political representation.[65] In Nigeria, for example, experts believed that the 1951 census, the last under colonial rule, undercounted the population, while the 1962 census, the first under independent self-government, overcounted it.[66] Nigeria's prime minister nullified the 1962 census, repeating the whole process in 1963. Tabulations of the 1962 data were never officially released. The 1963 census was just as controversial as the 1962 census had been, but the Nigerian government published it and sent tabulations to the UN and other international agencies, despite the fact that many Nigerian experts themselves rejected the figure for total population, which was 55.7 million, up from the 42 million counted in the 1962 census and the 36.5 million estimated just before.[67] Nigeria's 1973 census was also disputed, so the 1963 figures remained in use for official national and international purposes until the next census, in 1991.[68]

Other countries had their own political circumstances that affected census-making and the reporting of results. Lebanon did not take a census after 1932 because the ruling Christian majority in government (where representation was allocated on the basis of religion) feared revealing the emergence of a Muslim majority in the population.[69] After its revolution, China disallowed the publication of separate population data for Taiwan, claiming Taiwan as part of the People's Republic. In such situations, delegates to the UN decided that they "had to give priority to the political reality and not in the field of demography."[70] Just as censuses made citizens legible to states, they also made states legible to the UN and other international organizations, and some states resisted aspects of that legibility or used it strategically to assert their sovereignty.

Many of the 186 censuses that occurred as part of the 1950 UN World Census Program were incomplete.[71] By the time preparations began for the 1960 World Census Program, it had become clear that a considerable number of the world's countries would still be unable to enumerate the entirety of their populations. As an alternative, the UN Population Division began to encourage sample surveys.[72] Sampling is a statistical technique, developed in the first half of the twentieth century, whereby a small part of a population of interest—a sample—stands in for the whole.[73] Sampling was introduced into the U.S. Census in 1940 to ask questions about things like fertility and parental birthplace that were not feasible to inquire after for the entire population but could be asked of every twentieth person.[74] Early forms of sampling relied on supposedly representative populations, such as Muncie, Indiana, in Robert and Helen Lynd's famous *Middletown* studies, and Indianapolis in Social and Psychological Factors Affecting Fertility.[75] Because such studies as *Middletown* and Indianapolis aimed to identify the typical, however, they did not facilitate the study of systematic variation or deviation from the norm. To remedy this shortcoming, survey researchers developed methods of nationwide random sampling, reasoning that, when each member of a target population has an equal chance of being selected, the sample has the potential to capture the diversity of the larger population.

Random sampling made frequent nationally representative surveys feasible in countries whose populations were generally known and locatable, such as the United States. Under such conditions, statisticians could quantify the generalizability of results obtained from a sample and thereby optimize the trade-off between cost and quality in advance and return results with a quantitative estimate of their inferential validity. Random sampling, however, requires that samples be drawn from a known sampling frame comprising prior information about all potential sample units, whether those units are individuals, households, cities, or villages. A complete enumeration of sample units is therefore a prerequisite for a statistically valid sample. In countries that had not established this kind of statistical infrastructure, samples were usually determined "by the personnel available to analyze the results, the available transport, and by the money which a particular country is prepared to spend," rather than by calculations of statistical power.[76] Samples drawn using such methods were anything but random, representative, or generalizable, as they typically covered only the segments of the population that were particularly tractable to enumeration, such as those living in urban areas. UN demographers recognized that sample surveys were an inadequate substitute for complete enumeration but suggested that they could fill in temporarily and could "serve as an experimental census paving the way to a complete census to be executed in the near future."[77]

However, if census-making strengthened a country's sovereignty over its population, both practically and symbolically, the failure of census-making in many countries and the consequent need to substitute sample surveys challenged national sovereignty. Censuses are a governmental activity that can be completed only by states and that make populations tractable to governance in the process of constituting them. In contrast, sample surveys can be done by anyone with the requisite resources, and they produce the information desired by those who do the survey rather than information that might facilitate governance. Those who run the surveys control the dissemination of that information. By including the collation and publication of population data for every country of the world within its mandate, the UN opened up countries that could not complete their own censuses—or that could not provide data that were sufficiently convincing—to sample surveys conducted by private organizations or even by the governments of other countries. Over the next several decades, the failure of national censuses in many countries to meet the demands of the UN and other international agencies and nongovernmental organizations would justify the production of what Michelle Murphy has termed "postcolonial thick data" by the "thousands of NGOs that shadow the state" throughout the Global South.[78] Whereas censuses facilitated the planning for and planning of population by the governments that constituted those populations, sample surveys facilitated the planning for and planning of population by U.S.-based scientists and philanthropists, and eventually by the U.S. government and the UN.

MODELING THE WORLD'S POPULATIONS

As it became apparent that a world of national populations could not be instantiated through censuses alone, the UN Population Division turned to modeling as an alternative way to fill the remaining blanks in the *UN Demographic Yearbook*, at least until censuses and vital registration became more robust. For assistance, the Population Division called on OPR, where demographers were beginning to utilize demographic theory and models to develop sophisticated mathematical methods for smoothing the unruly data produced by sample surveys and incomplete censuses. Their primary tools for this project were the stable population model, which had been developed by Jim Lotka in the first half of the century, and demographic transition theory, which OPR demographers first articulated during World War II.

Notestein and his OPR colleagues developed demographic transition theory in response to the wartime challenge of predicting an unknown future on a much larger scale than they had ever done before. Their solution to this problem was a demographic corollary of modernization theory. Although it existed in many forms, modernization theory began to coalesce as a unifying social scientific principle in the United States during the war and served as a blueprint for the postwar world order.[79] It grew out of the stadial view of human progress that had originated two centuries earlier in the Scottish Enlightenment. Stadial theory conceptualized cultural difference as societal evolution, arraying the peoples of the world on a continuum from "advanced" (Western Europe) to "primitive" (those societies most different from Western Europe). Eighteenth-century conjectural historians looked to the present of non-European societies for evidence of the past of European societies. In the twentieth century, American social scientists flattened this continuum into a binary distinction between modern societies, those characterized by industrial economies, secular education, urban agglomerations, and specialization of functions, and traditional societies, those characterized by agricultural economies and kinship-based social institutions. Through this binary modernization paradigm, intellectuals understood the American present as the future of non-Western countries.

Although demographic transition theory was a collective accomplishment of the OPR team,[80] its initial articulation is often credited to Kingsley Davis, a sociologist recruited to OPR in 1942. Davis had completed his Ph.D. at Harvard University in 1936, working mainly with Talcott Parsons and Pitirim Sorokin. His background was therefore a bit different from that of other sociologists who were coming to identify as demographers between the wars, heavier on social theory and lighter on quantitative methods.

Demographic transition is a description of the demographic consequences of modernization in England. Demographic transition *theory* posits that modernization will have the same demographic implications everywhere. According to demographic transition theory, traditional societies have high rates of birth and death, with little overall population growth. Mortality is high because food is scarce, sanitation is rudimentary, antibiotics and vaccines are not available, and life is dangerous. Fertility is high because social institutions have evolved to promote large families. Davis reasoned that societies that did not privilege large families may have existed in the past, but only those in which high fertility balanced high mortality could have survived into the twentieth century. He had few empirical details about the specific institutions that fostered high fertility, but he nonetheless assumed that the family was the basic unit for most social and economic functions in all traditional societies, and that childbearing and childrearing were critical sources of power and prosperity.[81]

On the basis of England's history, Davis theorized that the early stages of the modernization process would reduce death rates as food became more secure, as new sanitation practices lessened the incidence of infectious disease, and as medical innovation made diseases less deadly, disrupting the pretransitional equilibrium between high fertility and high mortality and stimulating rapid population growth. The later stages of modernization would transform the social institutions that had promoted high birth rates, leading to smaller and smaller families, until low fertility balanced low mortality, restoring population equilibrium, but with lower birth and death rates and more people overall.[82]

The synthetic trajectory of demographic transition represented a kind of societal life cycle analogous to the human life cycle. Together these two life cycles facilitated population projection. The human life cycle represented age-specific rates of mortality and fertility (generally higher mortality at the beginning and end of life; higher fertility in the middle). The societal life cycle represented secular decline in mortality and fertility rates as a society underwent the transformation from tradition to modernity. The idea of a societal life cycle remained implicit rather than explicit in the work of OPR demographers, likely because it had been associated with the Italian statistician Corrado Gini between the wars or perhaps because American demographers did not want to suggest that posttransitional populations were nearing any kind of societal death. Rather, these were the societies that were to lead the rest of the world into the demographic future. The implication of a societal life cycle nonetheless naturalized the nation-state as the appropriate container within which population was to be measured, planned, and planned for. It also naturalized modernization and the demographic transition that was assumed to result, divorcing these processes from the material changes that were thought to drive them and casting demographic change purely as a function of time, just as the human life cycle was a function of advancing age.

Demographic transition theory suggested that national populations would grow along S-shaped trajectories similar to Pearl's logistic curve. When Notestein made his first global population projection in 1944, data for most of the world were so scarce that he derived future population numbers almost entirely from the stylized curve of demographic transition.[83] Conceptually, however, demographic transition theory diverged radically from Pearl's logistic law. It relied on the aggregate ontology of population that underpinned vital rate indices and the cohort component projection method rather than the organic ontology that drove the logistic law. Moreover, while Pearl's model was Malthusian—assuming that population growth is entirely driven by food availability or scarcity—demographic transition theory is post-Malthusian. It posits that modernization begins a process by which societies are freed from the so-called Malthusian trap. Modernization simultaneously allows for rapid population growth and severs the connection between population growth and resource availability, such that population growth can slow even as resources remain abundant. Demographic transition theory rested on the belief that modernization would overcome any natural limits on the number of people a territory could support and that the population growth it engendered was self-regulating, producing a new equilibrium as social institutions adjusted to technological advance. The end result was not the "saturation" Pearl had predicted but the stationarity demographers had anticipated between the wars for the countries of North America and Western Europe. Demographic transition theory reinterpreted that stationarity as the pinnacle of modernization rather than Malthusian overpopulation or mercantilist stagnation.

Demographic transition theory, like modernization theory, was grounded in the cultural racism that supplanted biological racism in the United States and Europe after World War II.[84] By 1945, when Davis edited a collection of essays titled *World Population in Transition*, mortality had begun to decline in parts of Asia, stimulating the rapid population growth associated with demographic transition. Davis assured readers who feared this growth that it did not spell the end of Euro-American world hegemony. He explained that "the existing civilization of the Orient is not fixed in the genes of the Asiatic races" but "is rather a historical stage resembling in some respects the medieval civilization of Europe," that would "pass irretrievably as the Asiatic peoples become westernized."[85] Asians were not biologically different from Europeans, he argued; they were just living in an archaic society. Although people of Asian descent might outnumber those of European descent at the global level, Davis predicted that European institutions and practices would still predominate. OPR demographers understood demographic transition to be inseparable from "the nexus of cultural traits that are valued as 'progress.'" They believed these "traits" were in the process of diffusing from Northwest Europe to the rest of the world "along the lines of communication . . . assisted by the presence of natural resources appropriate to industrialization, and . . . checked by natural and cultural barriers" but having "gained a solid foothold even among non-European peoples."[86]

Demographic transition theory explained the patterns that population observers had begun to identify between the wars: slowing population growth in Western Europe, North America, and Oceania, coinciding with accelerating population growth in Southern and Eastern Europe and South and East Asia. It predicted that population growth would abate in Eastern Europe and Asia as advancing modernity remade social institutions in the North American and Western European image. It also predicted that, as modernization spread to other parts of the world, they too would break free from the Malthusian trap and experience a brief period of rapid population growth before the assimilation process brought with it the values that had produced small family norms in Western Europe and North America.[87]

Davis illustrated this prediction by explaining that Japan had gone "farther than any other Oriental people in borrowing Western culture and thus increasing her power; but, as a consequence, her fertility also began to drop, so that, although her population will grow very rapidly for a while, she too will eventually approach a stationary population."[88] Demographers gave no indication that this expected growth would strain global resources or present any other problems. They viewed it simply as part of what they considered the natural and beneficial modernization process. Any population growth stimulated by modernization was temporary by definition. It would be halted not by rising mortality (the Malthusian trap) but by falling fertility (the demographic hallmark of modernity). In contrast to interwar observers, who feared that supposedly inferior nonwhite populations would replace supposedly superior white populations,[89] the racism of OPR demographers during World War II was a cultural racism that predicted and celebrated Westernization. According to this racial logic, nonwhite people might exceed white people numerically, but European culture would remain hegemonic.

Demographic transition theory was operationalized by Ansley Coale, a wartime graduate student at OPR whose mathematical capabilities exceeded those of his mentors. It was Coale who figured out how to apply demographic transition theory to practical demographic problems: projecting future population where current population was known and estimating current population where it was unknown. Coale had been an undergraduate economics major at Princeton during the Depression, waiting tables in the dining hall to pay living expenses that were not covered by his scholarship.[90] After graduating in 1939, he stayed to complete a Ph.D. in economics under Notestein's direction at OPR as the second Milbank Fellow.

During the war Coale worked with Notestein's team on the European population projections commissioned by the League of Nations, formalizing demographic transition theory as a practical guide to forecasting future changes in fertility and mortality rates. To do so, he reconceptualized cross-sectional variation (geographic difference) in fertility and mortality rates as a universal longitudinal trajectory (change over time).[91] Demographic transition theory cast the world as "anachronistic space" and the demographic variation within it as "panoptical time," terms coined by the postcolonial literary scholar Anne McClintock to describe a vantage point from which the whole of human history—in this case the history of human population—can be read in a single glance, either on a map or from a statistical table.[92] Coale assumed that countries with higher rates of mortality and fertility were at an earlier stage of demographic transition, and those with lower rates of mortality and fertility were at a later stage, arranging contemporary vital rates into synthetic trajectories of a supposedly universal demographic process. Those at the higher end of the continuum represented the past of those at the lower end, and those at the lower end represented the future of those at the higher end.

Once Coale had constructed these synthetic trajectories, Notestein and his colleagues could predict future mortality and fertility for any country by locating its current vital rates on the synthetic trajectory and reading from left to right,[93] a nearly literal example of what demographer Arland Thornton has termed "reading history sideways": the practice of interpreting cross-sectional variation as chronological progress through a universal human history.[94] Vital rates came to stand in for levels of progress, so demographers could predict future population change without requiring a prediction of any of the other supposed signals of modernization. This approach naturalized demographic transition and modernization itself as universal processes that were already in motion everywhere, however latent they may have been in some places, and that could be expected to unfold apace. OPR demographers of this period never attempted to correlate mortality or fertility with any other markers of modernization. Their population projections took as inputs only population and time, making superfluous the social and economic transformations that were thought to bring about demographic transition.[95]

Demographic transition theory served an important wartime purpose for OPR demographers, providing them with a systematic method of predicting future mortality and fertility rates for the countries of Europe, where current rates were well documented. Data from censuses and vital registration provided baselines from which demographers could project population change on the basis of demographic transition theory. But while baseline data were readily available for the United States and much of Europe, the failure of the UN's efforts to promote censuses and vital registration worldwide meant that, even two decades after the end of World War II, demographers did not have appropriate baselines for projecting population in many countries of the world. Coale would eventually develop solutions to that problem as well.

In the midst of projecting Europe's demographic future, Coale paused his graduate education to join the war effort. He had received a low draft number, but morally objected to serving in combat or using his mathematical training for ballistic purposes. Notestein turned to Osborn for advice about what his student should do, assuring Osborn that Coale was "quite willing, even glad to serve in the medical corps of the army" or in any other capacity "directed to saving rather than taking life."[96] Likely following advice from Osborn and Notestein, Coale didn't wait to be drafted. Instead he volunteered for a scientific position in the navy and ended up in the Radiation Laboratory at MIT, where his research focused on reducing vulnerability to atomic warfare. In 1947 Princeton accepted Coale's wartime research on atomic vulnerability as his dissertation and hired him as an assistant professor of economics.[97]

Over the next decade, Coale focused on the relationship between population growth and economic development, producing evidence—which will be discussed at greater length in the next chapter—suggesting that rapid population growth inhibited economic growth.[98] But just as Coale's research was generating anxiety about population growth rates in developing countries, the UN's efforts to promote census-making and vital registration were failing to produce the data demographers needed even to generate a picture of the current population of many developing countries, much less to project future growth. To create this baseline, or at least a working facsimile of a baseline, Coale began to develop mathematical methods for synthesizing data to fill the gaps in the UN's statistical tables, culminating in the 1967 publication of the UN's *Manual IV: Methods of Estimating Basic Demographic Measures from Incomplete Data*.[99] *Manual IV* provided demographers with tools to estimate current vital rates, calculate net reproduction rates and total fertility rates (a summary of age-specific fertility rates indicating the total number of children the average woman is expected to bear over her lifetime),[100] and project future population growth from the sparse data available in sample surveys or partial censuses.

The methods described in *Manual IV* emerged from two large-scale projects Coale carried out simultaneously during the 1960s. The first, known as the Princeton European Fertility Project, was a seminal study in the then-emerging subfield of historical demography.[101] Inverting conjectural history, which had looked to non-Western societies to fill in for the unknown European past, historical demography looked to the European historical record to better understand contemporary population dynamics in countries that lacked data but were thought to be pretransitional, an epistemological move made possible by demographic transition theory. Historical data for some parts of Europe were more complete than were contemporary data for many countries in Africa, Asia, and Latin America, and they covered a much longer time span.[102] On the basis of historical data, mostly from Europe, Coale created model life tables and model stable populations that could be used to estimate vital rates in countries that lacked adequate data of their own.[103]

Model life tables are premised on the observation that life tables made from detailed empirical data show strong regularities in the age patterns of mortality. That is, the curve of age-specific mortality in a high-mortality population has the same shape as the curve of age-specific mortality in a low-mortality population, as shown in Figure 3.1. With the historical data he was able to find, Coale developed model life tables representing all levels of mortality from expectation of life at birth of twenty years to seventy-five years, in five-year increments.[104] If a sample survey determined mortality rates among a subset of a given population, a demographer could identify the appropriate model life table and thereby estimate the overall mortality level of the population in question.

Closely related to model life tables are model stable populations. The concept of a stable population was developed by Lotka between 1907 and 1925 to describe "a material system in which the physical conditions vary with time" such that "certain individual constituent elements may have a transitory existence *as such*, each lasting just so long as its conditions and those of its neighborhood continue within certain limits."[105] Lotka's language was deliberately vague, as he intended his stable population model to describe any set of living or nonliving things where the individual things—whether people or industrial components—are subject to wear and eventual retirement (or death). A stable population is one that is subject to constant rates of addition (fertility) and subtraction (mortality) and is closed to migration (or, in the industrial example, does not permit the addition of used components or the removal of components that are still functional). When

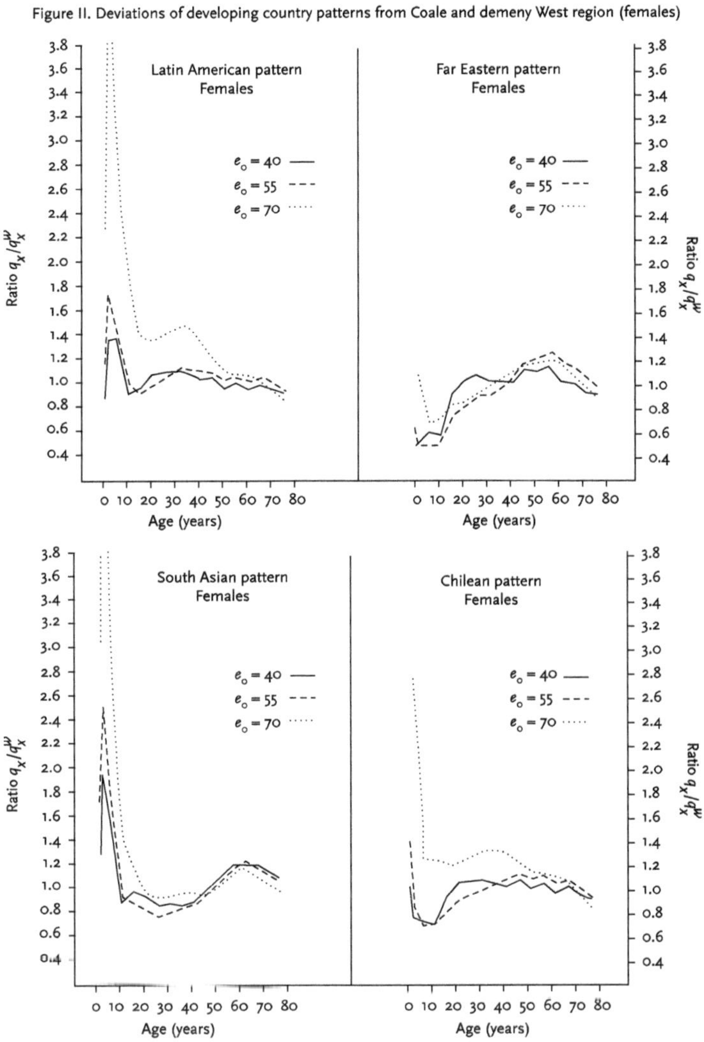

Figure 3.1 Model age-specific mortality curves for females in Latin America, East Asia, South Asia, and Chile, expectation of life at birth forty years (high mortality), fifty-five years (medium mortality), and seventy years (low mortality).

Source. Model Life Tables for Developing Countries, by UN Department of International Economic and Social Affairs, © United Nations 1982. Reprinted with the permission of the United Nations.

rates of fertility and mortality remain constant over long periods of time, in the absence of migration, populations grow at a constant rate (which may be positive, negative, or zero), and the proportions in each age group remain constant (stable). The stable population model therefore links the mortality, fertility, and age structure of a population, such that any two of these pieces of information are sufficient to calculate the third.[106] For any given population that can be presumed stable, once a model life table has been selected, the analyst needs only a sense of the fertility rate or rate of natural increase to select the appropriate model stable population, which provides age-specific fertility rates. Coale's collaborator and former student Paul Demeny later described this work as figuring out "how to make silk out of [a] sow's ears, namely, how to do demographic estimates from limited bad data."[107] With model life tables and model stable populations, the determination of vital rates no longer depended on governmental surveillance practices. Instead it could be done by foreign demographers using very limited samples.

The Princeton European Fertility Project provided Coale with the raw materials for model life tables and model stable populations. Simultaneously with that project, Coale led a large-scale study in sub-Saharan Africa that investigated the application of model life tables, model stable populations, and other methods to derive detailed age-sex distributions and vital rates from the sparse data produced by sample surveys and partial censuses. Published in 1968 as *The Demography of Tropical Africa*, the project was instigated by Frank Lorimer, who had already done substantial research in Africa and established institutional connections there.[108] Preliminary analysis had "indicate[d] the exciting possibility that African fertility is higher than that observed in any other large population in the past," suggesting that Africa's demographic trajectory might differ from that of Europe, which had previously been presumed universal.[109] The 1960(ish) round of censuses appeared to show high rates of population growth in African countries over the previous decade, but census coverage and enumeration methods had also improved. It was therefore likely that larger proportions of the populations of African countries were being counted in 1960 than in 1950.[110] Determining actual growth over the decade would thus require some knowledge of vital rates. Coale explained to the project's funders that, in the near absence of vital registration in Africa, demographers needed alternative methods "for obtaining reliable information on fertility, mortality and migration in situations where one cannot reasonably expect a rapid development of effective vital registration systems of a classic type in the near future."[111] The project was not simply about Africa; the countries it examined were to stand in for uncounted and unregistered populations in general.

William Brass, a medical demographer at the London School of Hygiene and Tropical Medicine who had previously worked in the British Colonial Service's East African Statistical Office, took the lead on developing methods of "abstracting valid information from bad data."[112] The methods he devised, now known as indirect estimation methods or simply

Brass methods, relied on a small set of questions that could be asked of a sample of women to identify the appropriate model life tables and stable populations for the countries they were thought to represent.[113] By 1988 Brass had become so well-known for having developed a method to estimate just about any measure for which data were lacking that, when rain broke out at an OPR picnic, one student joked that they "should use the Brass method for keeping off the rain drops."[114] Even then, two decades after the publication of *The Demography of Tropical Africa*, many developing countries still lacked reliable censuses and vital registration systems.

Model life tables and model stable populations described what demographers considered to be every possible demographic regime from the high mortality and high fertility of pretransitional traditional societies to the low mortality and low fertility of posttransitional modern societies. With just a few data points—a small number of questions asked of a small sample of people—indirect estimation methods allowed demographers to place any country along the model trajectory, using demographic transition theory to fill in its current age-sex structure and vital rates. Demographic transition theory suggested that model life tables and model stable populations are sequential, so an analyst could move through the synthetic series—from high to low mortality and fertility—to imagine a population's past and predict its future. Demographers thereby estimated the demographic present and projected the demographic future in a single step.

Demographers could use model stable populations to estimate unknown population figures because demographic transition theory cast the populations of developing countries as pretransitional and therefore stable (closed to migration and having constant age-specific rates of fertility and mortality) or quasi-stable (fertility still constant, but mortality beginning to decline). By characterizing these societies as being in a natural or primordial state of high fertility and high (or recently-high) mortality, demographic transition theory and the stable population model wiped away hundreds of years of history—including histories of colonization, which often involved tremendous demographic upheaval—and positioned the countries of the Global South as ready to embark, unencumbered by the past, on the universal path to demographic, economic, social, and political modernity paved by the countries of the Global North.

The numbers produced by sample surveys and model stable populations were intended as a stopgap, filling statistical tables until all of the world's populations had become countable. They were thus what Martha Lampland terms "provisional numbers": numbers that stand in for unknown values to facilitate "formalizing practices,"[115] such as the publication of the *UN Demographic Yearbook*. Lampland argues that provisional numbers are often used when an actual value is unknown but some number is needed to get on with the task at hand. In the case of population data in the early postwar period, the task at hand was the administrative organization of an international community comprising sovereign states governing national populations and managing national economies. These "provisional numbers" facilitated the calculation of per capita GNP and allowed national governments, international agencies, and nongovernmental organizations to get on with efforts to plan for population or to promote economic development through population control.

With demographic transition theory, the stable population model, and indirect estimation methods, UN demographers could finally represent the world as a community of national populations. Yet they had also fundamentally changed the nature of population. The demographers of the UN Population Commission had initially conceived of populations as objects of governance, constituted through the governmental practices of census-making and vital registration, which would in turn produce national sovereignty over populations. In reality, however, the postwar world of populations came into view not through the establishment of liberal democratic governments worldwide but through the development and application of demographic theory and methods. Populations were thus constituted as natural objects of science rather than political objects of governance. Accounting for population with demographic models rather than national censuses challenged the sovereignty of governments over their populations and legitimated international intervention into their management.

CHAPTER 4
Population Consensus

Almost as soon as the demographers of Princeton's OPR articulated demographic transition theory, new data coming in to the UN Population Division began to suggest that actual populations in both modern (posttransitional) and traditional (pretransitional) societies were growing in ways that the theory had not predicted. In the countries of North America, Western Europe, and Oceania, which had appeared to be on the brink of stationarity between the wars due to rapidly falling fertility, birth rates were rising. In the countries of Asia and Latin America, death rates were falling, but in the absence of the social, political, and economic changes that demographers had expected would trigger demographic transition.

Demographers were embarrassed by their failure to predict what came to be known as the "baby boom." What really worried them, however, was population growth in Asia and Latin America, where death rates had dropped precipitously, with no indication that birth rates would soon follow. Unless those societies modernized quickly, demographers warned, their expanding populations would be increasingly vulnerable to economic shocks and environmental depredations. Drawing on demographic transition theory and interwar contraceptive research, demographers initially recommended economic assistance to rapidly growing countries as a means of stimulating modernization. They expected that demographic transition would accompany modernization, eventually halting population growth. Over the next two decades, however, a very different consensus emerged among demographers, philanthropists, businessmen, diplomats, and policymakers in both the United States and developing countries. The

Building the Population Bomb. Emily Klancher Merchant, Oxford University Press (2021). © Oxford University Press.
DOI: 10.1093/oso/9780197558942.003.0005

consensus posed rapid population growth as the primary barrier to economic development in what was coming to be known as the Third World, and presented family planning as the most effective way to slow population growth and thereby stimulate modernization.

POPULATION GROWTH

The U.S. birth rate spiked during World War II, catching American demographers by surprise. It had fallen steadily over the first three decades of the twentieth century, and demographers had expected that this trend would continue. Each population projection made by Pat Whelpton and Warren Thompson between 1928 and 1938 was lower than the previous one (see Figure 2.2). In 1940 the net reproduction rate (NRR) was below replacement (1.0), meaning that each new generation was smaller than its parents'. But the crude birth rate (births per thousand population) increased by 20% over the next two years, and by 1942 the NRR was well above replacement.[1] Thompson and Whelpton updated their projections roughly every two years in the 1940s to keep up with increases in the birth rate, but—as demographer Ronald Freedman would later say of those projections—"by the time they got to the Government Printing Office, they were wrong."[2]

American demographers were professionally humiliated by the fact that they hadn't seen this "baby boom" coming, but it neither undermined their authority over population projection nor posed an insurmountable challenge to demographic transition theory. Led by Whelpton, demographers responded by developing a new approach to measuring fertility. Previously they had used only what are now called *period* rates, which cover a specific moment in time.[3] In the calculation of crude birth rates and age-specific fertility rates, period measures are straightforward, referring to births in a particular year or set of years. But the calculation of summary indices, such as NRR or TFR (total fertility rate, the average number of children a woman will bear across her lifetime), from period measures involves constructing synthetic cohorts. A synthetic cohort represents the current population as if it were one set of people moving through the life course (that is, it treats the people who are currently forty-five years old as older versions of the people who are currently fifteen). A period TFR for 1945 is calculated by summing the age-specific fertility rates for 1945 over all ages, assuming that the average woman would bear children at the 1945 rates over the whole span of her reproductive life.

Demographers recognized, however, that the age-specific fertility rates of the mid-1940s were anomalous. The wartime and postwar economic boom allowed older couples who had put off childbearing during the Great Depression to finally complete their families, and it allowed couples who had come of age during World War II to start their families at younger ages than they would have been able to do earlier in the century.[4] The convergence of late childbearing among the Depression generation and early childbearing among the World War II generation produced a period TFR that was impossibly high, suggesting a rate of childbearing of more than one baby per year.[5] In response, demographers began to calculate TFR and NRR on a *cohort* basis, using age-specific fertility rates for actual cohorts of women born in the same year but having babies in different years rather than synthetic cohorts of women born in different years but having babies in the same year.[6]

Cohort fertility rates indicated that, although Americans were—on average—having more children each year than they had done in the recent past, the average number of children born to a given couple was not increasing. American families were not getting larger; what was changing was the age at which parents had their children. High period fertility rates in the 1940s suggested that children born during the baby boom would experience crowding in classrooms and job markets,[7] but they did not indicate that the population of the United States was poised for dramatic growth over the long term. Given interwar anxiety about depopulation, demographers generally welcomed the baby boom as compensation for the birth deficit of the 1930s. They expected that population growth would stimulate economic growth: higher fertility would mean more consumption and more effective demand, reducing the amount of government deficit spending that economists and policymakers had by then accepted as necessary to promote economic growth in a stationary population.[8]

The baby boom was not limited to the United States. Other English-speaking countries and, to a lesser extent, most of Western Europe also experienced a rise in fertility between the early 1940s and the early 1950s. It was not, however, the primary cause of global population growth after World War II. Even before the war ended, some parts of the world where fertility and mortality had remained high well into the twentieth century, primarily in Asia and Latin America, began to see dramatic declines in death rates, producing rapid population growth as high birth rates remained unchanged. Demographic transition theory predicts that, in the early stages of modernization, death rates will go down before birth rates do, resulting in population growth. What demographers were seeing in Asia and Latin

America troubled them, however, because it departed from the European demographic transition template.

Figure 4.1 compares the "classic" demographic transition, as experienced in Western Europe and North America, on the left, with postwar demographic trends in Asia and Latin America, on the right. It shows that birth rates were higher in Asia and Latin America than they had been in North America and Western Europe prior to their demographic transitions, due to earlier marriage for women and higher proportions of women marrying overall.[9] As a result of inexpensive public health interventions, death rates in these parts of the world were falling much more rapidly than they had done in North America and Western Europe during demographic transitions in those regions, producing higher rates of overall growth than the countries of North America and Western Europe had experienced. What concerned demographers the most was that the countries where death rates were falling were not experiencing the kind of modernization they had predicted would trigger demographic transition. In the absence of industrialization, urbanization, and secular education, there could be no expectation that birth rates would eventually come into balance with reduced death rates, raising the specter of the infinite growth of poor—and likely disaffected—populations.

In the course of their wartime work for the U.S. Department of State, Princeton University demographers Frank Notestein and Kingsley Davis had discovered that modernization was a global process that affected

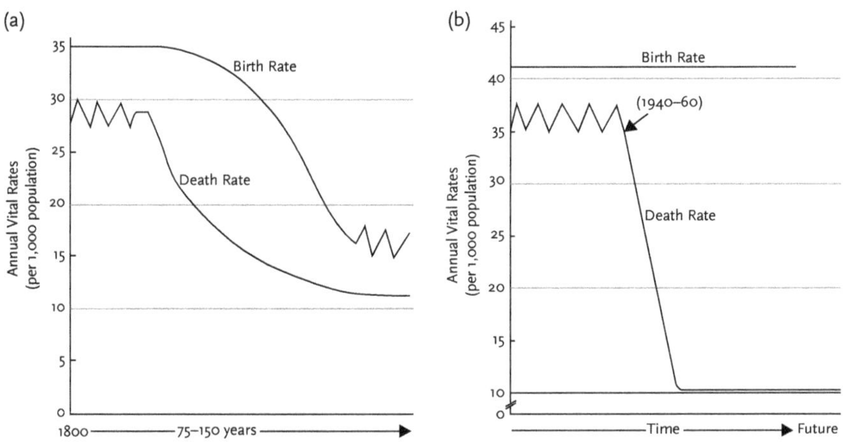

Figure 4.1 Demographic transition in Western Europe and North America (left) and postwar demographic trends in Asia and Latin America (right).

Source: National Academy of Sciences, The Growth of World Population: Analysis of the Problems and Recommendations for Research and Training (Washington, D.C.: National Academies Press, 1963), 10, 15.

demographic regimes in the countries of primary production as well as in industrial countries. Many agricultural regions of Africa and South and Southeast Asia still belonged to European empires, with land and production largely controlled by a small number of expatriates and local elites. The "dollar diplomacy" of the U.S. government leveraged the sovereign debt of independent countries in East Asia and Latin America to promote political regimes and economic policies favorable to American corporations rather than the people of those countries.[10] Notestein and Davis recognized that these colonial and quasi-colonial territories had "been developed by technologically advanced countries primarily as sources of agricultural and mineral raw materials, often of a specialized kind, and as markets for manufactured goods."[11] Multinational corporations extracted labor value and raw materials from the countries of primary production, then sold manufactured goods to people in those countries at a large profit. For that reason, economic development of the interwar variety (extraction and marketing of raw materials) did not necessarily produce economic development in the postwar sense (modernization and improved living conditions).

Notestein and Davis found that death rates had recently fallen in many countries of primary production because the extraction of natural resources "required the introduction of strong government, improved transportation, simple sanitation, and a modicum of epidemic control."[12] Yet the denizens of those countries were not becoming an urban bourgeoisie that valued small families. Rather, they had become what Davis described as "a rural proletariat, working often for bare subsistence and thus reaping few of the potential advantages of participation in the world economy."[13] Notestein and Davis argued that, among this "rural proletariat," colonial and quasi-colonial regimes had preserved "native customs, religions, and social organization" that had developed under conditions of high mortality and therefore "foster[ed] the maintenance of high fertility."[14] The result was an expanding population ever more reliant on a small number of commodities and therefore increasingly vulnerable to the vicissitudes of the natural environment and global economy.

Notestein and Davis contended that the bifurcation of the global economy between industrial countries and those of primary production was unsustainable, as it produced a dual demographic regime in which the populations of industrial countries grew smaller as their share of global wealth grew larger, while those of agricultural countries grew larger and poorer, threatening to destabilize the geopolitical order. Notestein and Davis did not see this pattern as a challenge to demographic transition theory. Rather, they saw demographic transition theory as a scientific critique of imperialism and global capitalism, which stalled the supposedly natural process of demographic transition at the point of maximum population growth by extending only partial modernization to colonial and quasi-colonial territories.

Many high-fertility countries were sparsely populated and could support substantial growth in human numbers. Others were already densely settled. Notestein warned that, in these places, the incomplete demographic transition produced by formal imperialism and informal economic domination (or the structural inequality of the global capitalist economy) had the potential to produce Malthusian crises. Large populations living on the margins of subsistence, dependent on a single commodity in the global market, were nearly assured of frequent catastrophes stemming from natural disasters or even small economic shocks. As populations continued to grow, he predicted, catastrophes would become more frequent and more devastating.[15] Notestein and Davis contended that the only way out of the dilemma was to help rapidly growing countries complete their demographic transitions by promoting political and economic independence and full modernization.

Population growth was not the primary problem facing these countries, and Notestein and Davis did not recommend direct efforts to slow it. Population growth was simply a symptom of stalled modernization, they argued, so jump-starting modernization would facilitate the completion of the demographic transition. They conceded that making available existing forms of birth control—condoms, diaphragms, and spermicides—could help, but they cautioned that these technologies were neither sufficient nor even necessary to reduce birth rates in the aggregate. Interwar research suggested that "populations whose social institutions and personal aspirations are those developed in high mortality [traditional] cultures are little interested in contraception," whereas "populations whose institutions and personal aspirations are those of modern individualistic cultures will control their fertility in substantial degree with or without the assistance of modern contraceptive techniques."[16] They also worried that supplying birth control where there was little demand for it could be a political faux pas. Davis warned that efforts to promote contraception in colonial territories and postcolonial states "may be construed as an attempt to limit the power and freedom of the nation." Even worse, "since 'overpopulation' is a relative matter, it can be taken as merely an excuse for not effecting other improvements of a nondemographic kind."[17] Notestein and Davis acknowledged that the remedies they recommended would stimulate further mortality decline before producing spontaneous fertility decline, and that total population would grow even more rapidly in the interim. They did not see this growth as a problem, however, as it would occur within the supposedly natural process of demographic transition, as a result of the modernization that they expected would release countries from the Malthusian trap and generate higher standards of living, even for larger populations.

In the second half of the 1940s, Notestein and Davis each changed their views on population growth in the Global South, moving in different directions. Notestein began to suggest that high fertility was not a *symptom* of stalled modernization in the Global South but its *cause*, and that yet-to-be-developed contraceptive technologies could, if disseminated through appropriate family planning programs, reduce aggregate birth rates and thereby stimulate modernization.[18] Davis began to see high fertility as a threat to the global environment, contending that preservation of the Earth's ecosystems required an immediate cessation of population growth, which could not be accomplished without more direct intervention.[19] Histories of population thought and policy in the twentieth century have overlooked the differences between Notestein and Davis after 1945.[20] This may be because, over the next two decades, each position generated popular support and material resources for the other, synergistically producing a global consensus that the world's population was growing too quickly and that family planning programs could solve this new "population problem." Notestein and Davis aligned themselves with separate nongovernmental organizations—Davis with the Population Reference Bureau and Notestein with the Population Council—but these organizations worked together to shape public opinion and government policy regarding population, both in the United States and in what was coming to be known as the Third World.

THE POPULATION REFERENCE BUREAU

Davis's version of the postwar population problem originated with the Population Reference Bureau, which exercised strong influence over American public opinion regarding population through much of the twentieth century. The Bureau was founded in 1929 by Guy Irving Burch, who after World War I had "decided to make it [his] chief, if not only interest to discover the causes and cures (if possible) of such unreasonable things as wars, hunger, etc."[21] Influenced by the popular anti-immigrant and racist publications of the time, such as *The Passing of the Great Race* by Madison Grant (1916), *The Rising Tide of Color against White World-Supremacy* by Lothrop Stoddard (1920), *Mankind at the Crossroads* by Edward East (1923), and *Standing Room Only?* by Edward A. Ross (1927), Burch identified increasing population quantity and decreasing population quality as the fundamental causes of all of the world's misery and strife.[22]

Though never a public figure himself, Burch was extraordinarily gifted in the shaping of public opinion. He recognized the growing authority of science in both the public sphere and the policy arena, but he also recognized that most people, citizens and legislators alike, had little direct contact with scientists or their work. Rather, their understanding of science was shaped by the media. Burch established the Population Reference Bureau to promote press coverage of the emerging science of population and to influence how the media reported on population issues. As the only organization that regularly produced and circulated summaries of demographic research in a form that journalists could easily understand and pass along to their audiences, the Bureau strongly influenced public and policy understandings of population science. It issued frequent press releases to publicize demographic research and to promote interpretations that supported eugenic policies. In 1940 it also began to produce a periodic *Population Bulletin* that Burch circulated to the media, educational institutions, businessmen, philanthropists, and politicians.

Burch publicly claimed that the materials he produced simply communicated scientific findings rather than advocating any political position, securing tax-exempt status for the Bureau as a scientific and educational organization.[23] Yet he admitted privately that "we do not confine our activities to research or the gathering of the research of others, but attempt to coordinate and synthesize the results into a workable philosophy of life, and then explain such a program in simple terms that the man in the street can understand."[24] This "philosophy of life" was rooted in the racial eugenics that had begun to fall out of popular favor in the 1930s and that Fred Osborn was attempting to replace with his supposedly democratic eugenic program. With his *Population Bulletin* and other publications, Burch aimed to "stimulate interest in the [population] problem among the practical politicians and public" and thereby "make it easier for academic and government organizations to carry on" with research and policy in support of eugenics.

Despite Burch's claims to expertise in population, the materials he produced for the media and other audiences were out of step with then-current research in demography. Burch continued to promote outdated theories, such as Pearl's logistic law and Francis Amasa Walker's displacement principle, long after demographers had rejected them. As a result, these concepts lived on as common knowledge among the U.S. public and policymakers. As late as 1949 Burch opposed the immigration of Europeans dislocated by World War II to the United States because "it can be shown through qualified studies that the population of the United States has already passed its economic optimum, and that additional immigration (with the exception of a few hundred experts) will compete with people already here and tend to displace them, or lower the level of living."[25] Warren Thompson had made a similar argument in the early 1920s, but his generation of demographers abandoned their anti-immigrant sentiment and intra-European racism in the 1930s.

Burch coined the term "population explosion" in the 1930s to describe the out-of-control population growth he anticipated in the near future,[26] at the exact moment that the most prominent demographers in the United States and Western Europe—including Robert Kuczynski, Jim Lotka, Louis Dublin, Warren Thompson, and Pat Whelpton—predicted impending stationarity. Burch dismissed the vital rate indices these demographers developed—the true rate of natural increase and the NRR—which indicated an imminent cessation of natural increase and which, nearly a hundred years after their interwar introduction, remain staple measures in demography, as a conspiracy to undermine immigration restriction by "small-fry academics led by foreign born scientists such as Robert R. Kuczynski and Louis I. Dublin."[27] The population of the United States was indeed still growing in the aggregate between the wars, even as fertility rates fell. Demographers who understood the stable population model saw falling fertility as evidence of looming stationarity, but these metrics were beyond the ken of the general public and even other scientists. To them, aggregate growth appeared as convincing evidence that overpopulation was just around the corner.

Burch ran the Population Reference Bureau nearly singlehandedly during its first two decades, but he recognized that the organization's credibility depended on the reputation of the scientists associated with it. Most interwar demographers of the younger generation kept their distance, regarding Burch as well-meaning but not very savvy. Pearl described him as "an intelligent person but also a somewhat naïve and inexperienced one, in the field of his interest—population."[28] Pearl nonetheless joined the Bureau's scientific council, as did other natural scientists and members of the older generation of social scientists, those who continued to embrace a eugenic outlook informed by intra-European racism even after it had been abandoned by their younger and more quantitatively oriented colleagues. In addition to Pearl, members included Edward East, Henry Pratt Fairchild, Frank Hankins, Clarence Cook Little, and Edward A. Ross.[29] In the 1940s Burch took on as an assistant the mostly home-schooled geneticist Robert C. Cook, who was also the editor of the eugenicist *Journal of Heredity*, a post for which he had been appointed on the recommendation of family friend Alexander Graham Bell.[30] Cook shared Burch's passion for eugenics and his understanding of the importance of science journalism in legitimating eugenic policy.[31]

As World War II came to an end, Burch saw a new opportunity to promote immigration restriction and eugenic sterilization. Historians of eugenics have demonstrated that, contrary to popular belief, eugenics did not simply disappear after World War II and the horrors of the Holocaust. Instead eugenics organizations adopted a new approach, de-emphasizing sterilization and refocusing on medical genetics and marital counseling.[32] But even overt advocacy for eugenic sterilization continued in some quarters, notably the Population Reference Bureau.

In 1945 Burch and sociologist Elmer Pendell self-published the book *Population Roads to Peace or War*, which was republished by Penguin two years later under the title *Human Breeding and Survival*. Both versions recommended the same eugenic programs Burch had supported between the wars. In the wake of the Holocaust, however, Burch and Pendell presented these familiar initiatives as means of promoting global peace and democracy in the face of impending overpopulation. Though today an obscure work, the influence of *Human Breeding and Survival* on postwar public opinion regarding population cannot be overstated. It laid out the conceptual foundation for the extreme approach to population control aired on *Bill Nye Saves the World* and inspired those who would go on to advocate explicit restrictions on childbearing.

In *Human Breeding and Survival*, Burch and Pendell described population growth as the greatest threat to global peace and the spread of democracy in the second half of the twentieth century. Referencing the "Four Freedoms" from Franklin D. Roosevelt's 1941 State of the Union address, the book included chapters titled "Freedom from Want Requires Population Limitation," "Freedom from War Requires Population Limitation," and "Democracy Requires Population Limitation." Burch and Pendell described the global calamities of the first half of the twentieth century—war, depression, fascism, and more war—as inevitable outcomes of the basic Malthusian dilemma: population growth creates increasing competition for the Earth's scarce resources. This explanation reduced world history to natural history. It attributed the extreme disparities of wealth and power within and between countries to increasing human competition for resources and reduced the complicated geopolitics of great power conflict to the simple biopolitics of population size.[33] If the world's calamities were caused by the biological fact of human numbers, Burch and Pendell reasoned, then immigration restriction, sterilization, and the promotion of birth control were the obvious political, scientific, and technological solutions.

Human Breeding and Survival argued that the Earth, and every part of it, was already overpopulated. The number of humans on the planet had been estimated at nearly 2.5 billion in 1940, so Burch and Pendell assumed that this was the number "the technologists" of the time had in mind when they "[told] us that we possess the technical ability to produce enough for everyone."[34] Although this was probably not the intent of "the technologists," Burch and Pendell took their assurances to mean that 2.5 billion was the Earth's absolute limit, and that the planet could support no more people than that. As evidence that the Earth had already exceeded its capacity, Burch and Pendell cited the fact that "two-thirds of the earth's inhabitants are now living in a chronic state of serious want,"[35] neglecting the fact that many people had been in a similar state of want in 1940, when, according to their premise, resources had definitely existed to provide for everyone. Describing overpopulation as a "disease," Burch and Pendell claimed that the United States had but "a mild case," evident in the soil erosion that had erupted in the dust storms of the 1930s, while Europe was "a very sick continent," and Asia was "in the very last stages."[36]

Burch and Pendell argued that a lasting peace would require the spread of democracy, which they described as "a flower that cannot survive where the weeds of overpopulation crowd."[37] In their account, fascism had come to Germany, Italy, and Japan when the populations of those countries grew to the "must expand or explode" stage, at which point only "regimentation" could preserve order.[38] They did not explain why the fascist governments of those countries had pursued pronatalist policies.

Germany, Italy, and Japan were but the most extreme examples of "regimentation." Burch and Pendell characterized any regulation of economic activity as both a threat to democracy and a necessary response to overpopulation. Even the New Deal, according to Burch and Pendell, was a sign of creeping totalitarianism, an antidemocratic response to resource limitation caused by the lack of political will to reduce population growth in the United States.[39] Perhaps they expected their readers would not recall that experts in the 1930s had been worried about depopulation and agricultural overproduction, not overpopulation and scarcity, and that many had attributed the Great Depression itself to falling birth rates. Burch and Pendell's critique of the New Deal provides a glimpse into the motives behind their book. They hoped to preserve the economic autonomy of the wealthy in the United States by limiting the size of populations that might advocate for regulation, redistribution, or welfare. Their targets were the poor and nonwhite in the United States and people in other countries who might want to migrate to the United States or who might agitate for a greater share of the world's territory or resources.

Human Breeding and Survival evoked such interwar Malthusian texts as *Mankind at the Crossroads* in that it proposed qualitative solutions to supposedly quantitative problems. Burch and Pendell described population *quantity* as a threat to peace and democracy, contending that "blind population forces are the most persistent influences barring the way to the world-wide attainment of freedom from want and from war, and the attainment of government by the people."[40] The solutions they proposed, however, targeted population *quality*. They recommended restrictions on international migration, income-based limitations on marriage, compulsory sterilization according to social and economic criteria, and birth control primarily for those at the lower end of the socioeconomic spectrum.

Burch and Pendell went to great lengths to redeem involuntary sterilization. They described Nazi sterilization policy as a beneficial measure that had failed to prevent war because the hundreds of thousands of sterilizations it had accomplished were simply not enough.[41] They acknowledged that "there is evidence that the Nazis also used sterilization as a political tool" but argued that this fact should not discredit sterilization itself. They reassured readers that "it is well to remember that in the hands of a dictatorial and unscrupulous government any social control device may be *abused*."[42] In a further attempt to normalize coercive sterilization, they argued that "wages or taxes may be used for political purposes, and in Germany they have been so used; but that fact can hardly serve to discredit wages or taxes."[43] Referencing Walker's displacement principle, Burch and Pendell contended that sterilization of the supposedly unfit would "make room for children of other people—those desirable people who are earliest to trim their birth rates as our quasi-quota is approached," thereby raising overall population quality.[44]

Burch and Pendell proposed that population control measures be enforced by the United Nations, reasoning that it was "in a position to insist that the conquered countries pass such laws, and that the laws be administered under Allied supervision for a given period as a prerequisite to autonomy."[45] Anticipating concerns from readers that the restrictions they proposed on immigration, marriage, and childbearing themselves curtailed democracy and individual freedom, Burch and Pendell contended that these regulations were of a different order. As they put it, "population control is not part and parcel of the march toward dictatorship; but is instead a counteracting move, a move whereby a few rules that only rarely touch directly any citizen's life would make obsolete a vast network of irritating regulations that now harass us every day."[46] Burch and Pendell reasoned that, if population was, in fact, the ultimate cause of war and totalitarianism, nearly any degree of restriction on its movement and growth could be justified as a lesser intrusion. Their disregard for the humanity of those they sought to sterilize and their valuation of the economic freedom of the world's wealthy above the bodily autonomy and integrity of the world's poor was evident in their description of population control as "a few rules that only rarely touch directly any citizen's life."

Human Breeding and Survival tried hard to pass for a scientific text. It was replete with numbers, calculations, and references to respected authorities, from Plato to Notestein. Always eager to exaggerate his expertise, Burch described himself on the back cover of the Penguin edition as "a charter and organizing member of the Population Association of America" and "a director of the American Eugenics Society."[47] Scientists, however, were not impressed with the book. The *American Sociological Review* predicted that sociologists would "classify it as propaganda rather than an objective scientific statement."[48] Natural scientists were no more enthusiastic. The *Quarterly Review of Biology* described the book as "loose and uncritical in analysis of opinion," continuing that "of unfounded opinion and bias there seems to be a considerable amount."[49] By the end of 1948, however, *Human Breeding and Survival* had sold approximately forty-three thousand copies, which Burch—with his penchant for exaggeration—claimed was "about as large a distribution of a population book as any since Malthus' *Principle of Population*."[50]

Burch's ideas about population circulated much more widely than did his book through his influence on two more popular books published in 1948. *Our Plundered Planet* by Henry Fairfield ("Fair") Osborn Jr. (first cousin of Fred Osborn) and *Road to Survival* by William Vogt were international bestsellers and have been widely credited with launching the modern environmental movement.[51] Both books sold millions of copies. In November 1948 an article in *Time* declared that "their influence has already reached around the world."[52] *Our Plundered Planet* was eventually translated into thirteen languages; *Road to Survival*, translated into eleven languages, was selected for the Book-of-the-Month Club and remained the most popular environmental book until the 1962 publication of *Silent Spring* by Rachel Carson.[53]

Road to Survival and *Our Plundered Planet* presented the increasingly visible degradation of the natural world and depletion of natural resources—a topic on which Burch and Pendell had only just touched—as evidence of overpopulation. Vogt and Osborn called for population control as a prerequisite for protecting the Earth's ecosystems. They vividly described the destruction human activity had visited on the natural environment, warning that resource consumption and soil erosion were rapidly undermining the basis for human life and prosperity. In 1948 the idea that humans were part of the natural world and that they depended on their environment while simultaneously posing a threat to its integrity was new to most Americans.[54]

Vogt and Osborn attributed global environmental degradation to unrestrained capitalism, demonstrating that the rapacious pursuit of profit had depleted and destroyed the resources on which humans depended not only for their livelihoods but for their lives. A reviewer in the *New Republic* declared that "both of these writers are barking up the right tree. They have put their finger on the soil and water robber. This robber is an economic and business system which makes it profitable to destroy the elements that give us our food, our clothes, our houses and our gadgets."[55] Vogt and Osborn did not blame the system itself, however, but rather the size to which it had grown, and they attributed the growth of the global economy to the world's rising human numbers rather than recognizing expansion as an inherent feature of capitalism. They reasoned that the system could be rendered sustainable, if only the size of the world's population could be kept down. Both men had backgrounds in animal ecology, and both were heavily influenced by the work of Aldo Leopold.[56] Vogt and Osborn drew on Burch and Pendell's *Human Breeding and Survival* and other Population Reference Bureau publications to extend Leopold's theories to human populations. Just as violence and starvation had been irrefutable proof of overpopulation for Burch and Pendell, ecosystem degradation proved for Vogt and Osborn that the world's human population had exceeded its natural limit. Their favored solution was not regulation of industry or conservation of natural resources but population control.

While Osborn took a more measured approach, Vogt made clear that he saw no value in the lives of the indigenous inhabitants of the countries of primary production, where population was growing most rapidly and where population growth threatened the access of U.S.-based corporations to raw materials. He denounced recent advances in medicine and sanitation as being even more destructive than the diseases they cured or prevented because they fostered population growth. Vogt compared hybrid corn to syphilis, arguing that, because the former promoted life while the latter destroyed it, the former caused more misery in the long run, attributing the plight of the world's poor to their simply being alive in too large a quantity.[57] He recommended that the U.S. government withhold aid to countries that didn't have population control measures in place and ridiculed demographers' claims that the distribution of birth control in and of itself would not slow population growth. Vogt envisioned a futuristic contraceptive that could cheaply and easily control world population growth. He made no bones about his desire to focus such efforts on the world's poor and nonwhite. Vogt became national director of the Planned Parenthood Federation of America in 1951, signaling the organization's move into global population control.

Despite the immense popularity of *Road to Survival* and *Our Plundered Planet*, scientists—of both natural and social varieties—were no more enthusiastic about these books than they had been about *Human Breeding and Survival*. Karl Brandt of Stanford University's Food Research Institute described Vogt's book as "deliberate propaganda" and expressed concern that "while the book is written in the style of lyrical fiction, which it actually is, certain scientific trimmings are attached which impress the non-professional reader as much as the quack's white laboratory uniform impresses the gullible patient."[58] Demographers spent a considerable portion of the 1949 PAA meeting critiquing these books.[59] But not all scientists shared these negative evaluations. One of Vogt and Osborn's most enthusiastic readers, biologist Paul Ehrlich, then an undergraduate student at the University of Pennsylvania, would later adopt the same claims and tactics in his efforts to control human population growth. Kingsley Davis was also impressed by Vogt and Osborn's Malthusian arguments. Davis left Princeton in 1948, when he received an offer from Columbia University that included a large raise and promotion to full professor.[60] In the same year, Fair Osborn, in partnership with Laurance Rockefeller, established the Conservation Foundation, an organization that aimed to promote environmental protection through population control.[61] The Conservation Foundation immediately became a source of research funding for Davis and his students at Columbia. Davis's work simultaneously began to focus on the environmental effects of population growth, though it is unclear whether this shift preceded or followed his association with the Conservation Foundation.[62]

Road to Survival and *Our Plundered Planet* brought public attention to the Population Reference Bureau and provided support to Burch's population theories. These books also attracted to the Bureau a powerful new champion, businessman and peace activist Hugh Everett Moore, who had grown wealthy by inventing the Dixie Cup. Recognizing that war threatened U.S. business interests abroad, Moore used his largesse to establish the Hugh Moore Fund for International Peace in 1944.[63] In 1948 he read Vogt's *Road to Survival* and followed the footnotes to Burch's *Human Breeding and Survival*, which convinced him that population was "the most basic reason for recent and possibly future wars."[64] Moore initiated a frequent correspondence with Burch, which would continue until Burch's death, to learn more about the work of the Population Reference Bureau.

Before donating his own money to the Bureau, Moore sought additional information. He sent a copy of Burch's book to Frank Boudreau, former director of the Health Organization of the League of Nations, who had become executive director of the Milbank Memorial Fund in 1936. Boudreau warned Moore that Burch's book was "not regarded very seriously by the real authorities in the field of population and agriculture" because "the authors are not real authorities on the subject; their knowledge is second hand." He even offered to "pick out for [Moore] statement after statement which would not stand critical analysis."[65] Moore nonetheless persisted in his support for Burch, replying to Boudreau that "while appreciating the information you give me about him, I must still give him credit, along with William Vogt, for really waking me up!"[66] As Moore explained, he was less interested in population research and more interested in "education," by which he meant the education of the U.S. public and policymakers about the dangers population growth abroad posed to U.S. interests.[67] Moore made his first contribution to the Population Reference Bureau before the end of 1948.[68] He may have been swayed by the fact that Clarence Cook Little, a member of the Bureau's scientific council, had been a classmate of his at Harvard, and by a personal appeal he received from California land developer and eugenicist Charles M. Goethe. Goethe, a founding member of the Northern California Eugenics Society, had worked with the Human Betterment Foundation to lobby the state of California to restrict immigration from Mexico and sterilize poor women.[69] He explained to Moore that he had supported the Population Reference Bureau from its beginning with monthly checks in the range of $1,600 to $2,500, which he considered a business expense because "it is really insurance against excessive taxation, as well as against the future of any business."[70] Goethe's explanation of the importance of the Bureau's work echoed Burch's publications, which described population control as necessary for the expansion of U.S. business enterprises worldwide.

Moore did contribute to the Population Reference Bureau, but he also recognized that his connections in the business, philanthropic, and diplomatic communities could facilitate the building of a much broader, wealthier, and more influential base of support for overseas population control. To solicit backing, Moore sent copies of Burch's book to several of his friends, urging them to consider "whether over-population will not, in fact, be the basic cause of future wars and also of the spread of tyranny and Communism."[71] But Moore's friends were not immediately convinced. Several had read a critique of Vogt's and Osborn's books in *Time* that described them as "scare books" and reassured readers that "to the real agricultural scientists, close to the soil and its sciences, such pessimism sounds silly or worse. Every main article of the Neo-Malthusian creed, they say, is either false or distorted or unprovable."[72] Upon receipt of Burch's book from Moore, the journalist Clarence Streit replied that it "rubs my fur the wrong way by the high percentage of fallacious reasoning, and ill-considered dogmatic assertions, and dubious implications."[73]

As the one world envisioned by the United Nations began to divide into the three worlds of the Cold War, Burch's warnings about the relationship between population growth and communism began to seem more prescient, and Moore's appeals to his friends became more insistent. In his 1949 inaugural address, President Harry Truman announced that the United States would extend technical assistance to Third World countries as a means of launching them down the path of free-market development. Burch explained to Moore that foreign aid of the type Truman promised "could cause an explosion in world population which could easily bankrupt the United States in its efforts to support the large increase in population to prevent these areas from becoming communistic."[74] Moore warned members of the diplomatic-industrial community that development assistance could backfire if its effects on vital rates were not carefully considered.[75] If aid from the United States reduced mortality rates without simultaneously curtailing fertility, he cautioned, it could generate population growth on an order that might undermine the process of economic development. In the 1950s a new organization joined the scene to take a scientific approach to this dilemma.

THE POPULATION COUNCIL

The Population Council was established in 1952 by John D. Rockefeller III (older brother of Laurance Rockefeller), with the assistance of Fred Osborn and Frank Notestein, following a secretive meeting with some of the country's most prominent scientists. Already by the end of 1945 Notestein had begun to offer a new prescription for the rapidly growing countries of Asia and Latin America. Only a year earlier he had argued that decolonization and foreign aid for economic development would complete the demographic transition, halting population growth. When these claims were met with skepticism from social scientists affiliated with the Rockefeller Foundation—which had recently replaced the Milbank Memorial Fund as OPR's primary patron[76]—Notestein began to recommend family planning instead. What Notestein meant by family planning in the Global South was analogous to what Fred Osborn had meant by family planning in the interwar context of American eugenics: the legalization and spread of contraception, together with a variety of social and economic mechanisms that would influence who used it and how. Just as Osborn had proposed the Indianapolis Study as a way to determine policy approaches that would promote larger families among the native white middle class and smaller families among the poor, nonwhite, and immigrants in the United States,

Notestein began to propose demographic research to figure out how to popularize the use of contraceptives overseas. He also proposed biomedical research to develop new contraceptive technologies that would require less effort on the part of potential users, compensating for the individualistic modern values that were thought to be absent from traditional societies.[77] If fertility couldn't be reduced through the spread of modern values, perhaps it could be reduced through the spread of modern technology.

Notestein became more confident in the need for research into new contraceptive technologies and social stimulus to their use in 1948, when he and his OPR colleague Irene Taeuber joined Rockefeller Foundation officers on a tour of East Asia. There Notestein attributed the poverty he witnessed not to the economic domination of the countryside by the city or the East by the West, but rather to population density.[78] He believed that agrarian couples could be convinced that smaller families would benefit them economically, but continued to doubt that they would adopt existing contraceptive methods or that they would be able to use them correctly even if they wanted to adopt them.

After his trip to Asia, Notestein stopped calling for an end to imperialism and economic exploitation of agricultural countries as the surest means of promoting modernization and thereby triggering demographic transition.[79] Instead he called for the development of new contraceptive technologies that would be attractive even to couples who lacked the socioeconomic incentives for small families that had led to the adoption of birth control in Western Europe and North America. The right technology, Notestein reasoned, could reduce fertility without requiring social change, thereby alleviating population pressure even in the absence of decolonization or modernization. The ideal birth control method, he believed, would be one that required more effort *not* to use.

By the early 1950s it had become clear that the Rockefeller Foundation, though it eagerly funded OPR, would not sponsor the development of new contraceptive technologies or research on how to popularize them in agrarian societies.[80] Nonetheless John D. Rockefeller III, who became chairman of his family's foundation in 1952, took a personal interest in the project. He was the grandson of John Davison Rockefeller ("Senior"), who had founded Standard Oil in 1870 and the Rockefeller Foundation in 1913. The eldest son of Senior's only son, John D. III was tapped to take over the family's philanthropic work. As early as 1934 he told his father that he wanted to focus his efforts on birth control.[81] Between the wars this meant legalizing contraception and making it more widely available in the United States.[82] By 1934 the birth control and eugenics movements had fully converged, with Margaret Sanger embracing eugenics from the birth control side and Fred Osborn embracing birth control from the eugenics side. The Osborn cousins, Fred and Fair, had been frequent guests in the home of John D. Jr. while the third generation of Rockefellers—Abby, John D. III, Nelson, Winthrop, Laurance, and David—was growing up. The Osborns piqued the interest of John D. III in population and Laurance in conservation. Laurance served alongside Fair on the board of the New York Zoological Society and was environmental advisor to every president from Dwight D. Eisenhower to George W. Bush.[83] Fred impressed upon John D. III the relationship between birth control and eugenics beginning in the late 1930s and, a decade later, the potential role of birth control in mitigating the threat of population growth in Asia.[84]

In February 1952 Leland DeVinney, head of the Rockefeller Foundation's Social Science Division, warned Rockefeller that, as birth control was still politically dangerous, public efforts to promote it, either at home or abroad, would encounter resistance. He suggested, however, that "a private individual willing to do so can make an especially useful contribution" to the "limitation of population growth."[85] John D. III's financial advisor, Lewis Strauss, a former commissioner and future chair of the U.S. Atomic Energy Commission, suggested that Rockefeller hold a small meeting of experts behind closed doors to explore how he might make such a contribution.[86] The meeting took place over three days in June 1952 at the Rockefeller-owned Colonial Williamsburg Inn under the auspices of the National Academy of Sciences. NAS president Detlev Bronk, who was soon to become president of the Rockefeller Institute for Medical Research, chaired the meeting, which was paid for by a direct grant to the NAS from Rockefeller.

The Williamsburg meeting brought together the two emerging postwar positions on population. William Vogt, Fair Osborn, and Kingsley Davis represented the Malthusian perspective of the Population Reference Bureau and the Conservation Foundation: they claimed the world's human population had already exceeded Earth's capacity to provide, requiring an immediate cessation of growth achieved through political pressure on high-fertility countries from the United States and the United Nations. Fred Osborn, Frank Notestein, and several other demographers represented the modernizationist perspective that would come to characterize the Population Council, that modernization and the resulting demographic transition had stalled out in many of the countries of Africa, Asia, and Latin America and could be jump-started by family planning programs that distributed innovative contraceptive technologies. Other participants in the meeting—including embryologist George Corner, physicist and former MIT president Karl Taylor Compton, and geneticists Lewis Stadler and Hermann J. Muller—claimed to know nothing about human population.

It was nonetheless clear that they had imbibed the Population Reference Bureau's message that the world as a whole, including the United States, was already in a state of overpopulation. Whelpton did his best to assure them that the high birth rate in the United States was but a temporary phenomenon.[87]

Even if population growth *in* the United States was not a problem, however, all participants saw population growth in other parts of the world as a problem *for* the United States, a threat to American political and economic interests. Some worried that investment in Africa, Asia, and Latin America—whether in agriculture, transport, manufacturing, or education and whether by the U.S. government, the UN, businesses, or philanthropies—would not produce the desired results (financial returns, either to investors or to the local economy) unless accompanied by a reduction in birth rates. Others worried that rising levels of poverty and starvation in nonaligned countries—which they uncritically attributed to population growth—would make those countries more vulnerable to communist revolution. Those present in Williamsburg discussed the need to combat "communist propagandists who are filtering into the villages" promising "other ways out of the problem" of poverty.[88] Specifically, communism offered state control of land and natural resources and the promise of directing industrialization to produce maximum benefit for workers, solutions that had the potential to support a growing population at higher standards of living but that threatened the prevailing geopolitical and world economic order that benefited U.S. industry.

Participants in the Williamsburg meeting never agreed on the nature of "the population problem." For Notestein, it was a problem only in select parts of the world where demographic transition had to be helped along; for Davis it was global. Nonetheless, by the end of the meeting, they had agreed that population and natural resources needed to be brought into balance with one another. No thought at all was given to conservation or redistribution of resources. Participants only considered ways to either increase the quantity of resources or reduce the number of people. Some had high hopes that aquaculture, genetic engineering of food crops and animals, and solar power could provide for the world's growing population, but they conceded that these innovations were decades in the future. Organizations like the Rockefeller Foundation were already working toward more attainable advances in agriculture, which would soon be realized in the Green Revolution. Demographer Dorothy S. Thomas, an expert on internal migration in the United States, made the unpopular suggestion that international migration could help to even out population density on a global level. She quickly admitted, however, that racism and xenophobia in what she called "over-developed" countries would make such a scheme politically impossible.[89] Even Warren Thompson, who had advocated for the international redistribution of population between the wars, thought this idea impractical. Something needed to be done in the shorter term to slow population growth, certainly in countries that were already densely settled and possibly in the world as a whole.

Everyone present at Williamsburg believed that fertility rates had to come down. The challenge was that nobody knew how to do it. OPR demographer Irene Taeuber, who knew more about population dynamics in Asia than anyone else in the United States, admitted that "if we can take the villagers of India, or if we take the villagers of Ceylon, if we take even the peasants of Japan, we won't know what the cultural values involved in fertility are. We won't know what the resistances to change are."[90] In the formulation of demographic transition theory, demographers had deduced that social institutions in all traditional societies promoted high birth rates, as societies that lacked such institutions would have already died out. But they didn't know the specifics of those institutions or how resistant (or amenable) they were to change. They also seem to have been unaware of the eugenically oriented birth control programs that had been established in many parts of the world before World War II.[91] Thomas pointed out that the African American birth rate had fallen dramatically in conjunction with the Great Migration but conceded that "how the Negroes are controlling their family size we don't know, because we haven't asked them."[92] Research on fertility in the United States had focused on the members of the population whose fertility demographers hoped to *increase*, not those whose fertility some hoped to *decrease*. The demographers at Williamsburg called for more research into the childbearing practices of couples in developing countries but felt unqualified to carry it out. Such research, they argued, "must be done by people, themselves, the members of the culture, who can do studies with the understanding that is required."[93]

Interwar research in the United States had suggested that a couple's ability to limit childbearing depended both on what contraceptive technologies were available and on how motivated the couple was to use them. The stronger a couple's desire to avoid conception, the more willing they would be to use difficult and unpleasant methods. Williamsburg participants assumed that desire to avoid conception was low among the denizens of agricultural countries, reasoning that contraception would likely offend their cultural mores and interfere with their sexual pleasure. They therefore agreed that demographic change in the absence of large-scale social change would require developing the perfect contraceptive. Paul Henshaw, research director of the Planned Parenthood Federation of

America (of which Vogt was then executive director), described this ideal technology as "an agent which can be taken orally or by inoculation"—importantly not during sexual activity—"which will have a known period, a reasonably known period of sterility, of complete safety [from conception], and a subsequent period during which there would be no impairment to reproduction, and this agent must be cheap. It must be so simple and so inexpensive that anybody can have it."[94] As DeVinney had put it prior to the meeting, what was needed was an "effective, cheap, foolproof contraceptive device suitable for use among ignorant peasants in backward areas."[95] Those present in Williamsburg generally shared DeVinney's perception that the targets of these technologies were too "ignorant" and "backward" to desire contraception and too "foolish" to use available methods even if they wanted to.

Planned Parenthood and the Conservation Foundation had already surveyed the relevant biomedical research, finding a few leads but nothing near ready for testing. Williamsburg participants nonetheless agreed that further inquiry into contraceptive physiology was the most promising approach to population control, as it could be done wholly within the United States. They recognized that implementing the resulting technology would require research into childbearing practices in target countries, but decided to cross that bridge later.

At the meeting's final session, Lewis Strauss proposed the creation of "an unofficial international council" to undertake the work discussed at Williamsburg: biomedical research to develop new contraceptive technologies and demographic research to determine how best to stimulate their acceptance and use. Although Strauss had envisioned an international organization in which "Americans would be the minority members,"[96] when the Population Council formed in November 1952, its board of trustees included only American scientists, businessmen, and philanthropists. Most had been at the Williamsburg meeting, including John D. Rockefeller III, Fred Osborn, Frank Notestein, Lewis Strauss, Detlev Bronk, Karl Taylor Compton, and former U.S. surgeon general Thomas Parran Jr., who had overseen racist syphilis experiments at Tuskegee and in Guatemala that would later be a focus of controversy, spurring the adoption of new norms regarding informed consent in medical research.[97]

Strauss had initially suggested an international council because most Williamsburg participants agreed that efforts to impose population control on other countries would fail, particularly if those efforts came from the United States. He and his associates therefore needed the buy-in of target countries. But they also recognized that, if their program was as unpopular as they expected it to be, trustees recruited from target countries would not acquiesce to it. As Warren Weaver, director of the Division of Natural Sciences at the Rockefeller Foundation, reminded the others, global population control made sense only "from the point of view of Western Protestant philosophy," which was, "from the point of view of this planet, a minority point of view." He cautioned that such a program would likely be impossible to implement under international leadership because "there are thousands and millions of people on this planet whose basic ethical principles would lead them to totally different ideas about what was worth doing in this field of population and resources."[98]

Williamsburg participants joked about ways to make their proposed council *look* like an international organization while remaining under their control. Strauss suggested that the Population Council hold its first official meeting overseas. Bronk seconded the idea, stating that "there are simple devices whereby one can have one's friends abroad take the initiative." Strauss ribbed, "We'll write the invitations in Sanscript [*sic*]," to which Kingsley Davis responded, "You might give the money to a Frenchman, who would give it to a Yugoslav, who would eventually give it back to the Council." Despite his doubt about the international ethics of population control, Weaver volunteered his considerable experience in "indirection," that is, "having international things initiated without their being aware of it," "their" presumably referring to the people on whose behalf such things were initiated.[99] The levity with which these statements were made (evidenced by notations of "laughter" in the meeting's transcript) suggests that the Population Council's founders had few qualms about acting in the world unilaterally under the guise of multilateralism.[100] They ultimately decided, however, that even this façade of international leadership was more likely to hinder the Council's activities than to facilitate them.

The Population Council's initial funding came from John D. III himself, and from the Rockefeller Foundation and the Rockefeller Brothers Fund.[101] On Notestein's recommendation, Rockefeller appointed Fred Osborn executive vice president. Finding a president for the new organization proved impossible. Men who had the right leadership experience lacked knowledge of population dynamics, and women were not even considered. Osborn insisted "that any person who takes this position should be a person who has convictions that population is a real problem,"[102] a conviction that had not yet become widespread. In his estimation, only Hauser, Notestein, and Whelpton had the appropriate credentials. Rockefeller, however, wanted someone better known, someone who could bring his own respectability to the organization's activities. He selected Brock Chisholm, a Canadian physician who had recently served as the first director-general of the World Health Organization, where he had faced considerable opposition in his efforts to include birth control in the WHO's program.[103] When Chisholm declined the appointment, Rockefeller asked Osborn to fill the post temporarily, which he did for nearly eight years, until Notestein succeeded him.[104]

Under the influence of Osborn and Notestein, the Population Council focused on their modernizationist version of "the population problem" (stalled demographic transition in the Global South) and on their preferred solution: family planning with new contraceptive technologies to jump-start the demographic transition and thereby stimulate modernization. As president, Osborn was able to insert his eugenic agenda into the Population Council's program and transfer at least some of the Council's social and intellectual legitimacy to the American Eugenics Society, of which he remained secretary for much of the second half of the twentieth century. During that time the AES shared office space with the Population Council at 230 Park Avenue in New York.[105] Throughout the 1950s the Population Council granted the AES $4,000 annually.[106] Osborn and others viewed the work of the two organizations as complementary. As one supporter put it, "the Population Council appears to be oriented toward the frightfully urgent control of racial quantity, while the Eugenics Society serves as a sort of Committee on Racial Quality."[107]

In its basic aims, Osborn's eugenic program had changed little since its interwar inception. It still combined "negative" eugenics (efforts to reduce family size among those considered genetically inferior) with "positive" eugenics (efforts to increase family size among those considered genetically superior). Unlike Burch's version of eugenics, it was silent with regard to immigration and sterilization. Family planning remained the primary vehicle for both positive and negative sides of the program. During and immediately after World War II, Osborn connected his negative program with the emerging field of medical genetics, which was searching for the genetic origins of some diseases.[108] Through the AES, Osborn promoted the incorporation of medical genetics into medical school curricula and helped to develop genetic counseling programs (including information about contraception and sterilization) for couples who had hereditary diseases or the genetic predisposition to them.[109] In the 1950s Osborn presented new Cold War justifications for his eugenic program: preserving the U.S. position of global leadership in the face of competition from the Soviet Union and animosity from the rapidly growing nonwhite and nonaligned portion of the world's population.[110]

Osborn was one of the strongest champions of eugenics in the postwar United States, but he was not alone. Prominent demographers served on the AES's board of directors during the 1950s and 1960s, incorporated eugenic analyses of population trends into their work, and published occasionally in eugenics journals.[111] The fertility differentials that had vexed interwar demographers were those between the middle class and poor, the white and nonwhite, and the native-born and foreign-born in the United States. After World War II, American demographers began to see differential fertility in global terms, with higher birth rates in Asia and lower birth rates in the United States threatening U.S. world hegemony. In Williamsburg, Thompson warned of "a very great danger of ruining our opportunities"—meaning those of the United States on the global stage—"if we have to compete with the populations which are going to grow rapidly."[112] Several years later, Dudley Kirk, the Population Council's first demographic director, stated that he had always viewed international population growth in eugenic terms:

> I think there's a real problem in the Western civilization in that we are approaching a stationary population and the rest of the world, the less developed world, is rapidly becoming an increasing proportion of the total population. Since I have a background in political science, I see that as a power problem too. Because as these countries get developed, and particularly as China gets developed, their large populations are going to be a tremendous asset. . . . I see us having to face a major readjustment in which power is going to go to other countries.[113]

In the context of demographic transition, Davis had argued that the growth of nonwhite populations would not threaten Western civilization, as their expansion would be a byproduct of their Westernization. Outside that context, demographers saw the growth of nonwhite populations as a clear and present danger to U.S. interests.

Since the Council's population control program and the eugenic program of the AES both relied on family planning, Osborn was readily able to advance both agendas simultaneously. Yet promoting family planning was still a controversial prospect. Birth control remained a taboo subject of conversation in the United States. Contraception was still illegal in some states and could not be discussed in the press, on the radio, or by the government.[114] Nelson Rockefeller, a younger brother of John D. III, worried about the impact John's activities would have on his political career.[115] Economists and policymakers worldwide still viewed population growth through the mercantilist lens, as a source of economic, political, and military strength. Pressure from the United States or a nongovernmental organization to limit growth could therefore appear to be an attempt to reduce that strength.[116] The UN Convention for the Prevention and Punishment of the Crime of Genocide, adopted by the General Assembly in 1948 and ratified by the requisite twenty member states in 1951, included in its definition of genocide "imposing measures intended to prevent births" when done "with intent to destroy, in whole or in part, a national, ethnical [*sic*], racial or religious group."[117] For all of these reasons, the Population Council worked quietly at first. Its staff was careful not to draw too much public attention to its activities. But the Council encountered much less resistance than its founders expected, as the work of Hugh Moore and the Population Reference Bureau smoothed the way for it in American public opinion.[118]

LEGITIMATING POPULATION CONTROL

Burch died in 1950 and was succeeded as director of the Population Reference Bureau by his former assistant Robert Cook. The Bureau's activities expanded following a three-year grant of $60,000 from the Ford Foundation in 1952,[119] representing Ford's initial foray into population activities. Moore remained a dedicated advocate and fundraiser for the Population Reference Bureau, having come to see population growth as a major threat to the postwar peace and the delicate balance that kept the Cold War from erupting into an all-out nuclear conflict. Before his death, Burch had explained to Moore that "in your lifetime and mine we (certainly our children) are faced with a tremendous world population explosion and also with an immediate atomic explosion." Though he hoped "the immediate atomic explosion is prevented," he warned that "if the population explosion continues (we are really already in it), the atomic explosion cannot be suppressed indefinitely."[120] Suppressing "the population explosion" became the focus of Moore's work.

Moore believed the Population Reference Bureau could make a larger dent in overseas population growth if it had more support from the American business and diplomatic communities. To that end, he and his associates Ellsworth Bunker, former president of the National Sugar Refining Company and U.S. ambassador to Argentina and Italy, and Will Clayton, founder of the world's largest cotton-trading company and former undersecretary of state for economic affairs, published a pamphlet in 1954 titled *The Population Bomb*. It expanded on Burch's contention that population growth in Africa, Asia, and Latin America would promote the spread of global communism and lead inevitably to nuclear war. It thus made a simple equation between overpopulation and communism, attributing to overpopulation the fact that "hundreds of millions of people in the world are hungry" and warning that "in their desperation, they are increasingly susceptible to Communist propaganda."[121] The solution it proposed was also simple: fewer people would mean less competition for food and other resources, eliminating the "desperation" that Moore and his associates believed made communism appealing.

Moore circulated *The Population Bomb* throughout the business, philanthropic, diplomatic, and policy communities. Cook published a summary of it under the same title in the *Bulletin of the Atomic Scientists* in 1956.[122] By the end of the decade, the connection between population growth and atomic detonation had become so ubiquitous that the January 11, 1960, issue of *Time* magazine was titled "That Population Explosion."[123] With nuclear war looming on the horizon, the population bomb concept was both terrifying and reassuring. It was terrifying because the world's population really was growing quite quickly. Although global demographic data were not sufficient to determine exact growth rates, each estimate was larger than the last, appearing to bring nuclear war ever closer. But the population bomb concept was also reassuring in that it suggested a simple way to defuse the threat of imminent atomic warfare: population control, which Moore and his associates presented as eminently possible, if only the U.S. government would make the decision to pursue it.

The founders of the Population Council agreed with Moore that overseas population growth threatened to undermine global political stability and U.S. economic hegemony. Whelpton encouraged Moore to "not stop with the one pamphlet which has been issued."[124] Geneticist (and eugenicist) Hermann J. Muller agreed that "the Communist movement is finding this situation [growth of poor populations] profitable to themselves and may be able to use it to gain world dominance if we do not succeed in helping the underdeveloped countries to check their population growth."[125] Yet the Population Council's leaders and advisors also recognized that overseas population control was not something the U.S. government could simply enact by brute force. Rather, they worried that any appearance of U.S. interest in population control could undermine the whole project. Muller warned Moore, Bunker, and Clayton that "many of these people have already been aroused by the Communists to such antagonism against us that the mere suggestion of our wanting them to change their ways in order to give us an advantage relative to the Communists would tend to throw them still further toward the Communist camp."[126] The Population Council consulted public opinion experts, who emphasized that any propaganda for population control needed to "be indigenous to the country concerned," cautioning that "materials that appear to be preaching from the outside can backfire dangerously."[127] It was particularly important to avoid the impression that these materials were coming from the United States.

But even as the Council's board recognized the political danger posed by involving the U.S. government in international population control, it also acknowledged that the government had considerably more money to throw at the problem than did the philanthropic community.[128] The board concluded that the U.S. government could successfully intervene in population growth in other countries only if the leaders of those countries saw population growth as a threat rather than an asset, and only if they requested U.S. assistance in dealing with it. The key was to convince the leaders and citizens of developing countries that population control was in their own interest by portraying population growth as the fundamental source of individual and societal poverty, and population control as a prerequisite for development.

Eugene Black, president of the World Bank, had an idea for just how to do it. He had become familiar with Moore's *Population Bomb* through Assistant Secretary of Commerce and Population Reference Bureau trustee Samuel W. Anderson, who had shared the pamphlet with him.[129] Black wrote the foreword to later editions of *The Population Bomb*[130] but recognized that it had the potential to cause deep offense or even to stimulate backlash if circulated in poor countries. He envisioned a different pamphlet, one written specifically for leaders of developing countries seeking World Bank aid, that would explain how rapid population growth prevented economic growth. When Black asked Notestein to produce such a pamphlet, however, Notestein responded that there was no empirical evidence that population growth necessarily would prevent economic development.[131] After all, modernization had occurred in North America, Europe, and Japan in the context of rapid population growth. To generate the evidence that would be required to produce the pamphlet he desired, Black made a two-year grant of $40,000 from the World Bank to OPR to fund a study on the relationship between population growth and economic development in low-income countries.[132]

Notestein's colleague and former student Ansley Coale carried out the study in collaboration with a CIA economist, Edgar Hoover. When the grant from the World Bank proved insufficient to complete it, the Population Council stepped in to take up the slack. Coale and Hoover focused on India, a critical node in the geography of the Cold War. For policymakers in the United States, India, the world's largest democracy, teetering on the brink between economic success and failure, was the focal point for testing the possibility of free-market development, particularly as its neighbor China pursued a state-led approach.[133] India's newly independent government welcomed the study. Nationalist economists had already begun to attribute poverty in India to overpopulation rather than colonial misrule, resulting in the inclusion of family planning in India's first five-year plan.[134]

India had a well-developed census infrastructure, so demographic data were readily available. Nonetheless, documenting a process of long-term growth at the scale of human generations would take decades, time the World Bank did not have if it was to use the results of the study to promote global population control. Coale and Hoover therefore turned to simulation. Coale projected the population of India over the next thirty years under assumptions of constant and declining fertility, representing future population with and without government-sponsored efforts to reduce birth rates. Hoover predicted the economic growth India could expect under each of Coale's fertility scenarios. He incorporated several assumptions about economic development that had been described theoretically by Coale's former classmate Harvey Leibenstein, a fellow student of Notestein at OPR.[135] Leibenstein theorized that industrialization was the engine of development. Industrialization required capital accumulation, which was driven by household savings. Household savings were directly related to fertility. With more children, households spent more on food and clothing and had less to save; lower saving rates meant less capital accumulation and slower industrialization, which translated into slower economic growth. As with any simulation, the assumptions fully determined the outcome. Coale and Hoover found that, after thirty years, per-capita national income would be 40% higher under the lower fertility scenario. They published these results in 1958 in a book titled *Population Growth and Economic Development in Low Income Countries: A Case Study of India's Prospects*.

Although it was a simulation, theory illustrated with numbers,[136] the Coale-Hoover Report, as it was informally known, was accepted by scientists, philanthropists, and policymakers as empirical evidence that rapid population growth poses an insurmountable barrier to economic development. Historians today uncritically cite it as such.[137] The problem with this reading is that the Coale-Hoover Report does not demonstrate that population growth would prevent economic development, only that reduced fertility could enhance economic growth. Even under the high-fertility scenario, Coale and Hoover projected that India's per-capita national income would increase by 38%,[138] suggesting that India would likely experience substantial economic growth even in the presence of high fertility. Nearly fifty years after its publication, Coale described the study as having pointed to "significant prospective economic progress even with continued high fertility, and significant if somewhat modest additional progress should fertility be substantially reduced in the next generation."[139]

At the time, however, Coale misrepresented the study as empirical evidence that "continued high fertility is an impediment if not a total barrier to economic and social development,"[140] and audiences generally received it that way. Instrumental in promoting this reading of the Coale-Hoover Report was the Population Reference Bureau, which quickly publicized it. The Bureau's *Population Bulletin* published a summary that inaccurately claimed that, if India's fertility were to continue unchanged, "economic development will be stifled by the sheer number of people, and India will not achieve that breakthrough to a better life for her people that her Five-Year Plans envision. Rather, she will be much more deeply engulfed in the morass of poverty and misery."[141] This summary had been vetted by Population Council demographic director Dudley Kirk, who regularly provided editorial oversight for the Population Reference Bureau's *Population Bulletin*.[142] The Population Council circulated the Bureau's summary and the report itself in Asia, encouraging governments to take India's lead in incorporating family planning into their nation-building projects and provide birth control to their citizens as a means of stimulating economic development. But the U.S. government still had to be convinced to provide assistance.

In the United States, birth control remained controversial. In the same year that Coale and Hoover published their report, President Eisenhower appointed a committee to study the U.S. military assistance program. Its chair, Maj. Gen. William Henry Draper Jr., had been undersecretary of the army during the U.S. occupation of Japan and had succeeded W. Averell Harriman as head of the Marshall Plan.[143] He had also founded the first venture capital firm in California and was a member of Moore's diplomatic-industrial circle. When Moore heard about the committee, he sent Draper copies of *The Population Bomb* for every member and referred Draper to the Population Reference Bureau's summary of the Coale-Hoover Report.[144] The Draper Commission's final report, issued in July 1959, concluded that military and economic aid were critical measures in the fight against global communism and recommended that the United States also provide assistance in slowing population growth if requested by aid-receiving countries.[145] The Roman Catholic Bishops of the United States quickly weighed in on the issue, announcing that they would oppose any public program to promote birth control, either at home or abroad.[146] Eisenhower responded at a press conference that birth control was not the responsibility of government, famously stating, "I cannot imagine anything more emphatically a subject that is not a proper political or governmental activity or function or responsibility,"[147] and urging private philanthropies to handle requests by other countries for family planning assistance.[148]

Eisenhower's science advisor, chemist George ("Kisty") Kistiakowsky, was frustrated by what he saw as religion and politics interfering in the implementation of a scientific recommendation.[149] Following his 1961 departure from the White House, Kistiakowsky founded and became the chair of the Committee on Government Relations within the NAS.[150] The NAS is a congressionally chartered organization of scientists that typically undertakes studies through its operational division, the National Research Council, at government request and with government funding. The Committee on Government Relations was different; it would allow NAS members to introduce scientific matters directly into the policy arena.

In late 1962 Kistiakowsky proposed global population growth as a topic for the Committee on Government Relations. He recognized that "whereas the Government may find it impossible for a number of reasons to enter into a study of population problems, and especially birth control, the Academy could make a scholarly study of the technological and even the social aspects of the subject in a world framework."[151] What he wanted was not so much a *study* of the causes and consequences of population growth as a *scientific appeal* for government action on population control. He hoped that, through a report issued by the NAS, "a great influence might be exerted toward putting the matter on such a basis that the Government could more freely concern itself explicitly with the problem" by transforming it from a political and religious question into a scientific one.[152] The National Science Foundation (NSF) had supported the Committee's previous work, but Kistiakowsky recognized that the population panel he envisioned—one that would lead to a recommendation that the government provide contraceptives to other countries—would be too controversial for the NSF. He instead turned to the Population Council, which eagerly agreed to provide the necessary funds.[153]

The Panel on Population Problems appointed by Kistiakowsky included Coale and two representatives of the Population Council. Although the panel's work was described as research, panelists knew in advance that they would determine world population growth to be a major threat and recommend the Population Council's program of population control through family planning with novel contraceptive technologies. Before its first meeting, the panel's chair, Johns Hopkins University biologist William McElroy, sent a memo to the other panel members describing their task as figuring out "what we should do to get various people, agencies, countries, etc. to 'face up' to this important problem of world population control."[154] Recognizing that the panel was preparing recommendations that would be controversial, NAS leadership shielded its activities from publicity until the panel had issued its final report.[155]

The NAS population panel worked quickly. By April 1963 it had prepared a report that summarized Coale and Hoover's findings and recommended to the government a plan of action that continued and expanded the Population Council's program. The report presented population growth as "an important barrier" to improving quality of life for "millions now living in privation," stating that "other than the search for lasting peace, no problem is more urgent." It cited the Coale-Hoover Report as evidence that rapid population growth prevented economic development and pointed to field studies funded by the Council (and described in chapter 5) as evidence that citizens of high-fertility countries wanted to have fewer children and were willing to accept family planning assistance. The report concluded that the problem of population growth was not insoluble; it could "be successfully attacked by developing new methods of fertility regulation, and implementing programs of voluntary family planning widely and rapidly throughout the world,"[156] exactly what the Population Council was already doing.

In effect, the report did what Paul Henshaw, research director of Planned Parenthood, had proposed a decade earlier in Williamsburg when he suggested that "one concrete step would be for the National Academy of Sciences to make a pronouncement saying in its view the problem of population and resource balance is the most important problem at this time and that work should be undertaken on it."[157] At that point, Davis—who would later be the first sociologist elected to the NAS—had warned that such a pronouncement would lead to the NAS being "attacked." Ten years later, however, after the publication of Moore's *Population Bomb* and the Coale-Hoover Report, the NAS could make exactly that pronouncement. Demography had transformed international population control from a potentially genocidal undertaking aimed at advancing U.S. interests into a humanitarian project aimed at promoting economic development in the Third World.

With the publication of the NAS report and the publicity it received in the press, President Kennedy could not avoid the topic.[158] Eager to demonstrate that he was responsive to science and not beholden to the Vatican, Kennedy announced immediately that the government of the United States would offer family planning assistance to countries that requested it. The U.S. Agency for International Development began a population program in 1965, distributing contraceptives abroad and funding such private organizations as the Population Council, Planned Parenthood, and the Pathfinder Fund.[159] Science had spoken, elevating the problem of population and the family planning solution above religion and national and global politics.

Moore and Draper attempted to push this success further by running a series of full-page advertisements in prominent newspapers, including the *New York Times*, the *Wall Street Journal*, and the *Washington Post*. Moore favored advertisements over earned media because "in paid space you can tell people what they should do, when they should do it and where."[160] Some of the ads appealed directly to President Kennedy—and later to President Johnson—to act on the threat of overseas population growth and were signed by a long list of prominent Americans. Others urged U.S. citizens to pressure the government to pursue international population control along with, or even instead of, foreign aid. Their aim, as described by Rockefeller Prentice, a cousin of John D. III and an associate of Moore, was to "get elected officials to realize that their stand on the population issue will mean their success or defeat at the polls" so that the United States would eventually "have men in office who can control policies as to birth control through clinics in this country and through foreign aid abroad, and implement such policies by the use of public funds of a magnitude that, admittedly, no single one of us could ever hope to match."[161]

Moore kept in regular contact with George Gallup at the American Institute of Public Opinion, who carried out surveys to assess the effects of Moore's efforts on U.S. public opinion and advised Moore on how to more effectively capture Americans' attention.[162] A 1965 Gallup poll found that 58% of respondents thought the U.S. government should help other countries slow their population growth; of those, 62% felt the aid should include contraceptive supplies. Americans rated "the world's population problem" as being less serious than the threat of nuclear war and the global spread of communism but thought population control more important than "aid to backward nations."[163] Yet public understanding of population dynamics remained vague: 66% answered correctly that the population of India was growing more rapidly than that of the United States, but 57% incorrectly reported that the population of Japan was also growing more rapidly than that of the United States.[164] To be fair, population data for much of the world were still inexact at best, but the large proportion who thought Japan was growing faster than the United States suggests a general perception among Americans that their country faced an imminent danger from the growth of the world's nonwhite populations and demonstrates a continued lack of general understanding of demographic measures or theories.

By that time the two postwar versions of "the population problem"—one promoted by the Population Council and the other by the Population Reference Bureau—had largely converged. The Population Council's modernizationist version of the problem suggested that incomplete modernization in countries of the Global South had stalled the demographic transition and that the resulting population growth prevented further modernization. It was rooted in the vital rate indices developed between the wars and linked to Fred Osborn's supposedly democratic and postracial eugenic project. The Population Reference Bureau's Malthusian version of the problem began from the premise that the Earth as a whole had already surpassed its natural human limit and that all of the world's ills stemmed from (and were thus evidence of) overpopulation. Its roots lay in the older racial version of eugenics, its biological understanding of the limits to population growth, and its commitment to immigration restriction. Both versions turned to numbers for support, but the actual size of the world's population and rates of fertility and mortality in the countries where population growth most concerned American observers remained shrouded in mystery. Appeals for population control therefore utilized figures that were highly aggregated—usually to the global level—and rounded to only one or two significant figures. They employed graphs with long time horizons, showing world population growing very slowly for hundreds of years, then shooting up in the twentieth century. As the two population problems merged into a consensus, they did so around a stylized story of world population growing ever more quickly, emphasizing the unprecedented nature of global population growth as evidence of the dangers it engendered and the necessity of halting it.

Although the Population Council and the Population Reference Bureau were not in complete agreement, neither challenged the other's version of the population problem. The Council produced scientific legitimacy for the Bureau's version and the Bureau generated public support for the Council's version. Demography, as shaped by the Population Council and filtered through the publications of the Population Reference Bureau, was central to public understanding of population, both in the United States and, as will be discussed in the next chapter, in high-fertility countries.

CHAPTER 5

Demography as Diplomacy

As the Population Council and its allies considered intervening in childbearing in other parts of the world, and as they urged the U.S. government to intervene as well, they did so gingerly. Recognizing the magnitude of what they were doing, the Council called on science to lead the way and to justify further efforts in the eyes of target individuals, leaders of high-fertility countries, and the international community. In a 1988 interview, Ansley Coale quoted Frank Notestein as having said that "coercive measures to force contraceptive practice are more likely to bring down the government than the birth rate."[1] It is unclear when or even if Notestein said this, but Coale's memory indicates a general perception among those involved in population control that their work could have serious unintended consequences.

The Population Council addressed this concern by putting demography out in front of its efforts to spread the new contraceptive technologies it helped to develop. Together with the Ford Foundation, the Population Council invested heavily in demography in the 1950s and 1960s, expanding the field dramatically and establishing the network of population research and training centers that characterizes demography today. Through these centers, the Ford Foundation and the Population Council funded the training of demographers from high-fertility countries in order to foster indigenous support for the establishment of family planning programs. The institutional location of population centers between rather than within traditional academic departments left them dependent on external funding, giving their patrons substantial influence over the research they carried out and focusing that research on fertility in Africa, Asia, and Latin

Building the Population Bomb. Emily Klancher Merchant, Oxford University Press (2021). © Oxford University Press.
DOI: 10.1093/oso/9780197558942.003.0006

America. Under the influence of the Population Council, U.S. demographers developed the fertility survey from a tool with which to plan *for* population into a tool with which to plan population itself. The Council embedded some of its first family planning initiatives in fertility surveys, presenting what might have been a controversial intervention in the more acceptable guise of scientific research and generating evidence of demand for family planning services. These efforts succeeded in convincing governments throughout the developing world to establish family planning programs or to allow nongovernmental organizations to provide family planning services for their citizens. Family planning programs, however, and the new contraceptive technologies they disseminated, were not designed to meet the needs of individuals or couples but rather to reduce aggregate fertility rates and thereby stimulate economic development.

DEMOGRAPHY AFTER WORLD WAR II

Demography was still a tiny field in the late 1940s. The Population Association of America held its annual meeting in a single room at the Princeton Inn, and only a few universities in the United States offered graduate-level courses in population. At the end of World War II, the only demography journal was *Population Index*, primarily a bibliography of scholarship published in other venues. When the U.K. Population Investigation Committee established *Population Studies* in 1947, it was the first English-language demography journal devoted to original research. Princeton and the universities of Chicago and North Carolina were the earliest loci of graduate training in demography. After the war, students of the initial cohorts of demographers fanned out to Brown, Cornell, and the universities of Pennsylvania, Michigan, and Wisconsin, establishing population-related courses in the sociology and economics departments there. Kingsley Davis moved to UC Berkeley in 1955, bringing demography with him and leaving Columbia without a strong presence in the field.

Demography expanded rapidly in the late 1950s and early 1960s as a result of funding from the Population Council and the Ford Foundation. The Ford Foundation made its first grant to the Population Council in 1954, amounting to $1 million over three years.[2] It quickly became the Council's largest donor, eventually granting over $88 million.[3] The Ford Foundation launched its own population program, in close coordination with the Population Council, in the 1960s. In 1964 it sponsored the establishment of a new journal, *Demography*, which immediately became the field's flagship publication.[4] The primary aims of the Ford Foundation and the Population Council were to fund research on fertility control in Africa, Asia, and Latin America and to sponsor the training of demographers from those regions. In support of research and training, the Population Council and Ford Foundation focused their resources on the universities that already had strengths in population, establishing population centers modeled on Princeton's OPR. These interdisciplinary centers housed graduate students and faculty with disciplinary homes in sociology and economics. By the end of the 1960s, the Ford Foundation had created twelve population centers at U.S. universities (some universities, including Chicago and Michigan, boasted two centers) and about half that number overseas.[5]

Generous private funding allowed population centers in the United States to attract top faculty with light teaching loads, ample statistical and computing support, and easy access to research funds. Centers lured students with generous fellowships at a time when there were few other opportunities to fund a Ph.D. in sociology or economics.[6] Students training in population centers were able to earn their degrees relatively quickly. Many who began with a B.A. completed a Ph.D. in three or four years; those coming in with a master's degree could do it in as few as two years.[7] Throughout the 1960s there were more jobs available for demographers than there were people qualified to fill those positions, so graduate students in sociology or economics could be assured that studying population would fund their education and lead to secure employment afterward.[8]

To receive foundation funding, population centers had to develop research programs in fertility control and train graduate students from high-fertility countries. In its first five years, the Population Council provided fellowships to sixty-nine students from twenty-one countries to study demography at U.S. universities.[9] The Ford Foundation also provided fellowships for students at the centers it endowed. At the University of Pennsylvania, tensions arose between the population center and the Sociology Department over the number of international students who were coming into the sociology graduate program through the population center.[10] This is not to say that international students were unqualified; many had already worked in government statistical agencies in their home countries. In the mid-1980s the Population Council's demographic director Dudley Kirk reported that over a third of the "leading demographers in less developed countries" had attended graduate school in the United States as Population Council fellows.[11] In 1971 Coale reflected back on his career, remembering that, in the 1950s, "we found few expert demographers in India and Mexico and fewer social scientists in other disciplines who had an expert knowledge of population." Since then, he continued, the field had grown immensely, and "an impressive fraction of the best of these [new] demographers—in the United States and in the less developed countries—were trained as Population Council fellows."[12] Many more were trained as Ford Foundation fellows.

The expectation that all countries would take regular censuses and report demographic data to the UN Population Division created a legitimate need for demographic training worldwide. Philip Hauser, director of the University of Chicago's Population Research and Training Center, recruited international students because "what was clear was that the most severe population problems were in the Third World. But in the Third World there was practically nobody who could be called a demographer, who could begin to provide the basic data for policy, which they badly needed."[13] With this statement Hauser conflated two separate issues: the dearth of demographic data in much of the world he had encountered while serving as U.S. representative to the UN Population Commission and the rapid population growth cast by the Coale-Hoover Report as the primary barrier to economic development. The colonial histories of many nonaligned countries accounted for both rapid population growth and the absence of reliable data with which to document it. Basic methods of data collection and analysis were at the heart of the training graduate students received in population research centers at U.S. universities. However, students were also taught to view population through the modernizationist lenses of demographic transition theory and the Coale-Hoover Report. Hauser and other center directors therefore expected that, in addition to developing their countries' infrastructure for demographic data collection and analysis, the students they trained would make the case to policymakers in those countries that too-rapid population growth was preventing economic development and that family planning programs could stimulate economic growth.[14] This approach to population control was analogous to the Ford Foundation's strategy of bringing Chilean economists to the University of Chicago for graduate training, after which they promoted U.S.-friendly policies in Chile.[15]

Decades later demographer John Caldwell argued that, through these research and training programs, the Ford Foundation and the Population Council had "literally talked down the birthrate" in the Global South by stimulating enough anxiety about population growth to lead to the establishment and promotion of family planning programs, exactly what the participants at John D. Rockefeller III's 1952 Williamsburg meeting had hoped to do.[16] Left out of Caldwell's account were the ways in which U.S.-led population control programs tapped into and built upon already existing family planning initiatives in target countries. Several countries of the Global South had already initiated programs aimed at controlling growth in certain segments of their populations.[17] In many countries, heads of state welcomed overtures made by the Population Council and the Ford Foundation as assistance in advancing their own population agendas. International students who came to the United States to study demography typically represented the most elite strata of their respective countries and were thus more likely than others to embrace alliances with American scientists and philanthropists aimed at limiting the growth of poorer and potentially more radical segments of their societies.

Three of these students—Mercedes Concepcion and Visid Prachuabmoh, who studied at the University of Chicago, and Nathanial Iskandar, who studied at Princeton—went on to direct population centers at universities in their countries of origin: the Philippines (Concepcion), Thailand (Prachuabmoh), and Indonesia (Iskandar).[18] The Ford Foundation provided initial multiyear grants to establish these centers but made continuation grants contingent on the centers securing matching funds from within their countries, incentivizing center directors and faculty to bring their work—and the problem of rapid population growth—to the attention of local governments.[19] Initially the core faculty of these population centers were educated in the United States and taught largely from American texts. Students of demography in Southeast Asia were therefore trained to analyze population through the theories, models, and ideologies developed by American demographers and their U.S.-based patrons.[20]

While the Ford Foundation sponsored centers in overseas universities, the Population Council provided the funds needed by the UN to finally establish the stand-alone centers for demographic training it had begun to plan in India, Chile, and Egypt after the 1950 World Census Program. Like the Ford-funded population centers, the UN centers funded by the Population Council were furnished with textbooks published in the United States and staffed by U.S.-trained demographers.[21] In the earliest days of these centers, instruction was provided by American faculty members on short-term contracts with the Population Council. These overseas sojourns gave American demographers personal experience with the widespread poverty in the countries where the UN centers were located, furthering their commitments to research on fertility control.[22]

In general, the UN population centers funded by the Population Council and the Ford-funded population centers at Southeast Asian universities seem to have met the aims of their patrons.[23] General Suharto, who became Indonesia's head of state after a 1966 military coup, was strongly influenced in favor of family planning by U.S.-trained technocrats, becoming a strong spokesman for population control throughout Asia.[24] Mercedes Concepcion, director of the population center at the University of the Philippines, organized conferences of prominent demographers and policymakers and placed articles about population growth in local newspapers, leading to the formation in 1968 of a governmental committee, which Concepcion directed, to "study the population problem with the idea of recommending a policy to the president." The Population Council's influence is evident in the committee's final report, which, as Concepcion described informally many years later, concluded that "we need to undertake a program of family planning so that each Filipino could partake of the fruits of national progress."[25] That is, the report presented family planning as the path toward equitable economic development. In 1971 President Ferdinand Marcos signed the proposed policy into law, creating family planning programs supported with funds from the U.S. Agency for International Development (USAID) and the UN Fund for Population Activities.[26] Fred Osborn credited the research of Carmen Miró, a Panamanian demographer and former Population Council fellow who had become the first director of the UN population center in Chile, with promoting the acceptance of family planning in Latin America and making Catholic Church leaders receptive to consideration of population control measures.[27]

In countries that did not already have population control aims, training local demographers at U.S. population centers was key to securing governmental support for the population control programs of the Population Council, the Ford Foundation, and USAID. Also critical to legitimating the population control activities of U.S. agencies was the international fertility research being done by American demographers. U.S. population centers informally carved up the world among themselves, with faculty at different centers specializing in different parts of the world.[28] The University of Michigan specialized in Taiwan, Brown University in Thailand, Cornell University in Latin America and the Caribbean, and the University of Pennsylvania in the whole continent of Africa. The key tool for international research on fertility and its control was the fertility survey, which had originated in Indianapolis between the wars and which postwar demographers developed in two directions, one for the United States and one for the Global South.

FERTILITY SURVEYS AT HOME AND ABROAD

In the decade after Indianapolis, American demographers launched two new fertility survey programs, one in the United States and one in the Caribbean. In the United States, the Growth of American Families study focused on planning *for* population. Beginning in 1955 and recurring every five years, it surveyed married women to find out how many children they planned to have in order to more accurately predict population growth over the remainder of the century. In the Caribbean, fertility surveys carried out in the first half of the 1950s focused on the planning *of* population. In contrast to the Indianapolis Study, which had aimed to identify the determinants of childbearing in order to increase family size among those whose childbearing was socially valued, fertility surveys in the Caribbean aimed to identify the determinants of contraceptive use in order to decrease family size among those whose childbearing was devalued by American scientists, philanthropists, and policymakers.

Growth of American Families was funded by the Rockefeller Foundation and the Population Council. It was directed by Pat Whelpton of the Scripps Foundation, who had also led the Indianapolis Study, and Ron Freedman of the University of Michigan, who had participated in the postwar analysis of Indianapolis data and used them to train his graduate students.[29] Growth of American Families was a response to the challenges the baby boom had posed to population projection. The baby boom had demonstrated that, in countries with very low mortality and little immigration, fertility is the primary determinant of population growth. It had also shown that the spread of birth control does not produce uniformly small families. Rather, it allows couples to adapt their childbearing plans to short-run economic fluctuations, having fewer babies when money is scarce and more babies when times are good. Freedman warned that such practices meant that "'bulges' and 'gaps' may be created at the bottom of the age structure which seriously affect many aspects of the society as they move inexorably up the pyramid of ages for the longer life expectancy of modern man."[30] When Freedman typed these words in 1961, observers had already blamed the baby boom for the overcrowded schools and teacher shortages of the 1950s. Forty years later that "bulge" would begin to near retirement age and would take the blame for existential threats to public and private pension systems.[31] The problem wasn't aggregate population size, but rather the unpredictability of such bulges. Freedman and Whelpton hoped that, by asking women on a regular basis how many children they planned to have, demographers could make better predictions of future fertility and overall population size.[32]

In contrast to the Indianapolis Study, which had interviewed couples in a single city, Growth of American Families interviewed a sample of married women that its directors claimed was nationally representative, though it included only white women. There was no need to interview men because the cohort component projection method modeled fertility as a function of the number of *women* in the childbearing ages. If their childbearing intentions were known, those of their husbands (or other men) were redundant. Female interviewers worked from rigid questionnaires and were expected to follow detailed instructions to the letter. Responses to open-ended questions were coded into a standard set of answers, either by interviewers on the spot or later by coders, to facilitate quantitative analysis.[33] Interviewers were instructed not to "take a stand for or against family limitation, or for or against a desirable family size."[34] They were explicitly told not to provide information about birth control, though it is impossible to know whether and in what ways interviewers departed from the specific language of their survey instruments. The questions they asked covered respondents' experience of marriage, childbearing, and contraceptive use, which was still illegal in some states and generally not discussed in polite company.

Interviewers found that most of the women sampled for Growth of American Families participated enthusiastically.[35] Americans had, by that time, become accustomed to responding to questionnaires and to learning about themselves and their neighbors through published survey reports.[36] Even personal questions were becoming fair game. Gallup and Roper polls began asking Americans about their attitudes toward contraception (but not their contraceptive practices) in 1936.[37] Alfred Kinsey published the reports of his detailed survey of male sexual behavior in 1948 and the companion volume on female sexual behavior in 1953.[38] These studies may have moved the Overton window regarding public and private discussions of sexuality, but they also generated considerable controversy, both for Kinsey and for his patrons, the Ford Foundation and the National Committee for Research in Problems of Sex.

To avoid the same fate, Whelpton and Freedman emphasized—to respondents, interviewers, patrons, and audiences—that Growth of American Families was a survey about *childbearing*, not a survey about *sexuality*. The questionnaire asked many detailed questions about women's childbearing intentions and contraceptive use, but none about their sexual practices. Although Kinsey had found that almost half of his female respondents had had sex outside of marriage,[39] Growth of American Families interviewed only married women, portraying conception as a function of heterosexual marriage rather than a consequence of sexual activity. Freedman and Whelpton simply assumed that women who were married were having sex regularly. The increasing availability of birth control reconciled any potential tension between the growing acceptability of premarital sex and the study's assumption that childbearing occurred only within marriage.

Growth of American Families approached the sexuality of its respondents so delicately that its questionnaire omitted the word "contraception" altogether and used the phrase "birth control" only as a probe. Freedman and Whelpton designed the survey so that discussion of contraception would occupy only about 10% of interview time.[40] Interviewers never named specific birth control methods, and respondents were given the opportunity to avoid naming them as well. They were told that "many married couples do something to limit the size of their families and to control when their children come" and were asked "how do you feel about that?" Interviewers also asked, "how does your husband feel about married couples limiting family size and controlling when children come?" and finally, "in your own case, have you or your husband ever done anything to limit the number of your children or to keep from having them at certain times?"[41] If the respondent answered this question in the negative, the interviewer followed with a probe, uttering the phrase "birth control" for the first time, only to assure the respondent that she was not accusing her of using birth control and to remind her of the scientific purpose of the study: "Some things couples do may not be considered birth control. Doctors and public health workers are interested in learning how many people use these methods. Have you ever made use of either of the methods on this card—you can tell me by the numbers on the card." The interviewer would then hand the respondent a card listing—by number—safe period (rhythm) and douche. If the respondent answered that she *had* "done something" to limit the number of children she had or to control when she had them, she was handed a different card, which listed by number the contraceptive methods then available (safe period; douche; withdrawal; abstinence; rubber condom; diaphragm; [spermicidal] jelly; vaginal suppository; foam tablets; tampon, vaginal cap, or stem pessary; lactation).[42] Respondents were asked simply to give the numbers corresponding to the methods they had used. Freedman and Whelpton had decided to use cards for this purpose after finding in pretests that some respondents were reluctant to name specific forms of birth control. Interviewers also reported that they preferred not having to name birth control methods.[43]

Women who responded to Growth of American Families generally reported wanting between two and four children. The study found quite widespread use of contraception: 70% of women surveyed had used some form of birth control in the past, and an additional 9% intended to do so in the near future. It also identified a strong desire among couples to limit their childbearing in times of economic stress. The recent pattern of fertility had followed the economic cycle, suggesting that Americans had begun to consider childbearing a consumer choice with potential alternatives.[44]

The 1955 Growth of American Families study was the first in a quinquennial series of American fertility surveys that continues to this day.[45] The 1960 wave was the first to include nonwhite women. In 1965 the study asked women their opinions regarding population growth in the United States and in the world as a whole, and whether they felt that the U.S. government should assist with family planning, either domestically or internationally. The survey found that 57% of respondents felt population growth in the United States was a problem. Of those, 81% stated that the federal government should support domestic family planning programs. On the global level, 78% felt that population growth was a problem. Of those, 68% said the U.S. government should support family planning in other countries. Fertility surveys in high-fertility countries were the first steps toward achieving that goal.

While Whelpton and Freedman worked on Growth of American Families, two of Kingsley Davis's graduate students at Columbia University, Joe Mayone Stycos and Judith Blake, carried out similar fertility surveys in Puerto Rico and Jamaica, sponsored by the Conservation Foundation and the Population Council.[46] These surveys answered the call of the Population Council's founders to study childbearing and contraceptive use in high-fertility countries in order to figure out how to reduce the former by increasing the latter. The Puerto Rico study was titled Family and Population Control, explicitly summarizing its goals. In contrast to Growth of American Families, which celebrated growth, Family and Population Control emphasized control and identified the family as the point at which control was to be applied. U.S. policymakers had long justified Puerto Rico's territorial status by pathologizing Puerto Ricans' sexuality and had elided colonial mismanagement by attributing widespread poverty to excessive reproduction.[47] The island's first democratically elected governor, Luís Muñoz Marín, in office from 1948 to 1964, shared this view and promoted birth control as a solution.[48] As American demographers began to configure population growth in other parts of the world as a barrier to economic development, Puerto Rico became a laboratory for research on fertility reduction, with Family and Population Control serving as a pilot for studies that would appear throughout Africa, Asia, and Latin America in the 1960s and 1970s.[49]

Overseas fertility surveys contained a central tension: study directors always described their purpose as *measuring* demand for family planning and *empowering* parents to have the number of children they wanted, but the studies themselves seem to have been designed to *increase* demand for family planning and *reduce* the number of children parents wanted. The line between their stated and unstated goals—measurement and empowerment on the one hand and population control on the other—slipped and blurred throughout the course of the Puerto Rico study.

In contrast to Growth of American Families, which simply collected information, Family and Population Control contained both survey and intervention components. Officially the survey was intended to measure demand for family planning, while the intervention was intended to empower families to use it, but the design of the study suggests that both components aimed to reduce the number of children parents wanted and to popularize the use of birth control. The survey attempted to reduce the number of children parents wanted by attributing poverty to excessive childbearing. Respondents were told to "suppose there is a couple called María and José. They are poor and have six children. María does not want to have any more children but José does not care how many children they have." Respondents were then asked if they thought María "should do something or not."[50] This question and others like it implied that limiting childbearing through the use of contraception would alleviate poverty and promoted the idea that women should take responsibility for birth control, even though existing contraceptive methods required the cooperation of both partners.

To popularize the use of birth control, interviewers were required to discuss each available method with respondents, asking whether they knew about each, whether they had used each, when, and to what effect.[51] Interviewers—local women who had been recruited from graduate programs in health education at the University of Puerto Rico—were expected to teach respondents about the methods with which they were not already familiar.[52] The influence of interviewers on respondents was not limited to the survey itself. Historian Laura Briggs has attributed the widespread use of birth control in Puerto Rico in the 1960s to the fact that "a huge array of Puerto Rican modernizing middle-class professionals took up the banner of overpopulation, advocating the idea that familial poverty was caused by too many children, and through a combination of educating, cajoling, and pressuring working-class women, succeed[ed] in raising the rate of birth control use."[53] Family and Population Control was one mechanism for producing this "array of Puerto Rican modernizing middle-class professionals" and deploying them to pressure poor couples to have fewer children.

Unlike Growth of American Families, Family and Population Control interviewed husbands as well as wives, as both members of a couple contributed to contraceptive decisions and fertility outcomes during this period, when available contraceptive methods required the participation of both parties.[54] In particular, the study aimed to correlate nonuse of birth control with a traditional culture of male dominance and female modesty. Interviewers asked women, "Many husbands forbid their wives to do certain things, don't they? What happens in your case? Does your husband forbid you to . . ." followed by six items, including using makeup, going out alone, and dancing with other men. Men were also asked about things they prohibited their wives to do. To gauge modesty, interviewers asked women how embarrassed they would be listening to "dirty" jokes, undressing in front of their husbands, being examined by a doctor or nurse, and talking with their husbands about menstruation or sex.[55] These questions and the theory informing them referenced colonial tropes that viewed male dominance and female subordination as signs of the supposed backwardness of nonwhite people.[56] Nonetheless they also suggest recognition—surprisingly unusual among demographers of the time—that gender relations influence childbearing.

The intervention component also targeted both husbands and wives. Participants were divided into three groups: one received their intervention in person, the second received pamphlets, and the third group—the controls—received neither. The in-person group was invited to a series of three meetings. The first focused on planning in general (with clothes shopping presented as an example), and the second featured a film produced by the U.S. Public Health Service and the Puerto Rico Department of Health, which contrasted an unhappy family with many children to a happy family with fewer children, promoting the idea that small families were superior.[57] Actual information about birth control was reserved for the third meeting. The series of pamphlets distributed among the second group paralleled the series of meetings, with the first one telling participants that "if things are planned, they end well," and the second contrasting large and small families through an analogy to planting banana trees "as far apart as one can support." The third pamphlet, titled *María Solves Her Problem*, referred back to the survey, detailing María's visit to the family planning clinic. As the doctor in the story explained various contraceptive methods to María, readers learned about them along with her.[58] Study directors claimed that they had to save information about birth control for the end so as to avoid offending participants' moral sensibilities: researchers would first prepare the ground by explaining why couples should limit their childbearing, then instruct them in how to do so.

Such an approach might have made sense if birth control were brand-new to Puerto Ricans, but it wasn't. Demographers from the mainland may not have known it, but contraception had long been available on the island, first through feminist and socialist programs connected to Margaret Sanger's organizations and later through government-sponsored public health programs that promoted contraception as a eugenicist solution to widespread poverty. However, the shift to government provision of family planning services had resulted in the replacement of more effective barrier methods with less effective spermicidal compounds, as program administrators and consultants believed condoms and diaphragms too complicated to be used properly by poor nonwhite men and women.[59] As a result, sterilization had increased in popularity as the most effective available method.

The Family and Population Control study found that knowledge and use of contraception were already widespread: 87% of respondents knew where to get free birth control supplies; of those, 54% had used them. Of the 87% of women who reported that they wanted no more children, 57% were already using birth control; of those, 41% had been sterilized.[60] Study directors claimed that the third meeting or pamphlet was the real intervention, the first two just preparing participants to receive the third. Given the high prevalence of contraceptive knowledge in Puerto Rico, however, it seems that the first two meetings or pamphlets were the real interventions, the ones that would convince participants to want smaller families and urge them to use the birth control methods with which they were already familiar. Investigators belied the purpose of their study by measuring the success of each intervention in terms of the number of couples who began to use contraception rather than the number who achieved their childbearing goals.[61]

Participants in the study seem to have found it largely irrelevant to their lives. They already knew about birth control, and those who wanted to use it were doing so. Of those selected for the in-person intervention, only 59% of women and only 40% of men attended at least one meeting, and only 16% of women and 8% of men attended all three. When asked why they did not attend, most cited inconvenience rather than opposition to the material. Men in particular said they needed to look for work during meeting times, attributing their own financial circumstances to low wages or lack of work rather than family size. Those who did attend typically arrived late, sometimes by an hour or more.[62]

The Family and Population Control study was not about introducing contraception into a setting where it had previously been unavailable, but rather about convincing people who already had access to contraception to use it. Even after the intervention, however, contraceptive prevalence rates remained lower than the Population Council's leaders would have liked. Perhaps the available methods of birth control were still too onerous, they reasoned. Throughout the 1950s the Council, in conjunction with Planned Parenthood, funded biomedical research aimed at developing the revolutionary contraceptive methods its founders had envisioned at the Williamsburg meeting. These investments began to bear fruit in the 1960s, resulting in technologies that worked directly on women's bodies. The availability of systemic contraceptive methods changed the approach the Council took to family planning and transformed the fertility surveys that continued to promote uptake of family planning services.

TECHNOLOGIES OF POPULATION CONTROL

The Population Council's biomedical research program continued the efforts begun by Planned Parenthood and the Conservation Foundation to find a contraceptive technology that would reliably bring down birth rates in agricultural countries where large families were still socially normative and economically beneficial. It therefore depended not only on the natural and medical sciences but also on demography to test the effects of new contraceptives on national birth rates in high-fertility countries. One candidate population control technology was the foaming spermicidal tablet, which could be inserted into the vagina by hand just before sex. These single-use tablets were developed specifically to work in the Global South. They were stable in hot climates and their use did not require running water (unlike a diaphragm). They were also thought to be simpler than diaphragms and less detrimental to male pleasure than condoms. In 1955 the Population Council sent Frank Notestein and Leona Baumgartner, New York City's commissioner of health, to India to consult with the government's family planning program, which had been established in 1952. Baumgartner, whose husband was the director of Durex, manufacturer of Durafoam spermicidal tablets, enthusiastically endorsed foaming tablets as an ideal birth control technology for India.[63]

Studies in the continental United States and Puerto Rico, however, indicated that spermicidal tablets were not very effective in preventing pregnancy.[64] Nor were they ever very popular. Only 1% of respondents in the 1955 wave of Growth of American Families reported having used them.[65] But advocates for the tablets contended that their ease of use relative to barrier methods compensated at the population level for their lower effectiveness at the individual level. They reasoned that, in the aggregate, a less effective technology that was easier to use, and therefore more likely to be used and more likely to be used correctly, would have a more dramatic effect on the birth rate than a more effective technology that was harder to use, and therefore less likely to be used and less likely to be used correctly. Spermicidal tablets were thus an early form of what feminist technology scholar Chikako Takeshita has called "birth control for a nation."[66] Their purpose was not to provide individuals or couples with reliable control over their childbearing but to reduce aggregate birth rates. The Population Council's founders, however, recognized a danger in this approach. If the method was not sufficiently reliable on an individual level, it would develop a bad reputation and people would stop using it.[67] Spermicidal tablets were therefore not an adequate technology for controlling the world's population.

The Population Council sought something that was better at preventing pregnancy and that required less agency on the part of users, who they did not trust to cooperate with their population control programs. In an early study in India, investigators were unable to assess the efficacy of spermicidal tablets because they could not distinguish between the acceptance of tablets by those to whom they were offered and their subsequent use by those who accepted them.[68] As political scientist Mahmood Mamdani found in a critical examination of the study, most participants had little interest in birth control but accepted the tablets as a matter of etiquette. One man showed Mamdani a sculpture he had made out of the tablets he accepted rather than using them for their intended purpose.[69] The Population Council's leaders reasoned that spermicidal tablets were ineffective because they left too much control in the hands of users, who could decide, with each act of sexual intercourse, whether or not to use them. The Council therefore focused its biomedical research program on methods of contraception that required less effort from users, especially methods that did not require any action during sex.

Feminist birth control activists also hoped to separate contraception from sex, but for the sake of increasing rather than decreasing women's agency in the realm of conception and contraception. As early as 1912 Sanger had envisioned a "magic pill" that would give women total control over their childbearing. By the early 1950s it had become clear to Sanger that, if her vision were ever to become reality, she would need to provide the impetus. The pill she sought depended on research in endocrinology, which had long lagged behind research in other bodily systems because of its association with sex.[70] Although the Rockefeller Foundation had funded endocrinological research earlier in the century through the National Committee for Research in Problems of Sex—the same committee that had funded Kinsey's research—this early work focused on overcoming infertility rather than preventing conception.[71]

In 1951 Sanger decided to take action and commissioned endocrinologist Gregory Pincus to develop an oral contraceptive pill. Pincus was something of an outsider in biology. After being denied tenure at Harvard as a result of controversial research on in-vitro fertilization in rabbits, he had established the Worcester Foundation for Experimental Biology and was constantly on the lookout for external funding.[72] It is likely that a scientist with a more secure flow of income would have turned down Sanger's relatively radical project.

In 1952, when Pincus went to Planned Parenthood to report his early success using an oral dose of progesterone to suppress ovulation in rabbits, William Vogt, who had recently become Planned Parenthood's executive director, refused to fund human testing.[73] The pill that Sanger and Pincus were developing was clearly a technology designed to increase the reproductive autonomy of middle-class white American women. Vogt doubted that it could effectively reduce birth rates in developing countries, expecting that nonwhite women would lack the foresight to take a daily pill, even if they did want to avoid pregnancy. He preferred to focus Planned Parenthood's resources on technologies that would reduce birth rates overseas rather than technologies that would make contraception more convenient for American women and thereby widen the global fertility differential. As Planned Parenthood's research director Paul Henshaw explained, "this organization in the past has been devoted primarily to maternal and family problems. The onrush of population growth, however, in those parts of the world where resources are limited, and a recognition of the eugenic, economic and security factors influenced by fertility control procedures, have necessitated consideration of the maternal and family problems involved in relation to world events."[74] In 1961 Planned Parenthood merged with the World Population Emergency Campaign, an organization Hugh Moore had founded to raise money for the International Planned Parenthood Federation, forming Planned Parenthood–World Population and emphasizing the organization's focus on overseas population growth.[75] Sanger's pill was a birth control technology. Planned Parenthood and the Population Council sought a population control technology.[76]

The Pill nonetheless became a reality at the end of the 1950s. Katharine McCormick, widow of the heir to the International Harvester fortune and a scientist and birth control activist, funded the research that Planned Parenthood would not support. Human testing began in 1954. Since birth control was still illegal in Massachusetts, Pincus turned to Puerto Rico, where he could utilize existing family planning infrastructure and the knowledgeability of local doctors in contraceptive techniques. Puerto Rico's territorial status afforded easy access to potential research subjects who had little legal protection.[77] Nearly immediately Pincus's team encountered severe criticism of its use of Puerto Rico as a laboratory to test drugs intended for women in the mainland United States. These critiques, however, were countered by positive press in such magazines as *Science*, *Time*, *Fortune*, *Reader's Digest*, *Saturday Evening Post*, and *Ladies' Home Journal*, in response to which middle-class white American women wrote to Pincus to offer themselves as test subjects.[78]

Although the Population Council was not involved in its development, testing of the Pill in Puerto Rico blurred the distinction between the birth control and population control projects, allowing each to cite the other in support of its own legitimacy. Those involved in research on the Pill at times tested it informally on their wives and daughters, signaling their perception that the Pill was a birth control technology intended for use by middle-class white American women.[79] Yet they publicly pointed to the perceived threat of overseas overpopulation to justify their efforts. John Rock, one of the doctors involved in testing the Pill, explained the need for it in 1954 by claiming that "overpopulation and communism are more than synchronous" and comparing an overpopulated country to a too-large family.[80] The popular perception that reproduction in Puerto Rico was out of control seemed to justify testing the Pill there. At the same time, leaders of the Population Council and Planned Parenthood could point to the development of the Pill and the excitement surrounding it in the United States to describe their population control efforts as simply providing women overseas with the same level of fertility control that middle-class white women in the United States eagerly sought.

Yet the leaders of those organizations never intended to place control over childbearing into the hands of women or couples in high-fertility countries. If they had perceived those women and couples as people who actively wanted to limit the size of their families, the Pill would have been adequate. Instead Notestein, who had become president of the Population Council in 1959, compared the Council's family planning efforts to public health work in a hypothetical world in which "malaria were as welcome as children":

> If a majority of young couples felt that they had really not justified their existence until they had undergone four or five attacks of malaria, which, moreover, they thoroughly enjoyed; if their fathers, mothers, mothers-in-law, uncles and aunts were constantly urging them to become exposed to the disease as soon as possible; if each new onslaught were welcomed with approbation by the whole community; and if to avoid this attractive disease, each deviant couple had to spray its own home with DDT acquired somewhat furtively.[81]

A birth control pill would not suffice in such a situation, as it would *facilitate* couples having the number of children they wanted. Instead the

Population Council needed a contraceptive technology that would *prevent* couples from having the number of children they wanted. The malaria analogy provided the Council with moral cover, suggesting that the technology it sought would allow couples to have the number of children that was in everyone's best interest.

The oral contraceptive initiated by Sanger and funded by McCormick took the form of a pill administered by women to themselves because Sanger and McCormick insisted that it do so and because they were the ones holding the checkbook. The users they imagined had access to doctors and could afford a monthly prescription. In contrast, when the Population Council and Planned Parenthood began to fund contraceptive research to develop a population control technology, their leaders were agnostic as to the form it would take and as to whether it would prevent conception from the male or female side. The only requirements were that it prevent pregnancy effectively and at low cost and require little or no action on the part of prospective parents, whom the leaders of the Population Council and Planned Parenthood imagined as being unmotivated to control the size of their families and possibly even ignorant as to where babies came from.[82] In fact, the users of these imagined contraceptive technologies were not individuals or couples but governmental or scientific authorities who would apply the technologies to specific populations to produce desired birth rates.

Developing a *birth control* technology was a *clinical* problem: all that mattered was how well it worked for the people who used it. Developing a *population control* technology was also a *demographic* problem: it needed to be tested for its aggregate effects as well as its individual effects. Contraceptive researchers had long distinguished between physiologic effectiveness (the effectiveness of a contraceptive technique under controlled laboratory conditions) and clinical effectiveness (its effectiveness as actually used). In 1959 Christopher Tietze, a physician with the National Committee on Maternal Health, which received funding from and would soon be absorbed by the Population Council, coined the term "demographic effectiveness" to describe "the reduction of childbearing among all couples who have been instructed in the use of a contraceptive method, including those who fail to use it as well as those who discontinue use after a shorter or longer period,"[83] that is, how effectively it reduced the birth rate of a nation. This was the metric that research efforts by Planned Parenthood and the Population Council sought to maximize. With a known demographic effectiveness, a government could calculate how many people needed to be given a particular contraceptive technology or instructed in a particular technique in order to produce the desired magnitude of change in the birth rate.

Planned Parenthood and the Population Council initially made grants to researchers studying various hormonal compounds that worked on both men and women. Ultimately, however, these organizations turned their focus exclusively to methods that acted on women, such as microorganisms that could be introduced into the vagina to prevent conception until an antidote was administered.[84] Contraceptive researchers claimed that the female reproductive system offered more opportunities for interruption than did the male system, but it was also likely that they simply felt more comfortable tinkering with female bodies than with male bodies.[85] Equally important, since women were the basis for calculating fertility rates and projecting future population growth, contraceptive technologies that worked on women's bodies had readily calculable demographic effects. When reports of successful contraception with intrauterine devices (IUDs) began to appear in the early 1960s, the Population Council and Planned Parenthood focused their attention and resources on the IUD's further development.

The IUD is an ancient contraceptive technology that involves inserting an object into the uterus through the cervix. The biological mechanism by which it prevents pregnancy is still unknown. In the first half of the twentieth century, the IUD was generally considered disreputable by the medical establishment because of its association with infection and excessive bleeding.[86] But the development of new forms of flexible plastic in the middle of the century revived medical interest, and the Population Council enthusiastically funded research. By the early 1960s several new IUDs had come onto the market, and the Population Council held patents on two of them, the Lippes Loop and Gynekoil.[87]

The Population Council worked hard to raise the profile of the IUD among the medical establishment. In 1962 it sponsored international conferences on intrauterine contraception, and in 1963 it launched the journal *Studies in Family Planning* to report on field experiments with the IUD in the United States and high-fertility countries. By the time the journal's third issue went to press, over fifty such studies had begun and IUDs had been placed in over 100,000 women.[88] For the IUDs on which the Population Council held the patent, the Council provided nonexclusive royalty-free licenses to pharmaceutical companies that would produce them at low cost for use by national and nongovernmental family planning programs in Africa, Asia, and Latin America.[89] By 1967 IUDs were being manufactured in Egypt, Hong Kong, India, Pakistan, South Korea, Taiwan, and Turkey. The Population Council provided molds and raw materials free of charge.[90]

The Council's leadership recognized, however, that acceptance of the IUD in overseas family planning programs hinged on its acceptance and use in the United States. Testing in the United States was also critical after the flak the developers of the Pill had caught as a result of experimentation in Puerto Rico.[91] For that reason, the Population Council funded large-scale cooperative testing of the IUD in the United States, largely through clinics provided by medical schools and other organizations for patients who could not afford private care, including clinics affiliated with Planned Parenthood.

IUDs were not regulated by the Food and Drug Administration, and U.S.-based pharmaceutical companies quickly realized that they could make large profits on these cheaply produced devices. Although early testing suggested that IUDs held immense promise, no model was quite satisfactory. Women who used them experienced pain and heavy bleeding and were more prone to infection than were women who did not. IUDs were not as effective at preventing pregnancy as their creators and users had hoped, and pregnancies that occurred with an IUD in place were nearly certain to incur complications. Pharmaceutical companies capitalized on these problems, continually inventing newer and supposedly better IUDs. Although they touted their new designs as improvements in order to boost sales in the United States, the innovations often caused more problems. Some of the most notoriously dangerous IUDs—such as the Majzlin Spring, which frequently embedded itself in the uterus of users, and the Dalkon Shield, which had a tail that wicked bacteria into the uterus—were sold primarily on the U.S. market.[92] It was partly in response to complaints about IUDs that the FDA began regulating medical devices in 1976.

The Population Council used IUD testing to help high-fertility countries establish national family planning infrastructures. In contrast to testing in the United States, which focused on safety and clinical efficacy, overseas testing examined demographic effectiveness and the feasibility of large-scale IUD delivery programs, the research question being how to most effectively insert as many IUDs as possible in a given area. A proposal for one such study in Egypt stated that "the idea is to show how effective the mass and quick attack of the I.U.C.D. [intrauterine contraceptive device] will deal with the problem of massive increase in the total number of population in a selected period of time taking the village as example."[93] The IUD was not being tested as a technology for the control of reproduction by individuals or couples, but rather as a technology for the control of population growth in the aggregate. The militaristic language suggests that individual fertility was an enemy to be combatted through the mass insertion of IUDs. One study found that, with an assembly-line-style approach, up to seventy IUDs could be inserted in an hour by a single doctor. Such a rapid procedure left no time to determine the right type of IUD for any given patient (or even if an IUD was right for any given patient), so studies experimented with different sizes and styles to find the one that would work best for the largest number of women.[94]

IUD studies also examined the rate at which IUDs were "lost" in various populations, with loss occurring through pregnancy with the device in place, spontaneous expulsion of the device, or removal at the request of the user for either medical or personal reasons, including a desire to get pregnant. The studies focused on identifying the lifespan of an IUD, glossing over the consequences of "lost" IUDs for the women involved. Population Council staff adapted demographic methods—life tables and the stable population model—to determine how many IUDs needed to be inserted each year in order to keep the desired number "in situ" in a given population.[95] Unlike Pill use, IUD insertion could be directly factored into population projections. Family planning programs hired "motivators," who were paid for each woman they convinced to accept an IUD, in order to achieve the requisite insertion rates.[96]

Although the Lippes Loop, the preferred IUD of overseas family planning programs, was safer than some of the newer IUDs on the U.S. market, it continued to carry the risk of infection, particularly in women with certain medical histories. Participants in the Population Council's conferences wondered about the ethics of large-scale insertion programs that did not take individual medical histories into account. J. Robert Wilson, chair of obstetrics and gynecology at Temple University, reasoned to other participants, "perhaps the individual patient is expendable in the general scheme of things, particularly if the infection she acquires is sterilizing but not lethal."[97] He likely understood that treating such infections often required surgery and antibiotics. He may or may not have realized that, for poor women in rural areas who lacked reliable access to medical care, any infection was much more likely to become lethal.

The leadership of the Population Council had high hopes that the IUD would turn out to be the ideal "birth control for a nation" they had envisioned at the Williamsburg meeting. At the Population Council's second international IUD conference in 1964, a staff member described the device as "a tremendous contribution to the welfare of individual families and national communities, with all that this means for the economic prosperity, the political stability, and the freedom of mankind."[98] For the Population Council, the IUD wasn't a birth control technology but a technology that could stimulate modernization throughout the Third World and prevent the spread of communism. It was a lot to expect from a tiny piece of plastic. At the end of 1967 IUDs had been inserted in 1.2 million women in Pakistan.[99] As of July 1968 over 2.5 million IUDs had been inserted in India.[100] By the end of 1969 IUDs had been inserted in 1.6 million women in South Korea and 635,000 women in Taiwan.[101] Between 1965 and 1969 a single clinic in Thailand had inserted over 40,000 IUDs.[102]

The Population Council officially promoted the IUD as a tool to help couples achieve their small-family desires, and for many users it undoubtedly did just that. The Council's leaders, however, recognized that the IUD could also *prevent* couples from achieving their large-family desires. In fact, its clinical effectiveness was slightly lower than that of the Pill, making it less reliable for individual women or couples. Its demographic effectiveness, however, was considerably higher, as a woman who accepted an IUD could not easily remove or choose not to use it. As one participant in a Population Council conference put it, "once the damn thing is in the patient cannot change her mind. In fact, we can hope she will forget it's there and perhaps in several months wonder why she has not conceived."[103] Such rhetoric demonstrates his low opinion of users and disregard for their childbearing desires.

It also illustrates where the Population Council drew the boundary between legitimate and coercive population control measures. Because the insertion and removal of IUDs is controlled by medical professionals, feminist technology scholars have referred to the IUD as an "imposable" contraceptive technology, in contrast to the Pill, which is under users' control.[104] The Population Council, however, classified IUD programs—including both the device itself and the propaganda disseminated to encourage its use—as noncoercive. Even if women were being paid to "motivate" others to accept IUDs, or if those who accepted could not readily find doctors to remove them when they wanted to have more children (or could no longer tolerate the side effects), the Council reasoned that women still had the choice of accepting an IUD or not. As long as no government agency or nongovernmental organization told women that they had to get an IUD or explicitly limited the number of children they bore, they were not being coerced. The IUD therefore offloaded coercion from the Council or a government agency to the technology itself. But the technology worked only if women accepted it in the first place. Fertility surveys and the advertising campaigns that accompanied them played a critical role in making IUDs available and securing their acceptance.

KNOWLEDGE, ATTITUDES, AND PRACTICES OF CONTRACEPTION

In the 1960s the Population Council launched a new fertility survey program in Africa, Asia, and Latin America, collectively known as Knowledge,

Attitudes, and Practices of Contraception, or KAP. The KAP program was led by the Population Council's new communications director and later president, Bernard Berelson, a propaganda and behavioral science expert who joined the Council in 1962. KAP focused on promoting acceptance of IUDs, which Berelson and Notestein viewed as a technology that could bring down the birth rate of a nation while leaving its social structure and gender system intact. By 1970 approximately four hundred KAP-style studies had been completed.[105]

When the Council's leaders first began to discuss recruiting a communications director in 1958, they were advised to seek not a scientist but "an information specialist who can determine the best, surest and simplest way of getting a story across, particularly when you must reach a large number of illiterates or semi-literates."[106] Berelson was just the man. He had earned a Ph.D. in library science at the University of Chicago in 1941 under the direction of Doug Waples, whose Rockefeller-funded research focused on propaganda communication. During World War II, Berelson served with the renowned behavioral scientist Harold Lasswell in the Foreign Broadcast Intelligence Service. He joined the Ford Foundation in 1951, developing its behavioral science program, which housed the Foundation's population activities until it fell victim to McCarthy-era censorship.[107]

Under Berelson's leadership, the Population Council launched mass communication campaigns overseas to promote the uptake of family planning services and particularly to encourage IUD acceptance. Berelson's goal was to create a small-family norm in high-fertility countries, both by publicizing the supposed benefits of small families and by making it easy for elites who were already inclined to do so to limit their family size, providing role models for those who looked up to them and forging a connection between small families and socioeconomic success. Whereas earlier efforts to promote contraception, such as the intervention in Puerto Rico, had been part of controlled experiments, Berelson's programs had no control. The Population Council circulated information through such public channels as the popular press, posters, leaflets, and broadcasts, turning all citizens of target countries into experimental subjects without their consent.

Population Council communications promoted family planning by associating small families with health and material prosperity.[108] Typical of these communications was a ten-minute animated film produced by Disney for the Population Council in 1968 (stills and quotes shown in Figure 5.1). The Council chose to work with Disney because "the Disney style is familiar throughout the world and its identification with wholesome family life is well-known." The film's main character, described by the Population Council as the "common man," was drawn to appear as "a composite of men

"Throughout the world of course, there are all sorts of men. They look different in different places and have different ways of life. But, basically, all men are the same. So to make things easier, let's put them together into one and let this one stand for all. He's a common man, just like you and me."

"Other animals are at the mercy of the world around them but, by his ability to reason, man has learned to improve his lot. Carrying him ever upward, this ability may someday make man master of all he surveys. Well, nearly all, for at his side, of course, is woman."

"To begin with, the number of people in the community remained about the same for many generations. There was almost a balance—a balance between the large number of babies born each year and the large number of people who died."

"Then, in the space of a single generation, man began to change these conditions. There was great progress in medical science, more food and better distribution, and vastly improved methods of health and sanitation."

"Now imagine that there is a house to live in and a plot of land which the father works to support them all. There is an ox to pull the plow and the land yields a good crop."

"Today, things have changed. Modern science has given us key that makes possible a new kind of personal freedom—family planning."

Figure 5.1 Stills and quotes from Disney family planning film.
Source: The Population Council, "The Disney Film on Family Planning," *Studies in Family Planning* 1, no. 26 (1968).

from the major regions of the world." The initial release included versions in twenty languages: Arabic (Moroccan and Tunisian versions), Bengali, Cantonese, English, Farsi, Filipino, French, Hindi, Indonesian, Korean, Malay, Portuguese, Spanish, Swahili, Taiwanese, Tamil, Thai, Turkish, and Urdu. The Disney film was intended to stimulate demand for family planning services, not to provide contraceptive education to audiences who already wanted it. The Population Council hoped it would "help to develop attitudes favorable to the small family norm; inform people as to the causes and consequences of the population problem; stimulate discussion of the matter; and, importantly, help to legitimate the very concept and practice of family planning throughout the developing world."[109] In contrast to family planning programs themselves, which targeted women, the implied audience for the film was male. It attempted to revise notions of masculinity to focus on wealth rather than virility, stating that "the real measure of a man is not how many children he can produce, but how well he takes care of them."[110] It encouraged parents to consider children as liabilities rather than assets and to view childbearing as Americans had begun to do: as a consumer choice with desirable alternatives.

KAP surveys served three purposes. First, they allowed demographers to assess vital rates and contraceptive prevalence in the countries where they were done, facilitating the projection of population change. By the time the KAP survey program launched, the UN had begun to promote sample surveys, together with indirect estimation methods, as the most expedient way to produce the demographic data that were not readily forthcoming from censuses and vital registration systems in much of the world. This need for data justified the nearly worldwide coverage of KAP surveys, which collected information that demographers could use to estimate vital rates at the same time that they measured contraceptive prevalence.[111]

Second, KAP surveys evaluated and boosted the effectiveness of the Population Council's mass communication programs. They measured the success of those programs in terms of how many respondents used or were willing to use contraception, and they were repeated at regular intervals so the effect could be tracked over time. Researchers correlated changes in contraceptive use with density of communication effort, figuring out how to most cost-effectively get the Council's message across.[112] Yet while some demographers, such as Donald Bogue at the University of Chicago, eagerly participated in research on family planning communication, others, such as Bogue's Chicago colleague Philip Hauser, felt that such research was beyond the boundaries of demography and more properly belonged to public health.[113]

The surveys themselves also supplemented those efforts by encouraging female respondents to visit family planning clinics and get IUDs, which they could use without their partners' cooperation or even knowledge, obviating the need for male approval. The Population Council's leaders viewed the IUD as a technological intervention into women's bodies that eliminated the need for social intervention in the gender relations of marriage. The KAP surveys of the 1960s therefore narrowed their scope to women and spent less time than did the fertility surveys of the 1950s trying to understand the gender dynamics of target societies. They focused instead on getting women into family planning clinics, where IUDs could be inserted, as this single act would reduce the number of women who could potentially bear children.[114]

The first KAP survey launched in 1963 in Taiwan, funded by the Population Council and directed by Ron Freedman.[115] Over the next twenty-three years, Taiwan became a kind of "overseas research laboratory" for the University of Michigan's Population Studies Center, generating a wealth of data for student and faculty research, even though few Michigan students or faculty members actually traveled to Taiwan or participated in data collection.[116] Like their predecessors in the Caribbean, KAP surveys educated respondents and interviewers about birth control and linked respondents to family planning clinics. Clinics in Taiwan offered women the full complement of contraceptive options but focused on systemic methods and de-emphasized the Pill in favor of the IUD, which was considerably cheaper for users, at 75 cents per IUD insertion compared to 75 cents per monthly pill cycle.[117] The Population Council estimated the cost to the program of each IUD acceptance at $4 to $8, which it deemed "far below the eventual economic value of each prevented birth, which has been estimated as being between one and two times the annual per capita income."[118] Such analyses likely influenced President Johnson's 1965 statement to the United Nations that "less than five dollars invested in population control is worth a hundred dollars invested in economic growth."[119] The Taiwan KAP survey spent considerable time discussing the Lippes Loop with respondents, asking what they had heard about it and whether their friends or neighbors were using it. Interviewers even asked women, "Do you know where you can get an insertion of the loop?"[120] and gave out 50%-off coupons to women who expressed interest.[121]

As a form of program evaluation, the KAP surveys endowed the Population Council's propaganda efforts with scientific authority. KAP studies, however, were more like market research than social science. The question they asked was not whether the provision of family planning services improved quality of life or stimulated economic development. It was how effectively the Council's communications promoted the acceptance of IUDs or other methods of contraception. Between the first two waves of the nationwide version of the Taiwan KAP study, carried out in 1965 and 1967 (the 1963 study covered Taichung only), the proportion of respondents with some knowledge of contraception increased from 14% to 21% and the proportion using IUDs increased from 11% to 18%.[122] Using IUD acceptance as a metric of success severed population control programs from the policy imperative from which they drew legitimacy: economic development. The goal of the KAP program was simply to reduce fertility, which had become an end in and of itself. The economic effects of fertility reduction were assumed in advance and remained untested.

The third purpose of the KAP survey program was political. It aimed to demonstrate existing demand for family planning services, and thereby to shape policy and international opinion in favor of family planning. There is no doubt that many people worldwide wanted better access to contraception in the 1960s. Yet KAP surveys clearly aimed to exaggerate demand in order to legitimate the Council's work and elicit buy-in from the governments of high-fertility countries. Berelson and Notestein reasoned that, if KAP surveys could at least produce the appearance of high demand, then the Council could pressure the governments of high-fertility countries to establish or expand family planning programs. By the time such programs were in place, the KAP surveys themselves, together with the communication efforts that accompanied them, would have produced the levels of demand they had claimed simply to quantify.

KAP surveys employed two measures of demand. The first was general approval of family planning. Questionnaires used vague language to assess this approval. Echoing the wording of the 1955 wave of Growth of American Families, interviewers in Taiwan told women that "nowadays, some married couples do something to keep from getting pregnant too often or having too many children," and asked, "Generally speaking, do you approve or disapprove of their doing this kind of thing?," without ever specifying what was meant by "this kind of thing."[123] An answer of yes could have signified anything from "you do you" to "please tell me how to do that." Berelson interpreted all positive answers as the latter. On the basis of responses to such questions, he described an approval rate in Turkey of 70% among men and 79% among women as "a striking mandate, virtually an instruction," and evidence that the Turkish people "very strongly wish that the government would organize a program to inform them about family planning."[124]

The second measure—and perhaps the most powerful and durable artifact of the KAP program—is a figure that has come to be known as the "KAP-gap." Calculated as the proportion of women who said that they did not want any more children but were not using a recognized method of birth control,[125] the KAP-gap was described by the Population Council's leadership as a measure of "unmet need" for family planning services. This measure too was inflated, as it included women who were pregnant (and therefore not able to conceive) or lactating (and therefore unlikely to conceive, particularly under less than ideal nutritional conditions).

Women who explicitly stated that they did not want to use birth control were also included in the KAP-gap. Framed in the language of "unmet need," these exaggerated demand measures served as a moral indictment of governments that did not provide family planning services on a scale deemed sufficient by the Population Council.

KAP surveys generated considerable critique in their own time, particularly among demographers who did not see the promotion of family planning as a legitimate social scientific endeavor. Focusing on the challenges of cross-cultural survey research, critics complained that KAP questionnaires were written by "foreign experts who know little of the local culture, do not even speak the local language or dialects, and have often lived only a few weeks in the country" and were delivered "at a very high speed" to "illiterate women" by "poorly trained interviewers." Some skeptical demographers dismissed the results as "self-fulfilling prophecies, as they nearly all show, in varying degrees, that the people interviewed have favorable opinions toward family planning."[126] This was, of course, the Population Council's goal.

Demographers' critiques of the KAP program suggest their perhaps inchoate awareness of the performativity of survey research. Surveys in the United States produced valid results not as a function of the sampling and interviewing methods themselves but rather because respondents had become familiar with the genre and knew how to play their role. As Sarah Igo has demonstrated, by the mid-twentieth century Americans, even those who had not participated in a survey, recognized the survey as a mode of eliciting generalizable information from a scientifically constructed sample of people.[127] The interaction between interviewer and respondent was a well-known social relationship. KAP surveys generally used the same interviewing methods as Growth of American Families, though they relied on convenience samples, since drawing nationally representative random samples was impossible in countries that lacked complete censuses. In contrast to the women surveyed for Growth of American Families, most KAP respondents had no prior experience with survey research, so the roles of interviewer and respondent and the framework for their interactions were not part of local social repertoires.[128] Whereas interviewers in the United States could draw on the authority of science and depend on respondents recognizing the survey as a scientific instrument, interviewers for KAP surveys tended to rely on the global power of the United States and on their own social status as well-educated and often bilingual elites to compel respondent participation.[129] Because respondents lacked familiarity with survey research in general and with the concept of family planning in particular, interviewers often found themselves "instruct[ing] the respondents concerning the meanings of questions and . . . direct[ing] them to relevant responses."[130]

Some demographers contended that thinking about family in quantitative terms was a novel practice for many KAP survey respondents. Questions about ideal or desired family size therefore elicited not long-held opinions but rather answers respondents thought up on the spot, if they answered at all. KAP interviewers also encountered considerable resistance. Many women refused to answer questions on their husbands' behalf, including questions about age, occupation, level of education, and previous marriages. Many respondents, suspicious that interviewers were government employees, refused to provide details about their income in order to avoid taxation. In some places, women would not answer questions regarding marriage or sex in their husbands' presence. Many simply refused to answer questions about whether or not they wanted another child or to express a preference for a particular number of children.[131] Some lied outright and even ridiculed interviewers, while others supplied the answers they knew interviewers wanted to hear.[132] As critical demographer Agnes Riedmann has pointed out, survey coding methods largely elided nonstandard answers, eliminating evidence of resistance from the data and the historical record.[133] In these moments, it is possible that American study directors, local interviewers, and survey respondents may all have had their own agendas that influenced the data collection in unpredictable ways. As Matthew Connelly has argued, international fertility surveys should be recognized "as making fieldworkers reliant on their respondents and providing opportunities for everyone concerned to subvert or reject what these exercises appeared to represent."[134]

The Population Council nonetheless mobilized contraceptive approval measures and KAP-gaps to back a 1966 resolution, drafted by Berelson, circulated worldwide by John D. Rockefeller III, and presented to the United Nations on Human Rights Day, classifying access to family planning services as a human right.[135] With this resolution, Berelson and Rockefeller leveraged demographic research to transform the Population Council's activities from potentially genocidal under the UN Convention for the Prevention of the Crime of Genocide to humanitarian, and made the governmental provision of family planning services a prerequisite for membership in the international community.

Although data marshaled to support the resolution derived from measures of individual demand, the resolution itself framed the right to family planning in terms of the necessity of slowing aggregate population growth. It attributed to population growth the challenges many countries were facing in their "efforts to raise living standards, to further education, to improve health and sanitation, to provide better housing and transportation, to forward cultural and recreational opportunities—and even in some countries to assure sufficient food." In that context, it declared that "the opportunity to decide the number and spacing of children is a basic human right."[136] The declaration did not present the empowerment of individuals and couples to achieve their desired family size as an end in and of itself. Rather, it was a means of controlling "unplanned population growth," which was necessary because "lasting and meaningful peace will depend to a considerable measure upon how the challenge of population growth is met."[137] This continual slippage between individual fertility control and aggregate population control suggests that, for many people working in family planning, there was no contradiction between the two: better control of individual fertility seemed a natural solution to the problems thought to be caused by aggregate growth. Yet if it was the threat of actual or impending overpopulation that permitted the individual reproductive autonomy that family planning programs promised, then birth control was merely a policy instrument, not a human right.

As the world transformed from one of empires to one of nation-states in the wake of World War II, the legitimacy of international population interventions relied on the consent of their targets. Fertility surveys secured or produced that consent. They were not the whole of demography during this period—and demographers certainly debated their merits—but they were major projects of the new population research centers that the Population Council and the Ford Foundation established at universities in the United States, Asia, and Latin America, and they continued with funding from the United States and the United Nations. By focusing on *how* to reduce fertility, these studies elided larger questions about *whether* fertility reduction would in fact alleviate poverty or promote economic development. Instead they advanced those claims in the eyes of policymakers, publics, and even demographers themselves by assuming in advance that they were correct.

In the second half of the twentieth century, science became a powerful idiom through which nonstate actors promoted their agendas in the making of U.S. domestic and foreign policy. In the case of demography, that science was not already there waiting to be put to use. Instead it was called into being by the same actors who cited demographic research to promote national policies and international programs aimed at controlling population growth. American businessmen and philanthropists had determined that population growth in Africa, Asia, and Latin America threatened their overseas interests. Funding the expansion of demography in the United States and internationally allowed these actors to influence the field's agenda, producing research that facilitated the projection of their power across international borders, legitimating their overseas population control activities and convincing leaders of developing countries to integrate them into their nation-building and economic development projects.

CHAPTER 6

Detonating the Population Bomb

In 1967, as in 1966, population growth and family planning were at the center of the UN's observance of Human Rights Day. At the suggestion of John D. Rockefeller III, Secretary-General U Thant once again celebrated the population resolution Bernard Berelson had drafted the previous year.[1] This time it was bound into a lovely keepsake pamphlet, with a foreword by Rockefeller that described "increasing recognition of and concern for the world population problem" among heads of state. The pamphlet said nothing of the Population Council's role in either generating that concern or producing the resolution, but U Thant's speech thanked Rockefeller for "his untiring efforts to secure ever wider acceptance of the Declaration."[2] By the end of 1967, thirty countries had signed on.

In the following year, the United Nations Association of the United States of America convened a panel to study how the UN could further the cause of global population control. Chaired by Rockefeller, the panel included David E. Bell, vice president of the Ford Foundation; Oscar ("Bud") Harkavy, the Ford Foundation's program officer in charge of population; John A. Hannah, director of USAID; demographers Frank Notestein and Ansley Coale; the chairman of the Continental Oil Company; and the president of the Campbell Soup Company. In their final report, issued in 1969, these elite American men described the UN as being "uniquely qualified to make an important practical contribution toward a solution to one of the world's most serious problems" because "it can act without arousing the fear that family planning is a device of the rich nations to avoid their obligations to the poor."[3] The panel recommended that the UN's population budget be expanded from its current level of $1.5 million

Building the Population Bomb. Emily Klancher Merchant, Oxford University Press (2021). © Oxford University Press.
DOI: 10.1093/oso/9780197558942.003.0007

to $100 million annually, laying the basis for the 1969 establishment of the UN Fund for Population Activities (today the UN Population Fund). In its first year, USAID provided 85% of the Fund's money,[4] cloaking U.S. efforts to reduce global population growth in "the multilateral approach," which Rockefeller acknowledged was "so much more acceptable,"[5] particularly in the face of growing international criticism of U.S. aggression in Southeast Asia.

These closing years of the UN's first "Development Decade" proved to be the high-water mark for the postwar population consensus. They also saw the beginning of its collapse. The two versions of "the population problem" that had come together in the 1950s began to diverge toward separate solutions at the end of the 1960s. On one side, the Population Council, the Ford Foundation, Planned Parenthood, and most American demographers—a group coming to be known as "the population establishment"—remained committed to family planning as the only legitimate solution to the problem of rapid population growth. On the other side, Hugh Moore and William Henry Draper Jr., joined by demographer Kingsley Davis and biologist Paul Ehrlich, repudiated family planning, arguing that enhancing the reproductive autonomy of individuals had not prevented any of the global or local calamities they attributed to population growth. They instead advocated for approaches that the population establishment classified as coercive, demanding policies at national and individual levels that would immediately halt growth, or at least bring fertility to the replacement level (NRR = 1.0). In so doing, they revived the Malthusianism of Burch, Vogt, and Osborn. contending that the world's population had already exceeded the Earth's capacity to provide for it. For scientific support, they turned away from demography and toward the natural sciences.

The United States was, by that time, in the midst of a social revolution at home and beginning to lose its grip on power internationally. Intellectuals in high-fertility countries, though generally embracing reproductive autonomy, challenged the theory that underpinned national and nongovernmental family planning programs, namely that rapid population growth presented the primary barrier to economic development and that reducing aggregate fertility rates would stimulate economic growth. This challenge was picked up by a new generation of demography graduate students in the United States, who began to critique their field's close association with the federal government and the population establishment. These realignments portended the end of the postwar population consensus, which exploded spectacularly at the 1974 World Population Conference in Bucharest.

A MANHATTAN PROJECT FOR POPULATION

Moore and Draper broke from the population consensus in the second half of the 1960s. One of the major tenets of the consensus had been that "strong political pressures [from within the United States] to effect population control in developing countries seems more likely to generate political opposition abroad than acceptance" and was "likely to boomerang against its own objective."[6] The Population Council and its allies had, all along, contended that family planning could defuse the threat posed by population growth, but that any more direct efforts to control population would arouse opposition. For Moore and Draper, however, the Population Council's family planning approach was not working quickly enough. Fertility surveys indicated that family planning services were being utilized primarily by older couples who had already achieved large families rather than younger couples who sought to plan small families. They revealed that couples worldwide continued to desire at least three children, which meant that empowering couples to have the number of children they wanted might slow population growth but would not halt it. In response, Moore and Draper demanded that the U.S. government take a stronger stance on global population control. In 1965 they established the Population Crisis Committee to put pressure on Congress to allocate more money to USAID's population program.[7]

Keeping with the theme of nuclear warfare initiated by his *Population Bomb*, Moore privately dubbed the Committee's public relations strategy the "Manhattan Project," though its official title was "Campaign to Check the Population Explosion."[8] The irony of the nickname appears to have eluded Moore. In contrast to his earlier approach, which had focused on population growth abroad as a threat to U.S. political and economic hegemony, the Manhattan Project aimed to bring "the population problem" home. Reasoning that "the average man is much more concerned with conditions he can see in this country than in far-away Asia,"[9] Moore developed a new set of explicitly Malthusian newspaper ads that blamed U.S. population growth for the poverty, urban strife, and pollution that had become major concerns of the Johnson administration after the 1964 election.[10]

Manhattan Project advertisements appeared at a moment when many Americans feared their country was coming apart. The Vietnam War had begun to seem unwinnable. Opinion regarding the war was rapidly dividing the United States and undermining the country's credibility worldwide. The failure of new civil rights legislation to measurably change the living conditions of African Americans engendered violent confrontations between citizens, law enforcement, and the National Guard across the nation's cities between 1965 and 1968. Industrial pollution was increasingly visible. The population of the United States had grown dramatically since the end of World War II, from about 140 million in 1945 to 200 million in 1968, an increase of about 1.5% per year.[11] Much of this growth had come from the baby boom and therefore corresponded to a more youthful age structure. The antiwar movement and the movements for civil and women's rights drew massive support from this younger generation, generating anxiety among older and more conservative Americans that recent population growth was producing the same kind of political instability in the United States that they feared it would produce in nonaligned countries.[12]

Moore's new advertising campaign began early in 1968 with a full-page spread in the *New York Times* showing a young man preparing to stab an elderly man. The text informed readers that "city slums—jam-packed with juveniles, thousands of them idle—breed discontent, drug addiction and chaos. And crime in the cities is not the only problem. We have air and water pollution in wide areas. And the quality of life in this great country of ours is deteriorating before our eyes with the rapid increase of people." Tying all of these issues to population, the ad concluded, "Is there an answer? Yes—birth control is one."[13] Another ad displayed a graph showing that crime had increased along an apparently exponential trajectory since 1960. The headline read, "This is the crime explosion." The sentence concluded under the graph, "and the population explosion is an underlying factor."[14] These ads and others like them offered up population growth as a simple explanation for crime, poverty, and pollution, eliding such factors as structural inequality, inadequate municipal services, and industrial practices that reduced employment and generated pollution.

Moore's associates also proposed ads that directly attributed poverty to large families, including one that showed a couple with eight children and the headline claiming, "We spend over $4 billion a year on welfare. Yet we spend only $24 million a year to get to the cause of the problem." This ad, shown in Figure 6.1, linked the older Malthusian trope attributing poverty to large families and the sexual indiscretion of the poor with the emerging trope of new welfare programs producing "dependency" among those they aimed to help and thereby multiplying the number of female-headed households that increasingly bore the brunt of social scientific explanations for poverty and social unrest.[15] Just the year before, Republican congressmen George H. W. Bush and Herman Schneebeli had introduced a family planning amendment to the Social Security Act that garnered bipartisan support as a way to defuse contentious partisan debates over welfare.[16]

Figure 6.1 Proposed advertisement for Hugh Moore and William Draper's Campaign to Check the Population Explosion.
Source: folder 25, box 16, Hugh Moore Fund Collection (MC153), Seeley G. Mudd Manuscript Library, Princeton University.

Moore and his associates took care to avoid publicly attributing the "population explosion" to nonwhite Americans. They aimed to avoid charges of racism by picturing only white people in their crime and poverty ads and by using such dog-whistle phrases as "inner cities" and "welfare" to signal race without actually naming it. Yet internal memoranda laid the blame for such problems not on population growth in general but on the supposedly indiscriminate reproduction of poor people and people of color. One memo claimed "this black population explosion is the cause of 99% of riots and crime. As long as our politicians condone multiple births to the illiterate and degenerate, our nation will suffer more and more before being destroyed from within, making it easy for the Russians and Red Chinese to take over without firing a shot."[17] Such rhetoric neatly tied domestic racism to the fear of global communist revolution that motivated Moore's efforts.

Manhattan Project ads focused public attention not only on crime and poverty but also on the natural environment, attributing the air and water pollution that were becoming a matter of growing concern for the U.S. public and U.S. government to the sheer number of people in the United States. A 1968 ad showed a man drinking a glass of water, with the headline "Warning: The water you are drinking may be polluted." The text below the image attributed pollution to the "population . . . rising so fast, water purification methods simply can't keep pace."[18] A proposed alternative headline for the same image, shown in Figure 6.2, read, "Every day we dump the waste products of 150 million people into our water. And then we drink it."[19] These ads elided industrial sources of pollution in the United States, presenting the problem as a direct consequence of the country's growing human numbers. Other ads situated environmental degradation within the larger complex of social issues troubling the United States at the end of the 1960s, making each of these issues inseparable from the others and attributing the whole tangle of knots to population growth. A 1969 ad asked readers, "How many people do you want in your country?"

> Let's take a look at conditions in our country as they exist today with our present population of 200 million Americans. Our waters—rivers, lakes and beaches—are polluted. We are literally deafened by noise, and poisoned by carbon monoxide from 100 million cars. Our city slums are packed with youngsters—thousands of them idle, victims of discontent and drug addiction. And millions more will pour into our streets in the next few years at the present rate of procreation. You go out after dark at your peril. Last year one out of every four hundred Americans was murdered, raped, or robbed.

But, the ad continued, "birth control is an answer."[20]

Over the next three years, Moore's advertising campaign received positive attention from the public and from policymakers, including officials in the Nixon administration, World Bank president and former secretary of defense Robert McNamara, and senators and representatives of both major parties.[21] Manhattan Project ads told readers that population growth "is your problem and *you can do something about it*. Tear out this

Figure 6.2 Proposed advertisement for Hugh Moore and William Draper's Campaign to Check the Population Explosion.
Source: folder 25, box 16, Hugh Moore Fund Collection (MC153), Seeley G. Mudd Manuscript Library, Princeton University.

ad and send it to anyone in Washington you think might be helpful. Urge the Government to initiate a *crash program* to deal with the population problem."[22] Moore never offered details about what this "crash program" might look like, but his advertisements implied that the family planning approach of the population establishment was not sufficient. In addition to the public pressure created by these ads, Moore and Draper put direct pressure on William Fulbright, chair of the Senate Foreign Relations Committee, who had engineered the 1967 passage of the Title X amendment to the Foreign Assistance Act earmarking funds for USAID's population program. Following the launch of Moore's Manhattan Project, these earmarks rose from $35 million in fiscal year 1968 to $121 million in fiscal year 1972. The overall USAID budget did not increase, so funding for overseas health care simultaneously fell from $131 million in fiscal year 1968 to just over $35 million in fiscal year 1972.[23]

Inspiration for Moore's new advertisements came from two popular Malthusian books published in 1967: *Famine 1975! America's Decision: Who Will Survive?* by brothers William and Paul Paddock and *Moment in the Sun: A Report on the Deteriorating Quality of the American Environment* by political scientists Robert Rienow and Leona Train Rienow.[24] The Paddocks, agronomist William and diplomat Paul, focused on the international arena, predicting that continuing population growth would produce serious famines in the upcoming decade. Food production in the United States, they warned, would not be sufficient to save all of the world's hungry people. The Paddocks therefore proposed a "triage" system, classifying the countries seeking food aid into three categories: those beyond saving, those that could get by without aid, and those that both needed and could be helped by U.S. efforts. Only those in the third category, they contended, should receive assistance, while those in the first should be allowed to perish.[25]

The Paddocks were just two among many Americans who were returning to Vogt's 1948 suggestion that "the population problem" in the Global South should be solved by raising mortality rates.[26] William Lindsay White, editor of the *Emporia Gazette* of Emporia, Kansas, recommended in private letters to Moore that "the United Nations . . . send out a task force to poison village wells" or that "the Ford Foundation . . . popularize cannibalism by distributing a book of recipes to be prepared by Julia Child."[27] The second suggestion is clearly a facetious reference to Jonathan Swift's "A Modest Proposal,"[28] but the first—poisoning village wells—was more or less serious. White predicted that "there would be some criticism of this," but wondered "what is the suggested alternative?"[29] A month later, he returned to the proposal, saying "it has only one merit, which is that it would probably work, and all of the alternatives of which I heard in my opinion certainly would not."[30] The question is, "work" for what end? The population consensus had presented family planning as a way to improve the well-being of people in developing countries. As Moore's ads began to convince Americans that population growth anywhere in the world posed a direct threat to them personally, the solution shifted to population control by any means necessary. Its targets became expendable, their well-being irrelevant.

The Rienows' book, *Moment in the Sun*, focused on the United States and its growing environmental concerns. One of Moore's associates described it as "the first attempt to bring all our various environmental crises together in one book and then to lay them squarely at the feet of their basic cause: The American obsession for uncontrolled, unthinking growth of the economy and the population."[31] The authors, however, placed much more emphasis on population growth than on unregulated economic growth as the primary cause of the environmental degradation that had become increasingly visible throughout the 1960s, precipitating the creation of the Environmental Protection Agency by President Nixon in 1970.

Although other scholars of the time acknowledged the role of policy and development in the growing environmental crisis, the Rienows did not. Their book neglected factors that scientists such as biologist Barry Commoner readily addressed. They never mentioned that sprawling suburbs and investment in the construction of highways rather than railroads meant more cars driving greater distances. Or that breaking ground for this construction released carbon into the atmosphere and exposed soil to erosion, leading to silt deposition in streams, rivers, and lakes. Or that agricultural specialization meant that feedlot operators had no crops on which to spread animal manure and crop producers could more cheaply fertilize their land with synthetic fertilizer, the production of which burned carbon and the application of which led to nitrogen runoff.[32] They instead blamed population growth.

The Malthusian tract that resonated most with the American public was *The Population Bomb*, published by Stanford University biologist Paul Ehrlich in 1968 at the behest of the Sierra Club. It sold over three million copies in its first decade.[33] *The Population Bomb* combined the domestic environmental concerns of the Rienows with the geopolitical concerns of the Paddocks. Ehrlich borrowed more than just the title from Moore. As Moore stated in a form letter that he enclosed when mailing Ehrlich's book to supporters, *The Population Bomb* "expresses my own view of the frightening prospects of the world population out of control." Moore pointed to Ehrlich's credentials to legitimate the claims he made in the book, informing readers that "Dr. Ehrlich is a scientist of repute, Professor of Biology at Stanford University, yet he states the case for population control as dramatically as any science-fiction writer could do."[34]

The Population Bomb was, in fact, largely a work of science fiction. It devoted considerable space to spinning out horrific and highly speculative futures, including global nuclear conflagration and massive famines. The only scenario that did not end in nuclear war involved the United States cutting off food aid to countries that were "beyond hope" (the Paddocks' triage plan), including India and Egypt, leading to massive "die back" and allowing for the formation of a world government with strict controls on population growth, agricultural development, and industrialization.[35] Such speculation clearly exceeded Ehrlich's expertise in butterfly biology. Few of his claims about the dangers of population growth were backed by empirical research. Nonetheless, within a year of its publication *The Population Bomb* became required reading in approximately two hundred college courses around the country.[36]

Ehrlich had first spoken publicly about environmental issues in January 1965, but turned his focus to population as the ultimate cause of environmental degradation, poverty, and other social issues only later that year, during a research trip to Asia. As had been the case for other scientists and population activists, Ehrlich was severely troubled by the poverty he encountered there. In *The Population Bomb*, he famously recounted his impressions during a taxi ride with his wife and daughter, describing the Delhi streets as "alive with people."

> People eating, people washing, people sleeping. People visiting, arguing, and screaming. People thrusting their hands through the taxi window, begging. People defecating and urinating. People clinging to buses. People herding animals. People, people, people, people. As we moved slowly through the mob, hand horn squawking, the dust, noise, heat, and cooking fires gave the scene a hellish aspect. Would we ever get to our hotel? All three of us were, frankly, frightened.[37]

In his fright, Ehrlich attributed the poverty that surrounded him to the poor people themselves: there were obviously too many of them. Population growth provided a convenient explanation for the poverty that confronted Ehrlich in India. That is, it offered a biological explanation with a technological solution.[38] The image of defecating and urinating in the streets evokes the wanton sexual behavior no doubt underlying this scene in Ehrlich's mind and indicates a fear that he and his family could be infected with India's poverty through the bodily waste of its inhabitants. It also hints at a fear that the poverty and desperation Ehrlich witnessed in India could spread to California if rapid population growth continued unabated. Ehrlich's description of overwhelming numbers of brown bodies suggests anxiety about immigration from poor countries to the United States, and particularly from Latin America and Asia to California, which had begun to increase in the wake of the 1965 Hart-Celler Immigration and Naturalization Act.[39]

Ehrlich also attributed the social, economic, and environmental ills of the United States to population growth. Despite his own history of anti-racist activism,[40] Ehrlich contended that overpopulation, not racism, was the cause of the country's recent urban uprisings. In contrast to the 1968 report of the Kerner Commission, which attributed urban unrest to segregation and discrimination, Ehrlich offered a biological analogy. He noted that "we know all too well that when rats or other animals are overcrowded, the results are pronounced and usually unpleasant. Social systems may break down, cannibalism may occur, breeding may cease altogether. The results do not bode well for human beings as they get more and more crowded."[41] Ehrlich's explanation dehumanized urban residents, elided a long history of residential segregation and discrimination in policing and the provision of public services, and neglected the fact that cities were expanding mainly through internal migration rather than reproduction, meaning that rural areas were losing population as metropolitan areas grew.[42]

Of the environment Ehrlich claimed that "the causal chain of deterioration is easily followed to its source. Too many cars, too many factories, too much detergent, too much pesticide, multiplying contrails, inadequate sewage treatment plants, too little water, too much carbon dioxide—all can be traced easily to *too many people*."[43] Draper evoked this powerful passage in his appeal to the Democratic Party to add population control to its 1968 presidential campaign platform, stating that "we have crowded schools, polluted air and water, traffic jams, unspeakable slums and large families living from one generation to another in poverty. The quality of life for many of our citizens is threatened by increasing population pressures."[44] But neither Draper nor Ehrlich actually traced the link between pollution or poverty and human numbers. Attempts to do so would have failed.[45] By leaving the connection unstated, however, they implied that the causal pathways from people to cars, factories, detergent, and pesticides, and to poverty, segregation, and urban violence, were obvious and unequivocal.

Ehrlich, like other Malthusians, recommended raising mortality rates as a way to reduce the world's population. Comparing population growth to the uncontrolled multiplication of cells characteristic of cancer, he argued that solving "the population problem" would require deaths from starvation or violence, which he compared to "the cutting out of the cancer."[46] In such passages, starvation and violence morphed from threats that could potentially be averted by population control into the very means of controlling population.

Ehrlich had begun to see population control as the solution to environmental degradation after his earlier efforts to regulate pesticide use in U.S. agriculture failed. His biological research had suggested that the dangers of agricultural pesticides, many of which were still unknown, far outweighed their benefits. On the basis of his scientific expertise, he had appealed to the U.S. Department of Agriculture for greater oversight of the use of pesticides, at least until their safety could be ensured.[47] When these efforts were foiled by the far greater lobbying capacities of the pesticide industry and its efforts to portray opponents as "communist sympathizers,"[48] he turned instead to population control. It was easier, he believed, to appeal to Americans to reduce their childbearing—and even to lobby the government for policies limiting family size—than to take on the pesticide industry. He reasoned that, with fewer people, there would be less agriculture and therefore less need for pesticides.[49] In changing his environmental strategy from industrial regulation to population control, Ehrlich implemented the anticonservationist logic presented by Vogt in *Road to Survival* and before him by Burch and Pendell in *Human Breeding and Survival*: controlling the childbearing of the poor, who lacked the political power to protest, rather than controlling the production and consumption of the wealthy, whose political voice was much louder. Ehrlich's exhortations to the American public elided the fact that, within the United States, pollution had far outpaced population growth in recent decades and, globally, the segments of the population that were growing the fastest were those that contributed the least to environmental degradation.[50]

ZERO POPULATION GROWTH

Publication of *The Population Bomb* immediately turned Ehrlich into a public figure. Over the next few years, he appeared on numerous television and radio talk shows promoting population control. By the end of 1968, he had helped found a new organization, Zero Population Growth (ZPG).[51] ZPG aimed to build a grassroots movement of young Americans dedicated to limiting their own reproduction and to bringing into power policymakers committed to limiting the reproduction of others. Although Ehrlich at times found himself in opposition to other ZPG leaders, he was the public face of the organization. ZPG's first newsletter in 1969 urged members to read *The Population Bomb* because "as our president, Paul's views, probably more so than anyone else's, can be considered those of ZPG."[52]

Ehrlich and ZPG's other leaders primarily presented the organization as an environmental one, calling for population control in the United States because "our air, water and soil are being polluted. The deterioration and despoliation of our environment is due to the demands placed upon it by increasing numbers of people."[53] Although ZPG also called for population control in Africa, Asia, and Latin America—and advocated more extreme measures there—it focused the majority of its attention on North America. ZPG's leaders viewed the environmental crisis in the United States as evidence that the country was "already overpopulated" and recognized that other countries would be loath to submit to population control programs initiated by the United States if the U.S. government were not also making efforts to control its own population.[54] A substantial proportion of the

U.S. public seemed receptive to this message. Like Moore's ads and books by Ehrlich, the Paddocks, and the Rienows, ZPG provided a single explanation for everything going wrong in the country and the world. Its message was relatively popular: a 1969 Gallup poll found that 54% of respondents believed U.S. population growth to be a serious problem and 44% believed that maintaining current living standards would eventually require population control.[55]

Viewing access to birth control, abortion, and employment opportunities for women as prerequisites for reducing population growth in the United States, ZPG allied with the feminist movement.[56] But while the grassroots of the organization generally supported reproductive autonomy, its leaders did not, contending that "voluntary family planning is not a population policy." The population of the United States was growing too rapidly, they believed, not because Americans lacked access to birth control but because they were "having the number of children they *want*."[57] ZPG briefly advocated removing income tax exemptions beyond the second child, a proposal that the population establishment classified as a legitimate means of manipulating the economic context within which childbearing decisions were made. Ehrlich, however, was sympathetic to critiques made by people of color and the poor that such measures selectively limited their childbearing while letting the wealthy continue to have large families. Ehrlich instead proposed legislation that would uniformly limit the number of children any American could bear, perhaps not realizing that even such nominally universal policies tend to have their greatest impact on the least powerful. He contended that "if we could find a way to enforce compulsory birth control it would be much more democratic than many of the other methods that are being proposed," as it would not allow parents who could afford more children to have them.[58] For the population establishment, however, telling people how many children they could have was the very definition of coercion. One member of ZPG's board who was also on the board of Planned Parenthood resigned from ZPG because its advocacy of compulsory family limitation conflicted with Planned Parenthood's voluntarist position.[59]

Although ZPG portrayed itself as an advocate for the environment, its ultimate aim was to eliminate the need for conservation measures, which ZPG literature described as "a reduction in personal freedoms."[60] ZPG's cofounder Richard Bowers stated in 1970 that the U.S. population, then numbering just over 203 million, must be reduced to 100 million because the world's natural resources were "not adequate to provide such items as a 9 room house (not to speak of a wilderness mountain retreat or a quest cottage by the sea), two cars, quality heating systems, a wide variety diet, elaborate wardrobe, etc. etc. which have been and are the hallmark of the successful person."[61] Far from critiquing such aspirations, Bowers called for the government to limit population growth in order to avoid the imposition of conservation measures that would prevent his attainment of these "hallmark[s] of the successful person." The organization's leaders saw environmental protection as a means to the end of population control rather than the other way around, as evident in their statement that "to the extent that we can protect the environment for future generations only at expense to the present generation in material standards, government controls and loss of freedom, or dependence upon foreign sources of supply, we will choose less environmental protection."[62] For ZPG, conservation of natural resources was not a legitimate means of protecting the world's environment, but rather a violation of individual liberty that needed to be prevented through population control.[63] Again taking a page from Burch and Pendell's *Human Breeding and Survival* and Vogt's *Road to Survival*, Bowers presented the freedom of the "successful" to pollute and consume as more valuable than the freedom of others to reproduce.

With slogans borrowed from Moore's Manhattan Project, including "how many millions more do YOU want in the United States?,"[64] ZPG aimed to recruit college and even high school students who had not yet started families and could therefore be persuaded to minimize their childbearing.[65] At $10 for a regular membership and only $4 for a student membership, the bar to entry was low.[66] ZPG aimed to capture the energy of the sexual revolution by selling earrings made from IUDs and Valentine's Day cards with red condoms enclosed.[67] The organization officially aligned itself with the antiwar movement in 1970, when it issued a press release condemning the Vietnam War as an "ecological catastrophe."[68] Membership grew by an average of one hundred people per day throughout the first half of 1970. By the end of that year, ZPG boasted over thirty thousand members in more than three hundred chapters.[69] The white middle-class students who flocked to those chapters were members of the baby boom generation. As children, they had taken the blame for housing scarcity and overcrowded schools and thus had little trouble believing that the world was overpopulated.[70] Population growth provided them with a simple and seemingly actionable explanation for the war in Vietnam and for poverty and racial conflict at home. To these students, having a vasectomy or getting an IUD seemed a tangible way to make a difference in the world.[71] Ehrlich himself publicized the fact that he had had a vasectomy after the birth of his only child, sometimes even wearing a button inviting people to "ask me about my vasectomy."[72]

But what was zero population growth? ZPG's leaders initially defined their goal as replacement-level fertility. That is, an NRR of one, which in a low-mortality society like the United States translated into a TFR of approximately 2.1, or a two-child average family. As a result of recent work in demography, ZPG's leaders understood that even the immediate achievement of replacement fertility would generate population growth for another seventy years or so as larger cohorts moved through the childbearing ages, a phenomenon known to demographers as population momentum. However, ZPG's executive director Shirley Radl emphasized the importance of giving people readily understandable information and feared that the details of demographic analysis would confuse the public and discourage action.[73] For that reason, ZPG's initial slogan was "Stop at two."[74] A 1970 statement of the organization's goals specified "zero population growth in the U.S. by 1980 and in the world by 1990," defining "zero population growth" as replacement fertility.[75] A survey of ZPG members demonstrated widespread public misunderstanding of demographic measures when it found that most respondents believed that the limitation of families to two children would immediately end population growth in the United States.[76]

Birth rates fell dramatically among younger Americans in the years following 1968, reflecting trends toward later marriage, the increasing availability of birth control, and new educational and occupational opportunities for women. Although population was still growing in the aggregate, newspapers in major cities around the country announced that, as a result of this fertility decline, the United States had fallen below zero population growth, following ZPG's lead in defining "zero population growth" as replacement fertility.[77]

As the birth rate fell in the United States, so too did membership in ZPG, dwindling from its 1970 high of thirty-two thousand to twenty-one thousand at the end of 1972. This decline may also have been driven by the growing realization among members that even the immediate cessation of population growth would likely not reverse the trend of environmental degradation and depletion of nonrenewable resources, which had outpaced population growth in recent decades.[78] Members may have begun to suspect that many of the organization's claims were simply untrue. For example, data from the UN Food and Agriculture Organization, publicized in 1971 by Australian agricultural economist Colin Clark, demonstrated that food production in the developing world was, in fact, keeping pace with population growth.[79]

Projecting that membership would continue to decline, ZPG's board of directors feared that the organization would not have the funds to sustain its programs beyond 1974. To try to revive public interest, ZPG's leaders took credit for the recent decline in the U.S. birth rate, and also changed their definition of "zero population growth" from replacement-level fertility to population stationarity, a balance of births and deaths. Membership recruitment letters announced that the success of the organization's work "has led to the mistaken but widely held notion that U.S. population has stopped growing and that growth is no longer a problem."[80] To combat this popular belief, ZPG tried to educate the public about population momentum. In 1974, when newspaper headlines announced that the total fertility rate in the United States had reached 1.9, ZPG instructed members to send letters to editors with the following text:

> In the article " " (date), you state that parents "are having 1.9 children, fewer than is needed to replace themselves; thus we have reached the era of zero population growth." I would like to point out that even if the present U.S. birth rate holds steady, we will not reach zpg for about 70 years. Children of the post-war baby boom are now entering their prime childbearing years, creating a potential parent boom. Their fertility patterns will determine to a large extent when—if ever—we reach zpg.[81]

As fertility declined further in the 1970s, the organization turned its attention to immigration, pointing out that, even at replacement fertility, immigration would continue to swell the U.S. population. Moreover, since the passage of the 1965 Hart-Celler Act, which abolished immigration quotas in the United States, the bulk of immigration was coming from Asia and Latin America, where fertility rates were higher than in the United States. ZPG's leaders warned that such immigration would increase the U.S. population beyond the number of migrants, contending that "it is likely that immigrants will bring their customary fertility patterns with them."[82] Despite Ehrlich's claims that ZPG's policy recommendations were not intended to be discriminatory—he emphasized that the organization promoted birth limitation and immigration restriction across the board—ZPG became increasingly associated in the public mind with racism and exclusion.[83]

Moore's Manhattan Project, Ehrlich's *Population Bomb*, and ZPG's publicity activities firmly linked social upheaval and environmental degradation to population growth in the American popular imaginary. Together they presented a coherent narrative in which population growth provided a powerfully simple explanation not only for poverty and strife in Africa, Asia, and Latin America but also for poverty, crime, pollution, and resource depletion in the United States. It attributed the traffic, smog, racial discrimination, political polarization, and suburban sprawl that were coming to characterize the United States to population growth not just among the poor and nonwhite but also among wealthy consumers. This narrative attracted support from both ends of the increasingly divided political spectrum, with the right wing seeing in population control a solution to growing government expenditures on welfare, municipal services, and policing, as well as a justification to limit immigration, and the left wing seeing in population control an answer to poverty, warfare, urban strife, and environmental degradation.

Kingsley Davis, then teaching at UC Berkeley, allied with Ehrlich and served on the board of ZPG. His support provided a modicum of demographic legitimacy to ZPG, Ehrlich's *Population Bomb*, and Moore's Manhattan Project, but these projects hardly needed it. Instead they could call on the authority of the natural sciences, as represented by Ehrlich and physicist John Holdren, who coauthored a weekly column with Ehrlich in the *Saturday Review*.[84] In the public mind, these men's scientific credentials authorized them to speak on anything related to the natural world, no matter how far from their own research specialties. But other scientists criticized them for exaggerating the rapidity of population growth and the gravity of its consequences, and accused them of overstepping the limits of their scientific expertise.[85] John Lear, science editor at the *Saturday Review*, received numerous complaints from well-known scientists that Ehrlich and Holdren misled readers and deliberately tried to "scare people into believing they face only one set of alternatives when in fact the true alternatives are several." Lear wrote to Ehrlich in 1971:

> I beg you not to assume that, simply because you have not seen it, serious criticism of your columns has not been received here. I cannot go into much detail because most of it has been on a private level in telephone calls and personal conversations with scientists I have known for many years. The critics include major scientific figures at one end of the spectrum and, at the other, students of yours who so far as I know have been devoted to you in the past. You are right in supposing that I am not concerned about criticism per se. I worry about it only where I feel there is some justification for it.[86]

The fact that Lear was bringing these critiques to Ehrlich's attention suggests he did feel them to be justified, but if Ehrlich wasn't aware of this scientific opposition, the American public was likely not aware of it either.

DEMOGRAPHY IN OPPOSITION

With the exception of Davis, most American demographers were dismayed by *The Population Bomb* and made no bones about their distaste for Ehrlich's approach to population control. Not only was his Malthusian version of "the population problem" contrary to the findings of demographic science, but his proposed solution crossed the line demographers had drawn between legitimate and coercive means of population control. Demographers feared that the publicity Ehrlich garnered, as well as that generated by Moore's Manhattan Project, could threaten the progress they believed the Population Council was making in slowing population growth through family planning.

Nearly as soon as Ehrlich published *The Population Bomb* and began calling for explicit population limitation policies in the United States (as opposed to policies to provide family planning services to the poor), demographers began speaking against him and against his proposed policies, though mainly among themselves. Ansley Coale devoted his presidential address at the 1968 PAA meeting to arguing against "a campaign for fewer births" in the United States, pointing out that, even if the U.S. population reached one billion, the country would still be populated at a lower density than much of Europe.[87] Implicitly citing Moore's newspaper ads and Ehrlich's *Population Bomb*, Coale decried the fact that "it has become fashionable to explain almost every national failure or shortcoming by rapid population growth."[88] He inverted Ehrlich's and Moore's attribution of urban poverty and strife to high fertility, instead contending that "fertility in the urban ghettos will fall if discrimination is alleviated, if educational and employment opportunities are equalized."[89] With regard to the environment, Coale refuted the equation of rising population with worsening pollution, pointing out that "a population one-half or three-quarters the size of the current one in the United States could [still] ruin the potability of our fresh water supplies and poison our atmosphere by discharge of waste."[90] The only appropriate remedy, according to Coale, was direct regulation of industrial emissions. Notestein seconded this argument at the 1970 PAA meeting, where he contended that the focus on stopping population growth as the primary solution to the problem of environmental degradation was "a distraction from an immediate attack on pollution" by more direct means.[91]

In a panel on zero population growth at the 1970 PAA meeting, Philip Hauser criticized the ZPG movement for presenting "the problems of environmental pollution and the population explosion . . . as a smoke screen to obscure other problems that should have priority, including the problems of the slums, racism, and the 'urban crisis' in general."[92] Hauser and other demographers attributed these problems not to population growth in the aggregate but to the geographical unevenness of population density that had resulted from internal migration. Demographers who participated in President Nixon's 1970–1972 Commission on Population Growth and the American Future, chaired by John D. Rockefeller III, found that, since the end of World War II, large numbers of young rural Americans had moved into the outskirts of growing metropolitan regions, where they were joined by members of the white middle class fleeing central cities. Migration from urban cores and rural peripheries swelled populations in the new suburbs, drawing businesses away from cities, increasing the average distance workers had to travel between jobs and homes, draining rural areas of their most dynamic and productive residents, and leaving those who could not move out of cities—particularly African Americans who were largely barred from homeownership in the growing suburbs by restrictive real estate covenants—without jobs or adequate public services.[93] In January 1971 Conrad Taeuber, Census Bureau demographer and supervisor of the 1970 Census, announced in a speech that "economic and social factors are more important than population growth in threatening the quality of American life."[94]

Demographers' opposition to the Malthusianism of Moore, Davis, and Ehrlich was open enough that, when asked in 1970 to review a book by Ehrlich and his wife, Anne, titled *Population, Resources, and Environment*, Notestein declined, explaining, "I've been saying such nasty things about Ehrlich and doing so publicly, my friends would never believe I could give him an honest break."[95] In an internal Population Council memorandum, Bernard Berelson described ZPG as "a cult paying lip service to ecology but rather lightly based in science and deeply rooted in emotion,"[96] echoing interwar critiques of intra-European racism. Notestein's and Berelson's feelings toward Ehrlich were no secret. Ehrlich knew as early as 1969 that "the Population Council (or at least its biggest wheels) hates my guts, those of Kingsley Davis, Garrett Hardin, and indeed anyone else who has taken an approach to population control except their 'go slow and use family planning' one."[97]

Ehrlich's statement points to the fundamental difference between the population establishment and the population bombers (Ehrlich, Moore, and Davis). For the population establishment, population growth in non-aligned countries was detrimental to the well-being of people in those countries and a threat to global political stability and American economic hegemony. Their goal was to slow population growth enough to defuse that threat without triggering political upheaval through their efforts. Family planning was the only safe way to do this, they believed, and any dent in population growth produced by family planning was better than nothing. For the population bombers, population growth anywhere in the world posed an existential threat to middle-class white Americans that far outweighed the dangers of political upheaval that might result from efforts to halt it.

The publicity the population bombers generated for their version of "the population problem" dealt a major blow to the postwar population consensus in the United States. Ehrlich's book was much more widely read than anything written by a member of the population establishment. Moore succeeded in getting his views into the public consciousness through newspaper ads and onto the agendas of policymakers through direct lobbying. The population establishment, on the other hand, did not have its own grassroots movement comparable to ZPG. As a result, U.S. public opinion on population was largely severed from demographic thought by the end of the 1960s. Demography and the organizations that supported it wielded much less influence over popular ideas and public policy in the 1970s than they had done in the previous decade.

Another challenge to the postwar population consensus came from demography itself and from intellectuals in countries receiving family planning assistance at the beginning of the 1970s. Whereas the population bombers rejected family planning as a means to the end of population control, a new generation of demography graduate students—inspired by critiques of modernization theory coming from Latin America—rejected population control of any kind as a means to the ends of alleviating global poverty, stimulating economic development, and protecting the natural environment.

Demography's internal critique emerged from what those involved would later describe as "a free-swinging rap session" at the 1969 PAA meeting among demography graduate students about the state of their field and its role in the world.[98] They were concerned that the private foundations that supported demography exercised too much control over its research agenda, and that the senior members of their field had become "uninformed propagandists in world-wide family planning programs"[99] in exchange for "very high salaries, consulting fees and prestige."[100] As a result of the public anxiety that the Population Crisis Committee and other organizations had created surrounding population growth, the U.S. government had recently begun to fund research and training in demography through the National Institute of Child Health and Human Development. Over the remainder of the twentieth century and into the twenty-first, this funding supported demographic research in the United States that was aimed more at improving health than reducing fertility, giving demographers alternatives to private foundations and ultimately helping them broaden the remit of their field. In 1969, however, the students who met at PAA wondered "whether an academic discipline which largely depended on handouts from the federal government could remain aloof from the effects of the genocidal war abroad and the increasing signs of repression at home."[101]

Some of the most senior and well-respected demographers of the time dismissed the students as spoiled children. Notestein, who had just retired as president of the Population Council, called them a disgrace to the profession.[102] Others were more encouraging. Columbia University demographer Abram Jaffe—who had previously worked at the U.S. Census Bureau as a liaison between the Bureau, the Department of State, and the UN Population Commission—sent a letter to the group letting them know "you are on the right track."[103] Otis Dudley Duncan, then president of the PAA, challenged the student dissidents to either leave the organization or work through formal channels to change it.[104] Over the next year those who took part in the 1969 discussion and others they recruited—including graduate students from Brown, Cornell, Temple, and the universities of Massachusetts, Michigan, and Wisconsin—formed a group known as the Concerned Demographers, which accepted Duncan's challenge and worked within the PAA to effect change. They organized a panel at the 1970 PAA meeting on the influence of public and private funding agencies on demographic research and lobbied for voting rights for student members.

Students from the University of Wisconsin initially took the lead, publishing the first five issues of the group's quarterly newsletter, *Concerned Demography*. A different student was listed as editor in each issue. The permanent executive editor, Ezekiel Cummings, better known to Wisconsin students as "Zeke," probably did not do much actual editing, as it would have been difficult to wield a blue pencil with his canine paws.[105] The University of Wisconsin's population center was a bit of an outlier: it received little support from the Ford Foundation and its research program focused on the United States. When the National Institute of Child Health and Human Development began funding population centers, Wisconsin's received one of its first grants, allowing director Norman Ryder to hire a crop of young faculty members who had recently completed their Ph.D.s at the University of Michigan.[106] These demographers had little interest in reducing fertility overseas. Their research focused instead on the United States and on determinants of fertility, changing family structure, racial segregation, socioeconomic inequality, and social mobility. One of their graduate mentors, Beverly Duncan, had become editor of *Demography* in

1968 and had shifted the journal's focus from international family planning to research on domestic social issues.[107]

Although this new generation of demographers and their students did not engage in the type of scholarship promoted by the Ford Foundation and the Population Council, they were nonetheless products of those organizations and of the population consensus they had created. The postwar population consensus attracted enormous sums of money toward organizations that promised to solve "the population problem," including university-based population research centers. Demography's patrons had oriented the research of those centers toward international fertility, but they imposed few restrictions on how their money could be spent. Since they donated more money than could possibly be absorbed by international fertility research or the training of international students, their grants also funded the training of American students and research in other areas of demography. As Ron Freedman, founder of the University of Michigan's Population Studies Center, put it in 1970, "qualified investigators can almost always get support for demographic research, irrespective of their political or scientific ideology" because "there is an acute shortage of minimally reasonable applications for the available funds."[108] Population centers and their patrons therefore helped demography grow well beyond its initial niche, contributing to the emergence of new subfields that were far removed from international population control.

The University of Wisconsin was a major locus of antiwar protest in the late 1960s and early 1970s. The Concerned Demographers described it as "a hotbed of radical thought," though this characterization may have been somewhat tongue-in-cheek.[109] Protests there focused on the co-optation of academic research by the U.S. government for military purposes. Faculty members would later recall being tear-gassed and seeing soldiers "marching around [campus] with fixed bayonets against the protesters."[110] The Concerned Demographers described themselves as "women and men of the left who believe in the development of a more egalitarian and democratic social structure at home and the encouragement of social revolution and economic development abroad."[111] Their name signaled alignment with the Union of Concerned Scientists, an organization founded in 1968 by faculty members and graduate students at MIT to advocate for peaceful rather than military applications of science by the U.S. government.[112] Its establishment indicates a growing sense among U.S.-based scientists that the U.S. government, which had become the world's largest funder of scientific research, could not be trusted to use scientific knowledge to improve the human condition. In the humanities and social sciences, the late 1960s saw calls for a radicalization of traditional disciplines, including attention to issues of race, gender, class, imperialism, and capitalism, and experimentation with alternatives to standard methods.

The Concerned Demographers critiqued demography's framing of family planning as a panacea for all of the world's problems and objected to its focus on individual factors as drivers of both fertility and poverty. They urged demographers to think structurally, about economic, social, and political institutions rather than individual behavior, in order to understand demographic patterns.[113] Like the older generation of demographers, the Concerned Demographers acknowledged the revolutionary potential of population growth. Unlike establishment demographers, they did not call for a slowing of growth to preserve the existing order, which they described as "a system of exploitation and inequality." Rather, they pointed out hopefully that population "growth reveals the inadequacies of an inflexible system and sharpens them. All the while it provides a weapon to the exploited by increasing their numbers."[114]

The Concerned Demographers advocated for global social justice within the practice of demography and for greater openness and democracy in demographers' own institutions. They called for the active recruitment of African American graduate students to population research centers[115] and proposed a resolution that the PAA condemn security tests of the type that had led to Hope Eldridge's dismissal from the UN Food and Agriculture Organization in 1952.[116] The Concerned Demographers critiqued demography's equation of family planning with women's rights and called out gender discrimination within demography, "where women are permitted to be clerical assistants but rarely are seen in the classroom."[117] The Concerned Demographers may not have realized it, but there were actually more opportunities for women in demography than in many other social and natural sciences at the time. Large-scale research projects created jobs for nonfaculty scientists, and there were also opportunities in government, where gender discrimination in research positions was less intense than in academia. Demography seems to have been particularly welcoming for women with undergraduate degrees in mathematics or statistics, and more female than male demographers seem to have had backgrounds in these fields.[118] But the Concerned Demographers were correct in that female demographers were largely barred from training future generations of researchers or from overseeing the research that influenced population policy—often policy that disproportionately affected women—worldwide. Perhaps inspired by the Concerned Demographers, women of the PAA established their own caucus in 1970.[119]

The Concerned Demographers wielded humor to critique their field. A satirical article offered advice to graduate students on how to approach the various types of demography "star" they would meet at the 1970 PAA meeting. It termed the family planning crowd "A.I.D. [Agency for International Development (USAID)] boys" and described their motto as "Give a poor family an I.U.D. and tomorrow they will be as wealthy as the Rockefellers." The article recommended that graduate students ingratiate themselves among this crowd by "wearing an I.U.D. on a chain around your neck" and saying "that you know of a family planning program that reduced a population growth rate." Because such experience was, in fact, so rare, the Concerned Demographers predicted:

> You will be immediately surrounded and bombarded with questions. . . . Perhaps a job advising a military dictatorship on population will be awaiting you. Another good conversation piece is the suggestion that you have a new model showing that one I.U.D. leads to more economic development than one tractor. Also, point out how your model shows how the production of I.U.D.'s in itself is a stimulant to economic development as long as the plants are operated by private enterprise.[120]

The Concerned Demographers were no kinder to the other types of demographic "star" they described. In general, they heaped equal criticism on the population establishment and the population bombers, accusing both factions of inaccurately attributing all of the world's problems to population growth and promoting population control as a means of maintaining the geopolitical hegemony of the United States and the global economic hegemony of U.S. businesses.

By 1975 *Concerned Demography* had ceased publication. It is unclear exactly what happened to the group, but it appears that most of its leaders finished their Ph.D. programs and landed faculty positions, becoming part of the establishment.[121] Concerned Demographer Avery ("Pete") Guest went on to edit *Demography*—the field's flagship journal—from 1991 to 1993 and Concerned Demographer Charlie Hirschman served as PAA president in 2005, though both men retained a reflexive orientation toward demography.[122]

Although it had a short print run, *Concerned Demography* called attention to demography's political allegiances and the effect of those allegiances on research, demanding that demographers account for their power in the world. Their work forced Notestein to reclaim the critique of imperialism he had made in the early 1940s.[123] The Concerned Demographers who integrated themselves into the mainstream of the demographic profession did not sell out. Their research continued to focus on structural inequality within the United States. Along with their mentors and students, they contributed to a broadening of demography's concerns well beyond fertility in the Global South. As they joined the population establishment, they also changed it from the inside.

The Concerned Demographers' assessment of demography and population control was, in large part, inspired by the work of Latin American demographers and economists, many of whom were affiliated with CELADE, the UN population research and training center in Chile, and CEBRAP, the Brazilian Center for Analysis and Planning in São Paulo. These scholars developed a critique of the Coale-Hoover model of population growth and economic development that was analogous to dependency theory's critique of modernization theory, arguing that citizens of agricultural countries were poor not because they had too many children but because the global economy was structured to their detriment. Latin American social scientists maintained that the mechanism linking fertility to economic growth in the Coale-Hoover model, the investment of household savings in capital accumulation, was not relevant to Latin America, where most households did not have enough income to save, regardless of how few children they had. Moreover, by focusing on per capita national income as its outcome, the Coale-Hoover model failed to account for extreme inequality in the distribution of income within countries.

Angel Fucaraccio of CELADE contended that the Coale-Hoover model was itself a tool to repress dissent among the poor, who were "the potential executioners of the current system." The swelling of their ranks posed a threat to the existing order, he maintained, because "the greater their number and the greater their share of the total population, the greater is their power, *ceteris paribus*,"[124] a point that the Concerned Demographers would reiterate. Argentinian demographer Susana Torrado de Ipola, who had earned her Ph.D. in Paris under the supervision of then-director of the UN Population Division Léon Tabah, extended this argument to the international arena. She contended that "the U.S. government does not *use* so much as it crudely manipulates those theories that postulate a decline in fertility as a prerequisite of economic and social development." The American approach to global poverty, she maintained, was not to change the conditions causing it, but rather "to prevent the absolute growth of the exploited groups," who posed a threat to the established geopolitical order.[125] Leftists in Honduras viewed family planning "as an imperialist maneuver backed by the United States with the purpose of maintaining the status quo" and supported population growth as a "contribut[ion] to the necessary conditions for revolution."[126]

In a 1974 report to the Ford Foundation, former Population Council fellow and founding director of CELADE Carmen Miró reported that "in the case of Latin America, the demographic phenomena considered by many as the most problematic . . . appear as having their main causes in the historical process which led to the formation of capitalistic dependent societies characterized by a growing internal heterogeneity."[127] She contended that Latin American countries were poor not because of their high fertility but rather were poor and had high fertility because "the differential manner of insertion of these societies into the world economy determined initially the formation in most countries of national economies dependent on exports of agricultural products, cattle, mineral products or other raw materials." This diagnosis sounded very similar to the one Notestein and Davis had abandoned in the second half of the 1940s.

UN delegates from countries in Africa, Asia, and Latin America voiced these critiques during the UN's second Development Decade, the 1970s. At the UN Conference on the Human Environment, held in Stockholm in June 1972,[128] Ambassador Miguel A. Ozorio de Almeida, head of Brazil's delegation, turned the tables on U.S.-led population control efforts, recommending that industrial countries be asked to "reduce their own demographic numbers and, if necessary, their industrial 'predation' upon nature so as to reduce their claim upon the natural resources of underdeveloped countries."[129] In the Environment Forum, a parallel conference of nongovernmental organizations, University of Colorado professor Kariba Munio, originally from Kenya, blamed pollution on capitalism and referred to population control as "nothing short of genocide."[130] Ehrlich's calls for zero population growth were "shouted down as 'nonsense' and 'genocide,'" and his microphone was turned off during a panel discussion.[131] He later complained that population had been "kicked under the rug" when it should have been "at the top of the issues" discussed at the conference.[132] Given the explosive nature of population talk at the 1972 conference, UN Secretary-General Kurt Waldheim proposed that the issue be tabled until the 1974 UN World Population Conference. However, instead of restoring and building on the population consensus established in the 1960s, the World Population Conference marked its demise.

BUCHAREST, 1974

The 1974 World Population Conference was the centerpiece of the UN's World Population Year. Its focus was the adoption of a World Population Plan of Action that would specify quantitative population control targets for all countries of the world. Although World Population Year, the World Population Conference, and the World Population Plan of Action were sponsored by the United Nations, the impetus for them came from the U.S. Department of State. In 1969 President Nixon appointed Draper U.S. representative to the UN Population Commission. Draper was the first nondemographer to hold this position; his appointment signaled that the U.S. government had turned from the population establishment to the population bombers for guidance on international population issues.[133] Deputy Assistant Secretary of State for Congressional Relations Philander Priestly Claxton Jr. was reassigned to a new position, special assistant to the secretary of state for population matters. He joined Moore and Draper's Population Crisis Committee, which Draper continued to head after Moore's death in 1972. It was Draper and Claxton who pushed the UN to designate 1974 as World Population Year.[134]

The 1974 World Population Conference was technically the third in a series, but the first and second, held in Rome in 1954 and Belgrade in 1965, had been scientific conferences focused on population accounting and projection. Draper and Claxton proposed that the 1974 conference, to be held in Bucharest, instead be organized as "a serious meeting of political leaders prepared to adopt targets or goals for reduced birth or population growth rates," which would be formalized in the World Population Plan of Action.[135] The Plan was drafted ahead of the meeting by the UN Population Commission with considerable input from the U.S. Department of State and from American demographers, particularly those aligned with the Population Council.[136] At the meeting it became the primary site of confrontation between the population bombers, represented by the U.S. Department of State; the population establishment, represented by American demographers and the Population Council; and the rest of the world.

In preparation for the conference, Draper and Claxton urged the State Department to designate population growth in other countries a matter of U.S. national security.[137] Claxton warned that "current unprecedented rapid population growth will lead to violence and conflicts in or among over-populated, poor countries which could involve the US and the USSR despite our desire to avoid it."[138] To avert this outcome, he and Draper pushed for the inclusion of quantitative fertility targets in the World Population Plan of Action. Recognizing that such targets would encounter resistance, Claxton recommended that Secretary of State Henry Kissinger use the time leading up to the conference for "quiet negotiations to obtain agreement from enough governments on the basic elements of the Plan of Action" to assure the formal adoption of a suitable version, preferably one that specified replacement fertility worldwide by the year 2000.[139]

Prior to the conference, the strongest resistance to quantitative fertility targets came not from other countries but from the Population Council and demographers aligned with the population establishment. Berelson, who had become president of the Population Council in 1968, warned Claxton that "a political 'backlash' has emerged in the past few years that needs to be taken seriously," and cautioned that "further 'pushing' by the United States on population issues or perceived 'pushing' may be seriously counterproductive."[140] For the population establishment, quantitative targets, whether imposed by the UN on member states or by governments on their citizens, were on the wrong side of the boundary between legitimate and coercive means of population control.

Although the Population Council classified as coercive directives from governments regarding how many children people could bear, it classified as legitimate government manipulation of the social and economic conditions under which people made childbearing decisions. Following this rubric, they passed no judgment on Romania's recent ban on birth control and abortion, which has been described by others as "one of the most repressive pronatalist policies known to the world."[141] On the eve of the 1974 conference, Population Council demographic director Paul Demeny deemed Romania's policy simply an effort "to modify individual behavior and make it conform to the perceived public interest" by altering the environment in which reproductive behavior occurred.[142] Outlawing birth control and abortion did not force people to have more children, he reasoned; it simply raised the cost of having fewer children. To reduce fertility in an analogous manner, Coale fantasized about an antifertility agent that could be added to public water supplies, with an antidote readily available at a government-controlled price.[143] By contrast, China's one-child policy, which would be adopted in 1979, was deemed coercive because it legislated the number of children each couple could have.

The Population Council's narrow definition of coercion also limited its definition of reproductive freedom. It advocated that couples be free to make their own decisions about childbearing *only under conditions engineered to produce aggregate birth rates deemed acceptable by scientists and governments*. The Council supported individual choice in the realm of childbearing but reserved for governments the right to set the conditions under which those choices were made, eliding the coercive effects of economic incentives and legal penalties. Its approval of Romania's population policy clarified the distinction between family planning and birth control. The UN resolution on population had designated *family planning* a human right, but the Population Council's definition of family planning included access to *birth control* only when birth rates were deemed too high. The

Population Council therefore did not oppose government programs to manipulate birth rates; it simply opposed explicit statements of target birth rates and efforts to achieve those targets by legislating the number of children people could have. Parents had to be allowed to determine the size of their families, but governments could decide which tools parents could use to achieve their childbearing goals.

The conflict between the Population Council and the Department of State prior to the conference over how best to reduce fertility in Africa, Asia, and Latin America paled in comparison to the resistance both sides faced from representatives of target countries at the conference itself, where 1,250 delegates, representing all UN member states, negotiated the terms of the World Population Plan of Action for nine days and nights.

The world had changed considerably over the preceding thirty years, and so had the UN. As new countries formed after the breakup of European empires, UN membership swelled, ballooning from 55 states in 1945 to 135 at the time of the conference. Most of these new member states were nonaligned countries of primary production with mostly nonwhite populations. By 1973, 132 countries (member and nonmember) and other administrative entities had adopted policies aimed at reducing the pace of population growth. Another 31 officially supported family planning programs for other reasons. On a global level, approximately $750 million was being spent annually on population control, with about one-third coming from international agencies, nongovernmental organizations, and the governments of industrial countries, and the rest from governments of high-fertility countries, suggesting that heads of state throughout the Global South had bought into the modernizationist population paradigm.[144]

Family planning, however, had not delivered on its promises. Over the previous twenty years, GNP had grown dramatically in many countries, those with high fertility as well as those with low fertility, suggesting that family planning had not been a prerequisite for development. But GNP had grown faster in industrial countries than in agricultural countries—regardless of birth rate—because commodity prices had fallen relative to the price of manufactured products. The gap between rich and poor countries had widened, despite economic growth. Within poorer countries, continued social inequality meant that the fruits of economic growth were not shared evenly and living conditions for most people remained poor, regardless of family size.[145]

In Bucharest, the U.S. State Department and the Population Council encountered multivocal resistance from much of the rest of the world. Claxton described the opposition as "a concerted, five pronged attack by Algeria, supported by a few African countries; Argentina, supported by three or four Latin American countries; an Eastern European group of eight socialist countries; the People's Republic of China, and the Holy See."[146] The diversity of the opposition indicates the difficulty of mapping population thought either along the lines of the First, Second, and Third Worlds or according to the UN's more developed/less developed binary. The common thread linking many of the anti-population control factions was support for the New International Economic Order, which had emerged from the UN Conference on Trade and Development, attributing the growing socioeconomic divide between the Global North and the Global South to control over commodity markets by consumers rather than producers, and demanding "economic sovereignty" for postcolonial states.[147] It advanced a social, political, and economic explanation for poverty and inequality, and a set of solutions that challenged the biological explanation of population growth and the technological solution of population control.

The U.S. delegation to Bucharest firmly opposed the New International Economic Order and worked hard to keep mention of it to a minimum in the World Population Plan of Action, which was finally passed by acclamation at the end of the conference following forty-seven unsuccessful votes.[148] The final version of the Plan contained no quantitative targets for fertility or overall population growth. It only called on UN member states "to help co-ordinate population trends and the trends of economic and social development," an ambiguous statement that could have signified either planning *for* population or planning *of* population.[149] The Plan proposed "universal solidarity in order to improve the quality of life of the peoples of the world," a suggestion that could have been interpreted very differently by the countries requesting solidarity and by those being implored to offer it.[150] Although the Plan explicitly mentioned the New International Economic Order only three times, it never attributed global poverty to population growth. Instead it acknowledged that "the present situation of the developing countries originates in the unequal process of socio-economic development which has divided peoples since the beginning of the modern era . . . and is intensified by the lack of equity in international economic relations with the consequent disparity in levels of living." Ameliorating this situation required "a more equitable distribution of wealth" on a global scale.[151]

The U.S. Department of State declared the meeting a success because a World Population Plan of Action had been adopted, even if it was not the plan Claxton and Draper had hoped for.[152] To Claxton and Draper's consternation, however, and in spite of numerous press briefings by the U.S. delegation throughout the conference, the American media continually described the meeting as a failure.[153] Demographers affiliated with the Population Council concurred with the press; they described the conference as having been "captured," both procedurally and ideologically, by "the Third World."[154] Though they acknowledged that the Plan of Action contained some sound points, they complained that these points had "to be diligently extracted from even more fruity double talk clichés, special pleading, allocations of blame, flat misstatements of fact, and other assorted forms of nonsense."[155] In a memo marked "not for publication," Notestein joked that "if the B.S. as distributed in that conference could be utilized as fertilizer, the world would have no food problems."[156]

American demographers resented that representatives of nonaligned countries had steered the conference from population to economics. One report described the meeting as "an ideological confrontation over the structure of the international economic order, with population issues pushed into the background,"[157] echoing Ehrlich's account of the 1972 Conference on the Human Environment. Demeny compared it to "a conference on, say, railroad transportation where most speakers insist on discussing general disarmament."[158] By then, demographers had spent nearly twenty years immersed in figuring out how to reduce fertility. They seem to have forgotten that the original rationale for reducing fertility was to stimulate economic development. Instead population control had become an end in itself, just as it had for the population bombers, though the two factions disagreed about the most appropriate way to effect it.

Notestein was particularly disappointed by John D. Rockefeller III's speech at the Population Tribune, a meeting of scientific and nongovernmental organizations held in parallel to the World Population Conference. In his speech, Rockefeller publicly renounced the population consensus, stating that rapid population growth was "a multiplier and intensifier" of the problems facing developing countries, not their cause. He admitted that, when he established the Population Council in 1952, family planning had seemed the easiest route to alleviating poverty in the Global South, and he conceded that the approach had not worked. He therefore called for a "deep and probing reappraisal of all that has been done in the population field . . . so that the years ahead may yield the results mankind so desperately wants." Rockefeller had realized that development planning "must be indigenous—created by the country and executed on the basis of its own initiative and wisdom." This had been the Population Council's official position from the beginning, but Rockefeller's statement of it in Bucharest as if it were a new idea indicates his acknowledgment that the Council had previously manipulated local knowledge in target countries by promoting demography training and research, rather than deferring to already existing expertise. To alleviate social inequality, Rockefeller requested "much greater attention than in the past to more equitable distribution of the fruits of progress throughout all levels of society." He extended the same principle to the natural environment. Instead of calling on high-fertility countries to reduce their birth rates as a means of achieving global balance between population and resources, he asked those in high-income countries to "substantially cut their own diets" and "moderate their levels of consumption."[159]

Population Council staff had not received advance copies of the speech and were aghast when they heard it. Council trustee W. David Hopper fielded a frantic phone call from Bucharest, imploring him to stop Rockefeller from making such comments.[160] In a private note to Berelson, Notestein interpreted Rockefeller's speech to mean that "he's given up on birth control." Notestein speculated that "the right-to-lifers and the priests and the communists are all greatly pleased" because "obviously he's joined their side." Notestein's reading differed from that of delegates from nonaligned countries, who decried Rockefeller's speech as "a diversionary tactic" and "a sophisticated pushing of the capitalist line."[161] They were right in the sense that the text of Rockefeller's speech did not sound much different from the official voluntarist position the Population Council had always taken. What Notestein recognized, however, was Rockefeller's admission that, although the Population Council had always paid frequent lip service to broader development goals, it had pursued population control as a substitute. Notestein declared Rockefeller's speech to have been "thoughtless and childish" and to have "undo[ne] much of the effort" of the Population Council.[162]

Notestein's reading was correct in that Rockefeller's speech did signal a shift in his understanding of population. Two years earlier he had begun to recognize that his approach to population was not, in fact, promoting greater well-being among its targets. At the insistence of his wife that he needed more female perspectives, Rockefeller hired Joan Dunlop in 1972 as his personal assistant for population matters. Dunlop had not attended college and had no previous experience with population, but Rockefeller viewed her inexperience as an advantage. The first assignment he gave her was to "take a year and go around and go to meetings and listen to people and tell me what you think is wrong" with his approach to population. Rockefeller's wife instructed Dunlop to "consider [her]self to be his equal" and to "tell him the truth" about his population work.[163]

Dunlop collaborated with Adrienne Germain, a former Population Council staffer who had recently moved to the Ford Foundation. In her initial interview at the Ford Foundation several years earlier, Germain had been told that, despite the fact that she had an undergraduate degree in sociology from Wellesley College and had done graduate work at UC Berkeley with Kingsley Davis and Judith Blake, the Foundation couldn't "even consider you for this job because you're married." In the minds of the Foundation's leadership, that meant "you'll just work with us for a year or two and then you'll go and have babies."[164] Germain instead accepted a job as a research assistant at the Population Council, where she was one of only three women working in a professional capacity. She later moved to the Ford Foundation after getting divorced and finishing her master's degree. Dunlop and Germain both found that, in all areas of the population establishment—from the offices of the Population Council to the halls of university-based population centers to the clinics of overseas family planning programs—women "were being treated as objects and a means to an end," a "vehicle" for the technocratic aims of economic development, with their own lives, health, and safety never considered.[165]

After her first conversation with Germain, Dunlop reported to Rockefeller that the population establishment "was shot through with unintended sexism and racism." She found that good new ideas were not being funded because money was controlled by three men (Reimert Ravenholt at USAID, Bud Harkavy at the Ford Foundation, and Bob Bates at the Rockefeller Brothers Fund) and ideas were controlled by another three men (Bernard Berelson at the Population Council, Ron Freedman at the University of Michigan's Population Studies Center, and Ansley Coale at Princeton's OPR), all of whom resisted new approaches.[166] With the assistance of Dunlop and Germain, Rockefeller's views on population had, in his words, "matured."[167] They helped him realize that contraceptive technologies, even if combined with propaganda, could not substantially reduce birth rates in the absence of economic development, and that smaller families did not automatically improve human welfare. Increasing well-being, Rockefeller decided, was ultimately more important than reducing fertility. He saw his 1974 Bucharest speech as a chance to insert some new ideas into the population field, and assigned its writing to Dunlop, who recruited Germain to assist her. When Berelson learned that Dunlop and Germain were writing Rockefeller's speech, he complained that "it would just set back the field who knows how many years," which was exactly Notestein's response to hearing it.[168]

In reality, Rockefeller's speech marked the end of the population consensus but did not bring about its demise. The consensus had been fragile to begin with, bridging demographers' relatively contained modernizationist understanding of overpopulation as a local effect of global capitalism with the popular and more capacious Malthusian understanding of overpopulation—voiced loudly by Burch, Vogt, Osborn, Moore, and

Ehrlich—as the primary source of all the world's ills. Demography had benefited immensely from this consensus, developing a global network of practitioners and expanding its research agenda worldwide. Demographers had promoted family planning as a solution to both Malthusian and modernizationist versions of overpopulation, creating the illusion of demand for contraception sufficient that individual reproductive autonomy would halt aggregate population growth, and disseminating propaganda to generate the demand they claimed already existed. Yet demography also sowed the seeds of dissensus. Fertility surveys, though demonstrating that people in many parts of the world wanted to have smaller families, also revealed that true reproductive choice would continue to swell the world's population. Meanwhile the growth of demography itself generated practitioners who would come to question the very scientific basis for population control.

By 1974 the population consensus had fragmented under pressure from two sides. On the right, the population bombers attacked the family planning solution to the population problem, contending that empowering couples to have the number of children they wanted would not bring about zero population growth, which was necessary to avert ecosystem catastrophe, widespread famine, social upheaval, and nuclear war. On the left, the Concerned Demographers and the Latin American intellectuals who had inspired them contended that even an immediate halt to population growth would not solve the world's problems because population growth had not produced those problems in the first place. From their perspective, family planning was simply a tactic to defuse valid criticism of the geopolitical and global economic order and avert revolution. The American demographers who had aligned themselves with the population establishment faced an identity crisis as the collapse of the postwar population consensus undermined their moral authority to prescribe family planning to the world's developing countries.[169]

Epilogue

More than forty years after Bucharest, the experts on Bill Nye's "Earth's People Problem" episode continued to engage in the debate that had divided the population establishment and the population bombers at the end of the 1960s: Can "the population problem" be solved through family planning alone, or will it require explicit limits on childbearing? The very terms of the debate exclude discussion of whether population growth is actually responsible for poverty or ecosystem degradation. This is not to say that nothing has changed since Bucharest. The field of demography has largely moved away from its association with the population establishment. It is now primarily economists who link population to development and natural scientists who link population to the environment. In the years since Bucharest, access to contraception and abortion has once again come under attack, this time from the religious faction of the Republican Party in the United States, whose power extends worldwide because of the role of the United States as family planning provider to the world. Perhaps as a result, some organizations that advocate women's health have aligned themselves with the population establishment in a coalition reminiscent of Margaret Sanger's interwar alliance with eugenics.

POPULATION SCIENCE AFTER BUCHAREST

Members of the population establishment—and even some population bombers—were chastened by their experience in Bucharest. The Population Crisis Committee changed its name to Population Action International and actively began to distance itself from population bomb rhetoric.[1] The

Building the Population Bomb. Emily Klancher Merchant, Oxford University Press (2021). © Oxford University Press.
DOI: 10.1093/oso/9780197558942.003.0008

Population Council underwent a reorganization that resulted in the resignation of both Frank Notestein and Bernard Berelson.[2] It began to emphasize input from high-fertility countries in its programs but continued to fund research on long-acting contraceptive technologies and to promote them as the surest route to economic development.[3] Changes at the Ford Foundation were more dramatic. By the end of the 1970s, it had replaced its population program with a new initiative called Child Survival/Fair Start for Children.[4] Overseas offices widened their remit from family planning to reproductive health.[5]

As the Ford Foundation retreated from population control, it also withdrew from its commitments to demography. Grants to population research and training centers were not renewed. The focus of the Ford Foundation's graduate fellowship programs—not just in demography but across the board—shifted from international students to American students of color, providing opportunities for those who had previously lacked access to graduate training and promoting diversity in academia.[6] New foundations stepped into the population void—first Mellon and Hewlett, later Gates—but these patrons emphasized research on family planning administration and delivery rather than demography. At the end of the 1970s, demography had far less foundation money at its disposal than it had had at the beginning of the decade.[7]

The National Institutes of Health (NIH) had, by that time, become demography's largest source of funding, and demography changed dramatically under its influence. NIH sponsored training only for U.S. citizens, and its research priorities focused the attention of demographers primarily on the United States. American fertility was quite low by then, but the incidence of teenage childbearing began to rise as the baby boom generation reached late adolescence—simply because there were so many teenagers—and became a focus of research funding for the National Institute of Child Health and Human Development.[8] NICHD also continued to fund the kind of research that had earlier been pursued primarily by demographers at the universities of Michigan and Wisconsin on social stratification, racial segregation, and family structure. The 1974 establishment of the National Institute on Aging created another source of funding for demography and expanded research in the social science of aging. Together, NICHD and the National Institute on Aging transformed demography from a field primarily concerned with reducing fertility in the Global South to one overwhelmingly focused on understanding social inequality and the social and economic determinants of health worldwide. In addition to funding research and training, these agencies built research infrastructure, facilitating the collection of large data sets that today serve as focal points for enormous interdisciplinary research communities. At the turn of the twenty-first century, NIH-funded studies were the first to integrate analysis of DNA and other biomarkers into social scientific survey research.[9] International demography research expanded from its earlier narrow focus on fertility to include reproductive health, mortality, and aging.[10] Research on fertility, meanwhile, began to take a sociological and psychological approach, attempting to develop a more nuanced account of how people make childbearing decisions.[11]

To be sure, many demographers continued to work on reducing fertility in the Global South, and USAID continued to support research on the effectiveness of family planning programs.[12] It funded new fertility surveys that continued and updated the KAP studies, first the World Fertility Survey, then the Demographic and Health Surveys, which continue today and are the major source of data for demography research in the Global South.[13] The sums available from USAID were vast in comparison to the money available from other sources, but demographers saw the work USAID funded as "applied" or "industrial" research that would not garner for them the prestige they needed to advance in academia.[14]

By the middle of the 1980s, even demographers had begun to question the theoretical foundation of population control, the Coale-Hoover Report. A 1986 study by the National Academy of Sciences, funded by USAID and overseen by economic demographer Sam Preston—who had completed his Ph.D. at OPR under Ansley Coale's supervision—found that many countries in the Global South had experienced dramatic increases in per capita income over the previous thirty years, even as their populations grew rapidly, but poverty was still rampant in much of the world because the gains from economic growth were not equitably shared.[15] In other words, population growth was not, in and of itself, a barrier to economic growth, and economic growth, in and of itself, did not improve the human condition. The study also determined that population growth was not the primary cause of resource depletion and environmental degradation. It pointed instead to "economic activity in the developed countries" as the major culprit and recommended as a solution "a market in pollution rights"—a cap-and-trade system.[16]

By that time, another set of economists outside of demography had begun to theorize that population growth actually had a positive effect on economies and the natural environment, and that free markets could solve the problems that scientists, activists, and policymakers had previously attributed to population growth. Market fundamentalism had been brewing since the middle of the twentieth century, and economists had been making the neoliberal case against population control even before the 1974 UN conference in Bucharest.[17] By the beginning of the 1970s, the United States appeared to be stagnating. The long period of postwar economic growth had come to an end, as had the baby boom. The fertility rate in the United States had fallen to replacement, suggesting that population growth was slowing and would soon stop or reverse course. Demographers and economists alike had long recognized that, in the absence of population growth, economic growth required government spending.[18] But Keynesianism had fallen out of favor, and neoliberal economists instead recuperated the mercantilist view of population, recommending population growth as a way to stimulate economic growth without government spending.[19]

The most extreme version of this "cornucopianism," as it was termed at the time, held that the scarcity caused by population growth would generate innovations that would lead to economic development in the Global South and protect the global environment by stimulating the replacement of scarce (and therefore expensive) resources with more abundant (and therefore cheaper) ones. Julian Simon, perhaps the most famous of the cornucopianists, publicly challenged Paul Ehrlich to a bet in 1980 that aimed to prove this latter point.[20] Americans who had grown weary of the dire Malthusian warnings of the population bombers eagerly embraced cornucopianism. Historian Paul Sabin has described the 1980 U.S. presidential election as a popular referendum on conservation (Carter) versus growth (Reagan), with Reagan's sweeping victory signaling a public preference for growth.

Cornucopianism didn't last long, however. New economic and environmental arguments for population control emerged around the turn of the twenty-first century. On the economic side, the concept of the demographic dividend rearticulated fertility decline to economic growth. A demographic dividend is a brief period of rapid economic growth made possible (but not guaranteed) by the age structure of a population undergoing demographic transition. Pretransitional populations have a youthful age structure, as few people live to old age. Perhaps counterintuitively, when mortality falls at the beginning of a demographic transition, the proportion of young people in the population increases because mortality declines are concentrated among children and childbearing women. If, however, demographic transition proceeds apace, these children will have fewer children of their own. As they get older, their generation will be larger than either the generations that came before or those that come after. It is when this "bulge" has reached the working ages that the possibility of a demographic dividend emerges. At that point, the society's dependency ratio (the number of children and elderly divided by the number of people in the working ages) reaches its all-time low. During this window of opportunity—before the bulge reaches old age and brings the dependency ratio back up—a society that makes sufficient investments in education, health, infrastructure, and industrialization can increase the productivity of its relatively larger workforce and thereby reap a one-time windfall in economic growth, possibly enough to push a country from the UN's "less developed" category into its "more developed" category. Economists and demographers alike attributed the so-called East Asian economic miracle to this demographic dividend.[21] The possibility of a demographic dividend has provided intergovernmental agencies such as the UN Population Fund (UNFPA) and nongovernmental organizations like RAND and the Gates Foundation with a new rationale to promote family planning in developing countries.[22] Their policy prescriptions, however, focus more on reducing birth rates to speed up the demographic transition than on the job creation and workforce development that will be necessary to convert demographic transitions into demographic dividends. [23]

Attention to age structure has also generated concern about fertility levels that are below replacement in some countries of Europe and East Asia. This concern focuses not on the well-being of families but rather on the economic effects of low birth rates. With total fertility rates (TFRs) below 1.5 in Germany, Hong Kong, Italy, Japan, Singapore, South Korea, and Spain, experts worry that, in the absence of immigration, old-age dependency ratios in these countries will become disastrously high, an issue Bill Nye mentioned but quickly moved past in "Earth's People Problem." In a 2019 debate between Alibaba founder Jack Ma and Tesla founder Elon Musk, one of the few points of agreement was that the world was headed not for overpopulation but for what Musk termed "population collapse."[24] In some countries, low period TFRs reflect a shift toward later childbearing rather than a trend toward smaller completed families, the opposite of the impossibly high period TFRs during the baby boom.[25] But in other countries, low period TFRs do signal a trend toward smaller families. Those "lowest-low" fertility rates seem to be the product of societies where women have access to education and rewarding careers but are still expected to do the bulk of household labor, thus creating a very high opportunity cost for childbearing.[26] In the United States, stagnating middle-class wages, rising student debt burdens, and the hollowing-out of the welfare state have produced TFRs that, while higher than those of the lowest-low countries, are consistently below the number of children Americans report wanting in fertility surveys.[27] Demographers contend that promoting gender equity, raising overall living conditions, and welcoming immigration will likely avert population decline.[28] Some worry, however, that countries that took coercive approaches to reducing fertility in the past may take equally coercive approaches to increasing fertility in the near future.[29]

At the same time that the demographic dividend breathed new life into economic arguments for population control, the concept of the Anthropocene revitalized environmental arguments. The term "Anthropocene," introduced by biologist Eugene F. Stoermer in the 1980s and popularized by Paul Crutzen and others in the current century, describes our present geological epoch as one in which human activity is the most powerful driver of biogeochemical change.[30] The Anthropocene designation usefully calls attention to the effects of certain human activities on the Earth, altering not just our land, water, and atmosphere but the very substance of the planet. However, the term also threatens to naturalize the human influence on the environment and to collapse distinctions between small-scale agriculture and the extraction and burning of fossil fuels.[31]

"Anthropocene," notably, is a term coined and popularized by natural scientists. Social scientists and humanists have proposed alternative terms, such as "Capitalocene" and "Plantationocene," to distinguish between human *being* and specific modes of human *doing* related to extractive and exploitative means of production.[32] Demographers—who began to investigate questions of population and environment in the 1990s—have complicated the assumed relationship between human numbers and environmental degradation, exploring complex recursive micro-level relationships between ecosystems and population processes.[33] Yet natural scientists continue to emphasize the macro-level coincidence of massive population growth and catastrophic ecosystem destruction since World War II, the period Anthropocene scholars describe as "the great acceleration."[34] By attributing biogeochemical trends to humanity and its expansion rather than to specific human activities, the Anthropocene concept focuses efforts to protect the environment on reducing the number of people on Earth rather than demanding change from the corporations and governments that control most of the world's resources and drive most greenhouse-gas-producing processes.[35]

POPULATION POLICY AFTER BUCHAREST

The collapse of the population consensus in Bucharest did not signal the end of population control, either through family planning or by more direct means. Some heads of state who demanded implementation of the New International Economic Order at Bucharest continued to pursue population control as a means of promoting economic development and reducing the size and political power of poor populations in their own countries. Their approaches became more openly coercive after 1974. In 1975 India's prime minister Indira Gandhi called a state of emergency to avoid resigning after being found guilty of violating electoral law. While the Constitution was suspended, the Indian government undertook a comprehensive population control program.[36] Quotas created what historian Matthew Connelly describes as "a nationwide market in which people bought and sold . . . the capacity to reproduce," resulting in over eight million sterilizations in the first year.[37] China implemented its one-child policy in 1979.[38] In the early 1980s, Indonesia's government launched a population control campaign that included mass IUD "safaris," during which rural women were pressured to accept IUDs in the absence of follow-up medical care or the possibility of later removal.[39] Such policies were not limited to the developing world. Involuntary sterilization statutes remained on the books in many parts of the United States, and the sterilizations they authorized continued apace.[40]

When the UN held its next world population conference, in Mexico City in 1984, it was no longer the governments of nonaligned countries that posed the greatest challenge to the population establishment or the population bombers, but the government of the United States. The Reagan administration announced at the conference that the U.S. government would no longer fund organizations that provided abortions or information about abortions, or that lobbied governments to legalize abortion, anywhere in the world. In the United States, the political backlash to abortion legalization had begun even before the Supreme Court ruled on *Roe v. Wade* in 1973. That year, the Helms Amendment to the Foreign Assistance Act prohibited the use of U.S. foreign aid funds to pay for abortions.[41] What would come to be known as the Mexico City Policy—or the Global Gag Rule—was much more restrictive.[42] Its major targets were the International Planned Parenthood Federation and UNFPA, both of which lost access to U.S. monies.[43] The Mexico City Policy also restricted the activities of USAID, which had, to that point, been distributing abortifacients overseas. When the Mexico City Policy forced USAID to end its research into nonsurgical abortion methods—specifically menstrual regulation and the drug that would come to be known as RU-486—USAID quietly encouraged private foundations to take over this work.[44]

The Mexico City Policy was designed to appease antiabortion voters, who had played a major role in bringing Reagan to the White House. The Republican Party officially adopted an antiabortion stance early in the 1970s, marginalizing the more liberal East Coast ("Rockefeller") wing of the party.[45] Following *Roe v. Wade* and a series of cases that subsequently struck down state-level restrictions on abortion, evangelical Christians united with Catholics in opposition to abortion, and the Republican Party made a concerted effort to recruit the religious right as a new voting bloc.[46] The Mexico City Policy remained in place until 1993, when President Clinton repealed it, and has become a political football since then, reinstated under every Republican president and repealed under every Democratic president. Under the Mexico City Policy, women worldwide lost access to the contraceptives they had previously relied upon to avoid pregnancy, ironically leading to increased numbers of abortions, many occurring under unsafe conditions.[47]

The Mexico City Policy posed an existential threat to population control organizations and became a key site of opposition for reproductive health advocates. These two sets of actors came together in a partnership that was cemented at the International Conference on Population and Development, held in Cairo in 1994.[48] At this meeting, reproductive health advocates voiced opposition both to conservative efforts to limit the availability of contraceptives and abortion services and to the coercive population control campaigns that continued in many parts of the world even after Mexico City. The newly formed reproductive justice movement, led by women of color, came to Cairo to demand for everyone "safe and dignified fertility management, childbirth, and parenting."[49] The Cairo Program of Action is often hailed as a paradigm shift in population policy because it emphasized individual reproductive health and gender equity, eschewing aggregate demographic targets. Yet although it incorporated some of the language of reproductive justice, it excluded the movement's substance. While reproductive justice repudiates populationism—the attribution of social, political, economic, and environmental ills to population—the Cairo Program of Action continued to describe reproductive health and gender equity as means to population stationarity and population stationarity as a prerequisite for sustainable development, a new concept that blended economic growth and environmental protection.[50]

While many observers described the Cairo Program of Action as a compromise between reproductive health organizations and the population establishment, critical science and technology scholar Saul Halfon contends that it was actually more of a "structured disunity," in which actors with very different goals agreed to "get along" to advance their own agendas.[51] In light of the longer history of population intervention, however, it was a clear victory for the population establishment. Since Cairo, the term "population policy" has played the same role that "family planning" did through much of the twentieth century. Between the world wars, "family planning" was a kind of boundary concept that could mean either eugenics or birth control legalization; after World War II it could mean either birth control access or population control.[52] At Cairo, reproductive health organizations attempted to redefine the term "population policy" to mean reproductive health and gender equity full stop. They succeeded to such an extent that, when medical historian Alison Bashford began research for what would become the book *Global Population*, she was surprised to learn that "population policy" had ever had any other meaning.[53] However, simply by virtue of using the term "population policy" participants in the Cairo consensus instrumentalized reproductive health and gender equity as means to achieve population stationarity, which remained the goal of key members of the population establishment, including the Population Council, USAID, UNFPA, and the Gates Foundation. For them, "population policy" signified slowing population growth through the promotion of reproductive health and gender equity.

Joining the feminist critique of coercive population control programs allowed members of the population establishment to distinguish themselves from the population bombers, who were sidelined at Cairo and who came to take the blame for all of the coercive measures that advocates of reproductive health deplored. The Cairo consensus allowed the population establishment to reaffirm its own definition of coercion as explicit limits on childbearing and to redefine the family planning it had long promoted as a feminist project and a straightforward synonym for birth control. In so doing, the population establishment elided its earlier support for government control over the types and quantity of family planning offered to citizens in order to manipulate birth rates and distanced family planning programs—including those that relied upon such imposable methods as IUDs and those that hired motivators to meet IUD insertion quotas—from the "population control" that the conference disavowed.[54] Even ZPG jumped on the Cairo bandwagon, changing its name to Population Connection and restating its mission in terms of individual rights rather than its iconic demographic target. By echoing the language of reproductive justice, these populationist organizations co-opted the networks built by reproductive justice activists to serve their population-level agenda.[55] The Cairo Program of Action set the terms for today's population debate, eliding questions about whether population stationarity was, in fact, a worthwhile goal and focusing instead on the most effective and humane way to accomplish it. In so doing, it silenced debate about the actual causes of poverty and environmental degradation and the most effective and equitable ways to address these serious problems.

Although demographic targets were roundly rejected at Cairo, several countries continued to impose them, using overtly coercive methods to achieve their goals. Other countries, including the United States, deployed contraception and sterilization in coercive ways to control certain segments of their populations.[56] In the more than twenty-five years since the International Conference on Population and Development, the existential threat posed by climate change has reinvigorated the population bombers, who contend that advancing reproductive health and gender equity is not, in and of itself, an adequate population policy. To be sure, some environmental organizations use the language of the Cairo consensus, attempting to cloak their aggregate goals in individual reproductive autonomy.[57] Those that call for more direct limits on childbearing tend to focus on the United States and other developed countries so as to deflect charges of racism. But the demographic targets that have returned to the international population agenda have been set only for developing countries. These emerged at the 2012 London Summit on Family Planning, a joint venture of USAID, UNFPA, the Gates Foundation, and the U.K. Department for International Development. These organizations laid out a program titled "Family Planning 2020," which aimed to increase the number of users of systemic contraceptives (mainly IUDs and implants) in the world's poorest countries (mainly in Africa and South and Southeast Asia) by 120 million over the next eight years. This target was adopted in the face of opposition by the reproductive health organizations that had rejected demographic targets in Cairo and in spite of warnings from feminist scholars of reproduction that such targets will open the door to new forms of coercion.[58]

THE REAL POPULATION PROBLEM

In 2011 the economist and demographer David Lam gave a presidential address to the Population Association of America titled "How the World Survived the Population Bomb: Lessons from 50 Years of Extraordinary Demographic History." In Lam's address, "the population bomb" referred to the immense growth in world population that occurred in the second half of the twentieth century, primarily in Africa, Asia, and Latin America. He contended that the "bomb" is behind us; we have already "survived." Population growth once threatened to outpace food production, prevent economic development, and deplete the world's resources, but family planning and capitalism prevailed. Even as population grew, per-capita food production increased, non-energy commodity prices fell, and population growth rates declined. Lam attributed this survival to capitalism (market responses, innovation, and globalization) and family planning.[59] He was silent on a few key points, however. Although global food production has outpaced global population growth, the market mechanisms through which it is distributed have not prevented numerous famines. Contraceptives are much more available now than they were in the mid-twentieth century, but many who wish to use them still lack access, even as systemic contraception, abortion, and sterilization continue to be foisted upon people who wish to have children. Climate change, caused by the fossil-fueled economic growth Lam celebrated, threatens to make much of our planet uninhabitable. These silences allowed Lam to tell a story of triumphant modernization undeterred by rapid population growth—a successful world demographic transition.

Yet if we consider "the population bomb" from a discursive perspective—not as population growth itself but as a narrative that attributes many of the world's social, political, economic, and environmental ills to population growth and promises that population control will ameliorate them—then it is very much still with us. This population bomb demonizes the world's most vulnerable inhabitants, elides the true causes of urgent and complex problems, and deters equitable and just solutions to them. The two scientists who perhaps did the most to advance the cause of population control, demographer Frank Notestein and biologist Paul Ehrlich, both turned to fertility limitation as a solution to global problems (poverty in Notestein's case and environmental degradation in Ehrlich's) when the more targeted solutions they had previously proposed—redistribution to alleviate poverty and regulation to protect the environment, solutions that would have addressed these problems by attacking their causes—were deemed politically infeasible. By abandoning the solutions to which their science pointed in favor of one that was more politically palatable (regardless of how unpalatable contraception may have been in the mid-twentieth century, redistribution and regulation were infinitely less palatable), they garnered the support of the powers that be at the expense of women, people of color, the world's poor, and the Earth itself.

Lam's story is one in which the population establishment defused the population bomb. As was evident on Bill Nye's "Earth's People Problem," however, these two approaches to "the population problem," though in tension with one another, both contribute to the perpetuation of the idea that population *is* a problem. This book has demonstrated the synergy between the population establishment and the population bombers and the way each assemblage has contributed to the perpetuation of the other, even when the two were most opposed. Together these assemblages have undermined efforts to achieve economic, environmental, and reproductive justice. By attributing poverty to too-large families and environmental degradation to too-high birth rates, they obscure the actual causes of these issues and elide the ways in which they disproportionately affect women and people of color. The population establishment and population bombers substitute family planning for redistributive and regulatory measures and deny poor people and people of color bodily autonomy, the right to have children, and the right to parent in safe communities and healthy environments.

For most Americans, the idea that population growth is the primary culprit for the world's problems and the belief that population control offers a solution seems obvious or commonsensical. As I have shown in this book, these ideas did not simply follow from the realization that the world's population was growing; they originated in specific political programs aimed at controlling that growth. They were transmitted through personal contacts and the mass media, often with money lubricating their path and science legitimating their messages. It is, perhaps, because of this history that some reproductive health organizations continue to include the term "population" in their name: there is more popular support for slowing population growth than for promoting the health or reproductive autonomy of women and others who are not currently served by our health systems. One hundred years ago the same was true of eugenics. To most Americans, eugenics seemed a commonsense solution to the problems of poverty, crime, and social strife. Margaret Sanger subordinated birth control to eugenics because there was much more popular support for the latter than for the former.

In July 2020, in the wake of protests following George Floyd's murder at the hands of the Minneapolis Police Department, Planned Parenthood of Greater New York removed Sanger's name from its Manhattan Health Clinic in order to distance the organization from its founder's eugenicist politics.[60] Sanger thus became the fourth person (that I know of) appearing in this book to have their name removed from a building or institution during the course of my writing.[61] Yet in Sanger's case, I believe this action misses the point. While we absolutely must criticize eugenics wherever we see it, simply removing Sanger's name from a Planned Parenthood clinic individualizes the connection between Planned Parenthood and eugenics (and later population control) in Sanger's person. It ignores the fact that birth control became legal and widely available in the United States only because of widespread support for eugenics (and later population control) among the scientists, medical professionals, jurists, and policymakers who had the power to make it happen. As this book has demonstrated, the very name "Planned Parenthood" was adopted over Sanger's protest in order to appease eugenicists on the organization's board. Today Planned Parenthood is at the forefront of promoting reproductive health worldwide, not to slow population growth but for its own sake. To truly come to terms with its past, however, it will need to account for its long history of privileging the reproductive rights of middle-class white women in the Global North over reproductive justice for poor women and women of color worldwide.

Calls for population control offer an individual solution to structural problems. As this book has shown, over the past one hundred years, and even going back to Malthus, those in power have invoked population and its control as a means of avoiding redistribution and regulation. Harnessing the persuasive idiom of science, they supported demographic research, funded graduate training, and shaped the communication of results. Yet demography never provided unequivocal support to any population control project, challenging again and again the idea that population growth is the cause of the problems that proponents of population control claim it will solve. In particular, demography challenged the population bomb narrative, which was born of and has largely been perpetuated by natural scientists who used their credentials to make claims about matters well beyond their scientific expertise.

Historian Michelle Murphy has argued that the concept of population is bankrupt and needs to be abandoned.[62] Yet this position conflates population *science* with population *control* and conflates planning *for* population with the planning *of* population. American demographers today do vitally important work aimed at alleviating poverty, promoting health (reproductive and otherwise), and ending racial inequality. In 2021 the annual meeting of the PAA will include sessions on racial disparities in aging, redistricting after the 2020 Census, the effects of the COVID-19 pandemic on racial inequality, the role of violence in reproductive health, and intersectionality in population health. The concept of population remains analytically and politically valuable. We still live in a world of nation-states, where governments need to be able to predict population growth so as to budget for and administer welfare programs, and demographers currently play an important role in that process. The concept of population also allows demographers to examine the distribution of social goods (such as health, education, and safety) and bads (poverty, illness, and environmental hazards) within and between populations and determine ways to make it more equitable.

Demographers have done considerable work in recent decades to fight for the continued legality and accessibility of contraception and abortion.[63] But they must also work to protect human population itself from being scapegoated for the world's problems or from being targeted by those peddling faux solutions to those problems that ultimately divert resources from the promotion of social justice. While demographers have spoken out against China's one-child policy and other extreme forms of reproductive coercion,[64] they have done little to discredit the still popular idea that population is a problem that needs to be solved.[65]

Demographers have a privileged position from which to speak about human population, but they are not the only ones who must work against the glossing of the world's most pressing problems in terms of the number of people on the planet. When we assert that human numbers—either the number of all people (quantity) or the number of certain people (quality)—are the fundamental source of such issues as poverty (scarcity of goods that humans need) or environmental degradation (excess of pollutants that humans emit), we naturalize the human activities that caused those problems in the first place. When we say that people are poor simply because there are too many of them, we elide the fact that the world's wealthy—who hold the resources necessary to feed and shelter the world's poor—got that way by actively impoverishing workers and the producers of raw materials. When we calculate per-capita carbon emissions, we elide the fact that most emissions are caused not by the activities of individuals but by those of corporations and governments. When we gloss these challenges as "the population problem," we look to population-related expertise for solutions, when instead we should be turning to expertise in economic, environmental, and reproductive justice.

NOTES

INTRODUCTION

1. "Earth's People Problem," IMDb, imdb.com/title/tt6566210/?ref_=ttep_ep23. Quotations are from the episode's closed captioning.
2. As estimated by the United Nations in the *2019 Revision of World Population Prospects,* population.un.org/wpp.
3. Rieder is a research scholar at the Herman Institute of Bioethics at Johns Hopkins University.
4. Snow is chief of population development at the UN Population Fund; Benfield is professor of family planning at Albert Einstein College of Medicine at Yeshiva University.
5. Natural scientists in this group include Paul Ehrlich and his allies (discussed later in the book) and proponents of the Anthropocene concept (also discussed later) who emphasize human numbers rather than human activities as the key driver of biogeochemical change. Ethicists who take this position include Travis Rieder, *Toward a Small Family Ethic: How Overpopulation and Climate Change are Affecting the Morality of Procreation* (Cham, Switzerland: Springer, 2016), and Sarah Conly, *One Child: Do We Have a Right to More?* (New York: Oxford University Press, 2018).
6. Matthew Connelly, *Fatal Misconception: The Struggle to Control World Population* (Cambridge, MA: Belknap, 2008); Derek S. Hoff, *The State and the Stork: The Population Debate and Policy Making in U.S. History* (Chicago: University of Chicago Press, 2012).
7. Alison Bashford, *Global Population: History, Geopolitics, and Life on Earth* (New York: Columbia University Press, 2014); Thomas Robertson, *The Malthusian Moment: Global Population Growth and the Birth of American Environmentalism* (New Brunswick, NJ: Rutgers University Press, 2012).
8. Connelly, *Fatal Misconception.*
9. Adele Clarke and Donna Haraway, eds., *Making Kin Not Population: Reconceiving Generations* (Chicago: Prickly Paradigm Press, 2018).
10. In rejecting those assumptions, it joins other recent works that take a similarly skeptical approach: Carole R. McCann, *Figuring the Population Bomb: Gender and Demography in the Mid-Twentieth Century* (Seattle: University of Washington Press, 2017); Michelle Murphy, *The Economization of Life* (Durham, NC: Duke University Press, 2017); Jade Sasser, *On Infertile Ground: Population Control and Women's Rights in the Era of Climate Change* (New York: New York University

Press, 2018); Susan Greenhalgh, *Just One Child: Science and Policy in Deng's China* (Berkeley: University of California Press, 2008).

11. I used topic modeling (latent Dirichlet allocation) to read and analyze the entire corpus of demography journal literature and to compare it to population-related scholarship outside of demography. Emily Klancher Merchant, "A Digital History of Anglophone Demography and Global Population Control, 1915–1984," *Population and Development Review* 43 (2017): 83–117.
12. Manuel De Landa, *Assemblage Theory* (Edinburgh: Edinburgh University Press, 2016).
13. Begun in 1973, the PAA Oral History Project (populationassociation.org/about/our-history/oral-history-project) includes interviews with more than fifty demographers who have served as president of the PAA since 1947. In the course of writing this book, I was invited to join the committee that carries out these interviews. I have also utilized oral histories collected by the Population and Reproductive Health Oral History Project (libraries.smith.edu/special-collections/research-collections/resources-lists/oral-histories/population-reproductive-health), archived at Smith College.
14. Matthew Connelly, "Population Control Is History: New Perspectives on the International Campaign to Limit Population Growth," *Comparative Studies in Society and History* 45, no. 1 (2003): 122–147.
15. In so doing, it joins such recent works as Jamie Cohen-Cole, *The Open Mind: Cold War Politics and the Sciences of Human Nature* (Chicago: University of Chicago Press, 2014); Paul Erickson, *The World the Game Theorists Made* (Chicago: University of Chicago Press, 2015); Joel Isaac, *Working Knowledge: Making the Human Sciences from Parsons to Kuhn* (Cambridge, MA: Harvard University Press, 2012); Rebecca Lemov, *World as Laboratory: Experiments with Mice, Mazes, and Men* (New York: Hill and Wang, 2005); Aldon Morris, *The Scholar Denied: W. E. B. Du Bois and the Birth of Modern Sociology* (Oakland: University of California Press, 2015); Alice O'Connor, *Poverty Knowledge: Social Science, Social Policy, and the Poor in Twentieth-Century U.S. History* (Princeton, NJ: Princeton University Press, 2009); Joy Rohde, *Armed with Expertise: The Militarization of American Social Research during the Cold War* (Ithaca, NY: Cornell University Press, 2013); Mark Solovey, *Shaky Foundations: The Politics-Patronage-Social Science Nexus in Cold War America* (New Brunswick, NJ: Rutgers University Press, 2013).
16. Other recent works on the history of the United States in global development include Nick Cullather, *The Hungry World: America's Cold War Battle against Poverty in Asia* (Cambridge, MA: Harvard University Press, 2010); David Ekbladh, *The Great American Mission: Modernization and the Construction of an American World Order, 1914 to the Present* (Princeton, NJ: Princeton University Press, 2010); Daniel Immerwahr, *Thinking Small: The United States and the Lure of Community Development* (Cambridge, MA: Harvard University Press, 2015); Michael E. Latham, *The Right Kind of Revolution: Modernization, Development, and U.S. Foreign Policy from the Cold War to the Present* (Ithaca, NY: Cornell University Press, 2011); Stephen J. Macekura, *Of Limits and Growth: The Rise of Global Sustainable Development in the Twentieth Century* (New York: Cambridge University Press, 2015).
17. "Reproductive Justice," Sister Song, sistersong.net/reproductive-justice. Loretta J. Ross and Rickie Solinger define reproductive justice a bit more capaciously, as "safe and dignified fertility management, childbirth, and parenting," in

Reproductive Justice: An Introduction* (Oakland: University of California Press, 2017), 9.

18. The UN *2019 Revision of World Population Prospects* found that, although the world's population is growing in the aggregate, population in many countries is declining, and in many others is growing at a decreasing rate.
19. Michelle Murphy, "Against Population, towards Alterlife," in *Making Kin Not Population: Reconceiving Generations*, ed. Adele Clarke and Donna Haraway (Chicago: Prickly Paradigm Press, 2018), 101–123.
20. Demographers conceptualize populations as human aggregates delineated by administrative boundaries. The word "population" therefore means something very different to a demographer than it would to a biologist or geneticist, and I intend to defend only the demographic concept of population.
21. Clarke and Haraway, *Making Kin Not Population.*
22. David Satterthwaite, "The Implications of Population Growth and Urbanization for Climate Change," *Environment and Urbanization* 21 (2009): 62–69.
23. Joni Seager, "The 6-Billionth Baby: Designated Green Scapegoat," *Environment and Planning A* 32 (2000): 1712.
24. It is not a history of population thought in the broad sense, nor does it consider other scientific fields that invoke concepts of population, such as population ecology or population genetics.
25. United Nations, *2019 Revision* of *World Population Prospects.*

CHAPTER 1

1. Bernard Mallet, "Opening Address," in *World Population Conference Held at the Salle Centrale, Geneva, August 29th to September 3rd, 1927*, ed. Margaret Sanger (London: Edward Arnold, 1927), 2.
2. The IUSIPP was the forerunner of today's International Union for the Scientific Study of Population (IUSSP).
3. Jean H. Baker, *Margaret Sanger: A Life of Passion* (New York: Hill and Wang, 2011).
4. For earlier concerns about population in the United States, see Hoff, *The State and The Stork*, and David M. Wrobel, *Global West, American Frontier: Travel, Empire, and Exceptionalism from Manifest Destiny to the Great Depression* (Albuquerque: University of New Mexico Press, 2013). For the world as a whole, see Bashford, *Global Population.* The frequency with which "the population problem" appears in print increases dramatically after 1920 in both JSTOR Data for Research and Google N-Grams. In JSTOR, it appears only 51 times between 1864 and 1919, but 354 times between 1920 and 1929, and 712 times between 1930 and 1939. In Google Books, the prevalence of the phrase nearly quadruples from 1915 to 1920 and again between 1920 and 1940.
5. Mike Davis, *Late Victorian Holocausts: El Niño Famines and the Making of the Third World* (London: Verso, 2001).
6. For instance, see Daniel T. Rodgers, *Atlantic Crossings: Social Politics in a Progressive Age* (Cambridge, MA: Harvard University Press, 2009); Glenda Elizabeth Gilmore, ed., *Who Were the Progressives?* (New York: Bedford/St. Martin's, 2002); Arthur Stanley Link and Richard L. McCormick, *Progressivism* (Hoboken, NJ: Wiley-Blackwell, 1983); Michael E. McGerr, *A Fierce Discontent: The Rise and Fall of the Progressive Movement in America, 1870–1920* (New York: Oxford University Press, 2005).

7. Thomas C. Leonard, *Illiberal Reformers: Race, Eugenics and American Economics in the Progressive Era* (Princeton, NJ: Princeton University Press, 2016).
8. The word "eugenics," coined by Charles Darwin's cousin Francis Galton in 1883, literally means "good breeding." Galton introduced the concept earlier, in an 1865 series of articles in *MacMillan's Magazine* that was republished in 1869 as *Hereditary Genius: An Inquiry into Its Laws and Consequences* (London: Macmillan, 1869). Galton's theory was based on the observation that, in England, prominence tended to run in families. The conclusions he drew from that observation conflated prominence with natural ability and elided the passing of social privilege from parent to child. Daniel J. Kevles, *In the Name of Eugenics: Genetics and the Uses of Human Heredity* (New York: Knopf, 1985).
9. A vast quantity of historical scholarship on eugenics, much of it published in the 1990s, has documented eugenics programs in the United States, Latin America, Europe, Asia, Africa, and Australia. Notable examples include Chloe Campbell, *Race and Empire: Eugenics in Colonial Kenya* (New York: Manchester University Press, 2007); Allan C. Carlson, *The Swedish Experiment in Family Politics: The Myrdals and the Interwar Population Crisis* (New Brunswick, NJ: Transaction, 1990); Yuehtsen Juliette Chung, *Struggle for National Survival: Eugenics in Sino-Japanese Contexts, 1896–1945* (New York: Routledge, 2002); Sarah Hodges, "Indian Eugenics in an Age of Reform," in *Reproductive Health in India: History, Politics, Controversies*, ed. Sarah Hodges (New Delhi: Orient Longman, 2006), 115–138; William H. Schneider, *Quality and Quantity: The Quest for Biological Regeneration in Twentieth-Century France* (New York: Cambridge University Press, 2002); Nancy Leys Stepan, *"The Hour of Eugenics": Race, Gender, and Nation in Latin America* (Ithaca, NY: Cornell University Press, 1991); Alexandra Minna Stern, *Eugenic Nation: Faults and Frontiers of Better Breeding in Modern America* (Berkeley: University of California Press, 2005). For eugenic internationalism, see Stefan Kühl, *For the Betterment of the Race: The Rise and Fall of the International Movement for Eugenics and Racial Hygiene,* trans. Lawrence Schofer (New York: Palgrave Macmillan, 2013).
10. Michael Willrich, "The Two Percent Solution: Eugenic Jurisprudence and the Socialization of American Law, 1900–1930," *Law and History Review* 16 (1998): 63–111.
11. Garland E. Allen, "The Eugenics Record Office at Cold Spring Harbor, 1910–1940: An Essay in Institutional History," *Osiris* 2 (1986): 225.
12. Bruce Curtis coined the term "census-making" as an alternative to "census-taking." It emphasizes the active role of the state in producing the population enumerated by a census. Bruce Curtis, *The Politics of Population: State Formation, Statistics, and the Census of Canada, 1840–1875* (Toronto: University of Toronto Press, 2002).
13. Hyman Alterman, *Counting People: The Census in History* (New York: Harcourt, Brace & World, 1969); Rebecca Jean Emigh, Dylan Riley, and Patricia Ahmed, *Antecedents of Censuses from Medieval to Nation States: How Societies and States Count* (New York: Springer, 2016).
14. Margo J. Anderson, *The American Census: A Social History* (New Haven, CT: Yale University Press, 1988).
15. Prior to 1880, "Indians not taxed" were excluded from the U.S. census. Although living within the territory controlled by the U.S. government, they were not subject to its authority. Diplomatic and military personnel are usually counted in the country of their citizenship, not the country of their residence.

16. For this distinction, see Oz Frankel, *States of Inquiry: Social Investigations and Print Culture in Nineteenth-Century Britain and the United States* (Baltimore, MD: Johns Hopkins University Press, 2006).
17. In the remainder of the text, I will not use scare quotes around the word "quality" or the phrase "population quality," but readers should keep in mind that these are actor categories, not analytic categories.
18. Notable histories of these projects include Glenda Elizabeth Gilmore, *Gender and Jim Crow: Women and the Politics of White Supremacy in North Carolina, 1896–1920* (Chapel Hill: University of North Carolina Press, 1996); Mae M. Ngai, *Impossible Subjects: Illegal Aliens and the Making of Modern America* (Princeton, NJ: Princeton University Press, 2004); Brian Gratton and Emily Klancher Merchant, "Immigration, Repatriation, and Deportation: The Mexican-Origin Population in the United States, 1920–1950," *International Migration Review* 47 (2013): 944–975.
19. Stuart Hall, "Race, Articulation, and Societies Structured in Dominance," in *Sociological Theories: Race and Colonialism*, ed. Marion O'Callaghan (Paris: UNESCO, 1980), 305–346.
20. Madison Grant, *The Passing of the Great Race: Or, the Racial Basis of European History* (New York: Scribner, 1916). For a thorough account of Grant, his followers, and his critics, see Jonathan Spiro, *Defending the Master Race: Conservation, Eugenics, and the Legacy of Madison Grant* (Burlington: University of Vermont Press, 2009).
21. During her exile, Sanger befriended the birth control activist Marie Stopes, who organized a collective letter to U.S. president Woodrow Wilson on Sanger's behalf, describing the benefits of birth control to the "white race." Jane Carey, "The Racial Imperatives of Sex: Birth Control and Eugenics in Britain, the United States and Australia in the Interwar Years," *Women's History Review* 21 (2012): 733–752.
22. Secretary of the American Birth Control League to Raymond Pearl, December 23, 1921, folder "Margaret Sanger #1," box 24, Raymond Pearl Papers (Mss.B.P312), American Philosophical Society Library, Philadelphia [hereafter RPP].
23. Kevles, *In the Name of Eugenics*.
24. Louis Israel Dublin, "Fallacious Propaganda for Birth Control," *Atlantic Monthly*, February 1926, 145–157.
25. Dennis Hodgson, "Ideological Currents and the Interpretation of Demographic Trends: The Case of Francis Amasa Walker," *Journal of the History of the Behavioral Sciences* 28 (1992): 28–44.
26. Trent MacNamara, "Why 'Race Suicide'? Cultural Factors in U.S. Fertility Decline, 1903–1908," *Journal of Interdisciplinary History* 44 (2014): 475–508.
27. Edward A. Ross, "The Causes of Race Superiority," *Annals of the American Academy of Political and Social Science* 18 (1901): 67–89, 89.
28. Many prominent eugenicists were also prominent conservationists and vice versa, most notably President Theodore Roosevelt and his close associates Madison Grant and Henry Fairfield Osborn. In 1918 Osborn and Grant cofounded the Save-the-Redwoods League and the Galton Society for the Study of the Origin and Evolution of Man. For more on the close connection between eugenics and conservation in the early twentieth-century United States, see Stern, *Eugenic Nation*, and Spiro, *Defending the Master Race*.
29. Leopold would codify this approach to wildlife management in a 1925 article titled "Ten New Developments in Game Management," but the principles it

embodied had already been laid out by eugenicist and conservationist Madison Grant through the activities of his various conservation organizations over the previous ten years. Spiro, *Defending the Master Race*.

30. Margaret Sanger to Raymond Pearl, November 7, 1923, folder "Margaret Sanger #2," box 24, RPP. East attributed soil depletion to the size of the U.S. population, not to the agricultural industry that was strip-mining the soil to export grain all over the world, in the process undercutting markets for more sustainable growing methods in other countries.
31. Little left his post as president of the University of Michigan in 1929, after his public calls for immigration restriction, antimiscegenation laws, and eugenic sterilization caused conflict with the Board of Regents. In the 1950s he would direct the Scientific Advisory Board of the Tobacco Industry Research Committee, which would promulgate the idea that lung cancer had only genetic causes and was unrelated to smoking. In 2018 the University of Michigan removed Little's name from a science building. Lauren Love, "U-M to Remove Little, Winchell Names from Campus Facilities," *University Record*, March 29, 2018.
32. Sharon E. Kingsland, "Raymond Pearl: On the Frontier in the 1920's: Raymond Pearl Memorial Lecture, 1983," *Human Biology* 56 (1984): 4, 10.
33. Elazar Barkan, "Reevaluating Progressive Eugenics: Herbert Spencer Jennings and the 1924 Immigration Legislation," *Journal of the History of Biology* 24 (1991): 91–112.
34. Kingsland, "Raymond Pearl." Pearl stayed at the University of Michigan as a lecturer until 1905. While in Ann Arbor, he met and married biologist Maud Mary De Witt, who became a frequent collaborator, as eventually did their daughter Ruth. Herbert Spencer Jennings, "Biographical Memoir of Raymond Pearl 1879–1940," *National Academy of Sciences of the United States of America: Biographical Memoirs* 22 (1943): 295–345.
35. Pearson described Pearl as "the most original and powerful of the younger Americans who have taken up biometric work." Karl Pearson to the Carnegie Institution, October 28, 1909, folder "Karl Pearson UCL Copies #3," box 22, RPP.
36. As a result of their falling-out, Pearson dropped Pearl from the editorial board of his journal *Biometrika*, which he had established specifically to advance the ancestral inheritance theory. Raymond Pearl to Karl Pearson, January 27, 1909, folder "Karl Pearson UCL Copies #3," box 22, RPP. For more on the debate between ancestral inheritance and Mendelian heredity, see Sahotra Sarkar, *Genetics and Reductionism* (Cambridge: Cambridge University Press, 1998). For the synthesis between the two perspectives, see Sahotra Sarkar, "Evolutionary Theory in the 1920s: The Nature of the 'Synthesis,'" *Philosophy of Science* 71 (2004): 1215–1226.
37. Michael A. Little and Ralph M. Garruto, "Raymond Pearl and the Shaping of Human Biology," *Human Biology* 82 (2010): 77–102.
38. Thomas Robert Malthus, *An Essay on the Principle of Population as It Affects the Future Improvement of Society with Remarks on the Speculations of Mr. Godwin, M. Condorcet and Other Writers* (London: J. Johnson, 1798). I do not engage with Malthus in any depth in this book, as it is my contention that twentieth-century American demographers took little interest in Malthus. My approach was, however, partly inspired by Karl Marx's critique of Malthus, as laid out in Ronald L. Meek, *Marx and Engels on Malthus* (London: Lawrence and Wishart, 1953). For excellent recent work on Malthus, see McCann, *Figuring the Population*

Bomb; Alison Bashford and Joyce E. Chaplin, *The New Worlds of Thomas Robert Malthus: Rereading the "Principle of Population"* (Princeton, NJ: Princeton University Press, 2016); and Robert J. Mayhew, ed., *New Perspectives on Malthus* (New York: Cambridge University Press, 2016).

39. Bashford, *Global Population*.
40. Sharon E. Kingsland, *Modeling Nature: Episodes in the History of Population Ecology* (Chicago: University of Chicago Press, 1995).
41. Raymond Pearl and Lowell J. Reed, "On the Rate of Growth of the Population of the United States since 1790 and Its Mathematical Representation," *Proceedings of the National Academy of Sciences of the United States of America* 6 (1920): 275–288, 282.
42. Raymond Pearl and F. C. Kelly, "Forecasting the Growth of Nations," *Harper's Monthly Magazine*, May 1921, 704.
43. Kingsland, "Raymond Pearl."
44. Kingsland, *Modeling Nature*.
45. Benedict Anderson, *Imagined Communities: Reflections on the Origin and Spread of Nationalism*, revised edition (New York: Verso, 2006).
46. Raymond Pearl, "The Aging of Populations," *Journal of the American Statistical Association* 35 (1940): 277–297.
47. Raymond Pearl, *The Biology of Death* (Philadelphia: J. B. Lippincott, 1922), 250–253.
48. Pearl did eventually determine that the growth of the indigenous population of Algeria had traced a full logistic "cycle" between 1886 and 1921. Raymond Pearl, *The Biology of Population Growth* (New York: Knopf, 1925).
49. Pearl, *The Biology of Population Growth*, 4–5.
50. Pearl also used *Drosophila* in experiments on aging and longevity. Kingsland, "Raymond Pearl."
51. Raymond Pearl, "World Overcrowding: Saturation Point for Earth's Population Soon Will Be in Sight, with the Safety Limit for the United States Estimated at 200,000,000 People—How the Nations Grow," *New York Times*, October 8, 1922.
52. For the United States, East calculated that, with a requirement of 2.5 acres per person, the country's 800 arable acres could support a population of 320 million (close to the size of the actual U.S. population in the year 2010), with another 11 million supported by forests and grazing. Edward Murray East, *Mankind at the Crossroads* (New York: Charles Scribner's Sons, 1923).
53. Pearl, "World Overcrowding." There is another argument for birth control that Pearl could have made but didn't. If, as his logistic law proposed, population size was entirely determined by the availability of resources, then, given the same population size and resource base, a population with lower birth rates (that is, one that practiced birth control) would have lower mortality rates than would a population with higher birth rates (that is, one that did not practice birth control). This argument was certainly available to Pearl, as it is exactly the argument Malthus had made, though Malthus had advocated for late marriage rather than contraception. Malthus contended that societies that practiced the "preventive check" of late marriage (England) were much less vulnerable to the "positive checks" of famine, war, and epidemic than were those that did not (China). Pearl therefore could have advocated for birth control as a mortality-reducing measure, as in fact neo-Malthusians would do for high-fertility countries after World War II. The fact that Pearl did not make this argument indicates that his vision was firmly fixed on population size and growth in the

aggregate rather than the vital processes that determined aggregate size and growth.

54. For instance, see Edwin B. Wilson to Raymond Pearl, December 14, 1924, folder "National Academy of Sciences #4," box 20, RPP.
55. Edwin B. Wilson to Raymond Pearl, January 13, 1925, folder "Edwin B. Wilson #2," box 29, RPP.
56. Edwin B. Wilson and W. J. Luyton, "The Population of New York City and Its Environs," *Proceedings of the National Academy of Sciences* 11 (1925): 137–143.
57. Edwin B. Wilson to Raymond Pearl, November 14, 1924, folder "National Academy of Sciences #4," box 20, RPP.
58. Edwin B. Wilson to Raymond Pearl, November 14, 1924.
59. Raymond Pearl to Edwin B. Wilson, December 4, 1924, folder "National Academy of Sciences #4," box 20, RPP; Raymond Pearl to Edwin B. Wilson, January 8, 1925, and January 12, 1925, folder "Edwin B. Wilson #2," box 29, RPP.
60. Kingsland, "Raymond Pearl"; Edmund Ramsden, "Carving Up Population Science: Eugenics, Demography and the Controversy over the 'Biological Law' of Population Growth," *Social Studies of Science* 32 (2002): 857–899.
61. Jennings, "Biographical Memoir of Raymond Pearl."
62. Kingsland, "Raymond Pearl."
63. Little and Garruto, "Raymond Pearl and the Shaping of Human Biology."
64. Raymond Pearl to Margaret Sanger, April 19, 1926, and May 8, 1926, folder "Margaret Sanger #7," box 24, RPP.
65. Margaret Sanger, *My Fight for Birth Control* (London: Faber & Faber, 1932).
66. Adele Clarke, *Disciplining Reproduction: Modernity, American Life Sciences, and "the Problems of Sex"* (Berkeley: University of California Press, 1998).
67. Raymond Pearl to Margaret Sanger, October 21, 1926, and November 3, 1926, and Margaret Sanger to Raymond Pearl, November 1, 1926, folder "Margaret Sanger #8," box 24, RPP.
68. Margaret Sanger to Raymond Pearl, May 6, 1926, folder "Margaret Sanger #7," box 24, RPP. Henry Pratt Fairchild, Wesley C. Mitchell, and Franklin Giddings had all assured Sanger that this was a good idea. Also see Bernard Mallet to Raymond Pearl, March 7, 1927, folder "Sir Bernard Mallet #1," box 18, RPP.
69. Margaret Sanger, ed. *Proceedings of the World Population Conference Held at the Salle Centrale, Geneva, August 29th to September 3rd, 1927* (London: E. Arnold, 1927).
70. When it was suggested that Harry Olson, chief justice of the Municipal Court of Chicago, be invited to the conference, Pearl refused, saying "he is not a scientific man, he knows nothing whatever about the population question, and is a ridiculous, intemperate, unscientific propagandist for eugenics, who seeks every opportunity for association with scientific men as a means of self advertisement." Raymond Pearl to Juliet Rublee, March 28, 1927, folder "Margaret Sanger #9," box 24, RPP.
71. Raymond Pearl, "Sterilization of Degenerates and Criminals Considered from the Standpoint of Genetics," *Eugenics Review* 11 (1919): 6.
72. Raymond Pearl, "The Biology of Superiority," *American Mercury*, November 1927, 266.
73. Quoted in Melissa Hendricks, "Raymond Pearl's 'Mingled Mess,'" *Johns Hopkins Magazine*, April 2006.
74. Garland E. Allen, "Old Wine in New Bottles: From Eugenics to Population Control in the Work of Raymond Pearl," in *The Expansion of American Biology*,

ed. Keith R. Benson, Jane Maienschein, and Ronald Rainger (New Brunswick, NJ: Rutgers University Press, 1991), 231–261; Ramsden, "Carving Up Population Science."

75. Quoted in Pearl, "The Biology of Superiority," 262.
76. Elazar Barkan has written at length about the contradiction between Pearl's public egalitarianism and private racism and anti-Semitism. Elazar Barkan, *The Retreat of Scientific Racism: Changing Concepts of Race in Britain and the United States between the World Wars* (New York: Cambridge University Press, 1992).
77. Raymond Pearl to Edwin B. Wilson, March 7, 1925, folder "Edwin B. Wilson #2," box 29, RPP; Hendricks, "Raymond Pearl's 'Mingled Mess.'"
78. Raymond Pearl to Edwin B. Wilson, December 17, 1927, folder "Edwin B. Wilson #2," box 29, RPP.
79. Raymond Pearl to Wesley C. Mitchell, March 6, 1929, folder "SSRC #3," box 25, RPP.
80. Raymond Pearl to Edward M. East, 1929, folder "E. M. East #7," box 7, RPP. For more on the Milbank Memorial Fund, see Daniel M. Fox, "The Significance of the Milbank Memorial Fund for Policy: An Assessment at Its Centennial," *Milbank Quarterly* 84 (2006): 5–36.
81. Frank W. Notestein, "Oral History Interview with Anders Lunde, 27 April 1973," in *Demographic Destinies: Interviews with Presidents and Secretary-Treasurers of the Population Association of America*, vol. 1, no. 1, ed. Jean Van Der Tak (Washington, DC: Population Association of America, 2005), 6–17; Frank W. Notestein and Frederick H. Osborn, "Reminiscences: The Role of Foundations, the Population Association of America, Princeton University and the United Nations in Fostering American Interest in Population Problems," *Milbank Memorial Fund Quarterly* 49 (1971): 67–85.
82. Clyde V. Kiser, *The Milbank Memorial Fund: Its Leaders and Its Work, 1905–1974* (New York: Milbank Memorial Fund, 1975).
83. Gail Ralson, "Andover Stories: Thomas Cochran and Phillips Academy's 'Golden Decade,'" *Andover Townsman Online*, November 3, 2011.
84. Clyde V. Kiser, "The Work of the Milbank Memorial Fund in Population since 1928," *Milbank Memorial Fund Quarterly* 49 (1971): 15–66. This research program will be described at greater length in chapter 2.
85. Edward M. East to Raymond Pearl, 1928, folder "E. M. East #7," box 7, RPP; Frank Lorimer, "The Role of the International Union for the Scientific Study of Population," *Milbank Memorial Fund Quarterly* 49 (1971): 86–105.
86. Kiser, "The Work of the Milbank Memorial Fund in Population since 1928."
87. Dan Bouk, *How Our Days Became Numbered: Risk and the Rise of the Statistical Individual* (Chicago: University of Chicago Press, 2015); I. S. Falk, "Editorial: Louis I. Dublin: November 1, 1882–March 7, 1969," *American Journal of Public Health and the Nation's Health* 59 (1969): 1083–1085.
88. Kiser, "The Work of the Milbank Memorial Fund in Population since 1928."
89. For Lotka's time in Pearl's lab, see Raymond Pearl to Alfred J. Lotka, April 18, 1921, and May 28, 1921, folder "Alfred J. Lotka #1," box 17, RPP.
90. Barbara A. Anderson, *World Population Dynamics: An Introduction to Demography* (New York: Pearson, 2015), 44–46.
91. Anderson, *World Population Dynamics*, 396.
92. Louis Israel Dublin and Alfred James Lotka, "On the True Rate of Natural Increase: As Exemplified by the Population of the United States, 1920," *Journal of the American Statistical Association* 20 (1925): 305–339.

93. Louis Israel Dublin, review of *Mankind at the Crossroads*, by Edward M. East, *Journal of the American Statistical Association* 19 (1924): 249–253.
94. Frank W. Notestein, "Draft Biographical Statement for the Collection of Alfred James Lotka, Princeton University Library," 1951, folder 12, box 4, Alfred J. Lotka Papers (MC032), Seeley G. Mudd Manuscript Library, Princeton University [hereafter AJLP].
95. Paul Vincent, "Lotka Obituary for *Population*, January–March 1950," folder 12, box 4, AJLP.
96. Kingsland, *Modeling Nature*, 86.
97. For the definition of a stationary population, see Anderson, *World Population Dynamics*, 370. Throughout this book I use the terms "stationary population" to refer to a population of constant size and "population stationarity" to refer to the unchanging size of a stationary population. While the terms "stable population" and "population stabilization" may be more familiar to some readers, these terms have different meanings to demographers, and I will be referring to them in their demographic sense later in the book.
98. For a more sustained discussion of mercantilism, see Anderson, *World Population Dynamics*, 8.
99. Louis Israel Dublin, "The Statistician and the Population Problem," *Journal of the American Statistical Association* 20 (1925): 1–12.
100. Notestein, "Draft Biographical Statement."
101. Dublin, "The Statistician and the Population Problem," 3.
102. Dublin, "The Statistician and the Population Problem," 10.
103. Dublin, review of *Mankind at the Crossroads,* 252.
104. For the animosity between Pearl and Dublin, see correspondence between Raymond Pearl and Margaret Sanger, February 18–March 3, 1925, folder "Margaret Sanger #5," box 24, RPP. Despite Dublin's expressed opposition to birth control, he and Sanger were on cordial terms, and Sanger welcomed his critique of birth control as a friendly challenge. She invited him to the 1925 International Neo-Malthusian and Birth Control Conference in New York to make the case against birth control legalization.
105. Anderson, *World Population Dynamics*, 251–255.
106. The NRR purports to describe the rate at which women bear daughters, but since age-specific fertility rates are usually not available by sex of the child, this is estimated by applying the sex ratio at birth (boys born per 100 girls born) to age-specific fertility rates undifferentiated by sex of child. Samuel Preston, Patrick Heuveline, and Michel Guillot, *Demography: Measuring and Modeling Population Processes* (Oxford: Blackwell, 2001).
107. Kuczynski also worked with a gross reproduction rate (GRR), which is also part of today's demographers' toolkit. GRR measures fertility only and does not account for mortality. It therefore represents *all* the daughters a woman is expected to have, not just those who will live long enough to have their own children. Two populations with the same NRR will have very different GRRs if one has a much higher rate of mortality than the other. Anderson, *World Population Dynamics*, 251.
108. This choice had important consequences for the way demographers modeled population growth and conducted fertility research, and for the development after World War II of systemic methods of contraception that worked directly on women's bodies, which will be discussed at greater length in later chapters.

109. Richard A. Soloway, *Demography and Degeneration: Eugenics and the Declining Birthrate in Twentieth-Century Britain* (Chapel Hill: University of North Carolina Press, 1990); Carl Ipsen, *Dictating Demography: The Problem of Population in Fascist Italy* (New York: Cambridge University Press, 1996).
110. Karl Ittmann, *A Problem of Great Importance: Population, Race, and Power in the British Empire, 1918–1973* (Berkeley: University of California Press, 2013).
111. Alfred James Lotka, review of *The Balance of Births and Deaths, Volume I*, by Robert René Kuczynski, *Journal of the American Statistical Association* 24 (1929): 332–333; Alfred James Lotka to Raymond Pearl, November 28, 1932, folder 4, box 14, AJLP. For interwar France, see P. H. Karmel, "The Relations between Male and Female Reproduction Rates," *Population Studies* 1 (1947): 249–274.
112. Edwin G. Nourse to Alfred J. Lotka, September 28, 1931, folder 4, box 14, AJLP.
113. Frank Hankins, review of *Fertility and Reproduction*, by Robert R. Kuczynski, *American Economic Review* 23 (1933): 165–166.
114. Dublin and Lotka described the true rate as a measure of "reproductive vitality" in "On the True Rate of Natural Increase," 322.
115. Bashford, *Global Population*.
116. Corrado Gini, Shiroshi Nasu, Oliver Edwin Baker, and Robert René Kuczynski, *Population (Lectures on the Harris Foundation, 1929)* (Chicago: University of Chicago Press, 1930).
117. E. B. Reuter, review of *Population*, by Corrado Gini, Shiroshi Nasu, Oliver E. Baker, and Robert R. Kuczynski, *American Journal of Sociology* 36 (1931): 647.
118. Raymond Pearl to Bernard Mallet, December 27, 1929, folder "Sir Bernard Mallet #8," box 18, RPP.
119. Raymond Pearl to Bernard Mallet, August 11 and 21, 1930, folder "Sir Bernard Mallet #10," box 18, RPP. Mallet felt that the choice of Gini as the IUSIPP's next president would be no more popular in England or France than in the United States. Bernard Mallet to Raymond Pearl, February 28, 1930, folder "Sir Bernard Mallet #9," box 18, RPP.
120. For the relocation of the General Assembly, see Raymond Pearl to Bernard Mallet, September 19, 1930, and Bernard Mallet to Raymond Pearl, October 3, 1930, folder "Sir Bernard Mallet #10," box 18, RPP. Close was chosen for his experience with international organizations and the expectation that he would be able to raise funds for the IUSIPP. Bernard Mallet to G. H. L. F. Pitt-Rivers, folder "Sir Bernard Mallet #10," box 18, RPP; Raymond Pearl to Bernard Mallet, December 30, 1930, folder "Sir Bernard Mallet #11," box 18, RPP.
121. Raymond Pearl to Corrado Gini, June 13, 1931, folder "Corrado Gini #7," box 8, RPP.
122. Raymond Pearl to Bernard Mallet, October 22, 1928, folder "Sir Bernard Mallet #5," box 18, RPP.
123. Charles Close to Eugen Fischer, 1933, folder "IUSIPP #10," box 15, RPP.
124. Charles Close to Raymond Pearl, February 8, 1936, folder "IUSIPP #11," box 15, RPP.
125. Frank H. Hankins, "German Policies for Increasing Births," *American Journal of Sociology* 42 (1937): 630–652.
126. Charles Close to Raymond Pearl, February 8, 1936. For Campbell's politics, see "U.S. Eugenist Hails Nazi Racial Policy," *New York Times*, August 28, 1935; Clarence G. Campbell, "The German Racial Policy," *Eugenical News* 21 (1936): 25–29.

127. Landis MacKellar and Bradley W. Hart, "Captain George Henry Lane-Fox Pitt-Rivers and the Prehistory of the IUSSP," *Population and Development Review* 40 (2014): 653–675.
128. Raymond Pearl to Charles Close, February 21, 1936, folder "IUSIPP #11," box 15, RPP.
129. David Victor Glass, "The Berlin Population Congress and Recent Population Movements in Germany," *Eugenics Review* 27 (1935): 208.
130. For more on this distinction, see Barkan, *The Retreat of Scientific Racism*.
131. "Minutes of the Meeting of the Research Committee of the PAA, December 30–31, 1935," folder "Alfred J. Lotka #9," box 17, RPP.
132. Raymond Pearl to Alfred J. Lotka, January 28, 1936, folder "Alfred J. Lotka #9," box 17, RPP. See also Raymond Pearl to Charles Close, February 21, 1936.
133. Charles Close to Raymond Pearl, February 8, 1936.
134. Sandrine Bertaux, "Reproduce or Perish? The Artefact of the Fertility Concept and the French School of Demography," *Historical Social Research/Historische Sozialforschung* 36 (2011): 120–139.
135. MacKellar and Hart, "Captain George Henry Lane-Fox Pitt-Rivers," 664.

CHAPTER 2

1. Henry Pratt Fairchild, "Report on Preliminary Conference on a Population Association for the United States," December 15, 1930, folder 12, box 3, AJLP. Fairchild was, at that time, president of the American Eugenics Society and hoped that the new organization could unite the eugenics and birth control agendas.
2. The PAA officially dates its founding to this 1931 meeting, though an organizing meeting took place in December 1930 in Fairchild's office at New York University.
3. Dennis Hodgson, "The Ideological Origins of the Population Association of America," *Population and Development Review* 17 (1991): 1–34. Hodgson describes the early PAA as a coalition of eugenicists, immigration restrictionists, birth control activists, and population scientists, though he acknowledges that these categories blurred and overlapped, and that opponents of each political program were also involved.
4. Notestein and Osborn, "Reminiscences."
5. The first and second generations of demographers loved telling this story, which, as Carole McCann points out, came to serve as an origin myth of the birthing of demography from birth control, and the science's simultaneous rejection of its political mother. McCann, *Figuring the Population Bomb*.
6. Irene B. Taeuber, "Oral History Interview with Anders Lunde, 28 April 1973," in Van Der Tak, Demographic Destinies, vol. 1, no. 1, 74–80.
7. Christine I. Oaklander, "Jonathan Sturges, W. H. Osborn, and William Church Osborn: A Chapter in American Art Patronage," *Metropolitan Museum Journal* 43 (2008): 173–194.
8. Theodore Roosevelt, "My Life as a Naturalist: With a Presentation of Various First-Hand Data on the Life Histories and Habits of the Big Game Animals of Africa," *American Museum Journal*, May 1918.
9. Mary McAleer Vizard, "If You're Thinking of Living In: Garrison, NY: Concern for Environment on the Hudson," *New York Times*, October 22, 1995.
10. "Background Note," Frederick Henry Osborn Papers (Mss.Ms.Coll.24), American Philosophical Society Library, Philadelphia [hereafter FHOP].

11. Notestein, "Oral History Interview."
12. Frederick Henry Osborn, "The Development of Eugenic Policies," 1935, folder "Frederick Osborn—Papers #5," box 17, American Eugenics Society Records (Mss.575.06Am3), American Philosophical Society Library, Philadelphia [hereafter AESR]; Frederick Henry Osborn, "A Eugenics Program for the United States," 1935, folder "Frederick Osborn—Papers #3," box 17, AESR.
13. For more on the Johnson-Reed Act, see Mae M. Ngai, "The Architecture of Race in American Immigration Law: A Reexamination of the Immigration Act of 1924," *Journal of American History* 86 (1999): 67–92.
14. Frederick Henry Osborn, "History of the American Eugenics Society," 1971, folder "Frederick Osborn—History of the American Eugenics Society #1," box 17, AESR.
15. For more on the abandonment of scientific racism in the interwar United States, see Barkan, *The Retreat of Scientific Racism*.
16. Allen, "The Eugenics Record Office at Cold Spring Harbor."
17. Isabel Grossner, "Oral History Interview with Frederick Osborn for the Columbia University Oral History Office," 1967, folder "Osborn—Biography #1," box 3, FHOP; Edmund Ramsden, "Frank W. Notestein, Frederick H. Osborn, and the Development of Demography in the United States," *Princeton University Library Chronicle* 65 (2004): 282–316.
18. Frederick Henry Osborn, "Absolute Weapons—the American Reply," 1961, folder "Frederick Osborn—Papers #21," box 18, AESR; Frederick Henry Osborn, "Eugenics Credo," folder "Frederick Osborn—Papers #15," box 17, AESR. Osborn was a founding member and first secretary of the overtly racist Pioneer Fund, which was established by Wickliffe Draper in 1937 and is now classified by the Southern Poverty Law Center as a hate group. Ramsden, "Frank W. Notestein, Frederick H. Osborn, and the Development of Demography in the United States."
19. Frederick Henry Osborn, "Implications for the New Studies in Population and Psychology for the Development of Eugenic Philosophy," 1937, folder "Frederick Osborn—Papers #8," box 17, AESR.
20. Frederick Henry Osborn, "Major Aspects of Eugenic Selection," 1936, folder "Frederick Osborn—Papers #7," box 17, AESR.
21. Frederick Henry Osborn, "Notes for Eugenic Program," 1934, folder "Frederick Osborn—Papers #4," box 17, AESR.
22. Frederick Henry Osborn, "Moral Responsibilities of Parenthood," 1936, folder "Frederick Osborn—Papers #6," box 17, AESR.
23. Daniel Kevles termed Osborn's brand of eugenics "reform" eugenics, though Alexandra Minna Stern has argued that "reform" eugenics was just as repressive to many people as was "mainline" eugenics. The Eugenics Society of Great Britain also disavowed intra-European racism in the 1930s under the direction of Carlos P. Blacker. Kevles, *In the Name of Eugenics*; Stern, *Eugenic Nation*.
24. Osborn, "Moral Responsibilities of Parenthood."
25. Osborn, "Major Aspects of Eugenic Selection," emphasis mine.
26. Osborn, "Moral Responsibilities of Parenthood."
27. Osborn, "Moral Responsibilities of Parenthood."
28. "The Development of Eugenic Policies: A Memorandum by the American Eugenics Society," *Eugenics Review* 29 (1937): 120.
29. Frederick Henry Osborn, "Memorandum of Remarks at Birth Control Meeting at Mrs. Roland Redmond's House," 1937, folder "Frederick Osborn—Papers #8," box 17, AESR.

30. Osborn, "Major Aspects of Eugenic Selection."
31. Osborn, "A Eugenics Program for the United States."
32. Lemov, *World as Laboratory*.
33. Frank Lorimer and Frederick Osborn, *Dynamics of Population: Social and Biological Significance of Changing Birth Rates in the United States* (New York: Macmillan, 1934).
34. George J. Stolnitz, "Oral History Interview with Jean Van Der Tak, 20 January 1988," in Van Der Tak, Demographic Destinies, vol. 1, no. 3, 141–160.
35. Norman B. Ryder, "Oral History Interview with Jean Van Der Tak, 11 May 1988," in Van Der Tak, Demographic Destinies, vol. 1, no. 2, 250–277.
36. Frank Lorimer, "Letter to Members of the Population Association of America," December 19, 1934, folder "PAA #1," box 22, RPP.
37. Alfred James Lotka to Mortimer Spiegelman, December 5, 1941, folder 11, box 4, AJLP; Frank W. Notestein, "Memorandum Re Previous Recommendations of Terminology" and "Memorandum to the Committee on Uniform Scientific Terminology," and Alfred James Lotka, "Some General Principles in Framing an Acceptable Terminology," 1941, folder 11, box 4, AJLP.
38. Frank Lorimer to Raymond Pearl, September 6, 1934, and November 5, 1934, folder "PAA #1," box 22, RPP. This bibliography would eventually become the quarterly publication *Population Index*.
39. Harold Dodds, "Albert G. Milbank and His Relationship to Princeton," 1952, folder 22, box 26, series II, Milbank Memorial Fund Records (MS 845), Yale University Library [hereafter MMFR].
40. "School of Public and International Affairs, 1930 Report," folder 40, box 4, School of Public and International Affairs (P655.737.499), Seeley G. Mudd Manuscript Library, Princeton University [hereafter SPIA].
41. Cohen-Cole, *The Open Mind*.
42. Notestein, "Oral History Interview."
43. Dewitt Clinton Poole to Harold Dodds, December 11, 1935, folder 12, box 9, SPIA.
44. Thanks to demographer Emily Marshall for pointing this out to me.
45. "Princeton University President's Reports, 1936–1940," folder 12, box 4, SPIA; Dewitt Clinton Poole to William Church Osborn, April 4, 1936, folder 13, box 9, SPIA; Milbank Memorial Fund to Dewitt Clinton Poole, March 23, 1936, folder 21, box 15, SPIA; "Statement of Account," October 24, 1939, folder 21, box 15, SPIA; Notestein, "Oral History Interview."
46. John D. Durand, "Oral History Interview with Abbott Ferriss, 11 August 1979," in Van Der Tak, Demographic Destinies, vol. 1, no. 2, 6–12.
47. Ansley J. Coale, "Interview with Anders Lunde for the PAA Oral History Project" April 27, 1979, folder 5, box 1, Ansley J. Coale Papers (MC208), Seeley G. Mudd Manuscript Library, Princeton University [hereafter AJCP].
48. "Milbank Memorial Fund Fellows at the Office of Population Research for the Period 1936–1968," folder 5, box 1, Frank W. Notestein Papers (MC184), Seeley G. Mudd Manuscript Library, Princeton University [hereafter FWNP].
49. For an exception, see Merchant, "A Digital History of Anglophone Demography."
50. Frank W. Notestein to Frederick Henry Osborn, April 22, 1968, folder "Frank W. Notestein," box 3, FHOP.
51. The Recent Social Trends project has been the subject of a large quantity of historical scholarship: Robert C. Bannister, *Sociology and Scientism: The American Quest for Objectivity, 1880–1940* (Chapel Hill: University of North

Carolina Press, 1987); Martin Bulmer, "The Methodology of Early Social Indicator Research: William Fielding Ogburn and 'Recent Social Trends,' 1933," *Social Indicators Research* 13 (1983): 109–130; David L. Featherman and Maris Vinovskis, eds. *Social Science and Policy-Making: A Search for Relevance in the Twentieth Century* (Ann Arbor: University of Michigan Press, 2001); Michael Lacey and Mary Furner, *The State and Social Investigation in Britain and the United States* (Cambridge: Cambridge University Press, 1993); Mark C. Smith, *Social Science in the Crucible: The American Debate over Objectivity and Purpose, 1918–1941* (Durham, NC: Duke University Press, 1994).

52. Together with Lester Frank Ward, William Graham Sumner, and Albion Small. This Eurocentric vision of sociology's founding excludes W. E. B. Du Bois, who was also one of the originators of the field. Morris, *The Scholar Denied*.
53. Charles Camic and Yu Xie, "The Statistical Turn in American Social Science: Columbia University, 1890–1915," *American Sociological Review* 59 (1994): 773–805.
54. Anthony Oberschall, "The Institutionalization of American Sociology," in *The Establishment of Empirical Sociology*, ed. Anthony Oberschall (New York: Harper and Row, 1972), 187–251.
55. Bannister, *Sociology and Scientism*.
56. Warren Simpson Thompson, *Population: A Study in Malthusianism* (New York: Columbia University, 1915).
57. Mike Payne, *Scripps Gerontology Center: A Legacy of Leadership (A History of the Scripps Gerontology Center)* (Oxford, OH: Scripps Gerontology Center, Miami University, 2005).
58. Merchant, "A Digital History of Anglophone Demography."
59. Warren Simpson Thompson to Raymond Pearl, October 10, 1923, folder "Warren S. Thompson," box 27, RPP.
60. Warren Simpson Thompson to Raymond Pearl, October 19, 1923, folder "Warren S. Thompson," box 27, RPP.
61. Clyde V. Kiser, "Contributions of P. K. Whelpton to Demography," *Biodemography and Social Biology* 20 (1973): 438–447.
62. Warren Simpson Thompson, "Population Facts for the United States and Their Interpretation," *Journal of the American Statistical Association* 18 (1923): 575–587.
63. Pascal Kidder Whelpton, "Population of the United States, 1925 to 1975," *American Journal of Sociology* 34 (1928): 253–270.
64. Whelpton was not the first to use the basic mechanics of this method. British economists Edwin Cannan and Arthur Lyon Bowley had used it previously, Cannan in 1895 to forecast the 1931 population of London for the Metropolitan Water Commission (Edwin Cannan, "The Probability of a Cessation of Growth of Population in England and Wales during the Next Century," *Economic Journal* 5 [1895]: 505–515) and Bowley in 1924 to calculate the fertility rates that would be necessary for England and Wales to avoid population decline over the twentieth century (Arthur Lyon Bowley, "Births and Population in Great Britain," *Economic Journal* 34 [1924]: 188–192). In contrast to Whelpton, who employed vital rates that he expected to obtain in the future and that changed over time, Cannan assumed constant mortality rates and numbers of births and Bowley assumed constant mortality rates and zero overall natural increase.
65. Anderson, *World Population Dynamics*, 384.

66. Later in the century, critics would argue that the accuracy of vital data at the time, particularly for subsets of the population, did not warrant the precision with which Whelpton presented those estimates. George F. Mair, "Population Projection: The State of an Art," Ph.D. diss., Princeton University, 1957.
67. By this time Thompson saw the major problem facing the world as uneven population growth—rapid growth in some countries combined with slow growth in others—and recommended that global population be equalized through large-scale schemes of immigration from high-density countries to low-density countries and land transfer from sparsely populated countries, such as Australia and certain British colonies in Africa, to densely populated countries, such as India and Japan. Warren Thompson, *Danger Spots in World Population* (New York: Knopf, 1929).
68. China's leaders would use this method in the 1970s to develop the one-child policy. Susan Greenhalgh, "Science, Modernity, and the Making of China's One-Child Policy," *Population and Development Review* 29 (2003): 163–196.
69. "The Population Forecasts of the Scripps Foundation," *Population Index* 14 (1948): 188–195.
70. Derek S. Hoff describes these measures as "stable population Keynesianism" in *The State and the Stork*, though they would be more accurately described as "stationary population Keynesianism."
71. Warren Simpson Thompson and Pascal Kidder Whelpton, *Population Trends in the United States* (New York: McGraw, 1933), 126.
72. Thompson and Whelpton, *Population Trends in the United States*, 171.
73. Ross and Solinger, *Reproductive Justice*, 36–37.
74. For the relationship between demography and the welfare state, see Dan Bouk, "Generation Crisis: How Population Research Defined the Baby Boomers," *Modern American History* 1 (2018): 321–342.
75. "Minutes of the PAA Annual Meeting," 1934, folder "PAA #1," box 22, RPP.
76. Notestein, "Oral History Interview," 8.
77. Clyde V. Kiser, C. Horace Hamilton, and Joseph J. Spengler, "Oral History Interview with Harry Rosenberg, 15 December 1976," in Van Der Tak, Demographic Destinies, vol. 1, no. 1, 99–115.
78. Alfred James Lotka, "Population Trends in the United States," 1940, folder 16, box 20, AJLP.
79. Pascal Kidder Whelpton, "The Population Prospect," in *Proceedings of the Third International Conference of Agricultural Economists, Held at Bad Eilsen, Germany, 26 August to 2 September 1934* (London: Oxford University Press, 1935), 250–263.
80. Paraphrased in C. C. McGuire, review of *Population*, by Corrado Gini, Shiroshi Nasu, Robert R. Kuczynski, and Oliver E. Baker, *Political Science Quarterly* 46 (1931): 443.
81. Lotka, "Population Trends in the United States."
82. Milbank Memorial Fund, "Technical Committee Minutes," 1941, folder 83, box 11, series I, MMFR.
83. Milbank Memorial Fund, "Division of Population Problems," 1932, folder 74, box 29, series II, MMFR.
84. Frank W. Notestein to Frederick Henry Osborn, folder 21, box 15, SPIA; Clyde V. Kiser, "The Fund's Work in Population," folder 86, box 29, series II, MMFR; "Report of the Division of Population Problems," 1932, folder 74, box 29, series II, MMFR.
85. Charles F. Westoff, "The Changing Focus of Differential Fertility Research: The Social Mobility Hypothesis," *Milbank Memorial Fund Quarterly* 31 (1953): 24–38.

86. Frank W. Notestein, "The Fertility of Population Supported by Public Relief," *Milbank Memorial Fund Quarterly* 41 (1936): 37–49.
87. Milbank Memorial Fund, "Press Release," May 13, 1931, folder 177, box 22, series I, MMFR.
88. These theories were discussed at the 1931 IUSIPP Assembly in London. G. H. L. F. Pitt-Rivers, ed., *Problems of Population: Being the Report of the Proceedings of the Second General Assembly of the International Union for the Scientific Investigation of Population Problems* (London: Kennikat Press, 1932).
89. For the history of this research, see Clarke, *Disciplining Reproduction*.
90. Milbank Memorial Fund, "Division of Population Problems."
91. Milbank Memorial Fund, "Technical Committee Minute Book," November 17, 1932, folder 79, box 11, series I, MMFR.
92. Of the sixty-two population-related articles published in the *Milbank Memorial Fund Quarterly* in the 1930s, fully half were on fertility, with more than half of those specifically addressing differential fertility. Many of these studies are cited in Westoff, "The Changing Focus of Differential Fertility Research."
93. Milbank Memorial Fund, "Minutes of the Technical Committee," May 16, 1940, folder 82, box 11, series I, MMFR.
94. Regine Kronacher Stix and Frank W. Notestein, *Controlled Fertility: An Evaluation of Clinic Service* (Baltimore, MD: Williams & Wilkins, 1940).
95. Notestein found that about 95% of women who sought clinical assistance with birth control had previously used contraception on their own—mostly withdrawal—with a 75% success rate. Milbank Memorial Fund, "Press Release," January 22, 1934, folder 177, box 22, series I, MMFR; Regine Kronacher Stix and Frank W. Notestein, "Effectiveness of Birth Control: A Study of Contraceptive Practice in a Selected Group of New York Women," *Milbank Memorial Fund Quarterly* 12 (1934): 57–68. Feminist scholar Carole McCann has pointed out a serious flaw in Notestein's methodology. He assumed that, in the absence of birth control, women would continue to bear children at the same rate they did during their first year of marriage. This meant that a woman married at age twenty would experience a total of fourteen pregnancies before reaching menopause at age forty-five. This assumption exaggerated the number of pregnancies a woman would experience in the absence of birth control and thereby exaggerated the efficacy with which couples could prevent pregnancy in the 1930s. McCann contends that such exaggeration minimized the need to make birth control more widely available or develop more effective methods. McCann, *Figuring the Population Bomb*.
96. Quoted in Frank Lorimer, "The Development of Demography," in *The Study of Population: An Inventory and Appraisal*, ed. Philip M. Hauser and Otis Dudley Duncan (Chicago: University of Chicago Press, 1959), 160.
97. "Birth Control Ban Opposed (Press Clipping)," March 14, 1934, folder 185, box 22, series I, MMFR.
98. For the development of middle management, see Alfred Dupont Chandler, *The Visible Hand: The Managerial Revolution in American Business* (Cambridge, MA: Belknap, 1977).
99. Raymond Pearl, "Contraception and Fertility in 4,945 Married Women: A Second Report on a Study of Family Limitation," *Human Biology* 6 (1934): 355–401.
100. Stix and Notestein, *Controlled Fertility*.
101. This suggestion spurred research on spermicidal compounds by the National Committee on Maternal Health, resulting in a Milbank program to test the

distribution of spermicides in Logan County, West Virginia. Milbank Memorial Fund, "Minutes of the Technical Committee."

102. Frederick Henry Osborn to Frank W. Notestein, December 20, 1940, folder 5, box 8, FWNP.
103. Frank W. Notestein to Frederick Henry Osborn, January 6, 1941, folder 5, box 8, FWNP.
104. For the Bush family's relationship to Planned Parenthood, see Pema Levy, "How the Bush Family Aided Planned Parenthood's Rise," *Mother Jones*, August 11, 2015.
105. Quoted in Ramsden, "Frank W. Notestein, Frederick H. Osborn, and the Development of Demography in the United States," 302.
106. Surveys in this vein include Charles Booth's turn-of-the-century study of London's poor, W. E. B. Du Bois's *The Philadelphia Negro: A Social Study* (Philadelphia: University of Pennsylvania, 1899), the 1907–1908 Pittsburgh Survey, and Robert and Helen Lynd's *Middletown: A Study in Contemporary American Culture* (New York: Harcourt, Brace, 1929).
107. Jean M. Converse, *Survey Research in the United States: Roots and Emergence 1890–1960* (New York: Routledge, 2017).
108. In 2020 Princeton's Board of Trustees again renamed the school, reverting back to SPIA, in response to student protests regarding Wilson's segregationist policies. Lori Aratani, "Princeton Says It Will Remove Woodrow Wilson's Name from Its Public Policy School," *Washington Post*, June 28, 2020.
109. John F. Kantner, "Oral History Interview with Jean van der Tak, 22 March 1988," in Van Der Tak, Demographic Destinies, vol. 1, no. 3, 91–104.
110. Milbank Memorial Fund, "Technical Committee Minutes."
111. Pascal K. Whelpton and Clyde V. Kiser, "Social and Psychological Factors Affecting Fertility, Part III: The Completeness and Accuracy of the Household Survey of Indianapolis," *Milbank Memorial Fund Quarterly* 23 (1945): 259–260.
112. Clyde V. Kiser, "The Indianapolis Fertility Study—An Example of Planned Observational Research," *Public Opinion Quarterly* 17 (1953): 496–510.
113. This finding was consistent with the results of similar research in interwar Sweden that provided intellectual support for Sweden's combined eugenic/contraceptive/pronatalist program. Karl Arvid Edin, "The Fertility of the Social Classes in Stockholm in the Years 1919 to 1929," in Pitt-Rivers, *Problems of Population*, 91–104.
114. Gary S. Becker, "An Economic Analysis of Fertility," in *Demographic and Economic Change in Developed Countries*, ed. National Bureau of Economic Research (New York: Columbia University Press, 1960), 209–240; Judith Blake, "Are Babies Consumer Durables? A Critique of the Economic Theory of Reproductive Motivation," *Population Studies* 22 (1968): 5–25.
115. Clyde V. Kiser and Pascal K. Whelpton, "Resume of the Indianapolis Study of Social and Psychological Factors Affecting Fertility," *Population Studies* 7 (1953): 107.
116. Richard A. Williams, "Indianapolis Revisited: A New Look at Social and Psychological Factors Affecting Fertility," Ph.D. diss., University of Wisconsin, 1986.
117. Kiser, "The Indianapolis Fertility Study," 509.
118. Susan Greenhalgh, ed. *Situating Fertility: Anthropology and Demographic Inquiry* (New York: Cambridge University Press, 1995).

119. Frederick Henry Osborn, "Oral History Interview with Richard D. McKinzie for the Harry S. Truman Library and Museum," July 10, 1974, trumanlibrary.gov/library/oral-histories/osbornf.
120. Frederick Henry Osborn, "Eugenics and National Defense," *Journal of Heredity* 32 (1941): 203.
121. Osborn, "Eugenics and National Defense," 204.
122. Frank W. Notestein, "Frederick Osborn: Demography's Statesman on His Eightieth Spring," *Population Index* 35 (1969): 367–371.
123. For instance, see Thompson, *Danger Spots in World Population*.

CHAPTER 3

1. Robertson, *The Malthusian Moment*, 33.
2. In the United States, the data that made it possible to measure "the economy" became available only in the 1930s with the New Deal's revenue acts. Timothy Mitchell, "Economentality: How the Future Entered Government," *Critical Inquiry* 40 (2014): 479–507.
3. A notable exception is Warren Thompson, who in his 1929 book, *Danger Spots in World Population*, argued that rapid population growth in Japan and India could provoke a geopolitical crisis if people from those places were not allowed to emigrate to sparsely settled countries elsewhere in the world, specifically Australia and the British colonies of East Africa.
4. Mark Mazower, *Governing the World: The History of an Idea, 1815 to the Present* (New York: Penguin, 2012).
5. Princeton Office of Population Research, "Progress Report of: The Office of Population Research, to: The Carnegie Corporation of New York. On: Study of Demographic Problems of the Postwar Years," March 15, 1942, folder 21, box 15, SPIA. These projects resulted in the publication of several books: Frank W. Notestein et al., *The Future Population of Europe and the Soviet Union, 1940–1970* (Princeton, NJ: Princeton University Press, 1944); Frank Lorimer, *The Population of the Soviet Union: History and Prospects* (Princeton, NJ: Princeton University Press, 1946); Dudley Kirk, *Europe's Population in the Inter-War Years* (Princeton, NJ: Princeton University Press, 1946); Irene B. Taeuber, *The Population of Japan* (Princeton, NJ: Princeton University Press, 1958); Kingsley Davis, *The Population of India and Pakistan* (Princeton, NJ: Princeton University Press, 1951).
6. Inter American Statistical Institute, *The Story of the 1950 Census of the Americas: An Account Prepared by the Inter American Statistical Institute in Cooperation with the General Bureaus of Statistics and the National Census Offices of the American Nations* (Washington, DC: Inter American Statistical Institute, 1953).
7. "Total Population for Each Area of the World According to the Latest Census, Latest Official Estimate, and at Midyear 1946," March 1, 1948, folder 6, box 5, series 920, United Nations Archives, New York [hereafter UNA].
8. Walter Willcox, *Studies in American Demography* (Ithaca, NY: Cornell University Press, 1940), 511.
9. Frank W. Notestein, "Population—the Long View," in *Food for the World*, ed. Theodore Schultz (Chicago: University of Chicago Press, 1945), 38.
10. Robert René Kuczynski, *Colonial Population* (London: Oxford University Press, 1937); Robert René Kuczynski, *Demographic Survey of the British Colonial Empire* (London: Oxford University Press, 1948).

11. "Verification of Published Sources: Kenya" and "Verification of Published Sources: Cameroons (British)," folders 1-52, box 11, Series 920, UNA.
12. Quoted in Kuczynski, *Colonial Population*, 12.
13. For other mechanisms, see Ann Laura Stoler, *Race and the Education of Desire: Foucault's History of Sexuality and the Colonial Order of Things* (Durham, NC: Duke University Press, 1995).
14. Kuczynski, *Demographic Survey of the British Colonial Empire*, 14.
15. Kuczynski, *Demographic Survey of the British Colonial Empire*, 6–7.
16. For comparison, Megan Vaughan explores how colonial governments managed disease en masse rather than at the level of individual patients, in Megan Vaughan, *Curing Their Ills: Colonial Power and African Illness* (Stanford, CA: Stanford University Press, 1991).
17. Frederick Cooper, "Conflict and Connection: Rethinking Colonial African History," *American Historical Review* 99 (1994): 1533.
18. For political arithmetic, see Andrea A. Rusnock, "Biopolitics: Political Arithmetic in the Enlightenment," in *The Sciences in Enlightened Europe*, ed. William Clark, Jan Golinski, and Simon Schaffer (Chicago: University of Chicago Press, 1999), 113–138.
19. Hauser was thoroughly briefed on the positions he should take prior to each meeting. For instance, see Abram J. Jaffe to Ellsworth Bunker, March 10, 1949, and Abram J. Jaffe to Philip M. Hauser, March 10, 1949, folder 3, box 10, Philip M. Hauser Papers, Special Collections Research Center, University of Chicago Library [hereafter PMHP].
20. For a detailed description of this work, see Joseph W. Ryan, *Samuel Stouffer and the GI Survey: Sociologists and Soldiers during the Second World War* (Knoxville: University of Tennessee Press, 2013).
21. Philip M. Hauser to Christopher Tietze, August 11, 1945, folder 2, box 2, PMHP.
22. For other job offers, see 1945 correspondence between Hauser and Robert C. Angell, folder 1, box 2, PMHP. For Hauser's resignation from the Census Bureau, see Hauser to A. W. von Struve, June 27, 1947, and Hauser to J. C. Capt, September 10, 1947, folder 2, box 10, PMHP.
23. Philip M. Hauser to Gilberto Loyo, August 10, 1949, folder 13, box 2, PMHP.
24. Philip Hauser to Frank Notestein, April 11, 1950, folder 5, box 13, AJCP.
25. Frank Notestein Affidavit, April 14, 1950, folder 5, box 13, AJCP.
26. United Nations Administrative Tribunal, Judgment 32, digitallibrary.un.org/record/496696.
27. For more on the globalization of the New Deal, see Elizabeth Borgwardt, *A New Deal for the World: America's Vision for Human Rights* (Cambridge, MA: Harvard University Press, 2005).
28. Bruno Latour, *Science in Action: How to Follow Scientists and Engineers through Society* (Cambridge, MA: Harvard University Press, 1987).
29. Philip M. Hauser, "The Early Years of the Population Commission," *Population Bulletin of the United Nations* 19 (1986): 3.
30. Bashford, *Global Population*.
31. "Draft of Position Paper for Fourth Session of UN Population Commission, Sent by Abram Jaffe to Philip Hauser," March 10, 1949, folder 3, box 10, PMHP.
32. Quoted in S. A. Aluko, "How Many Nigerians? An Analysis of Nigeria's Census Problems, 1901–63," *Journal of Modern African Studies* 3 (1965): 371.
33. H. W. Arndt, *Economic Development: The History of an Idea* (Chicago: University of Chicago Press, 1987).

34. Mitchell, "Economentality," 507. See also Timothy Mitchell, *Carbon Democracy: Political Power in the Age of Oil* (London: Verso, 2011); Daniel Hirschman, "Inventing the Economy (or, How We Learned to Stop Worrying and Love the GDP)," Ph.D. diss., University of Michigan, 2016; Murphy, *The Economization of Life*; Marion Fourcade, "The Construction of a Global Profession: The Transnationalization of Economics," *American Journal of Sociology* 112 (2006): 145–194.
35. Mitchell, "Economentality."
36. Latour, *Science in Action*, 227.
37. Theodore M. Porter, "Thin Description: Surface and Depth in Science and Science Studies," *Osiris* 27 (2012): 209–226.
38. Wendy Espelend and Mitchell L. Stevens, "Commensuration as a Social Process," *Annual Review of Sociology* 24, no. 1 (1998): 315.
39. Espelend and Stevens, "Commensuration as a Social Process," 316.
40. For more on human classification, see Geoffrey C. Bowker and Susan Leigh Star, *Sorting Things Out: Classification and Its Consequences* (Cambridge, MA: MIT Press, 2000); Ian Hacking, "Making Up People," in *Reconstructing Individualism: Autonomy, Individuality, and the Self in Western Thought*, ed. Thomas C. Heller, Morton Sosna, and David E. Wellbery (Stanford, CA: Stanford University Press, 1986), 222–236.
41. Anderson, *World Population Dynamics*, 67.
42. If country A has a high rate of temporary migration to country B and one country has a *de jure* census and the other a *de facto* census, then migrants could be counted twice (if the census in country A is *de jure* and that in country B is *de facto*) or not counted at all (if the census in country A is *de facto* and that in country B is *de jure*).
43. The term "data friction" was coined by Paul Edwards to denote "the great difficulty, cost, and slow speed of gathering large numbers of records in one place in a form suitable for massive calculation." Edwards, *A Vast Machine: Computer Models, Climate Data, and the Politics of Global Warming* (Cambridge, MA: MIT Press, 2010), 80.
44. Abram J. Jaffe, "Population Commission—4th Session (Committee on Provisional Agenda)," March 7, 1949, folder 3, box 10, PMHP.
45. "United Nations Population Commission, Fourth Session (Draft)," April 25, 1950, folder 8, box 10, PMHP.
46. Inter American Statistical Institute, *The Story of the 1950 Census of the Americas*.
47. Jacob Darwin Hamblin, *Arming Mother Nature: The Birth of Catastrophic Environmentalism* (New York: Oxford University Press, 2013).
48. U.S. Bureau of the Census, "Program Review Report: January 1, 1949–June 30, 1949 Cooperation with the American Republics Program of the Bureau of the Census," 1949, folder 5, box 10, PMHP.
49. Calvert L. Dedrick, "Cultural Differences and Census Concepts," *Milbank Memorial Fund Quarterly* 27 (1949): 283–288.
50. United Nations, *Yearbook of the United Nations, 1946–1947* (New York: United Nations, 1947), 512. This was not the first attempt at international standardization of censuses. Nearly one hundred years earlier, a series of International Statistical Congresses convened for the same purpose, but these attempts primarily involved European countries and were ultimately derailed by the growing nationalism of the late nineteenth century. Nico Randeraad, "The

International Statistical Congresses (1853–1876): Knowledge Transfers and Their Limits," *European History Quarterly* 41 (2011): 50–65.

51. United Nations Population Division, *Population Census Methods* (New York: United Nations Department of Social Affairs, 1949), 3.
52. United Nations, *Yearbook of the United Nations, 1946–1947*, 567.
53. Dedrick, "Cultural Differences and Census Concepts."
54. Notwithstanding the inclusion of military and diplomatic personnel living abroad, the guide emphasized a territorial definition of population, recommending the inclusion of all people living within the borders of a state, even if they were outside its social, economic, and political framework, such as indigenous or nomadic groups. United Nations Population Division, *Population Census Methods*, 6–7.
55. United Nations Population Division, *Manual I: Methods of Estimating Total Population for Current Dates* (New York: United Nations Department of Social Affairs, 1952); William R. Leonard, "General Assessment of International Statistics and Outlook for the Future," *Milbank Memorial Fund Quarterly* 27 (1949): 332–337.
56. As Judith Treas has put it, "greater precision in reckoning age is the result of embedding chronological age in administrative practice. When age really mattered in practice, individual precision in reporting chronological age swiftly followed." Judith Treas, "Age in Standards and Standards for Age," in *Standards and Their Stories: How Quantifying, Classifying, and Formalizing Practices Shape Everyday Life*, ed. Martha Lampland and Susan Leigh Star (Ithaca, NY: Cornell University Press, 2009), 66.
57. Aluko, "How Many Nigerians?," 379.
58. United Nations, *Yearbook of the United Nations, 1951* (New York: United Nations, 1951), 569.
59. Myron Gutmann, Evan Roberts, and I have defined "big historical data" as data that are increasingly granular; in the realm of censuses, granularity reaches its limit with universal data collection and analysis. Myron Gutmann, Evan Roberts, and Emily Klancher Merchant, "'Big Data' in Economic History," *Journal of Economic History* 78 (2018): 268–299.
60. Additional questions about work were asked of everyone fourteen and older; questions about family formation and education were asked of every fifth person.
61. Steven Ruggles and Diana L. Magnuson, "Capturing the American People: Census Technology and Institutional Change, 1790–2020" (Minneapolis: Minnesota Population Center Working Papers, June 14, 2018).
62. Philip M. Hauser to Howard A. Meyerhoff, April 20, 1951, folder 3, box 3, PMHP.
63. United Nations Population Division, "The Past and Future Population of the World and Its Continents," in *Proceedings of the World Population Conference, Rome, 1954* (New York: United Nations, 1954), 265–281.
64. $70 million for population and agriculture and $15 million for housing. "General Questionnaire on Status of the 1950 Census Program in the Americas," folder 2, box 10, PMHP.
65. Aluko, "How Many Nigerians?," 376.
66. Babatunde A. Ahonsi, "Deliberate Falsification and Census Data in Nigeria," *African Affairs* 87 (1988): 553–562.
67. Aluko, "How Many Nigerians?," 385.
68. Ahonsi, "Deliberate Falsification and Census Data in Nigeria."

69. Donald P. Warwick, *Bitter Pills: Population Policies and Their Implementation in Eight Developing Countries* (New York: Cambridge University Press, 1982), 23–24.
70. Kuczynski, *Demographic Survey of the British Colonial Empire*, 8.
71. United Nations, *United Nations Demographic Yearbook 1962* (New York: Statistical Office of the United Nations, 1962). This number includes colonial territories as well as sovereign countries.
72. United Nations Population Division, *1960 World Population Census Programme: Sampling Methods and Population Censuses* (New York: Statistical Office of the United Nations, 1957).
73. Alain Desrosières, *The Politics of Large Numbers: A History of Statistical Reasoning* (Cambridge, MA: Harvard University Press, 2002).
74. This "sample line" approach was a precursor to the "long form," which was employed in the censuses of 1960–2000.
75. For more on the *Middletown* studies, see Sarah E. Igo, *The Averaged American: Surveys, Citizens, and the Making of a Mass Public* (Cambridge, MA: Harvard University Press, 2009).
76. United Nations Population Division, *1960 World Population Census Programme*, 79–80.
77. United Nations Population Division, *1960 World Population Census Programme*, 77.
78. Murphy, *The Economization of Life*, 59–60.
79. Ekbladh, *The Great American Mission*; Nils Gilman, *Mandarins of the Future: Modernization Theory in Cold War America* (Baltimore, MD: Johns Hopkins University Press, 2003); Michael E. Latham, *Modernization as Ideology: American Social Science and "Nation Building" in the Kennedy Era* (Chapel Hill: University of North Carolina Press, 2000); Latham, *The Right Kind of Revolution*.
80. Demographic transition theory also had interwar roots, most apparent in Warren Simpson Thompson, "Population," *American Journal of Sociology* 34 (1929): 959–975, and Adolphe Landry, *La Révolution Démographique* (Paris: Sirey, 1934). Dennis Hodgson, "Demography as Social Science and Policy Science," *Population and Development Review* 9 (1983): 1–34, and Simon Szreter, "The Idea of Demographic Transition and the Study of Fertility Change: A Critical Intellectual History," *Population and Development Review* 19 (1993): 659–701, assert that Thompson "discovered" demographic transition theory between the wars and that OPR demographers independently "rediscovered" it on the basis of their wartime studies of population in Europe and Asia. This chronology, however, overlooks the fact that Notestein and his OPR colleagues were familiar with Thompson's earlier work and in constant communication with Thompson through the PAA and as a result of interwar collaboration between OPR and the Scripps Foundation. They didn't need to "rediscover" his theories because they already knew them. Moreover, given the absence of reliable population data for much of the world, it is more likely that the formulation of demographic transition theory facilitated OPR's wartime population analysis than that OPR's wartime research revealed the pattern of spreading demographic transition.
81. Kingsley Davis, "Reproductive Institutions and the Pressure for Population," *Sociological Review* a29 (1937): 289–306; Frank W. Notestein, "Problems of Policy in Relation to Areas of Heavy Population Pressure," *Milbank Memorial Fund Quarterly* 22 (1944): 424–444.
82. Kingsley Davis, "The World Demographic Transition," *Annals of the American Academy of Political and Social Sciences* 237 (1945): 1–11.

83. Notestein, "Population—The Long View," 57.
84. For the distinction between biological and cultural racism, see Etienne Balibar and Immanuel Wallerstein, *Race, Nation, Class: Ambiguous Identities* (New York: Verso, 1991).
85. Davis, "The World Demographic Transition," 7.
86. Dudley Kirk, "Population Changes in the Postwar World," *American Sociological Review* 9 (1944): 28-29.
87. Although midcentury demographers thought that modernization had contributed to the rise of a small-family norm and nuclear-family living arrangements in Northern and Western Europe, the emergent field of historical demography would soon demonstrate that Northern and Western Europeans had been living in nuclear families as far back as the historical record went. They soon began to theorize that it was this nuclear-family living arrangement that spurred industrialization rather than the reverse. Myron Gutmann and Emily Klancher Merchant, "Historical Demography," in *Handbook of Population*, 2nd edition, ed. Dudley L. Poston Jr. (Cham, Switzerland: Springer Nature, 2019), 669–695.
88. Davis, "The World Demographic Transition," 7.
89. For instance, see Lothrop Stoddard, *The Rising Tide of Color against White World-Supremacy* (New York: Blue Ribbon Books, 1920).
90. Ansley J. Coale, "Oral History Interview with Anders Lunde, 27 April 1979, and Jean Van Der Tak, 11 May 1988," in Van Der Tak, *Demographic Destinies*, vol. 1, no. 2, 136.
91. Kirk, "Population Changes in the Postwar World."
92. Anne McClintock, *Imperial Leather: Race, Gender, and Sexuality in the Colonial Context* (New York: Routledge, 1995).
93. Notestein et al., *The Future Population of Europe and the Soviet Union.*
94. Arland Thornton, *Reading History Sideways: The Fallacy and Enduring Impact of the Developmental Paradigm on Family Life* (Chicago: University of Chicago Press, 2005).
95. To this day, population projections take into account only current population and expert judgments regarding future trajectories of mortality and fertility, excluding data about the economic or social hallmarks of modernization that are thought to drive demographic change. When OPR demographers did attempt to correlate fertility change with social and economic factors in the 1960s, they were unable to find consistent relationships.
96. Frank W. Notestein to Frederick H. Osborn, April 8, 1941, folder 5, box 8, FWNP.
97. This research was published as Ansley J. Coale, *The Problem of Reducing Vulnerability to Atomic Bombs* (Princeton, NJ: Princeton University Press, 1947).
98. Ansley J. Coale and Edgar M. Hoover, *Population Growth and Economic Development in Low Income Countries: A Case Study of India's Prospects* (Princeton, NJ: Princeton University Press, 1958). This research will be discussed at greater length in chapter 4.
99. United Nations Population Division, *Manual IV: Methods of Estimating Basic Demographic Measures from Incomplete Data* (New York: United Nations Department of Social Affairs, 1967).
100. Anderson, *World Population Dynamics*, 247.
101. Gutmann and Merchant, "Historical Demography"; Emily Klancher Merchant and J. David Hacker, "Historical Demography in the United States," in *A Global*

History of Historical Demography*, ed. Antoinette Fauve-Chamoux, I. Bolovan, and S. Sogner (Bern: Peter Lang, 2016), 655–670.

102. Prior to the introduction of censuses and vital registration, several European countries required churches to keep records of baptisms, marriages, and burials. Historical demographers of the 1950s and 1960s developed mathematical methods of calculating vital rates from these records. For details, see Gutmann and Merchant, "Historical Demography."
103. Ansley J. Coale and James Trussell, "The Development and Use of Demographic Models," *Population Studies* 50 (1996): 469–484.
104. Coale and his former student Paul Demeny specified four "families" of life tables, named for the regions of Europe from which their data originated. Ansley J. Coale and Paul Demeny, *Regional Model Life Tables and Stable Populations* (Princeton, NJ: Princeton University Press, 1966).
105. Alfred James Lotka, "Studies on the Mode of Growth of Material Aggregates," *American Journal of Science* 24 (1907): 199, emphasis in the original. For the demographic analogue, see Alfred James Lotka, "Relation between Birth and Death Rates," *Science* 26 (1907): 21–22. Contrary to recent usage by historians, a "stable" population in demography does not necessarily have a zero rate of growth. Rather, it has a constant rate of growth, which may be positive, negative, or zero. A stable population with zero growth is "stationary," and a stationary population is a special case of the stable population model.
106. Anderson, *World Population Dynamics*, 368–371.
107. Paul Demeny, "Oral History Interview with Jean Van Der Tak, 8 June 1988," in Van Der Tak, *Demographic Destinies*, vol. 1, no. 3, 222.
108. Lorimer first went to Africa on a mission for the Population Council. Etienne van de Walle, "Frank Lorimer, 1894–1985," *Population Index* 51 (1985): 635–642; William Brass to Frank Lorimer, October 1, 1961, folder 2, box 1, AJCP.
109. Ansley J. Coale to the Members of the Faculty Advisory Committee of the Office of Population Research, November 25, 1960, folder 2, box 1, AJCP.
110. Frank Lorimer, "Notes of African Population Studies," folder 2, box 1, AJCP.
111. Ansley J. Coale, "Memorandum on Experimental Studies of Population Dynamics in Areas without Effective Civil Registers—With Special Reference to Africa (Draft)," March 22, 1960, folder 2, box 1, AJCP.
112. Ansley J. Coale to the Members of the Faculty Advisory Committee of the Office of Population Research.
113. William Brass et al., *The Demography of Tropical Africa* (Princeton, NJ: Princeton University Press, 1968).
114. Coale, "Oral History Interview," 147.
115. Martha Lampland, "False Numbers as Formalizing Practices," *Social Studies of Science* 40 (2010): 378.

CHAPTER 4

1. Harold F. Dorn, "Pitfalls in Population Forecasts and Projections," *Journal of the American Statistical Association* 45 (1950): 311–334.
2. Ronald J. Freedman, "Oral History Interview with Anders Lunde, 5–6 April 1979, and Jean Van Der Tak, 12 June 1989," in Van Der Tak, Demographic Destinies, vol. 1, no. 2, 72.
3. Anderson, *World Population Dynamics*, 258.

4. Emily Klancher Merchant, Brian Gratton, and Myron P. Gutmann, "A Sudden Transition: Household Changes for Middle Aged U.S. Women in the Twentieth Century," *Population Research and Policy Review* 31 (2012): 703–726.
5. Notestein, "Oral History Interview," 13.
6. Pascal Kidder Whelpton, *Cohort Fertility: Native White Women in the United States* (Princeton, NJ: Princeton University Press, 1954); Norman B. Ryder, "Problems of Trend Determination during a Transition in Fertility," *Milbank Memorial Fund Quarterly* 34 (1956): 5–21.
7. Bouk, "Generation Crisis."
8. Frank W. Notestein, "As the Nation Grows Younger," *Atlantic Monthly*, October 1957, 131–136. Derek Hoff refers to government spending to promote economic growth in the absence of population growth as "stable population Keynesianism," but "stationary population Keynesianism" would be a more appropriate name, as a stable population is not necessarily stationary. (The stationary population is a special case of the stable population.) Hoff, *The State and the Stork*.
9. Demographers have long contrasted the marriage patterns of Western Europe, where women married later or not at all, with those in East Asia, where most women married and did so at younger ages. James Lee and Wang Feng have recently demonstrated that, although most women in China married and did so at relatively young ages, the same was not true for men, and that male nonmarriage kept birth rates lower than they would otherwise have been. James Z. Lee and Wang Feng, *One Quarter of Humanity: Malthusian Mythology and Chinese Realities, 1700–2000* (Cambridge, MA: Harvard University Press, 2001).
10. Latham, *The Right Kind of Revolution*.
11. Notestein, "Problems of Policy," 432.
12. Notestein, "Problems of Policy," 433.
13. Davis, "The World Demographic Transition," 6.
14. Notestein, "Problems of Policy," 433.
15. Notestein, "Problems of Policy."
16. Notestein, "Problems of Policy," 437.
17. Kingsley Davis, "Demographic Fact and Policy in India," *Milbank Memorial Fund Quarterly* 22 (1944): 276.
18. Frank W. Notestein, "A Positive Approach to the Problems of World Population," November 14, 1945, folder "OPR 1946–1948," box 82, series 200s, record group 1.1, Rockefeller Foundation Archives, Rockefeller Archive Center, Sleepy Hollow, New York [hereafter RFA].
19. Kingsley Davis, "Population and Resources in the Americas," in *Proceedings of the Inter-American Conference on Conservation of Renewable Natural Resources, Denver* (Washington, DC: U.S. Department of State, 1948), 88–97; Kingsley Davis, "Population Policy: Will Current Programs Succeed?," *Science* 158 (1967): 730–739.
20. For example, demographer Dennis Hodgson and historian Simon Szreter both trace the shift in Notestein's and Davis's thought between 1945 and 1955, but they present the shift as being the same for the two men, not recognizing that they were shifting in different directions and would, two decades later, find themselves in opposition. Dennis Hodgson, "Orthodoxy and Revisionism in American Demography," *Population and Development Review* 14, no. 4 (1988): 541–569; Szreter, "The Idea of Demographic Transition."

21. Guy Irving Burch to Hugh Everett Moore, August 25, 1948, folder 9, box 19, Hugh Moore Fund Collection (MC 153), Public Policy Papers, Department of Special Collections, Princeton University Library [hereafter HMFC].
22. Guy Irving Burch, "Headed for the Last Census? I. Overpopulation or Underpopulation? A Review of Conflicting Opinions," *Journal of Heredity* 28 (1937): 203–212.
23. Office of the Commissioner of Internal Revenue to the Population Reference Bureau, January 3, 1938 and December 1, 1939, folder 9, box 19, HMFC.
24. Guy Irving Burch to Hugh Everett Moore, October 16, 1948, folder 9, box 19, HMFC.
25. Guy Irving Burch to Francis E. Walker, March 23, 1949, folder 10, box 19, HMFC.
26. Burch, "Headed for the Last Census? I"; Guy Irving Burch, "Headed for the Last Census? II. The Differential Birthrate," *Journal of Heredity* 28 (1937): 241–254.
27. Guy Irving Burch to Hugh Everett Moore, June 10, 1949, folder 10, box 19, HMFC. Burch may have focused on Kuczynski and Dublin in this statement because both men were Jewish.
28. Raymond Pearl to the Social Science Research Council, January 28, 1930, folder "SSRC Population Committee #2," box 25, RPP.
29. Hugh Moore later referred to the board as "window dressing—responsible business men and scientists whose names on the letterhead certify to your probity." Hugh Everett Moore to Robert C. Cook, August 14, 1964, folder 12, box 19, HMFC.
30. Joan Cook, "Robert C. Cook, 92, a Longtime Scholar of Human Genetics," *New York Times*, January 9, 1991.
31. Cook claimed to have been a founder of the National Association of Science Writers. Population Reference Bureau, "Annual Report," 1952, folder 669, box 80, subseries 5, series 1, record group 5, John D. Rockefeller III Papers, Rockefeller Archive Center, Sleepy Hollow, New York [hereafter JDR3].
32. Stern, *Eugenic Nation*; Molly Ladd-Taylor, "Eugenics, Sterilisation and Modern Marriage in the USA: The Strange Career of Paul Popenoe," *Gender and History* 13 (2001): 298–327.
33. Alison Bashford echoes this view, though in a much more sophisticated way, in *Global Population*.
34. Guy Irving Burch and Elmer Pendell, *Human Breeding and Survival* (New York: Penguin, 1947), 4.
35. Burch and Pendell, *Human Breeding and Survival*, 28.
36. Burch and Pendell, *Human Breeding and Survival*, 24.
37. Burch and Pendell, *Human Breeding and Survival*, 36.
38. Burch and Pendell, *Human Breeding and Survival*, 44.
39. Burch and Pendell, *Human Breeding and Survival*, 32.
40. Burch and Pendell, *Human Breeding and Survival*, 100.
41. Burch and Pendell, *Human Breeding and Survival*, 90–91.
42. Burch and Pendell, *Human Breeding and Survival*, 92, emphasis in the original.
43. Burch and Pendell, *Human Breeding and Survival*, 92.
44. Burch and Pendell, *Human Breeding and Survival*, 94.
45. Burch and Pendell, *Human Breeding and Survival*, 100.
46. Burch and Pendell, *Human Breeding and Survival*, 119.
47. Burch and Pendell, *Human Breeding and Survival*, back cover.
48. Paul H. Landis, review of *Population Roads to Peace or War*, by Guy Irving Burch and Elmer Pendell, *American Sociological Review* 11 (1946): 126.

49. Bentley Glass, review of *Population Roads to Peace or War*, by Guy Irving Burch and Elmer Pendell, *Quarterly Review of Biology* 21 (1946): 128.
50. Guy Irving Burch to Hugh Everett Moore, December 16, 1948, folder 9, box 19, HMFC.
51. Pierre Desrochers and Christine Hoffbauer, "The Post War Intellectual Roots of the *Population Bomb*: Fairfield Osborn's *Our Plundered Planet* and William Vogt's *Road to Survival* in Retrospect," *Electronic Journal of Sustainable Development* 1 (2009): 73–97; Allan Chase, *The Legacy of Malthus: The Social Costs of the New Scientific Racism* (New York: Knopf, 1977); Robertson, *The Malthusian Moment*.
52. "Eat Hearty," *Time*, November 8, 1948, 29.
53. Desrochers and Hoffbauer, "The Post War Intellectual Roots of the *Population Bomb*," 75; Robertson, *The Malthusian Moment* 56.
54. Thomas Robertson, "Total War and the Total Environment: Fairfield Osborn, William Vogt, and the Birth of Global Ecology," *Environmental History* 17 (2012): 337.
55. Angus McDonald, "The Great Rat Race," *New Republic*, September 6, 1948, 25–26.
56. Robertson, "Total War and the Total Environment."
57. William Vogt, *Road to Survival* (New York: W. Sloane Associates, 1948), 33.
58. Karl Brandt, review of *Road to Survival*, by William Vogt, *Land Economics* 26 (1950): 88–90.
59. George F. Mair, ed. *Studies in Population: Proceedings of the Annual Meeting of the Population Association of America at Princeton, New Jersey, May 1949* (Princeton, NJ: Princeton University Press, 1949).
60. Roger Evans, "Memorandum of Meeting with Notestein at the Prince George Inn, Princeton," folder "OPR 1946–1948," box A82, series 200s, record group 1.1, RFA.
61. "Laurance" is not a typo. He seems to have been named for his grandmother, Laura Spelman Rockefeller.
62. Davis first engaged with the relationship between population and natural resources at the 1948 Inter-American Conference on Conservation of Renewable Natural Resources. Davis, "Population and Resources in the Americas."
63. "Hugh Moore Fund Collection, 1922–1972, Finding Aid, Princeton University Library Department of Rare Books and Special Collections," findingaids.princeton.edu/collections/MC153.pdf.
64. Hugh Everett Moore to Guy Irving Burch, October 13, 1948, folder 9, box 19, HMFC.
65. Frank Boudreau to Hugh Everett Moore, November 8, 1948, folder 17, box 14, HMFC.
66. Hugh Everett Moore to Frank Boudreau, November 9, 1948, folder 9, box 19, HMFC.
67. Hugh Everett Moore to the Princeton University Office of Population Research, November 2, 1948, folder 9, box 19, HMFC.
68. Hugh Everett Moore to Guy Irving Burch, November 10, 1948, folder 9, box 19, HMFC.
69. Alexandra Minna Stern, "Sterilized in the Name of Public Health: Race, Immigration, and Reproductive Control in Modern California," *American Journal of Public Health* 95 (2005): 1128–1138.
70. Charles M. Goethe to Hugh Everett Moore, October 23, 1948, folder 9, box 19, HMFC.

71. Hugh Everett Moore to John W. Gardner, November 9, 1948, folder 9, box 19, HMFC.
72. "Eat Hearty."
73. Quoted in Hugh Everett Moore to Guy Irving Burch, January 25, 1949, folder 10, box 19, HMFC.
74. Guy Irving Burch to Hugh Everett Moore, June 30, 1959, folder 10, box 19, HMFC.
75. "Draft of Position Paper for Fourth Session of UN Population Commission, Sent by Abram Jaffe to Philip Hauser," March 10, 1949, folder 3, box 10, PMHP.
76. Robert Redfield to Joseph H. Willits, July 21, 1944, and Robert Warren to Joseph H. Willits, August 3, 1944, folder "OPR 1943–1945," box A82, series 200s, record group 1.1, RFA.
77. Notestein, "A Positive Approach to the Problems of World Population."
78. Marshall C. Balfour, *Public Health and Demography in the Far East: Report of a Survey Trip, September 13–December 13, 1948* (New York: Rockefeller Foundation, 1950).
79. Notestein would later claim that his professional stance on demographic transition theory had never changed. He apparently continued to believe that modernization was the surest route to low fertility but embraced family planning as the most expedient.
80. Donald T. Critchlow, *Intended Consequences: Birth Control, Abortion, and the Federal Government in Modern America* (New York: Oxford University Press, 1999).
81. John D. Rockefeller III, "Population Growth: The Role of the Developed World," *Population and Development Review* 4 (1978): 509–516.
82. John D. Rockefeller Jr. had funded birth control development and legalization through the Bureau of Social Hygiene, the National Committee on Maternal Health, and the National Research Council's Committee for Research in Problems of Sex.
83. Laurance died in 2004 at age ninety-four. Michael T. Kaufman, "Laurance S. Rockefeller, Passionate Conservationist and Investor, Is Dead at 94," *New York Times*, July 12, 2004. In 1991 he received the Congressional Gold Medal for his conservation efforts. Robin W. Winks, *Laurance S. Rockefeller: Catalyst for Conservation* (Washington, DC: Island Press, 2013).
84. John Ensor Harr and Peter J. Johnson, *The Rockefeller Conscience: An American Family in Public and in Private* (New York: Scribner, 1991), 457.
85. Leland C. DeVinney, "Memorandum—Luncheon Conference with JDR III on February 13, 1952," February 15, 1952, folder 674, box 81, subseries 5, series 1, record group 5, JDR3.
86. Connelly, *Fatal Misconception*, 155.
87. National Academy of Sciences, "Conference on Population Problems, Morning Session, Friday, June 20, 1952," folder 720, box 85, subseries 5, series 1, record group 5, JDR3, 81.
88. National Academy of Sciences, "Conference on Population Problems, Afternoon Session, Saturday, June 21, 1952," folder 722, box 85, subseries 5, series 1, record group 5, JDR3.
89. National Academy of Sciences, "Conference on Population Problems, Evening Session, Saturday, June 21, 1952," folder 721, box 85, subseries 5, series 1, record group 5, JDR3, 19.

90. National Academy of Sciences, "Conference on Population Problems, Afternoon Session, Saturday, June 21, 1952," 83.
91. For instance, see Hodges, "Indian Eugenics in an Age of Reform"; Jill Briggs, "'As Fool-Proof as Possible': Overpopulation, Colonial Demography, and the Jamaica Birth Control League," *Global South* 4 (2010): 157–177; Ittmann, *A Problem of Great Importance*.
92. National Academy of Sciences, "Conference on Population Problems, Evening Session, Saturday, June 21, 1952," 4.
93. National Academy of Sciences, "Conference on Population Problems, Afternoon Session, Saturday, June 21, 1952," 55.
94. National Academy of Sciences, "Conference on Population Problems, Evening Session, Friday, June 20, 1952," folder 720, box 85, subseries 5, series 1, record group 5, JDR3, 41.
95. DeVinney, "Memorandum."
96. National Academy of Sciences, "Conference on Population Problems, Morning Session, Sunday, June 22, 1952," folder 721, box 85, subseries 5, series 1, record group 5, JDR3, 42–43.
97. In 2018 the University of Pittsburgh decided to rename Thomas Parran Hall, the building that houses its public health program, because of Parran's involvement in the Tuskegee syphilis experiment. Scott Jaschik, "Ending Honor for Disgraced Scientist," *Inside Higher Ed*, June 29, 2018.
98. National Academy of Sciences, "Conference on Population Problems, Morning Session, Sunday, June 22, 1952," 38.
99. National Academy of Sciences, "Conference on Population Problems, Morning Session, Sunday, June 22, 1952." This kind of intentional "indirection" was not unusual in U.S. foreign policy at the time. For instance, see Audra Wolfe, *Freedom's Laboratory: The Cold War Struggle for the Soul of Science* (Baltimore, MD: Johns Hopkins University Press, 2018); Inderjeet Parmar, *Foundations of the American Century: The Ford, Carnegie, and Rockefeller Foundations in the Rise of American Power* (New York: Columbia University Press, 2012); Hugh Wilford, *The Mighty Wurlitzer: How the CIA Played America* (Cambridge, MA: Harvard University Press, 2008); Frances Stonor Saunders, *Who Paid the Piper? The CIA and the Cultural Cold War* (London: Granta, 1999).
100. This would not be the only time representatives of the Natural Academy of Sciences were engaged in this kind of misdirection. See Wolfe, *Freedom's Laboratory*.
101. Cordelia Scaife May, an heiress to the Mellon fortune, was also an early supporter of the Population Council, but she broke with the organization after 1974, joining the population bomb faction that originated with the Population Reference Bureau and will be described at greater length in chapter 6. Nicholas Kulish and Mike McIntire, "Why an Heiress Spent Her Fortune Trying to Keep Immigrants Out," *New York Times*, August 14, 2019.
102. "Population Council Memorandum," January 21, 1953, folder 1, box 10, FWNP.
103. Reimert Ravenholt, "Interview with Rebecca Sharpless for the Population and Reproductive Health Oral History Project," July 18–20, 2002, Sophia Smith Collection, Smith College [hereafter SSC], 129.
104. Rockefeller Foundation, "Frederick Osborn Interview Report," September 4, 1964, folder 494, box 73, subseries 4, series 3, record group 5, JDR3.

105. Frederick Henry Osborn to Dudley Kirk, October 24, 1966, folder 1796, box 97, record group IV3B4.5, Population Council Archives, Rockefeller Archive Center, Sleepy Hollow, New York [hereafter PCA].
106. Dudley Kirk, "Proposals for Board of Trustees Meeting of May 13, 1959," May 4, 1959, folder 42, box 4, record group IV3B4.2, PCA.
107. P. S. Barrows to Frederick Henry Osborn, May 4, 1965, folder 1796, box 97, record group IV3B4.5, PCA.
108. Andrew J. Hogan, *Life Histories of Genetic Disease: Patterns and Prevention in Postwar Medical Genetics* (Baltimore, MD: Johns Hopkins University Press, 2016); Nathaniel C. Comfort, *The Science of Human Perfection: How Genes Became the Heart of American Medicine* (New Haven, CT: Yale University Press, 2012).
109. Frederick Henry Osborn, "Eugenics: Retrospect and Prospect," March 26, 1959, folder "Osborn—Concerning Eugenics," box 4, FHOP. For more on the history of genetic counseling, see Alexandra Minna Stern, *Telling Genes: The Story of Genetic Counseling in America* (Baltimore, MD: Johns Hopkins University Press, 2012).
110. For instance, see Frederick Henry Osborn, "Population Quality—Speech at the Women's City Club," April 1, 1955, folder "Frederick Osborn—Papers #14," box 17, AESR; Frederick Henry Osborn, "Absolute Weapons—the American Reply," 1961 folder "Frederick Osborn—Papers #21," box 18, AESR.
111. Demographers Kingsley Davis, Dudley Kirk, Clyde Kiser, Frank Lorimer, Frank Notestein, Norman Ryder, and Pat Whelpton all served on the board of the AES. Ramsden, "Frank W. Notestein, Frederick H. Osborn, and the Development of Demography in the United States."
112. National Academy of Sciences, "Conference on Population Problems, Morning Session, Friday, June 20, 1952."
113. Although this statement speaks most clearly to geopolitical rather than racial concerns, Kirk prefaced it with "there really is a eugenic aspect of this." Dudley Kirk, "Oral History Interview with Anders Lunde, 27 April 1979, and Jean Van Der Tak, 29 April 1989," in Van Der Tak, Demographic Destinies, vol. 1, no. 1, 130.
114. National Academy of Sciences, "Conference on Population Problems, Evening Session, Saturday, June 21, 1952."
115. Rockefeller Foundation, "Frederick Osborn Interview Report."
116. National Academy of Sciences, "Conference on Population Problems, Morning Session, Saturday, June 21, 1952," folder 723, box 85, subseries 5, series 1, record group 5, JDR3.
117. United Nations, "Convention for the Prevention and Punishment of the Crime of Genocide," 1948, un.org/en/genocideprevention/genocide-convention.shtml.
118. In the early 1960s Fred Osborn gratefully acknowledged that Moore's work had "created the public climate that enabled the great foundations to push forward in the field." Frederick Henry Osborn, "Organizations in the Population Field," 1966, folder 21, box 17, HMFC.
119. Population Reference Bureau, "Annual Report."
120. Guy Irving Burch to Hugh Everett Moore, July 2, 1950, folder 10, box 19, HMFC.
121. Hugh Everett Moore, *The Population Bomb*, 1954, folder 17, box 16, HMFC.
122. Robert C. Cook, "The Population Bomb," *Bulletin of the Atomic Scientists* 12 (1956): 295–298.
123. Desrochers and Hoffbauer, "The Post War Intellectual Roots of the Population Bomb," 74.

124. Pascal K. Whelpton to Hugh Everett Moore, January 10, 1955, folder 344, box 22, record group IV3B4.2, PCA.
125. H. J. Muller to Bruce Barton, Will Clayton, and Hugh Everett Moore, January 31, 1957, folder 344, box 22, record group IV3B4.2, PCA. For more on Muller, see Wolfe, *Freedom's Laboratory*.
126. Muller to Barton, Clayton, and Moore, January 31, 1957.
127. Edward W. Barrett, "Mass Opinion and Population Control: For Discussion at Population Council Ad Hoc Committee Meeting VI," November 16, 1956, folder 2, box 10, FWNP.
128. Rockefeller Prentice to Hugh Everett Moore, February 20, 1964, and John D. Rockefeller III to Hugh Everett Moore, January 2, 1968, folder 18, box 2, HMFC.
129. Samuel W. Anderson to Ellsworth Bunker, December 8, 1954, folder 8, box 16, HMFC.
130. Frances E. Walter to Hugh Everett Moore, August 9, 1961, folder 2, box 17, HMFC.
131. Coale, "Oral History Interview," 144.
132. Frank W. Notestein to Douglas J. Brown, 1954, folder 5, box 13, AJCP.
133. For the role of India in American Cold War thought and development efforts, see Cullather, *The Hungry World*.
134. Sarah Hodges, "Governmentality, Population and Reproductive Family in Modern India," *Economic and Political Weekly* 39 (2004): 1157–1163.
135. Harvey Leibenstein, *A Theory of Economic-Demographic Development* (Princeton, NJ: Princeton University Press, 1954).
136. Thanks to demographer Samuel Preston for this turn of phrase. Personal communication, 2016.
137. See, for example, Connelly, *Fatal Misconception*; Hoff, *The State and the Stork*.
138. Coale and Hoover, *Population Growth and Economic Development*, 280.
139. Ansley J. Coale, *Ansley J. Coale: An Autobiography* (Philadelphia: American Philosophical Society, 2000), 37.
140. Ansley J. Coale, "The Voluntary Control of Human Fertility," *Proceedings of the American Philosophical Society* 111, no. 3 (1967): 164.
141. Robert C. Cook, "India: High Cost of Fertility, Draft Sent to Dudley Kirk," 1958, folder 381, box 25, record group IV3B4.2, PCA.
142. Although the Population Council funded and served in an advisory role to the Bureau, it worked hard to maintain formal independence between the two organizations. For that reason, Fred Osborn declined an invitation to join the Bureau's board of trustees. Frederick Henry Osborn to Robert C. Cook, December 7, 1953, folder 382, box 25, record group IV3B4.2, PCA.
143. Phyllis Tilson Piotrow, "Interview with Rebecca Sharpless for the Population and Reproductive Health Oral History Project," September 16, 2002, SSC.
144. Hugh Everett Moore to William Henry Draper Jr., December 19, 1958, folder 28, box 15, HMFC. Donald Critchlow offers additional details of the pressure Moore put on Draper in *Intended Consequences*.
145. "Letter of Draper Committee on Foreign Aid," *New York Times*, July 24, 1959.
146. Farnsworth Fowle, "Eisenhower Backs Birth-Curb Aids," *New York Times*, November 10, 1964.
147. Quoted in Matthew Connelly, "Seeing Beyond the State: The Population Control Movement and the Problem of Sovereignty," *Past and Present* 193 (2006): 198.

148. Robert C. Toth, "Kennedy Would Give Out Data on Population Curbs," *New York Times*, April 25, 1963.
149. George Bogdan Kistiakowsky, *A Scientist in the White House: The Private Diary of President Eisenhower's Special Assistant for Science and Technology* (Cambridge, MA: Harvard University Press, 1976).
150. Frederick Seitz to Carl Albert, December 31, 1962, Committees and Boards, Committee on Science and Public Policy, General, National Academy of Sciences Archives, Washington, DC [hereafter NAS].
151. National Academy of Sciences, "Committee on Government Relations," November 27, 1961, Committees and Boards, Committee on Government Relations, Panels: Population Control, NAS.
152. National Academy of Sciences, "Committee on Government Relations."
153. S. D. Cornell to Frank Notestein, August 16, 1962, and Frank Notestein to S. D. Cornell, August 21, 1962, Committees and Boards, Committee on Government Relations, Panels: Population Control, NAS.
154. William D. McElroy, "Memo to Members of the NAS Panel on Population Problems," September 13, 1962, Committees and Boards, Committee on Government Relations, Panels: Population Control, NAS.
155. Robert E. Green to William D. McElroy, November 26, 1962, Committees and Boards, Committee on Government Relations, Panels: Population Control, NAS; William D. McElroy, "Memo to Members of the NAS Panel on Population Problems," November 29, 1962, Committees and Boards, Committee on Government Relations, Panels: Population Control, NAS.
156. National Academy of Sciences, *The Growth of World Population: Analysis of the Problems and Recommendations for Research and Training* (Washington, DC: National Academies Press, 1963).
157. National Academy of Sciences, "Conference on Population Problems," Afternoon Session, Saturday, June 21, 1952," 24.
158. "Transcript of the President's News Conference on Foreign and Domestic Matters," *New York Times*, April 25, 1963.
159. Ravenholt, "Interview with Rebecca Sharpless."
160. Hugh Everett Moore, "Mobilizing Public Opinion for Population Control," September 5, 1967, folder 23, box 21, HMFC.
161. Rockefeller Prentice to Hugh Everett Moore, February 20, 1964.
162. George Gallup to Hugh Everett Moore, August 14, 1963, folder 2, box 17, HMFC.
163. John F. Kantner, "American Attitudes on Population Policy: Recent Trends," *Studies in Family Planning* 1 (1968): 2.
164. Kantner, "American Attitudes on Population Policy," 6.

CHAPTER 5

1. Ansley J. Coale, "Interview with Jean Van Der Tak for the PAA Oral History Project," May 11, 1988, folder 5, box 1, AJCP.
2. Rockefeller Foundation, "Frederick Osborn Interview Report."
3. Oscar Harkavy, *Curbing Population Growth: An Insider's Perspective on the Population Movement* (New York: Plenum, 1995).
4. *Demography* would later receive additional funding from the National Science Foundation. Donald J. Bogue, "Oral History Interview with Jean Van Der Tak, 30 March 1989," in Van Der Tak, *Demographic Destinies*, vol. 1, no. 2, 39–67.
5. John Charles Caldwell and Pat Caldwell, *Limiting Population Growth and the Ford Foundation Contribution* (London: Pinter, 1986).

6. Fellows at the University of Michigan's Population Studies Center in 1970 received a stipend of $200 each month, plus $2.10 per hour in wages for twelve hours per week of work, totaling nearly $2,000 per month in 2019 dollars. "The Population Studies Center, University of Michigan," *Concerned Demography* 2 (1970): 39–41.
7. In a 1988 interview, Coale said he saw no reason why a Ph.D. should take longer than three years for a student coming in with a B.A. Coale, "Interview with Jean Van Der Tak for the PAA Oral History Project."
8. "Notes on JDR's Memo: Population Council Program—New Items and Items for Increased Emphasis," 1960, folder 41, box 4, record group IV3B4.2, PCA.
9. "Present Activities and Future Needs of the Demographic Division," 1958, folder 40, box 4, record group IV3B4.2, PCA.
10. Etienne van de Walle, "Oral History Interview with Jean Van Der Tak, 17 February 1993," in Van Der Tak, *Demographic Destinies*, vol. 1, no. 3, 426–460.
11. Kirk, "Oral History Interview," 120.
12. Ansley J. Coale to August Schou, October 29, 1971, folder "Nobel Prize, September 1971–1973," box AD25, accession 2, PCA.
13. Philip M. Hauser, "Oral History Interview with Jean Van Der Tak, 12 November 1988," in Van Der Tak, *Demographic Destinies*, vol. 1, no. 1, 40.
14. "Present Activities and Future Needs of the Demographic Division."
15. Juan Gabriel Valdes, *Pinochet's Economists: The Chicago School in Chile* (New York: Cambridge University Press, 1995).
16. Caldwell and Caldwell, *Limiting Population Growth*.
17. For British colonies, see Ittmann, *A Problem of Great Importance*. For other countries, see Raúl Necochea López, *A History of Family Planning in Twentieth-Century Peru* (Chapel Hill: University of North Carolina Press, 2014), and John P. DiMoia, "'Counting One's Allies': The Mobilization of Demography, Population, and Family Planning in East Asia, Late 1920s–Present," *East Asian Science, Technology and Society: An International Journal* 10 (2016): 355–376.
18. Mercedes Concepcion, "Interview with Rebecca Sharpless for the Population and Reproductive Health Oral History Project," August 17, 2004, SSC; Bogue, "Oral History Interview."
19. Concepcion, "Interview with Rebecca Sharpless."
20. Marion Fourcade has described a similar phenomenon in the field of economics during the same period. Fourcade, "The Construction of a Global Profession."
21. "Notes on JDR's Memo."
22. Bogue, "Oral History Interview," 41.
23. "Present Activities and Future Needs of the Demographic Division."
24. Betsy Hartmann, *Reproductive Rights and Wrongs: The Global Politics of Population Control* (Boston: South End Press, 1995), 74.
25. Concepcion, "Interview with Rebecca Sharpless," 16.
26. Concepcion, "Interview with Rebecca Sharpless," 17. As late as 2004, the majority of contraceptives in the Philippines came from USAID (36).
27. Rockefeller Foundation, "Frederick Osborn Interview Report."
28. Susan Greenhalgh, "The Social Construction of Population Science: An Intellectual, Institutional, and Political History of Twentieth-Century Demography," *Comparative Studies in Society and History* 38 (1996): 26–66.
29. Two of Freedman's graduate students wrote dissertations based on the Indianapolis Study. Ronald Freedman, "Oral History Interview," 71.

30. Ronald J. Freedman, "The Sociology of Human Fertility: A Trend Report and Bibliography," *Current Sociology* 10 (1962): 36.
31. Bouk, "Generation Crisis."
32. Ronald Freedman, Pascal K. Whelpton, and Arthur A. Campbell, *Family Planning, Sterility and Population Growth* (New York: McGraw-Hill, 1959); Harkavy, *Curbing Population Growth*, 20.
33. Ronald J. Freedman, Arthur A. Campbell, and Pascal K. Whelpton, *Growth of American Families 1955* [machine-readable data set] (Ann Arbor: Inter-university Consortium for Political and Social Research, 2009), doi.org/10.3886/ICPSR20000.v2.
34. "Instruction Booklet: A Study of the Growth of American Families (Preliminary)," November 5, 1954, folder 337, box 22, record group IV3B4.2, PCA.
35. Of those contacted, 91% responded to the survey. Interviewers classified 92% of respondents as having been "good" or "very good" participants. This percentage was higher among those who reported having used birth control than among those who did not, with 95% of users being classed as "good" or "very good" participants in contrast to 88% of nonusers. This difference may reflect interviewers' perceptions that women were lying about not having used birth control. Only ten respondents refused to answer the birth control questions. Author's analysis of Freedman, Campbell, and Whelpton, *Growth of American Families*.
36. Igo, *The Averaged American*.
37. "A Memorandum on Population Research at the University of Michigan," March 2, 1954, folder 294, box 18, record group IV3B4.2, PCA.
38. Alfred C. Kinsey, Wardell B. Pomeroy, and Clyde E. Martin, *Sexual Behavior in the Human Male* (Bloomington: Indiana University Press, 1948); Alfred C. Kinsey, *Sexual Behavior in the Human Female* (Bloomington: Indiana University Press, 1953).
39. Kinsey, *Sexual Behavior in the Human Female*, 286.
40. Ronald Freedman to Frederick Henry Osborn, December 14, 1954, folder 337, box 22, record group IV3B4.2, PCA.
41. Freedman, Campbell, and Whelpton, *Growth of American Families*; "Growth of American Families Questionnaire," January 4, 1955, folder 338, box 22, record group IV3B4.2, PCA.
42. Freedman, Campbell, and Whelpton, *Growth of American Families*.
43. Pascal K. Whelpton to Frederick Henry Osborn, January 4, 1955, and Ronald Freedman to Frederick Henry Osborn, December 13, 1954, folder 337, box 22, record group IV3B4.2, PCA.
44. Freedman, Whelpton, and Campbell, *Family Planning, Sterility and Population Growth*, 377.
45. In 1965 the study was taken over by the National Institute for Child Health and Human Development and renamed the National Fertility Survey. It continues today as the National Survey of Family Growth, sponsored by the Centers for Disease Control and Prevention.
46. J. Mayone Stycos and Judith Blake, "The Jamaican Family Life Project: Some Objectives and Methods," *Social and Economic Studies* 3 (1954): 342–349.
47. Laura Briggs, *Reproducing Empire: Race, Sex, Science, and U.S. Imperialism in Puerto Rico* (Berkeley: University of California Press, 2002), 112.

48. Daniel Immerwahr, *How to Hide an Empire: A History of the Greater United States* (New York: Farrar, Straus and Giroux, 2019).
49. Critchlow, *Intended Consequences*.
50. Reuben J. Hill, J. Mayone Stycos, and Kurt W. Back, *The Family and Population Control: A Puerto Rican Experiment in Social Change* (Chapel Hill: University of North Carolina Press, 1959), 432.
51. Kurt W. Back, Reuben Hill, and J. Mayone Stycos, *Family and Population Control Study: Puerto Rico, 1953–1954* [machine-readable data set] (Ann Arbor: Inter-university Consortium for Political and Social Research, 2009), https://doi.org/10.3886/ICPSR07062.v2.
52. Hill, Stycos, and Back, *The Family and Population Control*, 267.
53. Briggs, *Reproducing Empire*, 122.
54. In contrast to Growth of American Families, the Caribbean studies included both legally married couples and "consensual unions." Stycos and Blake, "The Jamaican Family Life Project."
55. Hill, Stycos, and Back, *The Family and Population Control*, 434–435.
56. For instance, see Philippa Levine, "What's British about Gender and Empire? The Problem of Exceptionalism," *Comparative Studies of South Asia, Africa, and the Middle East* 27 (2007): 273–274; Antoinette Burton, *Burdens of History: British Feminists, Indian Women, and Imperial Culture, 1865–1915* (Chapel Hill: University of North Carolina Press, 1994).
57. Hill, Stycos, and Back, *The Family and Population Control*, 263.
58. Hill, Stycos, and Back, *The Family and Population Control*, 263.
59. Briggs, *Reproducing Empire*. Raymond Pearl had expressed a similar opinion in his interwar birth control studies in the mainland United States: Pearl, "Contraception and Fertility in 4,945 Married Women."
60. Author's analysis of Back, Hill, and Stycos, *Family and Population Control Study*.
61. Hill, Stycos, and Back, *The Family and Population Control*, vii.
62. Hill, Stycos, and Back, *The Family and Population Control*, 277–278.
63. Ilana Löwy, "Defusing the Population Bomb in the 1950s: Foam Tablets in India," *Studies in History and Philosophy of Science Part C: Studies in History and Philosophy of Biological and Biomedical Sciences* 43 (2012).
64. Löwy, "Defusing the Population Bomb in the 1950s," 591.
65. Author's analysis of Freedman, Campbell, and Whelpton, *Growth of American Families*.
66. Chikako Takeshita, *The Global Biopolitics of the IUD: How Science Constructs Contraceptive Users and Women's Bodies* (Cambridge, MA: MIT Press, 2012).
67. National Academy of Sciences, "Conference on Population Problems, Afternoon Session, Saturday, June 21, 1952," 63.
68. John B. Wyon and John E. Gordon, *The Khanna Study: Population Problems in the Rural Punjab* (Cambridge, MA: Harvard University Press, 1971).
69. Mahmood Mamdani, *The Myth of Population Control* (New York: Monthly Review Press, 1973).
70. James Reed, *From Private Vice to Public Virtue: The Birth Control Movement and American Society since 1830* (New York: Basic Books, 1978); Clarke, *Disciplining Reproduction*.
71. Clarke, *Disciplining Reproduction*; Jonathan Eig, *The Birth of the Pill: How Four Crusaders Reinvented Sex and Launched a Revolution* (New York: Norton, 2014); Andrea Tone, *Devices and Desires: A History of Contraceptives in America* (New York: Macmillan, 2002).

72. Eig, *The Birth of the Pill*, 70–81.
73. Eig, *The Birth of the Pill*, 58.
74. Paul S. Henshaw, "Physiologic Control of Fertility," April 17, 1952, folder 667, box 80, subseries 5, series 1, record group 5, JDR3.
75. Critchlow, *Intended Consequences*, 32.
76. Tone, *Devices and Desires*, 215.
77. Tone, *Devices and Desires*, 221–222; Nelly Oudshoorn, *Beyond the Natural Body: An Archaeology of Sex Hormones* (New York: Routledge, 1994).
78. Tone, *Devices and Desires*, 223–226.
79. Eig, *The Birth of the Pill*.
80. John Rock, "Physiology and Fertility Control—Address at the Annual Luncheon of the Planned Parenthood Federation of America," May 6, 1954, folder 18, box 2, record group IV3B4.2, PCA.
81. Quoted in Bernard Berelson, "On Family Planning Communication," *Demography* 1 (1964): 95.
82. National Academy of Sciences, "Conference on Population Problems, Evening Session, Friday, June 20, 1952."
83. Christopher Tietze, "The Clinical Effectiveness of Contraceptive Methods," *American Journal of Obstetrics and Gynecology* 78 (1959): 650–656.
84. National Academy of Sciences, "Conference on Population Problems, Evening Session, Friday, June 20, 1952."
85. Sheldon J. Segal, "Contraceptive Research: A Male Chauvinist Plot?," *Family Planning Perspectives* 4 (1972): 21–25; Nelly Oudshoorn, *The Male Pill: A Biography of a Technology in the Making* (Durham, NC: Duke University Press, 2003).
86. Tone, *Devices and Desires*, 263–264.
87. Tone, *Devices and Desires*, 265.
88. "Report on Intra-Uterine Contraceptive Devices," *Studies in Family Planning* 1 (1964): 11–12; Bernard Berelson, "Application of Intra-Uterine Contraception in Family Planning Programs," in *Proceedings, Second International Conference on Intra-Uterine Contraception* (New York: Population Council, 1964), 9.
89. These agreements excluded Argentina, Australia, Canada, Israel, Japan, New Zealand, South Africa, and all of Europe. W. Parker Mauldin, "Copper T Devices for the Public Sector," June 20, 1975, folder 209, box 29, record group IV3B4.7, PCA.
90. Frank W. Notestein to Jan Myrdal, June 1, 1967, folder 1, box 20, FWNP.
91. Takeshita, *The Global Biopolitics of the IUD*.
92. Russel J. Thomsen, "Clinical Aspects of Intrauterine Contraceptive Device (IUD) Complications: Testimony Presented at the House Government Operations Committee Hearings May 30, 1973," folder 205, box 29, record group IV3B4.7, PCA.
93. M. Karim, "Research Plan for Intra Uterine Contraceptive Device," May 24, 1965, folder 145, box 11, record group IV3B4.2, PCA.
94. "Interim Report of Survey and Research Projects, Taiwan Provincial Institute of Family Planning," November 1969, folder "Mauldin—IUD," box AD46, accession 2, PCA.
95. W. Parker Mauldin, "Retention of IUD's: Work in Progress and Work Proposed," January 5, 1967, folder "Mauldin—IUD," box AD46, accession 2, PCA.
96. Penny Satterthwaite, "Diary Notes," November 19, 1969, folder "Mauldin—IUD," box AD46, accession 2, PCA.
97. Quoted in Connelly, *Fatal Misconception*, 202–203.

98. Berelson, "Application of Intra-Uterine Contraception in Family Planning Programs," 13.
99. "Pakistan: Report on the Family Planning Program by the UN/WHO Advisory Mission," *Studies in Family Planning* 1 (1969): 4–10.
100. Shri Govind Narain, "India: The Family Planning Program since 1965," *Studies in Family Planning* 1 (1968): 1–12.
101. John A. Ross et al., "Korea/Taiwan 1969: Report on the National Family Planning Programs," *Studies in Family Planning* 1 (1970): 1–16.
102. James T. Fawcett and Aree Somboonsuk, "Thailand: Using Family Planning Acceptors to Recruit New Cases," *Studies in Family Planning* 1 (1969): 1–4.
103. Quoted in Connelly, *Fatal Misconception*, 205.
104. Takeshita, *The Global Biopolitics of the IUD*.
105. Prior to 1974, at least one KAP study was carried out in each of the following countries: Afghanistan, Algeria, Argentina, Bangladesh, Barbados, Bolivia, Brazil, Chad, Chile, Colombia, Costa Rica, Ecuador, Egypt, Ethiopia, Ghana, Guatemala, Hong Kong, India, Indonesia, Iran, Jamaica, Jordan, Kenya, Lebanon, Malaysia, Mexico, Morocco, Nepal, Nicaragua, Niger, Nigeria, Pakistan, Panama, Paraguay, Peru, Philippines, Senegal, Sierra Leone, South Korea, Sri Lanka, Taiwan, Thailand, Togo, Trinidad and Tobago, Tunisia, Turkey, Uganda, Upper Volta, Venezuela, and Zambia. Albert I. Hermalin, Barbara Entwisle, and Lora G. Myers, "Some Lessons from the Attempt to Retrieve Early KAP and Fertility Surveys," *Population Index* 51 (1985): 194–208.
106. Francis A. Jamieson and Martha Dalrymple to John D. Rockefeller III, December 11, 1958, folder 40, box 4, record group IV3B4.2, PCA.
107. Grants recommended by program officers for Kinsey's sex research and for research on American Indian history and racial integration in St. Helena were vetoed by the board as too controversial, and the program dissolved in 1957. Solovey, *Shaky Foundations*.
108. Ronald Freedman and John Y. Takeshita, *Family Planning in Taiwan: An Experiment in Social Change* (Princeton, NJ: Princeton University Press, 1969).
109. Population Council, "The Disney Film on Family Planning," *Studies in Family Planning* 1 (1968).
110. Population Council, "Family Planning" (1968), youtube.com/watch?v=t2DkiceqmzU.
111. Hermalin, Entwisle, and Myers, "Some Lessons."
112. Bernard Berelson and Ronald J. Freedman, "A Study in Fertility Control," *Scientific American* 210 (1964): 29–37.
113. Caldwell and Caldwell, *Limiting Population Growth*.
114. Berelson described his overall approach to family planning in "On Family Planning Communication."
115. L. P. Chow, "A Programme to Control Fertility in Taiwan: Setting, Accomplishment and Evaluation," *Population Studies* 19 (1965): 155–166; Frank W. Notestein, "Statement in Support of Application by University of Michigan Population Studies Center for NIH Grant for its Program of Research on Fertility and Family Planning in Taiwan," March 30, 1967, folder 1, box 20, FWNP.
116. John C. Caldwell, "The Changing African Family Research Program," 1973, box AD25, accession 2, PCA, 74; Greenhalgh, "The Social Construction of Population Science."
117. Freedman and Takeshita, *Family Planning in Taiwan*, 123.

118. Berelson and Freedman, "A Study in Fertility Control," 37. For more on the economic value of averted births, see Murphy, *The Economization of Life*.
119. Quoted in Connelly, *Fatal Misconception*, 213. Connelly attributes the statement to the influence of the work of economist Stephen Enke, but Critchlow (in *Intended Consequences*) has also documented intense lobbying of President Johnson by John D. Rockefeller III following the 1964 election.
120. L. P. Chow, Hsiao-Chang Chen, and Ming-Cheng Chang, *Knowledge, Attitudes, and Practice of Contraception in Taiwan: First Province-Wide Fertility Survey (KAP I), 1965* [machine-readable data set] (Ann Arbor: Inter-university Consortium for Political and Social Research, 2005), doi.org/10.3886/ICPSR06862.v1.
121. Chow, Chen, and Chang, *Knowledge, Attitudes, and Practice of Contraception in Taiwan (KAP I)*.
122. L. P. Chow, Hsiao-Chang Chen, and Ming-Cheng Chang, *Knowledge, Attitudes, and Practice of Contraception in Taiwan: Second Province-Wide Fertility Survey (KAP II), 1967* [machine-readable data set] (Ann Arbor: Inter-university Consortium for Political and Social Research, 2005), doi.org/10.3886/ICPSR06863.v1.
123. Chow, Chen, and Chang, *Knowledge, Attitudes, and Practice of Contraception in Taiwan (KAP I)*.
124. Quoted in Anthony Marino, "KAP Surveys and the Politics of Family Planning," *Concerned Demography* 3 (1971).
125. Charles F. Westoff, "Is the KAP-Gap Real?," *Population and Development Review* 14 (1988): 225–232.
126. Quoted in Marino, "KAP Surveys and the Politics of Family Planning," 42.
127. Igo, *The Averaged American*.
128. Harvey M. Choldin, A. Majeed Kahn, and B. Hosne Ara, "Cultural Complications in Fertility Interviewing," *Demography* 4 (1967): 244–252.
129. Agnes Czerwinski Riedmann, *Science That Colonizes: A Critique of Fertility Studies in Africa* (Philadelphia: Temple University Press, 1993).
130. Choldin, Kahn, and Ara, "Cultural Complications in Fertility Interviewing," 247.
131. Choldin, Kahn, and Ara, "Cultural Complications in Fertility Interviewing," 248–250.
132. Philip M. Hauser, "Family Planning and Population Programs: A Book Review Article," *Demography* 4 (1967): 403–404.
133. Riedmann, *Science That Colonizes*.
134. Connelly, "Population Control Is History," 137.
135. In a letter dated December 14, 1966, Rockefeller thanked UN Secretary-General U Thant "for having personally issued the statement and for [his] own covering statement," saying that "it added much to its meaning and value." John D. III Rockefeller to U Thant, December 14, 1966, folder 5, box 4, series 857, UNA.
136. "World Leaders Declaration on Population Presented at the United Nations on Human Rights Day," December 1967, folder 9, box 19, series 288, UNA.
137. "Statement on Population by World Leaders," December 10, 1966, folder 5, box 4, series 857, UNA.

CHAPTER 6

1. John D. Rockefeller to U Thant, October 25, 1967, folder 9, box 19, series 288, UNA.
2. "World Leaders Declaration on Population Presented at the United Nations on Human Rights Day."

3. "UNA-USA Press Release: Rockefeller Panel Urges UN Action on Population," May 25, 1969, folder 6, box 4, series 857, UNA.
4. Ravenholt, "Interview with Rebecca Sharpless," 129.
5. John D. Rockefeller III to U Thant, May 21, 1969, folder 6, box 4, series 857, UNA.
6. Bernard Berelson, "Beyond Family Planning," *Science* 163 (1969): 536.
7. USAID's population director Reimert Ravenholt, finding the program woefully underfunded, had sought Moore's and Draper's help in getting funds specifically earmarked for population in USAID's budget. Ravenholt, "Interview with Rebecca Sharpless." For the establishment of the Population Crisis Committee, see Piotrow, "Interview with Rebecca Sharpless," 18.
8. "Manhattan Ad Schedule," February 2, 1968, folder 8, box 17, HMFC.
9. Hugh Everett Moore to Emerson Foote, Harry Hicks, and J. Drew Catlin, January 5, 1968, folder 8, box 17, HMFC.
10. The extent to which Draper participated in the Manhattan Project remains unclear. His former assistant, Dr. Phyllis Piotrow, assures me that Draper did not share Moore's affinity for explosive rhetoric.
11. In comparison, from the passage of the 1924 Johnson-Reed Act limiting immigration to the end of World War II, U.S. population grew by about 0.9% per year. Calculated by the author from Susan B. Carter et al., eds., *Historical Statistics of the United States*, Millennial Edition Online (New York: Cambridge University Press, 2020), Tables Aa6 and Aa7.
12. Not all young Americans were politically liberal; the conservative movement also drew its share of support from the baby boom generation. Although population growth in the Global South was caused by mortality decline rather than fertility increase, which was the primary cause of population growth in the United States, both changes produced a more youthful age structure, as the mortality decline in the Global South was concentrated among children and women in the childbearing ages.
13. Hugh Everett Moore, "Have You Ever Been Mugged?," *New York Times*, March 10, 1968.
14. Hugh Everett Moore, "This Is the Crime Explosion," *New York Times*, December 8, 1968.
15. Jill S. Quadagno, *The Color of Welfare: How Racism Undermined the War on Poverty* (New York: Oxford University Press, 1994); O'Connor, *Poverty Knowledge*.
16. Critchlow, *Intended Consequences*, 79.
17. "Memorandum," 1968, folder 24, box 16, HMFC.
18. Hugh Everett Moore, "Warning: The Water You Are Drinking May Be Polluted," *New York Times*, June 12, 1968.
19. "Advertisement Proposals," folder 25, box 16, HMFC.
20. Hugh Everett Moore, "How Many People Do You Want in Your Country?," *New York Times*, May 25, 1969.
21. See folders 11–12, box 17, HMFC.
22. "Are You Afraid to Go Out at Night?," May 25, 1968, folder 9, box 17, HMFC, emphasis in the original.
23. Public Law 90-137, 1967. Also see Piotrow, "Interview with Rebecca Sharpless," 29; Julian Simon, "Resources, Population, Environment: An Oversupply of False Bad News," *Science* 208 (1980): 1431–1437.
24. William Paddock and Paul Paddock, *Famine 1975! America's Decision: Who Will Survive* (Boston: Little, Brown, 1967) and Robert Rienow and Leona Train

Rienow, *Moment in the Sun: A Report on the Deteriorating Quality of the American Environment* (New York: Dial Press, 1967), cited in Moore to Foote, Hicks, and Catlin, January 5, 1968.

25. Wilbur L. Bullock, review of *Famine—1975! America's Decision: Who Will Survive?* by William and Paul Paddock, *Journal of the American Scientific Affiliation* 20 (1968): 126–127.
26. For a more recent fictional account of this approach, see Lionel Shriver, *Game Control: A Novel* (New York: Harper, 2007).
27. William Lindsay White to Hugh Everett Moore, August 14, 1968, and September 10, 1968, folder 9, box 17, HMFC.
28. Jonathan Swift, *A Modest Proposal: For Preventing the Children of Poor People in Ireland, from Being a Burden on Their Parents or Country, and for Making Them Beneficial to the Publick—1729,* Project Gutenberg, 2008, gutenberg.org/files/1080/1080-h/1080-h.htm.
29. White to Moore, August 14, 1968.
30. White to Moore, September 10, 1968.
31. "For Mr. Moore: Moment in the Sun," folder 25, box 16, HMFC.
32. "U.S. Department of Agriculture, Office of the Secretary," 1968, folder 25, box 16, HMFC; Barry Commoner, *The Closing Circle: Nature, Man, and Technology* (New York: Random House, 1971).
33. Michael Eagan, "Barry Commoner and the Science of Survival," Ph.D. diss., Washington State University, 2004, 174.
34. Hugh Everett Moore, "Form Letter," January 10, 1969, folder 5, box 17, HMFC.
35. Paul R Ehrlich, *The Population Bomb* (New York: Ballantine, 1968), 72–80.
36. Paul R. Ehrlich to Richard Bowers, March 3, 1969, folder 8, box 4, series 4, Paul R. Ehrlich Papers, Stanford University Library [hereafter PREP].
37. Ehrlich, *The Population Bomb*, 15. This is probably the most frequently cited passage in the book, but few who cite it comment on his obvious fear of brown bodies.
38. Robertson, *The Malthusian Moment*, 136–137.
39. For the Hart-Celler Act and its relationship to the civil rights movement, see John David Skrentny, *The Minority Rights Revolution* (Cambridge, MA: Harvard University Press, 2002).
40. Robertson, *The Malthusian Moment*, 130.
41. Ehrlich, *The Population Bomb*, 168.
42. Jack Rosenthal, "Census Expert Discounts Population Growth Issue," *New York Times*, January 14, 1971.
43. Ehrlich, *The Population Bomb*, 66–67, emphasis in the original.
44. William H. Draper Jr., "Testimony before the Platform Committee of the 1968 Democratic National Convention Committee," August 23, 1968, folder 47, fox 40, series 1, PREP.
45. Barry Commoner explained why population growth, in and of itself, was not responsible for ecosystem degradation in *The Closing Circle*.
46. Ehrlich, *The Population Bomb*, 166.
47. Ehrlich details this story in *The Population Bomb*. Science and technology studies scholars have described the idea of limiting unknown dangers as the "precautionary principle." Michel Callon, Pierre Lascoumes, Yannick Barthe, and Graham Burchell, *Acting in an Uncertain World,* trans. Graham Burchell (Cambridge, MA: MIT Press, 2011).
48. Ehrlich, *The Population Bomb*, 126. This episode is an example of efforts by industry to discredit science so as to avoid regulation, as described in

Naomi Oreskes and Erik M. Conway, *Merchants of Doubt: How a Handful of Scientists Obscured the Truth on Issues from Tobacco Smoke to Global Warming* (New York: Bloomsbury, 2010).

49. Robertson, *The Malthusian Moment*, 146–147.
50. Will Steffen, Wendy Broadgate, Lisa Deutsch, Owen Gaffney, and Cornelia Ludwig, "The Trajectory of the Anthropocene: The Great Acceleration," *Anthropocene Review* 2 (2015): 81–98.
51. "ZPG Statement of Purposes and Goals," 1969, folder 7, box 1, series 4, PREP. Kingsley Davis is often credited with having coined the phrase "zero population growth," but it was first used by demographer George J. Stolnitz in his "A Century of International Mortality Trends," *Population Studies* 9 (1955): 51.
52. "ZPG Communicator," March 1, 1969, folder 7, box 1, series 4, PREP.
53. "ZPG Brochure," 1969, folder 1, box 1, series 4, PREP.
54. "ZPG Newsletter," May 1, 1970, folder 4, box 1, series 4, PREP.
55. "California ZPG Newsletter," 1969, folder 7, box 1, series 4, PREP.
56. Paul R. Ehrlich to Leonard Ball, January 7, 1971, folder 3, box 1, series 4, PREP. Lucinda Cisler, chair of the National Organization for Women's Taskforce on Reproduction, served on the national board of ZPG. Robertson, *The Malthusian Moment*, 157–159.
57. "Declaration on Population and Food Prepared by the Environmental Fund for the UN World Population Meeting," 1974, folder 11, box 2, series 4, PREP.
58. Paul R. Ehrlich, "Response to Chasteen," 1/26/1970, folder 5, box 1, series 4, PREP.
59. [Illegible] to Richard Bowers, October 2, 1969, folder 8, box 1, series 4, PREP.
60. "A Recommended Population Policy for the United States," 1976, folder 6, box 3, series 4, PREP.
61. Richard Bowers, "100 Million Americans by the Year 2000?," 1970, folder 7, box 4, series 4, PREP.
62. "A Recommended Population Policy for the United States."
63. "ZPG Brochure."
64. "ZPG Brochure."
65. "ZPG Q&A," folder 3, box 1, series 4, PREP.
66. "Zero Population Growth: Program for Survival," 1970, folder 3, box 1, series 4, PREP.
67. Carol Oppenheim, "Big Zero for Zero Population's Goal," *Chicago Tribune*, December 14, 1978.
68. Shirley Radl, "Report to ZPG Board of Directors," May 6, 1970, folder 5, box 1, series 4, PREP.
69. Shirley Radl, "Report to Board of Directors, ZPG," July 21, 1970, folder 3, box 1, series 4, PREP.
70. Robertson, *The Malthusian Moment*, 160; Bouk, "Generation Crisis."
71. See, for example, Kenneth J. Fanucchi, "Youth Advised to Press for Population Control," *Los Angeles Times*, October 10, 1971; Keith Frye, "A Teacher's Sad Tale of Ecology and Young Activists," *Globe and Mail*, October 18, 1971.
72. Michael Dean, "Interview with Paul Ehrlich at Open University, England," 1972, folder 28, box 1, series 5, PREP.
73. Radl, "Report to Board of Directors, ZPG."
74. "ZPG Q&A."
75. "ZPG Draft Goals," 1970, folder 4, box 1, series 4, PREP.
76. Larry Barnett, "ZPG Membership Profile," folder 11, box 3, series 4, PREP.

77. For instance, see Jack Rosenthal, "Nation's Births Show Drop below Zero-Growth Level," *New York Times*, December 5, 1972; Jack Rosenthal, "New Census Study Projects Decline in the Rate of Births," *New York Times*, February 17, 1972; Jack Rosenthal, "The Panic as You Approach Zero: Population," *New York Times*, June 4, 1972.
78. Shirley Radl to Edgar Chasteen, folder 1, box 1, series 4, PREP; "Clipping from *Newsweek*," January 25, 1971, folder 7, box 16, series 1, PREP.
79. "Monday Conference, Australian Broadcasting Commission," August 30, 1971, folder 64, box 2, series 5, PREP.
80. "ZPG Recruitment Letter," March 19, 1979, folder 2, box 2, series 4, PREP.
81. "ZPG Media Target List," July 1, 1974, folder 1, box 3, series 4, PREP.
82. "A Recommended Population Policy for the United States."
83. See, for example, Norman Hartley, "Immigration Curb Plea Defended by Sponsors," *Globe and Mail*, April 25, 1975; Scott Young, "The ZPG Scare," *Globe and Mail*, April 15, 1975.
84. Holdren later served as science advisor to President Obama.
85. T. R. Parsons, the scientist-in-charge of the Environmental Research Group of the Fisheries Research Board of Canada, for example, critiqued an article Ehrlich published in *Saturday Review* titled "The Food-from-the-Sea Myth," pointing out, "Dr. Ehrlich is not a marine scientist, and his report was very much a compendium of well-known works dealing with specific subjects, rather than a fair appraisal of a problem." T. R. Parsons, "Response to 'Food-From-the-sea Myth,'" March 25, 1971, folder 100, box 23, series 1, PREP.
86. John Lear to Paul R. Ehrlich, March 25, 1971, folder 100, box 23, series 1, PREP.
87. Journalist Matthew Yglesias has recently argued that raising the U.S. population to one billion would produce advantageous economies of scale and that higher population densities would increase quality of life for most Americans. Matthew Yglesias, *One Billion Americans: The Case for Thinking Bigger* (New York: Penguin, 2020).
88. Ansley J. Coale, "Should the United States Start a Campaign for Fewer Births?," *Population Index* 34 (1968): 467.
89. Coale, "Should the United States Start a Campaign for Fewer Births?," 470.
90. Coale, "Should the United States Start a Campaign for Fewer Births?," 470.
91. Frank W. Notestein, "Zero Population Growth," *Population Index* 36 (1970): 445.
92. Philip M. Hauser, Judith Blake, and Paul Demeny, "Discussion," *Population Index* 36 (1970): 455.
93. *Population and the American Future: The Report of the Commission on Population Growth and the American Future* (New York: Signet, 1972).
94. "Clipping from *Newsweek*," January 25, 1971, folder 7, box 16, series 1, PREP.
95. Frank W. Notestein to Otis Dudley Duncan, April 11, 1970, folder 8, box 13, AJCP.
96. Bernard Berelson to Frank W. Notestein, November 11, 1970, folder 7, box 28, FWNP.
97. Paul R. Ehrlich to Richard Bowers, March 14, 1969, folder 8, box 4, series 4, PREP.
98. "*Concerned Demography* Looks Forward to Second Year," *Concerned Demography* 2, no. 1 (1970): 1–2. All issues of *Concerned Demography* are available on the PAA website: populationassociation.org/about/our-history/concerned-demography.
99. "Why a New Organization?," *Concerned Demography* 1, no. 1 (1969): 3.
100. "The PAA: A Time for Change," *Concerned Demography* 1, no. 4 (1970): 2.

101. "*Concerned Demography* Looks Forward to Second Year," 1.
102. Frank W. Notestein to the Concerned Demographers, December 10, 1969, folder "PAA 1970," box AD28, accession 2, PCA.
103. Abram J. Jaffe, "Letter to the Editor," *Concerned Demography* 1, no. 4 (1970): 10.
104. "Beginnings of Concerned Demographers," *Concerned Demography* 1, no. 1 (1969): 2–6.
105. Zeke was a dog. Emily Klancher Merchant, "PAA History: *Concerned Demography* and the Concerned Demographers," *PAA Affairs*, Winter 2017.
106. This group included Bob Hauser, Jim Sweet, David Featherman, and Larry Bumpass, all of whom had been strongly influenced by Michigan faculty members Dudley and Beverly Duncan. Some of them had also worked with Ronald Freedman, but Norman Ryder, who hired them at the University of Wisconsin, emphasized the Duncans' influence as the common denominator among them. Ryder, "Oral History Interview."
107. Emily Klancher Merchant, "A Digital Reading of Twentieth Century Demography: Toics by Journal," EmilyKlancher.com/digdemog/tmod/topjournal.html.
108. Ronald J. Freedman, "Relevance and Validity: Constraints and Controls in Demography," *Concerned Demography* 2, no. 2 (1970): 18.
109. "*Concerned Demography* Looks Forward to Second Year," 1.
110. Larry L. Bumpass, "Oral History Interview with Jean Van Der Tak, 21 March 1991," in Van Der Tak, *Demographic Destinies*, vol. 1, no. 3, 384.
111. "The PAA: A Time for Change," *Concerned Demography* 1, no. 4 (1970): 1–3.
112. Union of Concerned Scientists, "Founding Document: 1968 MIT Faculty Statement," ucsusa.org/about/founding-document-1968.html.
113. Charles Hirschman, "A New Look at Human Ecology and Marx," *Concerned Demography* 3, no. 2 (1970): 2–6.
114. Eric R. Weiss-Altaner, review of *Population, Resources, Environment*, by Paul and Anne Ehrlich, *Concerned Demography* 2, no. 3 (1971): 22.
115. "PAA Business Meeting: No Yawns This Year," *Concerned Demography* 1, no. 4 (1970): 8–9.
116. "*Concerned Demography* Looks Forward to Second Year," 3.
117. "Reader Response—Pro and Con," *Concerned Demography* 1, no. 4 (1970): 13.
118. Notable female demographers with mathematical or statistical backgrounds include Barbara Anderson, Margaret Hagood, Evelyn Kitagawa, Jane Menken, and Mindel Sheps.
119. "On Women in the Population Association: An Editorial," *Concerned Demography* 4, no. 1 (1974): 21.
120. "From the Waste Basket: Welcome to Convention '70," *Concerned Demography* 1, no. 4 (1970): 14.
121. Personal communication with Avery M. ("Pete") Guest.
122. Avery M. Guest, "Gatekeeping among the Demographers," in *Editors as Gatekeepers: Getting Published in the Social Sciences*, ed. Rita J. Simon and James J. Fyfe (Lanham, MD: Rowman and Littlefield, 1994), 85–106; Charles Hirschman, "Interview with the PAA History Committee," May 2014, populationassociation.org/about/our-history/oral-history-project.
123. Frank W. Notestein to the Concerned Demographers, December 10, 1969.
124. Paraphrased in Eric R. Weiss-Altaner, "Fertility Decline, Savings and Economic Growth," *Concerned Demography* 2, no. 3 (1971): 11.

125. Susana Torrado de Ipola, "A Contribution of the U.S. Department of State to the Latin American Population Conference, Mexico, 1970," *Concerned Demography* 2, no. 3 (1970): 4–5, emphasis in the original.
126. Axel I. Mundigo, "Latin American Attitudes on Birth Control: A Typology," *Concerned Demography* 3, no. 1 (1971): 95.
127. Carmen Miró, "Interrelationship of Population Policy and Aspects of Development," October 29, 1974, folder "Ford Foundation Conference on Social Science Research on Population and Development," box AD30, accession 2, PCA.
128. For a fuller account of the 1972 Conference on the Human Environment, see Perrin Selcer, *The Postwar Origins of the Global Environment* (New York: Columbia University Press, 2018).
129. Quoted in Barbara Ward, "The World: Pollution," *The Economist*, May 27, 1972, 68. Also see Claire Sterling, "U.S. Losing Argument with Poor Nations at Stockholm," *Washington Post*, June 8, 1972; "Prophets of Doom Come on Strong but Ecology Talks Sideline Them," *Los Angeles Times*, June 15, 1972.
130. Joe Alex Morris Jr., "World Population Issue Surfaces at Conference: Third World Nations Indicate That They Will Oppose Family Planning as Conspiracy," *Los Angeles Times*, June 10, 1972.
131. Morris, "World Population Issue Surfaces at Conference."
132. Paul Sabin, *The Bet: Paul Ehrlich, Julian Simon, and Our Gamble over Earth's Future* (New Haven, CT: Yale University Press, 2013), 56.
133. Previously the position had been held only by demographers: Philip Hauser (1946–1954), Kingsley Davis (1954–1961), and Ansley Coale (1961–1969).
134. "Telegram 3969 From the Embassy in Romania to the Department of State," August 31, 1974, D740242-0932, Central Foreign Policy Files, RG 59, National Archives, Washington, DC [hereafter NA], history.state.gov. historicaldocuments/frus1969-76ve14p1/d116.
135. Philander P. Claxton Jr., "Briefing Memorandum from the Secretary of State's Special Assistant for Population Matters (Claxton) to Secretary of State Kissinger," October 5, 1973, Department of State, Central Files 1970–73, SOC 13, RG 59, NA, history.state.gov.historicaldocuments/frus1969-76ve14p1/d108.
136. "Report of the Advisory Committee of Experts on the World Population Plan of Action on Its Third Meeting," February 25, 1974, folder "World Population Plan of Action 1974," box AD24, accession 2, PCA; "Advisory Committee of Experts on Global Population Strategy," June 19, 1972, folder 2, box 17, FWNP; "Airgram A-5913 From the Department of State to All Diplomatic Posts," July 11, 1973, Department of State, Central Files, 1970-73, SOC 13, RG 59, NA, history.state. gov.historicaldocuments/frus1969-76ve14p1/d107.
137. Philander P. Claxton Jr., "Memorandum of Conversation Regarding Population Matters," June 8, 1973, Department of State, Central Files 1970–73, SOC 13, RG 59, NA, history.state.gov.historicaldocuments/frus1969-76ve14p1/d104. Pestering by Draper led to a National Security Council study in 1974 on "the impact of world population growth on U.S. security and overseas interests." National Security Council, "National Security Study Memorandum 200," April 24, 1974, National Security Study Memoranda, NSSM 200, Box H-204, NCS Institutional Files (H-Files), Nixon Presidential Materials, NA, history.state. gov.historicaldocuments/frus1969-76ve14p1/d113. For Draper's role, see Brent Scowcroft, "Memorandum from the President's Deputy Assistant for National Security Affairs (Scowcroft) to the President's Assistant for National Security Affairs (Kissinger)," March 23, 1974, National Security Study Memoranda, NSSM

200, Box H-204, NCS Institutional Files (H-Files), Nixon Presidential Materials, NA, history.state.gov.historicaldocuments/frus1969-76ve14p1/d112.

138. Philander P. Claxton Jr., "Memorandum from the Executive Secretary of the Department of State (Eliot) to the President's Assistant for National Security Affairs (Kissinger)," June 13, 1973, Department of State, Central Files 1970–73, POL 7, USSR, RG 59, NA, history.state.gov.historicaldocuments/frus1969-76ve14p1/d105.
139. Claxton, "Briefing Memorandum from the Secretary of State's Special Assistant for Population Matters (Claxton) to Secretary of State Kissinger."
140. Bernard Berelson to Philander P. Claxton Jr., July 12, 1973, folder "World Population Plan of Action 1974," box AD24, accession 2, PCA.
141. Gail Kligman, *The Politics of Duplicity: Controlling Reproduction in Ceausescu's Romania* (Berkeley: University of California Press, 1998), 2.
142. Paul Demeny, "Population Policy on the World Agenda—1984," August 28, 1974, folder "Bucharest," box AD30, accession 2, PCA.
143. Coale, "Should the United States Start a Campaign for Fewer Births?"
144. Harkavy, *Curbing Population Growth*, 185.
145. Selcer, *The Postwar Origins of the Global Environment*, 215.
146. Philander P. Claxton Jr., "The World Population Conference: An Assessment," folder 15, box 29, FWNP.
147. Nils Gilman, "The New International Economic Order: A Reintroduction," *Humanity* 6 (2015): 3.
148. Caspar Weinberger, "Memorandum from Secretary of Health, Education, and Welfare Weinberger to Secretary of State Kissinger," September 19, 1974, National Security Study Memoranda, NSSM 200, box H-204, NSC Institutional Files, (H-Files), Nixon Presidential Materials, NA, history.state.gov.historicaldocuments/frus1969-76ve14p1/d117.
149. C. Chandrasekaran, "World Population Plan of Action," September 30, 1974, folder "Post-Bucharest," box AD24, accession 2, PCA.
150. Quoted in Claxton, "The World Population Conference: An Assessment."
151. W. Parker Mauldin, "Highlights of the Conference," folder "Bucharest," box AD30, accession 2, PCA.
152. Philander P. Claxton Jr., "Bucharest and the Future: Conference for Non-Governmental Organizations on the World Population Conference," October 10, 1974, folder 15, box 29, FWNP.
153. Weinberger, "Memorandum from Secretary of Health, Education, and Welfare Weinberger to Secretary of State Kissinger."
154. W. Parker Mauldin, "Outline of Report on the World Population Conference and Tribune, Bucharest, 1974," folder "Bucharest," box AD30, accession 2, PCA.
155. "The Plan of Action," September 30, 1974, folder "Post-Bucharest," box AD24, accession 2, PCA.
156. Frank W. Notestein, "Uninhibited Notes on Bucharest—Not for Publication," September 12, 1974, folder 13, box 29, FWNP.
157. Jason L. Finkle and Barbara B. Crane, "Ideology and Politics at Mexico City: The United States at the 1984 International Conference on Population," *Population and Development Review* 11 (1985): 1.
158. Demeny, "Population Policy on the World Agenda—1984."
159. John D. III Rockefeller, "Population Growth: The Role of the Developed World," 1974, folder 134, box 22, record group IV3B4.7, PCA.

160. Joan Dunlop, "Population Council April Staff Meeting: Closing Comments of Mr. Hopper," April 24, 1975, folder 491, box 72, subseries 4, series 3, record group 5, JDR3.
161. Bernard Berelson, "Memorandum to the File: World Population Conference, Bucharest—JDR's Speech," September 4, 1974, folder "Bucharest," box AD30, accession 2, PCA.
162. Frank W. Notestein to Bernard Berelson, 1974, folder "Post-Bucharest," box AD24, accession 2, PCA.
163. Joan Dunlop, "Interview with Rebecca Sharpless for the Population and Reproductive Health Oral History Project," April 14, 2004, SSC, 5.
164. Adrienne Germain, "Interview with Rebecca Sharpless for the Population and Reproductive Health Oral History Project," June 19, 2003, SSC, 18.
165. Dunlop, "Interview with Rebecca Sharpless," 6.
166. Dunlop, "Interview with Rebecca Sharpless," 7–8.
167. John D. Rockefeller III, "Introduction to Annual Report of the Population Council—Final Draft," April 4, 1977, folder 493, box 73, subseries 4, series 3, record group 5, JDR3.
168. Paraphrased in Germain, "Interview with Rebecca Sharpless," 50.
169. This identity crisis produced a number of reflexive articles by demographers, including Hodgson, "Orthodoxy and Revisionism in American Demography," and Paul Demeny, "Social Science and Population Policy, *Population and Development Review* 14, no. 3 (1988): 451–479.

EPILOGUE

1. Personal communication with Phyllis Piotrow, 2020.
2. Frank W. Notestein to John D. Rockefeller III, October 27, 1975; John D. Rockefeller III to Frank W. Notestein, October 31, 1975; and John D. Rockefeller III to Bernard Berelson, April 8, 1976, folder 15, box 13, AJCP.
3. The Population Council has contributed to the development of contraceptive rings (vaginal) and implants (arm), as well as new types of IUD.
4. Harkavy, *Curbing Population Growth*, 187.
5. Germain, "Interview with Rebecca Sharpless," 73–77.
6. Marta Tienda, "Interview with the PAA Oral History Committee for the PAA Oral History Project," 2013, populationassociation.org/about/our-history/oral-history-project.
7. Harkavy, *Curbing Population Growth*, 45–46.
8. Personal communication with Wendy Baldwin, 2016. Also see Kristin Luker, *Dubious Conceptions: The Politics of Teenage Pregnancy* (Cambridge, MA: Harvard University Press, 1996).
9. For instance, see the University of Michigan's Health and Retirement Study and the University of North Carolina's National Longitudinal Study of Adolescent to Adult Health.
10. Samuel Preston, "The Contours of Demography: Estimates and Projections," *Demography* 30 (1993): 593–606.
11. For instance, see Jennifer Johnson-Hanks, *Uncertain Honor: Modern Motherhood in an African Crisis* (Chicago: University of Chicago Press, 2006).
12. For instance, see John Bongaarts, W. Parker Mauldin, and James F. Phillips, "The Demographic Impact of Family Planning Programs," *Studies in Family Planning* 21 (1990): 299–310.

13. For the World Fertility Survey, see Kingsley Davis, "The World's Most Expensive Survey," *Sociological Forum* 2 (1987): 829–834. For the Demographic and Health Surveys, see John Cleland, "Fertility and Family Planning Surveys: Future Priorities in the Light of Past Experiences," *International Family Planning Perspectives* 12 (1986): 2–7.
14. Demeny, "Social Science and Population Policy."
15. National Research Council, *Population Growth and Economic Development: Policy Questions* (Washington, DC: National Academies Press, 1986), 34.
16. National Research Council, *Population Growth and Economic Development*, 36–37.
17. For the deeper roots of market fundamentalism, see Angus Burgin, *The Great Persuasion: Reinventing Free Markets since the Depression* (Cambridge, MA: Harvard University Press, 2012). For the origins of the neoliberal case against population control, see Hoff, *The State and the Stork*.
18. Hoff, *The State and the Stork*.
19. A newer (and non-neoliberal) version of this argument holds that, as per-capita GDP increases in such populous countries as China and India, increasing the size of the U.S. population will be the only way the United States can remain the world's largest economy. Yglesias, *One Billion Americans*.
20. Sabin, *The Bet*.
21. David E. Bloom and Jeffrey G. Williamson, "Demographic Transitions and Economic Miracles in Emerging Asia," *World Bank Economic Review* 12, no. 3 (1998): 419–455.
22. David E. Bloom, David Canning, and Jaypee Sevilla, *The Demographic Dividend: A New Perspective on the Economic Consequences of Population Change* (Santa Monica, CA: RAND, 2003).
23. Personal communications with Ellen Foley and Barbara Anderson, 2020.
24. Echo Huang, "Jack Ma and Elon Musk Are Pretty Worried about a Looming Population Collapse," *Quartz*, August 29, 2019.
25. Personal communication with Barbara Anderson, 2020.
26. James Feyrer, Bruce Sacerdote, and Ariel Dora Stern, "Will the Stork Return to Europe and Japan? Understanding Fertility within Developed Nations," *Journal of Economic Perspectives* 22, no. 3 (2008): 3–22.
27. Yglesias, *One Billion Americans*.
28. For instance, see Mikko Myrskylä, Hans-Peter Kohler, and Francesco C. Billari, "Advances in Development Reverse Fertility Declines," *Nature* 460 (2009): 741–743.
29. Personal communication with Dennis Hodgson, 2019.
30. Paul Crutzen, "Geology of Mankind," *Nature* 415 (2002): 23.
31. Andreas Malm and Alf Hornborg, "The Geology of Mankind? A Critique of the Anthropocene Narrative," *Anthropocene Review* 1 (2014): 62–69.
32. Donna Haraway, "Anthropocene, Capitalocene, Plantationocene, Chthulucene: Making Kin," *Environmental Humanities* 6 (2015): 159–165.
33. For instance, see work published in *Population and Environment* after 2005.
34. Steffen et al., "The Trajectory of the Anthropocene."
35. Ian Angus and Simon Butler, *Too Many People* (Chicago: Haymarket Books, 2011). Population bombers often cite the I=PAT equation as if it were a law of nature. It stands for the belief that the impact on the environment is the multiplicative product of population, affluence, and technology. For an excellent critique of this equation, and particularly of the way in which "P" lacks race, class, and gender, see H. Patricia Hynes, "Taking Population Out of the Equation: Reformulating

I=PAT," in *Dangerous Intersections: Feminist Perspectives on Population, Environment, and Development*, ed. Jael Silliman and Ynestra King (Cambridge, MA: South End Press, 1999), 39–73.

36. Rebecca Jane Williams, "Storming the Citadels of Poverty: Family Planning under the Emergency in India, 1975–1977," *Journal of Asian Studies* 73 (2014): 471–492.
37. Connelly, *Fatal Misconception*, 322.
38. Greenhalgh, *Just One Child.*
39. Hartmann, *Reproductive Rights and Wrongs*, 76–77.
40. Dorothy Roberts, *Killing the Black Body: Race, Reproduction, and the Meaning of Liberty* (New York: Vintage, 1998); Molly Ladd-Taylor, *Fixing the Poor: Eugenic Sterilization and Child Welfare in the Twentieth Century* (Minneapolis: University of Minnesota Press, 2020).
41. Its domestic analogue, the 1977 Hyde Amendment, prohibits federal funds from being used to pay for abortions in the United States, limiting the access of poor women to this medical procedure.
42. Dina Bogecho and Melissa Upreti, "The Global Gag Rule: An Antithesis to the Rights-Based Approach to Health," *Health and Human Rights* 9 (2006): 17–32.
43. Finkle and Crane, "Ideology and Politics at Mexico City."
44. Ravenholt, "Interview with Rebecca Sharpless." For more about menstrual regulation, see Michelle Murphy, *Seizing the Means of Reproduction: Entanglements of Feminism, Health, and Technoscience* (Durham, NC: Duke University Press, 2012).
45. Hoff, *The State and the Stork*. The term "Rockefeller Republican" refers to supporters of Nelson Rockefeller, younger brother of John D. III, who served as governor of New York from 1950 to 1973 and vice president under Gerald Ford.
46. Steven Waldman, *Sacred Liberty: America's Long, Bloody, and Ongoing Struggle for Religious Freedom* (New York: Harper and Collins, 2019); Ilyse Hogue and Ellie Langford, *The Lie That Binds* (Washington, DC: Strong Arm Press, 2020).
47. Karen L. Baird, "Globalizing Reproductive Control: Consequences of the 'Global Gag Rule,'" in *Linking Visions: Feminist Bioethics, Human Rights, and the Developing World*, ed. Rosemarie Tong, Anne Donchin, and Susan Dodds (Lanham, MD: Rowman & Littlefield, 2004), 133–145.
48. Dennis Hodgson and Susan Cotts Watkins, "Feminists and Neo-Malthusians: Past and Present Alliances," *Population and Development Review* 23 (1997): 469–523.
49. Ross and Solinger, *Reproductive Justice*, 9. For the activities of the reproductive justice movement at Cairo, see Loretta J. Ross, "Reproductive Justice as Intersectional Feminist Activism," *Souls* 19 (2017): 286–314.
50. For a definition and discussion of populationism, see Rajani Bhatia, Jade S. Sasser, Diana Ojeda, Anne Hendrixson, Sarojini Nadimpally, and Ellen E. Foley, "A Feminist Exploration of 'Populationism': Engaging Contemporary Forms of Population Control," *Gender, Place & Culture* 27 (2020): 333–350. For the history of the concept of sustainable development, see Macekura, *Of Limits and Growth.*
51. Saul E. Halfon, *The Cairo Consensus* (New York: Lexington Books, 2007).
52. I use the term "boundary concept" to mean something analogous to Star and Griesemer's "boundary object." Susan Leigh Star and James R. Griesemer, "Institutional Ecology, Translations, and Boundary Objects: Amateurs and Professionals in Berkeley's Museum of Vertebrate Zoology, 1907–39," *Social Studies of Science* 19 (1989): 387–420.

53. Bashford, *Global Population*. Also see Alison Bashford, "Population, Geopolitics, and International Organizations in the Mid Twentieth Century," *Journal of World History* 19 (2008): 327–347.
54. Bhatia et al., "A Feminist Exploration of 'Populationism.'"
55. Personal communication with Jade Sasser, 2020.
56. Bhatia et al., "A Feminist Exploration of 'Populationism'"; Roberts, *Killing the Black Body*; Susanne Schultz, "Redefining and Medicalizing Population Policies: NGOs and Their Innovative Contributions to the Post-Cairo Agenda," in *Markets and Malthus: Population, Gender, and Health in Neo-liberal Times*, ed. Mohan Rao and Sarah Sexton (Los Angeles: Sage, 2010), 173–214.
57. Sasser, *On Infertile Ground*.
58. Anne Hendrixson, "Population Control in the Troubled Present: The '120 by 20' Target and Implant Access Program," *Development and Change* 50 (2018): 786–804.
59. David Lam, "How the World Survived the Population Bomb: Lessons from 50 Years of Extraordinary Demographic History," *Demography* 48 (2011): 1231–1262.
60. Nikita Stewart, "Planned Parenthood in NY Disavows Margaret Sanger over Eugenics," *New York Times*, July 21, 2020.
61. The others were Woodrow Wilson, whose name was removed from Princeton University's School of Public and International Affairs; Clarence Cook ("C. C.") Little, whose name was removed from a science building at the University of Michigan; and Thomas Parran, whose name was removed from a building at the School of Public Health at the University of Pittsburgh.
62. Murphy, "Against Population."
63. For example, the Texas Policy Evaluation Project.
64. For instance, see Feng Wang, Yong Cai, Ke Shen, and Stuart Geitel-Basten, "Is Demography Just a Numerical Exercise? Numbers, Politics, and Legacies of China's One-Child Policy," *Demography* 55 (2018): 693–719; Susan Greenhalgh, "Making Demography Astonishing: Lessons in the Politics of Population Science," *Demography* 55 (2018): 721–731.
65. Demographer John Bongaarts of the Population Council even complained that the 2018 report of the Intergovernmental Panel on Climate Change did not pay enough attention to population control as a potential solution to climate change. John Bongaarts and Brian C. O'Neill, "Global Warming Policy: Is Population Left Out in the Cold?," *Science* 361 (2018): 650–652.

BIBLIOGRAPHY

Ahonsi, Babatunde A. "Deliberate Falsification and Census Data in Nigeria." *African Affairs* 87, no. 349 (1988): 553–562.

Allen, Garland E. "The Eugenics Record Office at Cold Spring Harbor, 1910–1940: An Essay in Institutional History." *Osiris* 2 (1986): 225–264.

Allen, Garland E. "Old Wine in New Bottles: From Eugenics to Population Control in the Work of Raymond Pearl." In *The Expansion of American Biology*, ed. Keith R. Benson, Jane Maienschein, and Ronald Rainger, 231–261. New Brunswick, NJ: Rutgers University Press, 1991.

Alterman, Hyman. *Counting People: The Census in History*. New York: Harcourt, Brace & World, 1969.

Aluko, S. A. "How Many Nigerians? An Analysis of Nigeria's Census Problems, 1901–63." *Journal of Modern African Studies* 3, no. 3 (1965): 371–392.

Anderson, Barbara A. *World Population Dynamics: An Introduction to Demography*. New York: Pearson, 2015.

Anderson, Benedict. *Imagined Communities: Reflections on the Origin and Spread of Nationalism*. Revised edition. New York: Verso, 2006.

Anderson, Margo J. *The American Census: A Social History*. New Haven, CT: Yale University Press, 1988.

Angus, Ian, and Simon Butler. *Too Many People*. Chicago: Haymarket Books, 2011.

Aratani, Lori. "Princeton Says It Will Remove Woodrow Wilson's Name from Its Public Policy School." *Washington Post*, June 28, 2020.

Arndt, H. W. *Economic Development: The History of an Idea*. Chicago: University of Chicago Press, 1987.

Back, Kurt W., Reuben Hill, and J. Mayone Stycos. *Family and Population Control Study: Puerto Rico, 1953–1954* [machine-readable data set]. Ann Arbor: Inter-university Consortium for Political and Social Research, 2009. doi.org/10.3886/ICPSR07062.v2.

Baird, Karen L. "Globalizing Reproductive Control: Consequences of the 'Global Gag Rule.'" In *Linking Visions: Feminist Bioethics, Human Rights, and the Developing World*, ed. Rosemarie Tong, Anne Donchin, and Susan Dodds, 133–145. Lanham, MD: Rowman & Littlefield, 2004.

Baker, Jean H. *Margaret Sanger: A Life of Passion*. New York: Hill and Wang, 2011.

Balfour, Marshall C. *Public Health and Demography in the Far East: Report of a Survey Trip, September 13–December 13, 1948*. New York: Rockefeller Foundation, 1950.

Balibar, Etienne, and Immanuel Wallerstein. *Race, Nation, Class: Ambiguous Identities*. New York: Verso, 1991.

Bannister, Robert C. *Sociology and Scientism: The American Quest for Objectivity, 1880–1940*. Chapel Hill: University of North Carolina Press, 1987.

Barkan, Elazar. "Reevaluating Progressive Eugenics: Herbert Spencer Jennings and the 1924 Immigration Legislation." *Journal of the History of Biology* 24, no. 1 (1991): 91–112.

Barkan, Elazar. *The Retreat of Scientific Racism: Changing Concepts of Race in Britain and the United States between the World Wars*. New York: Cambridge University Press, 1992.

Bashford, Alison. *Global Population: History, Geopolitics, and Life on Earth*. New York: Columbia University Press, 2014.

Bashford, Alison. "Population, Geopolitics, and International Organizations in the Mid Twentieth Century." *Journal of World History* 19, no. 3 (2008): 327–347.

Bashford, Alison, and Joyce E. Chaplin. *The New Worlds of Thomas Robert Malthus: Rereading the "Principle of Population."* Princeton, NJ: Princeton University Press, 2016.

Becker, Gary S. "An Economic Analysis of Fertility." In *Demographic and Economic Change in Developed Countries*, ed. National Bureau of Economic Research, 209–240. New York: Columbia University Press, 1960.

Berelson, Bernard. "Application of Intra-Uterine Contraception in Family Planning Programs." In *Proceedings, Second International Conference on Intra-Uterine Contraception*, ed. Sheldon Segal, 9–13. New York: Population Council, 1964.

Berelson, Bernard. "Beyond Family Planning." *Science* 163, no. 3867 (1969): 533–543.

Berelson, Bernard. "On Family Planning Communication." *Demography* 1, no. 1 (1964): 94–105.

Berelson, Bernard, and Ronald J. Freedman. "A Study in Fertility Control." *Scientific American* 210, no. 5 (1964): 29–37.

Bertaux, Sandrine. "Reproduce or Perish? The Artefact of the Fertility Concept and the French School of Demography." *Historical Social Research/Historische Sozialforschung* 36, no. 2 (2011): 120–139.

Bhatia, Rajani, Jade S. Sasser, Diana Ojeda, Anne Hendrixson, Sarojini Nadimpally, and Ellen E. Foley. "A Feminist Exploration of 'Populationism': Engaging Contemporary Forms of Population Control." *Gender, Place & Culture* 27, no. 3 (2020): 333–350.

Blake, Judith. "Are Babies Consumer Durables? A Critique of the Economic Theory of Reproductive Motivation." *Population Studies* 22, no. 1 (1968): 5–25.

Bloom, David E., David Canning, and Jaypee Sevilla. *The Demographic Dividend: A New Perspective on the Economic Consequences of Population Change*. Santa Monica, CA: RAND, 2003.

Bloom, David E., and Jeffrey G. Williamson. "Demographic Transitions and Economic Miracles in Emerging Asia." *World Bank Economic Review* 12, no. 3 (1998): 419–455.

Bogecho, Dina, and Melissa Upreti. "The Global Gag Rule: An Antithesis to the Rights-Based Approach to Health." *Health and Human Rights* 9, no. 1 (2006): 17–32.

Bogue, Donald J. "Oral History Interview with Jean Van Der Tak, 30 March 1989." In *Demographic Destinies: Interviews with Presidents and Secretary-Treasurers of the Population Association of America*, vol. 1, no. 2, ed. Jean Van Der Tak, 39–67. Washington, DC: Population Association of America, 2005.

Bongaarts, John, and Brian C. O'Neill. "Global Warming Policy: Is Population Left Out in the Cold?" *Science* 361 (2018): 650–652.

Bongaarts, John, W. Parker Mauldin, and James F. Phillips. "The Demographic Impact of Family Planning Programs." *Studies in Family Planning* 21, no. 6 (1990): 299–310.

Borgwardt, Elizabeth. *A New Deal for the World: America's Vision for Human Rights*. Cambridge, MA: Harvard University Press, 2005.

Bouk, Dan. "Generation Crisis: How Population Research Defined the Baby Boomers." *Modern American History* 1, no. 3 (2018): 321–342.

Bouk, Dan. *How Our Days Became Numbered: Risk and the Rise of the Statistical Individual*. Chicago: University of Chicago Press, 2015.

Bowker, Geoffrey C., and Susan Leigh Star. *Sorting Things Out: Classification and Its Consequences*. Cambridge, MA: MIT Press, 2000.

Bowley, Arthur Lyon. "Births and Population in Great Britain." *Economic Journal* 34, no. 134 (1924): 188–192.

Brandt, Karl. Review of *Road to Survival*, by William Vogt. *Land Economics* 26, no. 1 (1950): 88–90.

Brass, William, ed. *The Demography of Tropical Africa*. Princeton, NJ: Princeton University Press, 1968.

Briggs, Jill. "'As Fool-Proof as Possible': Overpopulation, Colonial Demography, and the Jamaica Birth Control League." *Global South* 4, no. 2 (2010): 157–177.

Briggs, Laura. *Reproducing Empire: Race, Sex, Science, and U.S. Imperialism in Puerto Rico*. Berkeley: University of California Press, 2002.

Bullock, Wilbur L. Review of *Famine—1975! America's Decision: Who Will Survive?* by William and Paul Paddock. *Journal of the American Scientific Affiliation* 20, no. 4 (1968): 126–127.

Bulmer, Martin. "The Methodology of Early Social Indicator Research: William Fielding Ogburn and 'Recent Social Trends,' 1933." *Social Indicators Research* 13, no. 2 (1983): 109–130.

Bumpass, Larry L. "Oral History Interview with Jean Van Der Tak, 21 March 1991." In *Demographic Destinies: Interviews with Presidents and Secretary-Treasurers of the Population Association of America*, vol. 1, no. 3, ed. Jean Van Der Tak, 375–397. Washington, DC: Population Association of America, 2005.

Burch, Guy Irving. "Headed for the Last Census? I. Overpopulation or Underpopulation? A Review of Conflicting Opinions." *Journal of Heredity* 28, no. 6 (1937): 203–212.

Burch, Guy Irving. "Headed for the Last Census? II. The Differential Birthrate." *Journal of Heredity* 28, no. 7 (1937): 241–254.

Burch, Guy Irving, and Elmer Pendell. *Human Breeding and Survival*. New York: Penguin, 1947.

Burgin, Angus. *The Great Persuasion: Reinventing Free Markets since the Depression*. Cambridge, MA: Harvard University Press, 2012.

Burton, Antoinette. *Burdens of History: British Feminists, Indian Women, and Imperial Culture, 1865–1915*. Chapel Hill: University of North Carolina Press, 1994.

Caldwell, John Charles, and Pat Caldwell. *Limiting Population Growth and the Ford Foundation Contribution*. London: Pinter, 1986.

Callon, Michel, Pierre Lascoumes, Yannick Barthe, and Graham Burchell. *Acting in an Uncertain World*. Translated by Graham Burchell. Cambridge, MA: MIT Press, 2011.

Camic, Charles, and Yu Xie. "The Statistical Turn in American Social Science: Columbia University, 1890–1915." *American Sociological Review* 59, no. 5 (1994): 773–805.

Campbell, Chloe. *Race and Empire: Eugenics in Colonial Kenya*. New York: Manchester University Press, 2007.
Campbell, Clarence G. "The German Racial Policy." *Eugenical News* 21, no. 2 (1936): 25–29.
Cannan, Edwin. "The Probability of a Cessation of Growth of Population in England and Wales during the Next Century." *Economic Journal* 5, no. 20 (1895): 505–515.
Carey, Jane. "The Racial Imperatives of Sex: Birth Control and Eugenics in Britain, the United States and Australia in the Interwar Years." *Women's History Review* 21, no. 5 (2012): 733–752.
Carlson, Allan C. *The Swedish Experiment in Family Politics: The Myrdals and the Interwar Population Crisis*. New Brunswick, NJ: Transaction, 1990.
Chandler, Alfred Dupont. *The Visible Hand: The Managerial Revolution in American Business*. Cambridge, MA: Belknap, 1977.
Chase, Allan. *The Legacy of Malthus: The Social Costs of the New Scientific Racism*. New York: Knopf, 1977.
Choldin, Harvey M., A. Majeed Kahn, and B. Hosne Ara. "Cultural Complications in Fertility Interviewing." *Demography* 4, no. 1 (1967): 244–252.
Chow, L. P. "A Programme to Control Fertility in Taiwan: Setting, Accomplishment and Evaluation." *Population Studies* 19, no. 2 (1965): 155–166.
Chow, L. P., Hsiao-Chang Chen, and Ming-Cheng Chang. *Knowledge, Attitudes, and Practice of Contraception in Taiwan: First Province-Wide Fertility Survey (KAP I), 1965* [machine-readable data set]. Ann Arbor: Inter-university Consortium for Political and Social Research, 2005. doi.org/10.3886/ICPSR06862.v1.
Chow, L. P. Hsiao-Chang Chen, and Ming-Cheng Chang. *Knowledge, Attitudes, and Practice of Contraception in Taiwan: Second Province-Wide Fertility Survey (KAP II), 1967* [machine-readable data set]. Ann Arbor: Inter-university Consortium for Political and Social Research, 2005. doi.org/10.3886/ICPSR06863.v1.
Chung, Yuehtsen Juliette. *Struggle for National Survival: Eugenics in Sino-Japanese Contexts, 1896–1945*. New York: Routledge, 2002.
Clarke, Adele. *Disciplining Reproduction: Modernity, American Life Sciences, and "The Problems of Sex."* Berkeley: University of California Press, 1998.
Clarke, Adele, and Donna Haraway, eds. *Making Kin Not Population: Reconceiving Generations*. Chicago: Prickly Paradigm Press, 2018.
Cleland, John. "Fertility and Family Planning Surveys: Future Priorities in the Light of Past Experiences." *International Family Planning Perspectives* 12, no. 1 (1986): 2–7.
Coale, Ansley J. *Ansley J. Coale: An Autobiography*. Philadelphia: American Philosophical Society, 2000.
Coale, Ansley J. "Oral History Interview with Anders Lunde, 27 April 1979, and Jean Van Der Tak, 11 May 1988." In *Demographic Destinies: Interviews with Presidents and Secretary-Treasurers of the Population Association of America*, vol. 1, no. 2, ed. Jean Van Der Tak, 135–163. Washington, DC: Population Association of America, 2005.
Coale, Ansley J. *The Problem of Reducing Vulnerability to Atomic Bombs*. Princeton, NJ: Princeton University Press, 1947.
Coale, Ansley J. "Should the United States Start a Campaign for Fewer Births?" *Population Index* 34, no. 4 (1968): 467–474.
Coale, Ansley J. "The Voluntary Control of Human Fertility." *Proceedings of the American Philosophical Society* 111, no. 3 (1967): 164–169.

Coale, Ansley J., and Paul Demeny. *Regional Model Life Tables and Stable Populations*. Princeton, NJ: Princeton University Press, 1966.
Coale, Ansley J., and Edgar M. Hoover. *Population Growth and Economic Development in Low Income Countries: A Case Study of India's Prospects*. Princeton, NJ: Princeton University Press, 1958.
Coale, Ansley J., and James Trussell. "The Development and Use of Demographic Models." *Population Studies* 50, no. 3 (1996): 469–484.
Cohen-Cole, Jamie. *The Open Mind: Cold War Politics and the Science of Human Nature*. Chicago: University of Chicago Press, 2014.
Comfort, Nathaniel C. *The Science of Human Perfection: How Genes Became the Heart of American Medicine*. New Haven, CT: Yale University Press, 2012.
Commoner, Barry. *The Closing Circle: Nature, Man, and Technology*. New York: Random House, 1971.
Conly, Sarah. *One Child: Do We Have a Right to More?* New York: Oxford University Press, 2018.
Connelly, Matthew. *Fatal Misconception: The Struggle to Control World Population*. Cambridge, MA: Belknap, 2008.
Connelly, Matthew. "Population Control Is History: New Perspectives on the International Campaign to Limit Population Growth." *Comparative Studies in Society and History* 45, no. 1 (2003): 122–147.
Connelly, Matthew. "Seeing Beyond the State: The Population Control Movement and the Problem of Sovereignty." *Past and Present* 193 (2006): 197–2003.
Converse, Jean M. *Survey Research in the United States: Roots and Emergence 1890–1960*. New York: Routledge, 2017.
Cook, Joan. "Robert C. Cook, 92, a Longtime Scholar of Human Genetics." *New York Times*, January 9, 1991.
Cook, Robert C. "The Population Bomb." *Bulletin of the Atomic Scientists* 12, no. 8 (1956): 295–298.
Cooper, Frederick. "Conflict and Connection: Rethinking Colonial African History." *American Historical Review* 99, no. 5 (1994): 1516–1545.
Critchlow, Donald T. *Intended Consequences: Birth Control, Abortion, and the Federal Government in Modern America*. New York: Oxford University Press, 1999.
Crutzen, Paul. "Geology of Mankind." *Nature* 415 (2002): 23.
Cullather, Nick. *The Hungry World: America's Cold War Battle against Poverty in Asia*. Cambridge, MA: Harvard University Press, 2010.
Curtis, Bruce. *The Politics of Population: State Formation, Statistics, and the Census of Canada, 1840–1875*. Toronto: University of Toronto Press, 2002.
Davis, Kingsley. "Demographic Fact and Policy in India." *Milbank Memorial Fund Quarterly* 22, no. 4 (1944): 256–278.
Davis, Kingsley. "Population and Resources in the Americas." In *Proceedings of the Inter-American Conference on Conservation of Renewable Resources, Denver*, 88–97. Washington, DC: US Department of State, 1948.
Davis, Kingsley. *The Population of India and Pakistan*. Princeton, NJ: Princeton University Press, 1951.
Davis, Kingsley. "Population Policy: Will Current Programs Succeed?" *Science* 158, no. 3802 (1967): 730–739.
Davis, Kingsley. "Reproductive Institutions and the Pressure for Population." *Sociological Review* a29, no. 3 (1937): 289–306.
Davis, Kingsley. "The World Demographic Transition." *Annals of the American Academy of Political and Social Sciences* 237 (1945): 1–11.

Davis, Kingsley. "The World's Most Expensive Survey." *Sociological Forum* 2, no. 4 (1987): 829–834.
Davis, Mike. *Late Victorian Holocausts: El Niño Famines and the Making of the Third World*. London: Verso, 2001.
Dedrick, Calvert L. "Cultural Differences and Census Concepts." *Milbank Memorial Fund Quarterly* 27, no. 3 (1949): 283–288.
De Landa, Manuel. *Assemblage Theory*. Edinburgh: Edinburgh University Press, 2016.
Demeny, Paul. "Oral History Interview with Jean Van Der Tak, 8 June 1988." In *Demographic Destinies: Interviews with Presidents and Secretary-Treasurers of the Population Association of America*, vol. 1, no. 3, ed. Jean Van Der Tak, 217–249. Washington, DC: Population Association of America, 2005.
Demeny, Paul. "Social Science and Population Policy." *Population and Development Review* 14, no. 3 (1988): 451–479.
Desrochers, Pierre, and Christine Hoffbauer. "The Post War Intellectual Roots of the *Population Bomb*: Fairfield Osborn's *Our Plundered Planet* and William Vogt's *Road to Survival* in Retrospect." *Electronic Journal of Sustainable Development* 1, no. 3 (2009): 73–97.
Desrosières, Alain. *The Politics of Large Numbers: A History of Statistical Reasoning*. Cambridge, MA: Harvard University Press, 2002.
DiMoia, John P. "'Counting One's Allies': The Mobilization of Demography, Population, and Family Planning in East Asia, Late 1920s–Present." *East Asian Science, Technology and Society: An International Journal* 10 (2016): 355–376.
Dorn, Harold F. "Pitfalls in Population Forecasts and Projections." *Journal of the American Statistical Association* 45, no. 251 (1950): 311–334.
Du Bois, W. E. B. *The Philadelphia Negro: A Social Study*. Philadelphia: University of Pennsylvania, 1899.
Dublin, Louis Israel. "Fallacious Propaganda for Birth Control." *Atlantic Monthly*, February 1926, 145–157.
Dublin, Louis Israel. Review of *Mankind at the Crossroads*, by Edward M. East. *Journal of the American Statistical Association* 19, no. 146 (1924): 249–253.
Dublin, Louis Israel. "The Statistician and the Population Problem." *Journal of the American Statistical Association* 20, no. 149 (1925): 1–12.
Dublin, Louis Israel, and Alfred James Lotka. "On the True Rate of Natural Increase: As Exemplified by the Population of the United States, 1920." *Journal of the American Statistical Association* 20, no. 151 (1925): 305–339.
Durand, John D. "Oral History Interview with Abbott Ferriss, 11 August 1979." In *Demographic Destinies: Interviews with Presidents and Secretary-Treasurers of the Population Association of America*, vol. 1, no. 2, ed. Jean Van Der Tak, 6–12. Washington, DC: Population Association of America, 2005.
Eagan, Michael. "Barry Commoner and the Science of Survival." PhD diss., Washington State University, 2004.
East, Edward Murray. *Mankind at the Crossroads*. New York: Charles Scribner's Sons, 1923.
Edin, Karl Arvid. "The Fertility of the Social Classes in Stockholm in the Years 1919 to 1929." In *Problems of Population: Being the Report of the Proceedings of the Second General Assembly of the International Union for the Scientific Investigation of Population Problems*, ed. G. H. L. F. Pitt-Rivers, 91–104. London: Kennikat Press, 1932.
Edwards, Paul. *A Vast Machine: Computer Models, Climate Data, and the Politics of Global Warming*. Cambridge, MA: MIT Press, 2010.
Ehrlich, Paul R. *The Population Bomb*. New York: Ballantine, 1968.

Eig, Jonathan. *The Birth of the Pill: How Four Crusaders Reinvented Sex and Launched a Revolution*. New York: Norton, 2014.

Ekbladh, David. *The Great American Mission: Modernization and the Construction of an American World Order, 1914 to the Present*. Princeton, NJ: Princeton University Press, 2010.

Emigh, Rebecca Jean, Dylan Riley, and Patricia Ahmed. *Antecedents of Censuses from Medieval to Nation States: How Societies and States Count*. New York: Springer, 2016.

Erickson, Paul. *The World the Game Theorists Made*. Chicago: University of Chicago Press, 2015.

Espelend, Wendy, and Mitchell L. Stevens. "Commensuration as a Social Process." *Annual Review of Sociology* 24, no. 1 (1998): 313–343.

Falk, I. S. "Editorial: Louis I. Dublin: November 1, 1882–March 7, 1969." *American Journal of Public Health and the Nation's Health* 59, no. 7 (1969): 1083–1085.

Fanucchi, Kenneth J. "Youth Advised to Press for Population Control." *Los Angeles Times*, October 10, 1971.

Fawcett, James T., and Aree Somboonsuk. "Thailand: Using Family Planning Acceptors to Recruit New Cases." *Studies in Family Planning* 1, no. 39 (1969): 1–4.

Featherman, David L., and Maris Vinovskis, eds. *Social Science and Policy-Making: A Search for Relevance in the Twentieth Century*. Ann Arbor: University of Michigan Press, 2001.

Feyrer, James, Bruce Sacerdoete, and Ariel Dora Stern. "Will the Stork Return to Europe and Japan? Understanding Fertility within Developed Nations." *Journal of Economic Perspectives* 22, no. 3 (2008): 3–22.

Finkle, Jason L., and Barbara B. Crane. "Ideology and Politics at Mexico City: The United States at the 1984 International Conference on Population." *Population and Development Review* 11, no. 1 (1985): 1–28.

Fourcade, Marion. "The Construction of a Global Profession: The Transnationalization of Economics." *American Journal of Sociology* 112, no. 1 (2006): 145–194.

Fowle, Farnsworth. "Eisenhower Backs Birth-Curb Aids." *New York Times*, November 10, 1964.

Fox, Daniel M. "The Significance of the Milbank Memorial Fund for Policy: An Assessment at Its Centennial." *Milbank Quarterly* 84, no. 1 (2006): 5–36.

Frankel, Oz. *States of Inquiry: Social Investigations and Print Culture in Nineteenth-Century Britain and the United States*. Baltimore, MD: Johns Hopkins University Press, 2006.

Freedman, Ronald J. "Oral History Interview with Anders Lunde, 5–6 April 1979, and Jean Van Der Tak, 12 June 1989." In *Demographic Destinies: Interviews with Presidents and Secretary-Treasurers of the Population Association of America*, vol. 1, no. 2, ed. Jean Van Der Tak, 68–100. Washington, DC: Population Association of America, 2005.

Freedman, Ronald J. "Relevance and Validity: Constraints and Controls in Demography." *Concerned Demography* 2, no. 2 (1970): 17–20.

Freedman, Ronald J. "The Sociology of Human Fertility: A Trend Report and Bibliography." *Current Sociology* 10 (1962): 35–68.

Freedman, Ronald J., Arthur A. Campbell, and Pascal K. Whelpton. *Growth of American Families 1955* [machine-readable data set]. Ann Arbor: Inter-university Consortium for Political and Social Research, 2009. doi.org/10.3886/ICPSR20000.v2.

Freedman, Ronald J., and John Y. Takeshita. *Family Planning in Taiwan: An Experiment in Social Change*. Princeton, NJ: Princeton University Press, 1969.
Freedman, Ronald J., Pascal K. Whelpton, and Arthur A. Campbell. *Family Planning, Sterility and Population Growth*. New York: McGraw-Hill, 1959.
Frye, Keith. "A Teacher's Sad Tale of Ecology and Young Activists." *Globe and Mail*, October 18, 1971.
Galton, Francis. *Hereditary Genius: An Inquiry into Its Laws and Consequences*. London: Macmillan, 1869.
Gilman, Nils. *Mandarins of the Future: Modernization Theory in Cold War America*. Baltimore, MD: Johns Hopkins University Press, 2003.
Gilman, Nils. "The New International Economic Order: A Reintroduction." *Humanity* 6, no. 1 (2015): 1–16.
Gilmore, Glenda Elizabeth. *Gender and Jim Crow: Women and the Politics of White Supremacy in North Carolina, 1896–1920*. Chapel Hill: University of North Carolina Press, 1996.
Gilmore, Glenda Elizabeth, ed. *Who Were the Progressives?* New York: Bedford/St. Martin's, 2002.
Gini, Corrado, Shiroshi Nasu, Oliver Edwin Baker, and Robert René Kuczynski. *Population (Lectures on the Harris Foundation, 1929)*. Chicago: University of Chicago Press, 1930.
Glass, Bentley. Review of *Population Roads to Peace or War*, by Guy Irving Burch and Elmer Pendell. *Quarterly Review of Biology* 21, no. 1 (1946): 128.
Glass, David Victor. "The Berlin Population Congress and Recent Population Movements in Germany." *Eugenics Review* 27, no. 3 (1935): 207–212.
Grant, Madison. *The Passing of the Great Race: Or, the Racial Basis of European History*. New York; Scribner, 1916.
Gratton, Brian, and Emily Klancher Merchant. "Immigration, Repatriation, and Deportation: The Mexican-Origin Population in the United States, 1920–1950." *International Migration Review* 47, no. 4 (2013): 944–975.
Greenhalgh, Susan. *Just One Child: Science and Policy in Deng's China*. Berkeley: University of California Press, 2008.
Greenhalgh, Susan. "Making Demography Astonishing: Lessons in the Politics of Population Science." *Demography* 55, no. 2 (2018): 721–731.
Greenhalgh, Susan. "Science, Modernity, and the Making of China's One-Child Policy." *Population and Development Review* 29 (2003): 163–196.
Greenhalgh, Susan, ed. *Situating Fertility: Anthropology and Demographic Inquiry*. New York: Cambridge University Press, 1995.
Greenhalgh, Susan. "The Social Construction of Population Science: An Intellectual, Institutional, and Political History of Twentieth-Century Demography." *Comparative Studies in Society and History* 39, no. 1 (1996): 26–66.
Guest, Avery M. "Gatekeeping among the Demographers." In *Editors as Gatekeepers: Getting Published in the Social Sciences*, ed. Rita J. Simon and James J. Fyfe, 85–106. Lanham, MD: Rowman and Littlefield, 1994.
Gutmann, Myron, and Emily Klancher Merchant. "Historical Demography." In *Handbook of Population*, 2nd edition, ed. Dudley L. Poston Jr., 669–695. Cham, Switzerland: Springer Nature, 2019.
Gutmann, Myron, Emily Klancher Merchant, and Evan Roberts. "'Big Data' in Economic History." *Journal of Economic History* 78, no. 1 (2018): 268–299.

Hacking, Ian. "Making Up People." In *Reconstructing Individualism: Autonomy, Individuality, and the Self in Western Thought*, ed. Thomas C. Heller, Morton Sosna, and David E. Wellbery, 222–236. Stanford, CA: Stanford University Press, 1986.

Halfon, Saul E. *The Cairo Consensus*. New York: Lexington Books, 2007.

Hall, Stuart. "Race, Articulation, and Societies Structured in Dominance." In *Sociological Theories: Race and Colonialism*, ed. Marion O'Callaghan, 305–346. Paris: UNESCO, 1980.

Hamblin, Jacob Darwin. *Arming Mother Nature: The Birth of Catastrophic Environmentalism*. New York: Oxford University Press, 2013.

Hankins, Frank. "German Policies for Increasing Births." *American Journal of Sociology* 42, no. 5 (1937): 630–652.

Hankins, Frank. Review of *Fertility and Reproduction*, by Robert R. Kuczynski. *American Economic Review* 23, no. 1 (1933): 165–166.

Haraway, Donna. "Anthropocene, Capitalocene, Plantationocene, Chthulucene: Making Kin." *Environmental Humanities* 6, no. 1 (2015): 159–165.

Harkavy, Oscar. *Curbing Population Growth: An Insider's Perspective on the Population Movement*. New York: Plenum, 1995.

Harr, John Ensor, and Peter J. Johnson. *The Rockefeller Conscience: An American Family in Public and Private*. New York: Scribner, 1991.

Hartley, Norman. "Immigration Curb Plea Defended by Sponsors." *Globe and Mail*, April 25, 1975.

Hartmann, Betsy. *Reproductive Rights and Wrongs: The Global Politics of Population Control*. Boston: South End Press, 1995.

Hauser, Philip M. "The Early Years of the Population Commission." *Population Bulletin of the United Nations* 19 (1986): 2–5.

Hauser, Philip M. "Family Planning and Population Programs: A Book Review Article." *Demography* 4, no. 1 (1967): 403–404.

Hauser, Philip M. "Oral History Interview with Jean Van Der Tak, 12 November 1988." In *Demographic Destinies: Interviews with Presidents and Secretary-Treasurers of the Population Association of America*, vol. 1, no. 1, ed. Jean Van Der Tak, 33–63. Washington, DC: Population Association of America, 2005.

Hauser, Philip M., Judith Blake, and Paul Demeny. "Discussion." *Population Index* 36, no. 4 (1970): 452–465.

Hendricks, Melissa. "Raymond Pearl's 'Mingled Mess.'" *Johns Hopkins Magazine*, April 2006.

Hendrixson, Anne. "Population Control in the Troubled Present: The '120 by 20' Target and Implant Access Program." *Development and Change* 50, no. 3 (2018): 786–804.

Hermalin, Albert I., Barbara Entwisle, and Lora G. Myers. "Some Lessons from the Attempt to Retrieve Early KAP and Fertility Surveys." *Population Index* 51, no. 2 (1985): 194–208.

Hill, Reuben, J. Mayone Stycos, and Kurt W. Back. *The Family and Population Control: A Puerto Rican Experiment in Social Change*. Chapel Hill: University of North Carolina Press, 1959.

Hirschman, Charles. "Interview with the PAA History Committee." May 2014. populationassociation.org/about/our-history/oral-history-project.

Hirschman, Charles. "A New Look at Human Ecology and Marx." *Concerned Demography* 3, no. 2 (1970): 2–6.

Hirschman, Daniel. "Inventing the Economy (or, How We Learned to Stop Worrying and Love the GDP)." PhD diss., University of Michigan, 2016.

Hodges, Sarah. "Governmentality, Population and Reproductive Family in Modern India." *Economic and Political Weekly* 39, no. 11 (2004): 1157–1163.
Hodges, Sarah. "Indian Eugenics in an Age of Reform." In *Reproductive Health in India: History, Politics, Controversies*, ed. Sarah Hodges, 115–138. New Delhi: Orient Longman, 2006.
Hodgson, Dennis. "Demography as Social Science and Policy Science." *Population and Development Review* 9, no. 1 (1983): 1–34.
Hodgson, Dennis. "Ideological Currents and the Interpretation of Demographic Trends: The Case of Francis Amasa Walker." *Journal of the History of the Behavioral Sciences* 28, no. 1 (1992): 28–44.
Hodgson, Dennis. "The Ideological Origins of the Population Association of America." *Population and Development Review* 17, no. 1 (1991): 1–34.
Hodgson, Dennis. "Orthodoxy and Revisionism in American Demography." *Population and Development Review* 14, no. 4 (1988): 541–569.
Hodgson, Dennis, and Susan Cotts Watkins. "Feminists and Neo-Malthusians: Past and Present Alliances." *Population and Development Review* 23, no. 3 (1997): 469–523.
Hoff, Derek S. *The State and the Stork: The Population Debate and Policy Making in U.S. History*. Chicago: University of Chicago Press, 2012.
Hogan, Andrew J. *Life Histories of Genetic Disease: Patterns and Prevention in Postwar Medical Genetics*. Baltimore, MD: Johns Hopkins University Press, 2016.
Hogue, Ilyse, and Ellie Langford. *The Lie That Binds*. Washington, DC: Strong Arm Press, 2020.
Huang, Echo. "Jack Ma and Elon Musk Are Pretty Worried about a Looming Population Collapse." *Quartz*, August 29, 2019.
Hynes, H. Patricia. "Taking Population Out of the Equation: Reformulating I=PAT." In *Dangerous Intersections: Feminist Perspectives on Population, Environment, and Development*, ed. Jael Silliman and Ynestra King, 39–73. Cambridge, MA: South End Press, 1999.
Igo, Sarah E. *The Averaged American: Surveys, Citizens, and the Making of a Mass Public*. Cambridge, MA: Harvard University Press, 2009.
Immerwahr, Daniel. *How to Hide an Empire: A History of the Greater United States*. New York: Farrar, Straus and Giroux, 2019.
Immerwahr, Daniel. *Thinking Small: The United States and the Lure of Community Development*. Cambridge, MA: Harvard University Press, 2015.
Inter American Statistical Institute. *The Story of the 1950 Census of the Americas: An Account Prepared by the Inter American Statistical Institute in Cooperation with the General Bureaus of Statistics and the National Census Offices of the American Nations*. Washington, DC: Inter American Statistical Institute, 1953.
Ipsen, Carl. *Dictating Demography: The Problem of Population in Fascist Italy*. New York: Cambridge University Press, 1996.
Isaac, Joel. *Working Knowledge: Making the Human Sciences from Parsons to Kuhn*. Cambridge, MA: Harvard University Press, 2012.
Ittmann, Karl. *A Problem of Great Importance: Population, Race, and Power in the British Empire, 1918–1973*. Berkeley: University of California Press, 2013.
Jaschik, Scott. "Ending Dishonor for Disgraced Scientist." *Inside Higher Ed*, June 29, 2018.
Jennings, Herbert Spencer. "Biographical Memoir of Raymond Pearl 1879–1940." *National Academy of Sciences of the United States of America: Biographical Memoirs* 22 (1943): 295–345.

Johnson-Hanks, Jennifer. *Uncertain Honor: Modern Motherhood in an African Crisis.* Chicago: University of Chicago Press, 2006.

Kantner, John F. "American Attitudes on Population Policy: Recent Trends." *Studies in Family Planning* 1, no. 30 (1968): 1–7.

Kantner, John F. "Oral History Interview with Jean Van Der Tak, 22 March 1988." In *Demographic Destinies: Interviews with Presidents and Secretary-Treasurers of the Population Association of America*, vol. 1, no. 3, ed. Jean Van Der Tak, 123–140. Washington, DC: Population Association of America, 2005.

Karmel, P. H. "The Relations between Male and Female Reproduction Rates." *Population Studies* 1, no. 3 (1947): 249–274.

Kaufman, Michael T. "Laurance S. Rockefeller, Passionate Conservationist and Investor, Is Dead at 94." *New York Times*, July 12, 2004.

Kevles, Daniel J. *In the Name of Eugenics: Genetics and the Uses of Human Heredity.* New York: Knopf, 1985.

Kingsland, Sharon E. *Modeling Nature: Episodes in the History of Population Ecology.* Chicago: University of Chicago Press, 1995.

Kingsland, Sharon E. "Raymond Pearl: On the Frontier in the 1920's. Raymond Pearl Memorial Lecture, 1983." *Human Biology* 56, no. 1 (1984): 1–18.

Kinsey, Alfred C. *Sexual Behavior in the Human Female*. Bloomington: Indiana University Press, 1953.

Kinsey, Alfred C., Wardell B. Pomeroy, and Clyde E. Martin. *Sexual Behavior in the Human Male*. Bloomington: Indiana University Press, 1948.

Kirk, Dudley. *Europe's Population in the Inter-War Years*. Princeton, NJ: Princeton University Press, 1946.

Kirk, Dudley. "Oral History Interview with Anders Lunde, 27 April 1979, and Jean Van Der Tak, 29 April 1989." In *Demographic Destinies: Interviews with Presidents and Secretary-Treasurers of the Population Association of America*, vol. 1, no. 1, ed. Jean Van Der Tak, 116–138. Washington, DC: Population Association of America, 2005.

Kirk, Dudley. "Population Changes in the Postwar World." *American Sociological Review* 9, no. 1 (1944): 28–35.

Kiser, Clyde V. "Contributions of P. K. Whelpton to Demography." *Biodemography and Social Biology* 20, no. 4 (1973): 438–447.

Kiser, Clyde V. "The Indianapolis Fertility Study—An Example of Planned Observational Research." *Public Opinion Quarterly* 17, no. 4 (1935): 496–510.

Kiser, Clyde V. *The Milbank Memorial Fund: Its Leaders and Its Work, 1905–1974.* New York: Milbank Memorial Fund, 1975.

Kiser, Clyde V. "The Work of the Milbank Memorial Fund in Population since 1928." *Milbank Memorial Fund Quarterly* 49, no. 4 (1971): 15–66.

Kiser, Clyde V., C. Horace Hamilton, and Joseph J. Spengler. "Oral History Interview with Harry Rosenberg, 15 December 1976." In *Demographic Destinies: Interviews with Presidents and Secretary-Treasurers of the Population Association of America*, vol. 1, no. 1, ed. Jean Van Der Tak, 98–114. Washington, DC: Population Association of America, 2005.

Kiser, Clyde V., and Pascal K. Whelpton. "Resume of the Indianapolis Study of Social and Psychological Factors Affecting Fertility." *Population Studies* 7, no. 2 (1953): 95–110.

Kistiakowsky, George Bogdan. *A Scientist in the White House: The Private Diary of President Eisenhower's Special Assistant for Science and Technology*. Cambridge, MA: Harvard University Press, 1976.

Kligman, Gail. *The Politics of Duplicity: Controlling Reproduction in Ceausescu's Romania*. Berkeley: University of California Press, 1998.
Kuczynski, Robert René. *Colonial Population*. London: Oxford University Press, 1937.
Kuczynski, Robert René. *Demographic Survey of the British Colonial Empire*. London: Oxford University Press, 1948.
Kühl, Stefan. *For the Betterment of the Race: The Rise and Fall of the International Movement for Eugenics and Racial Hygiene*. Translated by Lawrence Schofer. New York: Palgrave Macmillan, 2013.
Kulish, Nicholas, and Mike McIntire. "Why an Heiress Spent Her Fortune Trying to Keep Immigrants Out." *New York Times*, August 14, 2019.
Lacey, Michael, and Mary Furner. *The State and Social Investigation in Britain and the United States*. Cambridge: Cambridge University Press, 1993.
Ladd-Taylor, Molly. "Eugenics, Sterilisation and Modern Marriage in the USA: The Strange Career of Paul Popenoe." *Gender and History* 13, no. 2 (2001): 298–327.
Ladd-Taylor, Molly. *Fixing the Poor: Eugenic Sterilization and Child Welfare in the Twentieth Century*. Minneapolis: University of Minnesota Press, 2020.
Lam, David. "How the World Survived the Population Bomb: Lessons from 50 Years of Extraordinary Demographic History." *Demography* 48, no. 4 (2011): 1231–1262.
Lampland, Martha. "False Numbers as Formalizing Practices." *Social Studies of Science* 40, no. 3 (2010): 377–404.
Landis, Paul H. Review of *Population Roads to Peace or War*, by Guy Irving Burch and Elmer Pendell. *American Sociological Review* 11, no. 1 (1946): 125–126.
Landry, Adolphe. *La Révolution Démographique*. Paris: Sirey, 1934.
Latham, Michael E. *Modernization as Ideology: American Social Science and "Nation Building" in the Kennedy Era*. Chapel Hill: University of North Carolina Press, 2000.
Latham, Michael E. *The Right Kind of Revolution: Modernization, Development, and U.S. Foreign Policy from the Cold War to the Present*. Ithaca, NY: Cornell University Press, 2011.
Latour, Bruno. *Science in Action: How to Follow Scientists and Engineers through Society*. Cambridge, MA: Harvard University Press, 1987.
Lee, James Z., and Wang Feng. *One Quarter of Humanity: Malthusian Mythology and Chinese Realities, 1700–2000*. Cambridge, MA: Harvard University Press, 2001.
Leibenstein, Harvey. *A Theory of Economic-Demographic Development*. Princeton, NJ: Princeton University Press, 1954.
Lemov, Rebecca. *World as Laboratory: Experiments with Mice, Mazes, and Men*. New York: Hill and Wang, 2005.
Leonard, Thomas C. *Illiberal Reformers: Race, Eugenics and American Economics in the Progressive Era*. Princeton, NJ: Princeton University Press, 2016.
Leonard, William R. "General Assessment of International Statistics and Outlook for the Future." *Milbank Memorial Fund Quarterly* 27, no. 3 (1949): 332–337.
Levine, Philippa. "What's British about Gender and Empire? The Problem of Exceptionalism." *Comparative Studies of South Asia, Africa, and the Middle East* 27, no. 2 (2007): 273–274.
Levy, Pema. "How the Bush Family Aided Planned Parenthood's Rise." *Mother Jones*, August 11, 2015.
Link, Arthur Stanley, and Richard L. McCormick. *Progressivism*. Hoboken, NJ: Wiley-Blackwell, 1983.
Little, Michael A., and Ralph M. Garruto. "Raymond Pearl and the Shaping of Human Biology." *Human Biology* 82, no. 1 (2010): 77–102.

Lorimer, Frank. "The Development of Demography." In *The Study of Population: An Inventory and Appraisal*, ed. Philip M. Hauser and Otis Dudley Duncan, 124–179. Chicago: University of Chicago Press, 1959.

Lorimer, Frank. *The Population of the Soviet Union: History and Prospects*. Princeton, NJ: Princeton University Press, 1946.

Lorimer, Frank. "The Role of the International Union for the Scientific Study of Population." *Milbank Memorial Fund Quarterly* 49, no. 4 (1971): 86–105.

Lorimer, Frank, and Frederick Osborn. *Dynamics of Population: Social and Biological Significance of Changing Birth Rates in the United States*. New York: Macmillan, 1934.

Lotka, Alfred James. "Relation between Birth Rates and Death Rates." *Science* 26, no. 653 (1907): 21–22.

Lotka, Alfred James. Review of *The Balance of Births and Deaths, Volume I*, by Robert René Kuczynski. *Journal of the American Statistical Association* 24, no. 167 (1929): 332–333.

Lotka, Alfred James. "Studies on the Mode of Growth of Material Aggregates." *American Journal of Science* 24, no. 141 (1907): 199–216.

Love, Lauren. "U-M to Remove Little, Winchell Names from Campus Facilities." *University Record*, March 29, 2018.

Löwy, Ilana. "Defusing the Population Bomb in the 1950s: Foam Tablets in India." *Studies in History and Philosophy of Science Part C: Studies in History and Philosophy of Biological and Biomedical Sciences* 43, no. 3 (2012): 583–593.

Luker, Kristin. *Dubious Conceptions: The Politics of Teenage Pregnancy*. Cambridge, MA: Harvard University Press, 1996.

Lynd, Robert, and Helen Lynd. *Middletown: A Study in Contemporary American Culture*. New York: Harcourt, Brace, 1929.

Macekura, Stephen J. *Of Limits and Growth: The Rise of Global Sustainable Development in the Twentieth Century*. New York: Cambridge University Press, 2015.

MacKellar, Landis, and Bradley W. Hart. "Captain George Henry Lane-Fox Pitt-Rivers and the Prehistory of the IUSSP." *Population and Development Review* 40, no. 4 (2014): 653–675.

MacNamara, Trent. "Why 'Race Suicide'? Cultural Factors in U.S. Fertility Decline, 1903–1908." *Journal of Interdisciplinary History* 44, no. 4 (2014): 475–508.

Mair, George F. "Population Projection: The State of an Art." PhD diss., Princeton University, 1957.

Mair, George F., ed. *Studies in Population: Proceedings of the Annual Meeting of the Population Association of America at Princeton, New Jersey, May 1949*. Princeton, NJ: Princeton University Press, 1949.

Mallet, Bernard. "Opening Address." In *World Population Conference Held at the Salle Centrale, Geneva, August 29th to September 3rd, 1927*, ed. Margaret Sanger, 17–19. London: Edward Arnold, 1927.

Malm, Andreas, and Alf Hornborg. "The Geology of Mankind? A Critique of the Anthropocene Narrative." *Anthropocene Review* 1, no. 1 (2014): 62–69.

Malthus, Thomas Robert. *An Essay on the Principle of Population as It Affects the Future Improvement of Society with Remarks on the Speculations of Mr. Godwin, M. Condorcet and Other Writers*. London: J. Johnson, 1798.

Mamdani, Mahmood. *The Myth of Population Control*. New York: Monthly Review Press, 1973.

Marino, Anthony. "KAP Surveys and the Politics of Family Planning." *Concerned Demography* 3, no. 1 (1971): 36–75.

Mayhew, Robert J., ed. *New Perspectives on Malthus*. New York: Cambridge University Press, 2016.
Mazower, Mark. *Governing the World: The History of an Idea, 1815 to the Present*. New York: Penguin, 2012.
McCann, Carole R. *Figuring the Population Bomb: Gender and Demography in the Mid-Twentieth Century*. Seattle: University of Washington Press, 2017.
McClintock, Anne. *Imperial Leather: Race, Gender, and Sexuality in the Colonial Context*. New York: Routledge, 1995.
McDonald, Angus. "The Great Rat Race." *New Republic*, September 6, 1948, 25–26.
McGerr, Michael E. *A Fierce Discontent: The Rise and Fall of the Progressive Movement in America, 1870–1920*. New York: Oxford University Press, 2005.
McGuire, C. C. Review of *Population*, by Corrado Gini, Shiroshi Nasu, Robert R. Kuczynski, and Oliver E. Baker. *Political Science Quarterly* 46, no. 3 (1931): 441–444.
Meek, Ronald L. *Marx and Engels on Malthus*. London: Lawrence and Wishart, 1953.
Merchant, Emily Klancher. "A Digital History of Anglophone Demography and Global Population Control, 1915–1984." *Population and Development Review* 43, no. 1 (2017): 83–117.
Merchant, Emily Klancher. "PAA History: *Concerned Demography* and the Concerned Demographers." *PAA Affairs*, Winter 2017.
Merchant, Emily Klancher, Brian Gratton, and Myron P. Gutmann. "A Sudden Transition: Household Changes for Middle Aged U.S. Women in the Twentieth Century." *Population Research and Policy Review* 31, no. 5 (2012): 703–726.
Merchant, Emily Klancher, and J. David Hacker. "Historical Demography in the United States." In *A Global History of Historical Demography*, ed., Antoinette Fauve-Chamoux, I. Bolovan, and S. Sogner, 655–670. Bern: Peter Lang, 2016.
Mitchell, Timothy. *Carbon Democracy: Political Power in the Age of Oil*. London: Verso, 2011.
Mitchell, Timothy. "Economentality: How the Future Entered Government." *Critical Inquiry* 40, no. 4 (2014): 479–507.
Moore, Hugh Everett. "Have You Ever Been Mugged?" *New York Times*, March 10, 1968.
Moore, Hugh Everett. "How Many People Do You Want in Your Country?" *New York Times,* May 25, 1969.
Moore, Hugh Everett. "This Is the Crime Explosion." *New York Times*, December 8, 1968.
Moore, Hugh Everett. "Warning: The Water You Are Drinking May Be Polluted." *New York Times,* June 12, 1968.
Morris, Aldon. *The Scholar Denied: W. E. B. Du Bois and the Birth of Modern Sociology*. Oakland: University of California Press, 2015.
Morris, Joe Alex, Jr. "World Population Issue Surfaces at Conference: Third World Nations Indicate That They Will Oppose Family Planning as Conspiracy." *Los Angeles Times*, June 10, 1972.
Mundigo, Axel I. "Latin American Attitudes on Birth Control: A Typology." *Concerned Demography* 3, no. 1 (1971): 76–103.
Murphy, Michelle. "Against Population, towards Alterlife." In *Making Kin Not Population: Reconceiving Generations*, ed. Adele Clarke and Donna Haraway, 101–123. Chicago: Prickly Paradigm Press, 2018.
Murphy, Michelle. *The Economization of Life*. Durham, NC: Duke University Press, 2017.

Murphy, Michelle. *Seizing the Means of Reproduction: Entanglements of Feminism, Health, and Technoscience*. Durham, NC: Duke University Press, 2012.
Myrskylä, Mikko, Hans-Peter Kohler, and Francesco C. Billari. "Advances in Development Reverse Fertility Declines." *Nature* 460 (2009): 741–743.
Narain, Shri Govind. "India: The Family Planning Program since 1965." *Studies in Family Planning* 1, no. 35 (1968): 1–12.
National Academy of Sciences. *The Growth of World Population: Analysis of the Problems and Recommendations for Research and Training*. Washington, DC: National Academies Press, 1963.
National Research Council. *Population Growth and Economic Development: Policy Questions*. Washington, DC: National Academies Press, 1986.
Necochea López, Raúl. *A History of Family Planning in Twentieth-Century Peru*. Chapel Hill: University of North Carolina Press, 2014.
Ngai, Mae M. "The Architecture of Race in American Immigration Law: A Reexamination of the Immigration Act of 1924." *Journal of American History* 86, no. 1 (1999): 67–92.
Ngai, Mae M. *Impossible Subjects: Illegal Aliens and the Making of Modern America*. Princeton, NJ: Princeton University Press, 2004.
Notestein, Frank W. "As the Nation Grows Younger." *Atlantic Monthly*, October 1957, 131–136.
Notestein, Frank W. "The Fertility of Population Supported by Public Relief." *Milbank Memorial Fund Quarterly* 41, no. 1 (1936): 37–49.
Notestein, Frank W. "Frederick Osborn: Demography's Statesman on His Eightieth Spring." *Population Index* 35, no. 4 (1969): 367–371.
Notestein, Frank W. "Oral History Interview with Anders Lunde, 27 April 1973." In *Demographic Destinies: Interviews with Presidents and Secretary-Treasurers of the Population Association of America*, vol. 1, no. 1, ed. Jean Van Der Tak, 6–17. Washington, DC: Population Association of America, 2005.
Notestein, Frank W. "Population—The Long View." In *Food for the World*, ed. Theodore Schultz, 36–57. Chicago: University of Chicago Press, 1945.
Notestein, Frank W. "Problems of Policy in Relation to Areas of Heavy Population Pressure." *Milbank Memorial Fund Quarterly* 22, no. 4 (1944): 424–444.
Notestein, Frank W. "Zero Population Growth." *Population Index* 36, no. 4 (1970): 444–452.
Notestein, Frank W., and Frederick H. Osborn. "Reminiscences: The Role of Foundations, the Population Association of America, Princeton University and the United Nations in Fostering American Interest in Population Problems." *Milbank Memorial Fund Quarterly* 49, no. 4 (1971): 67–85.
Notestein, Frank W., Irene B. Taeuber, Dudley Kirk, Ansley J. Coale, and Louise K. Kiser. *The Future Population of Europe and the Soviet Union, 1940–1970*. Geneva: League of Nations, 1944.
Oaklander, Christine I. "Jonathan Sturges, W. H. Osborn, and William Church Osborn: A Chapter in American Art Patronage." *Metropolitan Museum Journal* 43 (2008): 173–194.
Oberschall, Anthony. "The Institutionalization of American Sociology." In *The Establishment of Empirical Sociology*, ed. Anthony Oberschall, 187–251. New York: Harper and Row, 1972.
O'Connor, Alice. *Poverty Knowledge: Social Science, Social Policy, and the Poor in Twentieth-Century U.S. History*. Princeton, NJ: Princeton University Press, 2009.

Oppenheim, Carol. "Big Zero for Zero Population's Goal." *Chicago Tribune*, December 14, 1978.
Oreskes, Naomi, and Erik M. Conway. *Merchants of Doubt: How a Handful of Scientists Obscured the Truth on Issues from Tobacco Smoke to Global Warming*. New York: Bloomsbury, 2010.
Osborn, Frederick Henry. "Eugenics and National Defense." *Journal of Heredity* 32, no. 6 (1941): 203–204.
Oudshoorn, Nelly. *Beyond the Natural Body: An Archaeology of Sex Hormones*. New York: Routledge, 1994.
Oudshoorn, Nelly. *The Male Pill: A Biography of a Technology in the Making*. Durham, NC: Duke University Press, 2003.
Paddock, William, and Paul Paddock. *Famine 1975! America's Decision: Who Will Survive*. Boston: Little, Brown, 1967.
Parmar, Inderjeet. *Foundations of the American Century: The Ford, Carnegie, and Rockefeller Foundations in the Rise of American Power*. New York: Columbia University Press, 2012.
Payne, Mike. *Scripps Gerontology Center: A Legacy of Leadership (A History of the Scripps Gerontology Center)*. Oxford, OH: Scripps Gerontology Center, Miami University, 2005.
Pearl, Raymond. "The Aging of Populations." *Journal of the American Statistical Association* 35, no. 209 (1940): 277–297.
Pearl, Raymond. *The Biology of Death*. Philadelphia: J. B. Lippincott, 1922.
Pearl, Raymond. *The Biology of Population Growth*. New York: Knopf, 1925.
Pearl, Raymond. "The Biology of Superiority." *American Mercury*, November 1927, 257–266.
Pearl, Raymond. "Contraception and Fertility in 4,945 Women: A Second Report on a Study of Family Limitation." *Human Biology* 6, no. 2 (1934): 355–401.
Pearl, Raymond. "Sterilization of Degenerates and Criminals Considered from the Standpoint of Genetics." *Eugenics Review* 11, no. 1 (1919): 1–6.
Pearl, Raymond. "World Overcrowding: Saturation Point for Earth's Population Soon Will Be in Sight, with the Safety Limit for the United States Estimated at 200,000,000 People—How the Nations Grow." *New York Times*, October 8, 1922.
Pearl, Raymond, and F. C. Kelly. "Forecasting the Growth of Nations." *Harper's Monthly Magazine*, May 1921, 704–713.
Pearl, Raymond, and Lowell J. Reed. "On the Rate of Growth of the Population of the United States since 1790 and Its Mathematical Representation." *Proceedings of the National Academy of Sciences of the United States of America* 6, no. 6 (1920): 275–288.
Pitt-Rivers, G. H. L. F., ed. *Problems of Population: Being the Report of the Proceedings of the Second General Assembly of the International Union for the Scientific Investigation of Population Problems*. London: Kennikat Press, 1932.
Population Council. "The Disney Film on Family Planning." *Studies in Family Planning* 1, no. 26 (1968).
Porter, Theodore M. "Thin Description: Surface and Depth in Science and Science Studies." *Osiris* 27, no. 1 (2012): 209–226.
Preston, Samuel. "The Contours of Demography: Estimates and Projections." *Demography* 30, no. 4 (1993): 593–606.
Preston, Samuel, Patrick Heuveline, and Michel Guillot. *Demography: Measuring and Modeling Population Processes*. Oxford: Blackwell, 2001.

Quadagno, Jill S. *The Color of Welfare: How Racism Undermined the War on Poverty*. New York: Oxford University Press, 1994.
Ralson, Gail. "Andover Stories: Thomas Cochran and Phillips Academy's 'Golden Decade.'" *Andover Townsman Online*, November 3, 2011.
Ramsden, Edmund. "Carving Up Population Science: Eugenics, Demography and the Controversy over the 'Biological Law' of Population Growth." *Social Studies of Science* 32, no. 5-6 (2002): 857–899.
Ramsden, Edmund. "Frank W. Notestein, Frederick H. Osborn, and the Development of Demography in the United States." *Princeton University Library Chronicle* 65, no. 2 (2004): 282–316.
Randeraad, Nico. "The International Statistical Congresses (1853–1876): Knowledge Transfers and Their Limits." *European History Quarterly* 41, no. 1 (2011): 50–65.
Reed, James. *From Private Vice to Public Virtue: The Birth Control Movement and American Society since 1830*. New York: Basic Books, 1978.
Reuter, E. B. Review of *Population*, by Corrado Gini, Shiroshi Nasu, Oliver E. Baker, and Robert R. Kuczynski. *American Journal of Sociology* 36, no. 4 (1931): 646–649.
Rieder, Travis. *Toward a Small Family Ethic: How Overpopulation and Climate Change Are Affecting the Morality of Procreation*. Cham, Switzerland: Springer, 2016.
Riedmann, Agnes Czerwinski. *Science That Colonizes: A Critique of Fertility Studies in Africa*. Philadelphia: Temple University Press, 1993.
Rienow, Robert, and Leona Train Rienow. *Moment in the Sun: A Report on the Deteriorating Quality of the American Environment*. New York: Dial Press, 1967.
Roberts, Dorothy. *Killing the Black Body: Race, Reproduction, and the Meaning of Liberty*. New York: Vintage, 1998.
Robertson, Thomas. *The Malthusian Moment: Global Population Growth and the Birth of American Environmentalism*. New Brunswick, NJ: Rutgers University Press, 2012.
Robertson, Thomas. "Total War and the Total Environment: Fairfield Osborn, William Vogt, and the Birth of Global Ecology." *Environmental History* 17, no. 2 (2012): 336–364.
Rockefeller, John D., III. "Population Growth: The Role of the Developed World." *Population and Development Review* 4, no. 3 (1978): 509–516.
Rodgers, Daniel T. *Atlantic Crossings: Social Politics in a Progressive Age*. Cambridge, MA: Harvard University Press, 2009.
Rohde, Joy. *Armed with Expertise: The Militarization of American Social Research during the Cold War*. Ithaca, NY: Cornell University Press, 2013.
Roosevelt, Theodore. "My Life as a Naturalist: With a Presentation of Various First-Hand Data on the Life Histories and Habits of the Big Game Animals of Africa." *American Museum Journal*, May 1918.
Rosenthal, Jack. "Census Expert Discounts Population Growth Issue." *New York Times*, January 14, 1971.
Rosenthal, Jack. "Nation's Births Show Drop below Zero-Growth Level." *New York Times*, December 5, 1972.
Rosenthal, Jack. "New Census Study Projects Decline in the Rate of Births." *New York Times*, February 17, 1972.
Rosenthal, Jack. "The Panic as You Approach Zero: Population." *New York Times*, June 4, 1972.
Ross, Edward A. "The Causes of Race Superiority." *Annals of the American Academy of Political and Social Science* 18, no. 1 (1901): 67–89.

Ross, John A., Oliver D. Finnigan III, S. M. Keeny, and George P. Cernada. "Korea/ Taiwan 1969: Report on the National Family Planning Programs." *Studies in Family Planning* 1, no. 54 (1970): 1–16.

Ross, Loretta J. "Reproductive Justice as Intersectional Feminist Activism." *Souls* 19, no. 3 (2017): 286–314.

Ross, Loretta J., and Rickie Solinger. *Reproductive Justice: An Introduction*. Oakland: University of California Press, 2017.

Ruggles, Steven, and Diana L. Magnuson. "Capturing the American People: Census Technology and Institutional Change, 1790–2020." Minneapolis: Minnesota Population Center Working Papers, June 14, 2018.

Rusnock, Andrea A. "Biopolitics: Political Arithmetic in the Enlightenment." In *The Sciences in Enlightened Europe*, ed. William Clark, Jan Golinski, and Simon Schaffer, 113–138. Chicago: University of Chicago Press, 1999.

Ryan, Joseph W. *Samuel Stouffer and the GI Survey: Sociologists and Soldiers during the Second World War*. Knoxville: University of Tennessee Press, 2013.

Ryder, Norman B. "Oral History Interview with Jean Van Der Tak, 11 May 1988." In *Demographic Destinies: Interviews with Presidents and Secretary-Treasurers of the Population Association of America*, vol. 1, no. 2, ed. Jean Van Der Tak, 250–277. Washington, DC: Population Association of America, 2005.

Ryder, Norman B. "Problems of Trend Determination during a Transition in Fertility." *Milbank Memorial Fund Quarterly* 34, no. 1 (1956): 5–21.

Sabin, Paul. *The Bet: Paul Ehrlich, Julian Simon, and Our Gamble over Earth's Future*. New Haven, CT: Yale University Press, 2013.

Sanger, Margaret. *My Fight for Birth Control*. London: Faber & Faber, 1932.

Sanger, Margaret, ed. *Proceedings of the World Population Conference Held at the Salle Centrale, Geneva, August 29th to September 3rd, 1927*. London: E. Arnold, 1927.

Sarkar, Sahotra. "Evolutionary Theory in the 1920s: The Nature of the 'Synthesis.'" *Philosophy of Science* 71 (2004): 1215–1226.

Sarkar, Sahotra. *Genetics and Reductionism*. Cambridge: Cambridge University Press, 1998.

Sasser, Jade. *On Infertile Ground: Population Control and Women's Rights in the Era of Climate Change*. New York: New York University Press, 2018.

Satterthwaite, David. "The Implications of Population Growth and Urbanization for Climate Change." *Environment and Urbanization* 21 (2009): 62–69.

Saunders, Frances Stonor. *Who Paid the Piper? The CIA and the Cultural Cold War*. London: Granta, 1999.

Schneider, William H. *Quality and Quantity: The Quest for Biological Regeneration in Twentieth-Century France*. New York: Cambridge University Press, 2002.

Schultz, Susanne. "Redefining and Medicalizing Population Policies: NGOs and Their Innovative Contributions to the Post-Cairo Agenda." In *Markets and Malthus: Population, Gender, and Health in Neo-liberal Times*, ed. Mohan Rao and Sarah Sexton, 173–214. Los Angeles: Sage, 2010.

Seager, Joni. "The 6-Billionth Baby: Designated Green Scapegoat." *Environment and Planning A* 32 (2000): 1711–1718.

Segal, Sheldon J. "Contraceptive Research: A Male Chauvinist Plot?" *Family Planning Perspectives* 4, no. 3 (1972): 21–25.

Selcer, Perrin. *The Postwar Origins of the Global Environment*. New York: Columbia University Press, 2018.

Shriver, Lionel. *Game Control: A Novel*. New York: Harper, 2007.

Simon, Julian. "Resources, Population, Environment: An Oversupply of False Bad News." *Science* 208, no. 4451 (1980): 1431–1437.

Skrentny, John David. *The Minority Rights Revolution*. Cambridge, MA: Harvard University Press, 2002.

Smith, Mark C. *Social Science in the Crucible: The American Debate over Objectivity and Purpose, 1918–1941*. Durham, NC: Duke University Press, 1994.

Solovey, Mark. *Shaky Foundations: The Politics-Patronage–Social Science Nexus in Cold War America*. New Brunswick, NJ: Rutgers University Press, 2013.

Soloway, Richard A. *Demography and Degeneration: Eugenics and the Declining Birthrate in Twentieth-Century Britain*. Chapel Hill: University of North Carolina Press, 1990.

Spiro, Jonathan. *Defending the Master Race: Conservation, Eugenics, and the Legacy of Madison Grant*. Burlington: University of Vermont Press, 2009.

Star, Susan Leigh, and James R. Griesemer. "Institutional Ecology, Translations, and Boundary Objects: Amateurs and Professionals in Berkeley's Museum of Vertebrate Zoology, 1907–39." *Social Studies of Science* 19, no. 3 (1989): 387–420.

Steffen, Will, Wendy Broadgate, Lisa Deutsch, Owen Gaffney, and Cornelia Ludwig. "The Trajectory of the Anthropocene: The Great Acceleration." *Anthropocene Review* 2, no. 1 (2015): 81–98.

Stepan, Nancy Leys. *"The Hour of Eugenics": Race, Gender, and Nation in Latin America*. Ithaca, NY: Cornell University Press, 1991.

Sterling, Claire. "U.S. Losing Argument with Poor Nations at Stockholm." *Washington Post*, June 8, 1972.

Stern, Alexandra Minna. *Eugenic Nation: Faults and Frontiers of Better Breeding in Modern America*. Berkeley: University of California Press, 2005.

Stern, Alexandra Minna. "Sterilized in the Name of Public Health: Race, Immigration, and Reproductive Control in Modern California." *American Journal of Public Health* 95, no. 7 (2005): 1128–1138.

Stern, Alexandra Minna. *Telling Genes: The Story of Genetic Counseling in America*. Baltimore, MD: Johns Hopkins University Press, 2012.

Stewart, Nikita. "Planned Parenthood in NY Disavows Margaret Sanger over Eugenics." *New York Times*, July 21, 2020.

Stix, Regine Kronacher, and Frank W. Notestein. *Controlled Fertility: An Evaluation of Clinic Service*. Baltimore, MD: Williams & Wilkins, 1940.

Stix, Regine Kronacher, and Frank W. Notestein. "Effectiveness of Birth Control: A Study of Contraceptive Practice in a Selected Group of New York Women." *Milbank Memorial Fund Quarterly* 12, no. 1 (1934): 57–68.

Stoddard, Lothrop. *The Rising Tide of Color against White World-Supremacy*. New York: Blue Ribbon Books, 1920.

Stoler, Ann Laura. *Race and the Education of Desire: Foucault's History of Sexuality and the Colonial Order of Things*. Durham, NC: Duke University Press, 1995.

Stolnitz, George J. "A Century of International Mortality Trends." *Population Studies* 9, no. 1 (1955): 24–55.

Stolnitz, George J. "Oral History Interview with Jean Van Der Tak, 20 January 1988." In *Demographic Destinies: Interviews with Presidents and Secretary-Treasurers of the Population Association of America*, vol. 1, no. 1, ed. Jean Van Der Tak, 141–160. Washington, DC: Population Association of America, 2005.

Stycos, J. Mayone, and Judith Blake. "The Jamaican Family Life Project: Some Objectives and Methods." *Social and Economic Studies* 3 (1954): 342–349.

Swift, Jonathan. *A Modest Proposal: For Preventing the Children of Poor People in Ireland, from Being a Burden on Their Parents of Country, and for Making Them Beneficial to the Publick—1729*. Project Gutenberg, 2008. Gutenberg.org/files/1080/1080-h/1080-h.htm.

Szreter, Simon. "The Idea of Demographic Transition and the Study of Fertility Change: A Critical Intellectual History." *Population and Development Review* 19, no. 4 (1993): 659–701.

Taeuber, Irene B. "Oral History Interview with Anders Lunde, 28 April 1973." In *Demographic Destinies: Interviews with Presidents and Secretary-Treasurers of the Population Association of America*, vol. 1, no. 1, ed. Jean Van Der Tak, 74–80. Washington, DC: Population Association of America, 2005.

Taeuber, Irene B. *The Population of Japan*. Princeton, NJ: Princeton University Press, 1958.

Takeshita, Chikako. *The Global Biopolitics of the IUD: How Science Constructs Contraceptive Users and Women's Bodies*. Cambridge, MA: MIT Press, 2012.

Thompson, Warren Simpson. *Danger Spots in World Population*. New York: Knopf, 1929.

Thompson, Warren Simpson. "Population." *American Journal of Sociology* 34, no. 6 (1929): 959–975.

Thompson, Warren Simpson. *Population: A Study in Malthusianism*. New York: Columbia University, 1915.

Thompson, Warren Simpson. "Population Facts for the United States and Their Interpretation." *Journal of the American Statistical Association* 18, no. 141 (1923): 575–587.

Thompson, Warren Simpson, and Pascal Kidder Whelpton. *Population Trends in the United States*. New York: McGraw, 1933.

Thornton, Arland. *Reading History Sideways: The Fallacy and Enduring Impact of the Developmental Paradigm on Family Life*. Chicago: University of Chicago Press, 2005.

Tienda, Marta. "Interview with the PAA History Committee." PAA, 2013. populationassociation.org/about/our-history/oral-history-project.

Tietze, Christopher. "The Clinical Effectiveness of Contraceptive Methods." *American Journal of Obstetrics and Gynecology* 78, no. 3 (1959): 650–656.

Tone, Andrea. *Devices and Desires: A History of Contraceptives in America*. New York: Macmillan, 2002.

Torrado de Ipola, Susana. "A Contribution of the U.S. Department of State to the Latin American Population Conference, Mexico, 1970." *Concerned Demography* 2, no. 3 (1970): 4–6.

Toth, Robert C. "Kennedy Would Give Out Data on Population Curbs." *New York Times*, April 25, 1963.

Treas, Judith. "Age in Standards and Standards for Age." In *Standards and Their Stories: How Quantifying, Classifying, and Formalizing Practices Shape Everyday Life*, ed. Martha Lampland and Susan Leigh Star, 65–87. Ithaca, NY: Cornell University Press, 2009.

Union of Concerned Scientists. "Founding Document: 1968 MIT Faculty Statement." ucsusa.org/about/founding-document-1968.html.

United Nations. *2019 Revision of World Population Prospects*. population.un.org/wpp.

United Nations. *United Nations Demographic Yearbook, 1962*. New York: Statistical Office of the United Nations, 1962.

United Nations. *Yearbook of the United Nations, 1946–1947*. New York: United Nations, 1947.

United Nations. *Yearbook of the United Nations, 1951*. New York: United Nations, 1951.
United Nations Population Division. *Manual I: Methods of Estimating Total Population for Current Dates*. New York: United Nations Department of Social Affairs, 1952.
United Nations Population Division. *Manual IV: Methods of Estimating Basic Demographic Measures from Incomplete Data*. New York: United Nations Department of Social Affairs, 1967.
United Nations Population Division. *1960 World Population Census Programme: Sampling Methods and Population Censuses*. New York: Statistical Office of the United Nations, 1957.
United Nations Population Division. "The Past and Future Population of the World and Its Continents." In *Proceedings of the World Population Conference, Rome, 1954*, 265–281. New York: United Nations, 1954.
United Nations Population Division. *Population Census Methods*. New York: United Nations Department of Social Affairs, 1949.
Valdes, Juan Gabriel. *Pinochet's Economists: The Chicago School in Chile*. New York: Cambridge University Press, 1995.
van de Walle, Etienne. "Frank Lorimer, 1894–1985." *Population Index* 51, no. 4 (1985): 635–642.
van de Walle, Etienne. "Oral History Interview with Jean Van Der Tak, 17 February 1993." In *Demographic Destinies: Interviews with Presidents and Secretary-Treasurers of the Population Association of America*, vol. 1, no. 3, ed. Jean Van Der Tak, 426–460. Washington, DC: Population Association of America, 2005.
Van Der Tak, Jean, ed. *Demographic Destinies: Interviews with Presidents and Secretary-Treasurers of the Population Association of America*. Washington, DC: Population Association of America, 2005.
Vaughan, Megan. *Curing Their Ills: Colonial Power and African Illness*. Stanford, CA: Stanford University Press, 1991.
Vizard, Mary McAleer. "If You're Thinking of Living In: Garrison, NY. Concern for Environment on the Hudson." *New York Times*, October 22, 1995.
Vogt, William. *Road to Survival*. New York: W. Sloane Associates, 1948.
Waldman, Steven. *Sacred Liberty: America's Long, Bloody, and Ongoing Struggle for Religious Freedom*. New York: Harper and Collins, 2019.
Wang, Feng, Yong Cai, Ke Shen, and Stuart Geitel-Basten. "Is Demography Just a Numerical Exercise? Numbers, Politics, and Legacies of China's One-Child Policy." *Demography* 55, no. 2 (2018): 693–719.
Ward, Barbara. "The World: Pollution." *The Economist*, May 27, 1972, 66–76.
Warwick, Donald P. *Bitter Pills: Population Policies and Their Implementation in Eight Developing Countries*. New York: Cambridge University Press, 1982.
Weiss-Altaner, Eric R. "Fertility Decline, Savings and Economic Growth." *Concerned Demography* 2, no. 3 (1971): 8–11.
Weiss-Altaner, Eric R. Review of *Population, Resources, Environment*, by Paul and Anne Ehrlich. *Concerned Demography* 2, no. 3 (1971): 22.
Westoff, Charles F. "The Changing Focus of Differential Fertility Research: The Social Mobility Hypothesis." *Milbank Memorial Fund Quarterly* 31, no. 1 (1953): 24–38.
Westoff, Charles F. "Is the KAP-Gap Real?" *Population and Development Review* 14, no. 2 (1988): 225–232.
Whelpton, Pascal Kidder. *Cohort Fertility: Native White Women in the United States*. Princeton, NJ: Princeton University Press, 1954.

Whelpton, Pascal Kidder. "Population of the United States, 1925 to 1975." *American Journal of Sociology* 34, no. 2 (1928): 253–270.
Whelpton, Pascal Kidder. "The Population Prospect." In *Proceedings of the Third International Conference of Agricultural Economists, Held at Bad Eilsen, Germany, 26 August to 2 September 1934*, 250–263. London: Oxford University Press, 1935.
Whelpton, Pascal K., and Clyde V. Kiser. "Social and Psychological Factors Affecting Fertility. Part III: The Completeness and Accuracy of the Household Survey of Indianapolis." *Milbank Memorial Fund Quarterly* 23, no. 3 (1945): 254–296.
Wilford, Hugh. *The Mighty Wurlitzer: How the CIA Played America*. Cambridge, MA: Harvard University Press, 2008.
Willcox, Walter. *Studies in American Demography*. Ithaca, NY: Cornell University Press, 1940.
Williams, Rebecca Jane. "Storming the Citadels of Poverty: Family Planning under the Emergency in India, 1975–1977." *Journal of Asian Studies* 73, no. 2 (2014): 471–492.
Williams, Richard A. "Indianapolis Revisited: A New Look at Social and Psychological Factors Affecting Fertility." PhD diss., University of Wisconsin, 1986.
Willrich, Michael. "The Two Percent Solution: Eugenic Jurisprudence and the Socialization of American Law, 1900–1930." *Law and History Review* 16, no. 1 (1998): 63–111.
Wilson, Edwin B., and W. J. Luyton. "The Population of New York City and Its Environs." *Proceedings of the National Academy of Sciences* 11 (1925): 137–143.
Winks, Robin W. *Laurance S. Rockefeller: Catalyst for Conservation*. Washington, DC: Island Press, 2013.
Wolfe, Audra. *Freedom's Laboratory: The Cold War Struggle for the Soul of Science*. Baltimore, MD: Johns Hopkins University Press, 2018.
Wrobel, David M. *Global West, American Frontier: Travel, Empire, and Exceptionalism from Manifest Destiny to the Great Depression*. Albuquerque: University of New Mexico Press, 2013.
Wyon, John B., and John E. Gordon. *The Khanna Study: Population Problems in the Rural Punjab*. Cambridge, MA: Harvard University Press, 1971.
Yglesias, Matthew. *One Billion Americans: The Case for Thinking Bigger*. New York: Penguin, 2020.
Young, Scott. "The ZPG Scare." *Globe and Mail,* April 15, 1975.

INDEX

For the benefit of digital users, indexed terms that span two pages (e.g., 52–53) may, on occasion, appear on only one of those pages.

Figures are indicated by *f* following the page number

www.ingramcontent.com/pod-product-compliance
Ingram Content Group UK Ltd.
Pitfield, Milton Keynes, MK11 3LW, UK
UKHW020848150926
475595UK00003B/77

9 780197 558942